When Hollywood loved Britain

MANCHESTER
UNIVERSITY PRESS

When Hollywood loved Britain

The Hollywood 'British' film 1939–45

H. MARK GLANCY

distributed exclusively in the USA by St. Martin's Press

MANCHESTER UNIVERSITY PRESS   Manchester and New York

Published by Manchester University Press
Oxford Road, Manchester M13 9NR, UK
and Room 400, 175 Fifth Avenue, New York, NY 10010, USA
http://www.man.ac.uk/mup

Distributed exclusively in the USA
by St. Martin's Press, Inc., 175 Fifth Avenue, New York,
NY 10010, USA

Distributed exclusively in Canada by
UBC Press, University of British Columbia, 6344 Memorial Road,
Vancouver, BC, Canada V6T 1Z2

British Library Cataloguing-in-Publication Data
A catalogue record is available from the British Library

Library of Congress Cataloging-in-Publication Data applied for

ISBN 0 7190 4852 4 *hardback*
ISBN 0 7190 4853 2 *paperback*

First published 1999
06   05   04   03   02   00   99   10   9   8   7   6   5   4   3   2   1

Typeset in Photina with Frutiger
by Northern Phototypesetting Co Ltd, Bolton
Printed in Great Britain
by Biddles Ltd, Guildford and King's Lynn

Contents

Illustrations

Acknowledgements

This book was originally conceived as Ph.D. thesis, and I am grateful to those who assisted and guided my research: the staff at the British Film Institute Library and the Public Record Office in London; Linda Beyer and the Wisconsin Center for Film and Theatre Research; Diana Brown and the Turner Entertainment Company; Ned Comstock and the Cinema and Television Library at the University of Southern California; Brigitte Kueppers and the Theatre Arts Library at the University of California at Los Angeles; Tibby Kull and the Widener Library of Harvard University; David Pfieffer and the Washington National Records Center; Howard Prouty and the Margaret Herrick Library of the Academy of Motion Pictures Arts and Sciences; Steven Ricci and the Film and Television Archive of the University of California at Los Angeles; and Ann Schlosser and the American Film Institute. Thanks are also due to Kevin Brownlow, Aljean Harmetz, Gavin Lambert, Thomas Schatz, Kristen Thompson and Catherine Wyler for answering queries and for aiding and abetting the research process. I am also grateful to the Department of History at Queen Mary and Westfield College, which provided research funding and a period of sabbatical leave in order to help me over the final hurdles, and to my colleagues in the department, who have been helpful and supportive throughout the past four years. Mark Connelly and Bernard Hrusa-Marlowe read the manuscript in its last stages and offered valuable suggestions that have influenced the final draft.

I am particularly indebted to Jeffrey Richards and Charles Barr, with whom I was fortunate enough to study. As an undergraduate at the University of Lancaster, I was introduced to the field of film history by Jeffrey Richards, who has remained a source of inspiration and insight ever since. As a student on the masters programme in film studies at the University of East Anglia, I was introduced to 'British' films by Charles Barr, who then guided me through three years of research and writing as my Ph.D. supervisor.

I am ever grateful to my parents, David Lucas Glancy and Eileen Glancy Brener, who have given me support of every kind over the years. Finally, I would like to dedicate this book to Roger Law, who made it all possible in the first place.

Abbreviations

BBFC   British Board of Film Censors
BMP   The Bureau of Motion Pictures of the Office of War Information
MoI   The British Ministry of Information
MPPDA   Motion Picture Producers and Distributors of America
OWI   The United States Office of War Information
PCA   Production Code Administration (of the MPPDA)
RAF   Royal Air Force
WAAF   Women's Auxiliary Air Force

The Hollywood film companies

Col   Columbia Pictures
Fox   Fox Films
MGM   Metro-Goldwyn-Mayer
Mon   Monogram Pictures
Par   Paramount Pictures
Rep   Republic Pictures
RKO   Radio-Keith-Orpheum Pictures
TCF   Twentieth Century-Fox Films
UA   United Artists Film Distributors
Uni   Universal Pictures
WB   Warner Bros. Pictures

Introduction

There was a time when Hollywood loved Britain. Between 1930 and 1945, over 150 'British' films were made in Hollywood. Whether based on British history or literature, or set geographically in the far outposts of the British Empire or in Britain itself, or located in time as period dramas or contemporary war films, Hollywood's 'British' films celebrated the most famous aspects of Britain's culture and history, and, in the films made between 1939 and 1945, they often portrayed the British war effort in the most heroic terms. The number of 'British' films is compellingly significant. No other foreign country was portrayed by Hollywood so often and with such apparent admiration. What is particularly striking about them, though, is that they include some of the most expensive and high-profile productions of this era, and many were both popular and critically acclaimed. One measure of this can be seen in the number of 'British' films that won the film industry's most coveted prize, the Academy Award for 'best picture' of the year. No fewer than five films – *Cavalcade* (1932), *Mutiny on the Bounty* (1935), *Rebecca* (1940), *How Green Was My Valley* (1941) and *Mrs Miniver* (1942) – won the award during these fifteen years, and a listing of the most popular films of these years would include not only those five films, but also *David Copperfield* (1934), *Lloyds of London* (1937), *A Yank at Oxford* (1938), *The Adventures of Robin Hood* (1938), *Goodbye Mr Chips* (1939), *Gunga Din* (1939), *Foreign Correspondent* (1940), *The Sea Hawk* (1940), *A Yank in the RAF* (1941), *Random Harvest* (1942), *The White Cliffs of Dover* (1944) and *National Velvet* (1945).

All of these productions fall into a category that can be known as 'British' films. Several determinants are used to define a film as 'British'. First, a 'British' film is one made by an American company, usually in California but occasionally in Britain. The films made by MGM-British in the late 1930s, for example, were shot at Denham Studios in Britain, but they were controlled entirely by MGM in Hollywood, and therefore they are 'British' rather than British. This particular determinant would be difficult to use in the post-war period, when the studio system broke down, filmmaking became decentralized, and films often received financial backing that was truly international. However, during the 1930s and the war years the production of American films was dominated, with considerable rigour, by the major Hollywood studios, so that it was far simpler to determine the nationality of a film. Thus, 'British' films are essentially American films, and they are not to be confused with actual British films.

The second determinant is that 'British' films are either based on British source material or set in Britain. A film such as *David Copperfield*, which is based on Dickens' novel and set in Britain, meets both criteria. *A Yank in the RAF* was based on an original screenplay written by Americans, but it is set in Britain and centres on the British war effort, and so it too is 'British'. A film such as *Gunga Din* can also be counted as 'British'. Although it is set in India and does not have a single scene set within Britain, the screenplay was derived from a story written by Rudyard Kipling, it centres upon British characters, and it concerns the activities of the British Army. By contrast, a film such as *Top Hat* (1935) would not be included in the 'British' category. Although *Top Hat* is set partly in London, it is based on an original screenplay written by Americans, it features a predominantly American cast, and it does not display the self-consciousness about its British setting that characterizes so many 'British' films.

The third determinant is that 'British' films have a significant number of British personnel among the credits. Hollywood had a large British community in the 1930s and the 1940s, and the British producers, directors, writers, stars and character actors who worked in Hollywood were used to give 'British' films a British perspective and some measure of authenticity. Of course, an American perspective was maintained at the same time. The films often have American stars or an American director, and the screenplays were often written in tandem by American and British writers. Yet a significant British presence was always pivotal to maintaining their transatlantic nature, and so Hollywood's Britons consistently found work in 'British' films. One of the most marked examples of this is *Rebecca*. Not only based upon a British novel and set in Cornwall, but also co-scripted by the British screenwriter Joan Harrison, the film was directed by Alfred Hitchcock and includes in its cast many of the most prominent actors in the Hollywood British community at this time: Laurence Olivier, Joan Fontaine, George Sanders, C. Aubrey Smith, Nigel Bruce, Gladys Cooper and Reginald Denny.

The fourth and often the strongest determinant is that Hollywood's Britain was seldom an average or ordinary Britain. Most of the films take a tourist's view of the country. The characters tend to be aged and venerable aristocrats, young officers and gentlemen, and their comical cockney servants. The settings are often grand manor houses, idyllic villages that have not been touched by the modern age, and a London marked by Big Ben, St Paul's Cathedral, Tower Bridge, and heavy and constant fog. In many instances, and particularly in the historical films and the literary adaptations, this is further compounded by a pronounced sense of patriotism. 'British' films often seem to be populated almost exclusively by the grandest historical figures, who are seen to be living lives of great national significance. *Lloyds of London*, for example, relates the story of the early days of the eponymous insurance company, which is seen to be an integral part of Britain's achievements and glories as a maritime power, and figures such as Lord Nelson, Benjamin Franklin and the Prince of Wales are represented to signify the historical importance of the story. In *Devotion* (1945), a film centred upon the Brontë sisters, Britain is seen to be a haven of great authors. One scene even shows William Thackeray, Charlotte Brontë and Charles Dickens meeting casually and by chance on a London street. In a similar vein, at the end of *Gunga Din*, Rudyard Kipling makes an appearance as a character observing the story, making it clear that the story just seen was witnessed by the great author himself and the lessons learned will inform the future of the British Empire. These are only a few examples of Hollywood's predilection for portraying the great and the good in 'British' films.

The author and film critic Graham Greene noted Hollywood's celebratory approach to British stories in his review of *Lloyds of London*:

The name of England is so freely on the characters' lips that we recognize at once an American picture. These people live, make love, bear children all from the most patriotic motives, and it's all rather like London in Coronation Week.[1]

Greene wrote this review when the film was released in 1937, a full two years before the beginning of the Second World War and four years before the United States entered the war. Yet Hollywood's celebration of Britain only grew stronger as the war approached, and of course Hollywood's patriotic approach enabled 'British' films to assume war themes with remarkable ease and speed. From 1940 onward, adaptations of British history became focused on past military triumphs and made timely historical parallels about Britain's ability to 'take it'. *A Yank at Oxford* was used as the basis for several films about 'Yanks' in the RAF, who witness the brave British war effort. Even Hollywood's preoccupation with the British upper classes took on a timely relevance, as the disparate classes were now portrayed as united in the common purpose of the war effort. While the United States remained, technically at least, a neutral country, Hollywood made its pro-British sympathies clear.

Why did American film-makers choose to make these films and, having chosen, why were they so numerous and in many cases made with such expensive production values? The most frequently cited explanation is that Hollywood was an industry of ardent Anglophiles, who filmed their favourite literary classics, dramatized proud moments in British history and later valorized the British war effort as a result of their profound Anglophilia. Yet this explanation hardly seems credible. The American film industry may have made sentimental films, but like any other major industry, it was not run for sentimental purposes. Furthermore, the industry was always wary of becoming involved in controversy and feared alienating any significant portion of its audience. Hollywood's 'British' films therefore cannot be understood merely as the products of Anglophiles, and, given that their patriotic tone was well established long before the outbreak of war, they cannot be explained as politically motivated propaganda films. This does not necessarily mean that the Anglophile theory must be entirely rejected. Many of those who made 'British' films may indeed have been Anglophiles, but it seems highly unlikely that this was the sole, or even the primary, consideration at work when 'British' films were made. Rather, 'British' films proliferated at a time when Americans remained fascinated by the British.

Actual British films were seldom popular in the United States, but Hollywood found that an American perspective on British stories provided a winning box-office combination. In fact, as Graham Greene's comment indicates, Hollywood's Britain is most often England, and it is an England that seems to exist mainly in the past. This is a crucial part of the films' American perspective. During the 1930s and the 1940s, many Americans still considered England to be a part of their heritage and, in the days before transatlantic journeys became common, their perspective on the country was a backward-looking one. Thus, many 'British' films dramatized the glories and achievements that were part of a shared Anglo-American heritage. Another aspect of this backward looking view, however, is that the films often focus on the rigidity of the class system, social snobbery, and Anglo-American differences. While Britain was never portrayed in an altogether unfavourable light, and Anglophobia exists only as an undercurrent in 'British' films, the American perspective on Britain conveyed a grateful awareness of the distance of both time and space. American audiences could revel in images of the old country, and at the same time be thankful that their forefathers had embarked for a new and more egalitarian world.

'British' films therefore require consideration on several different levels: why they were made, how they portray Britain, and what purpose they served during the war. The first three chapters of this book are concerned primarily with the film industry and the factors which gave rise to 'British' films in the 1930s and the earliest 'British' war films. Chapter One investigates the importance of foreign earnings to the Hollywood studios, and chronicles the changes which made Britain by far the most lucrative of all foreign markets in the 1930s. Chapter Two focuses on the Hays Office, and considers how the foreign market changes affected the political sympathies of American films from the 1930s to 1941. Chapter Three examines the 'British' films of one studio, MGM, which made many of the most successful 'British' films. MGM was certainly not the only studio to make such films, but it was clearly influential in establishing the transatlantic perspective of 'British' films, and the studio's financial records provide ample evidence of just how lucrative this formula could be.

Chapters Four to Six deal with the 'British' films made during the war years. The wartime films have been chosen for analysis because the most distinctive trait of 'British' films, their patriotic and celebratory approach to Britain, was most pronounced in these films. Furthermore, the wartime films are the key elements in Hollywood's reputation as an industry of Anglophiles: while Britain fought alone, Hollywood was seen to summon support from Americans and boost British morale. Analysis of the films' production records, the films themselves and their reception, however, reveals that they cannot simply be labelled as altruistic exercises on behalf of the beleaguered British. Chapter Four considers the earliest films, including *The Sea Hawk*, *That Hamilton Woman* (1941), *Foreign Correspondent*, *A Yank in the RAF* and

Eagle Squadron (1942). Chapter Five considers two wartime melo-dramas released in the summer of 1942, *This Above All* and *Mrs Miniver*, and their attempt to portray the 'new England' of the war years. Chapter Six focuses on one film, *Forever and a Day* (1943), which was made as a collective effort by the Hollywood British community, and considers the careers of Hollywood's leading British stars.

Finally, in Chapter Seven, the records of the Office of War Information (OWI) are used to offer another perspective on 'British' films. The OWI was the official propaganda agency of the United States during the Second World War, and it formed its opinions on how the British should be portrayed in feature films on the basis of public opinion polls rather than box-office results. While the Hollywood studios undoubtedly preferred to believe that their 'British' films were useful in building support for Britain among Americans, the OWI often thought that they were harm-ful and misleading. Indeed, the basic preoccupations of 'British' films – class, Empire, nostalgia for the past – were deemed in many instances to confirm prevailing American prejudices toward their British allies. The transatlantic perspective of 'British' films was seen to be inherently troublesome and, in this context, it becomes clear that Hollywood's love for Britain stemmed primarily from box-office considerations rather than ardent Anglophilia.

Hollywood's foreign markets

1

When the Second World War began in September 1939, the American film industry was thought to be facing a severe financial crisis. The film industry relied upon foreign earnings to make its films profitable, and with key foreign markets threatened by war, the future appeared bleak. It was well known that the Nazis were hostile to Hollywood, and this was confirmed as the Nazis moved throughout Europe, banning American films and seizing the industry's assets in all of the territories they occupied. On Wall Street, the result was that the value of the film companies' shares plunged during the first year of the war, while in Hollywood the trade papers reported war events as though they signalled the end of a golden era. Studio executives predicted job losses, as production cutbacks would have to match the cut in foreign earnings. Some predicted that the studios would begin to produce for the domestic market alone, indicating that production costs would be lower and films would be targeted specifically at the home audience. Others suggested hopefully that the burgeoning markets of Latin America eventually would compensate for the losses in Europe. All seemed to agree that the American film industry was dependent upon foreign earnings that were either severely threatened or already lost.[1]

In fact, Hollywood did lose many of its foreign markets as a result of the Second World War, in Europe and also in the Far East. Table 1 and table 2 indicate the scale of these losses, and the extent to which Hollywood's global distribution network was restricted by war. Table 1 lists the thirty leading export markets of 1933, based on the amount of film footage imported by each

Table 1 US motion picture exports in 1933 (exported footage of sound and silent film)

Country	Footage imported (feet)	
1. United Kingdom	13,620,160	
2. Argentina	12,706,152	
3. Spain	12,116,637	* (1936)
4. Brazil	9,151,956	
5. Panama	8,021,243	
6. Canada	7,413,851	
7. Mexico	6,655,066	
8. France	6,442,195	* (1940)
9. Bahamas	5,284,132	
10. Japan	5,139,190	* (1940)
11. India	5,020,717	
12. Australia	4,606,406	
13. South Africa	4,423,405	
14. Sweden	3,397,396	
15. New Zealand	3,137,233	
16. Cuba	3,063,110	
17. Chile	2,792,781	
18. Bermuda	2,628,825	
19. Netherlands	2,453,874	* (1940)
20. Poland	2,273,029	* (1940)
21. Philippines	2,225,988	* (1942)
22. Netherlands East Indies	2,059,230	* (1942)
23. Italy	2,043,718	* (1939)
24. Dominican Republic	2,036,285	
25. China	1,987,897	
26. British Malaya	1,959,157	* (1942)
27. Colombia	1,873,594	
28. Peru	1,852,383	
29. Belgium	1,788,935	* (1940)
30. Germany	1,548,689	* (1940)

* Indicates markets which would be lost within the next nine years, followed by the year in which they ceased to import American films (in brackets).

Source: T. Ramsaye (ed.), *The 1935–1936 Motion Picture Almanac*, pp. 997–1034.

country.[2] In 1933 the foreign market was truly global, but, over the course of the next nine years, eleven of the countries listed as major export markets would become closed to American films. Table 2 lists the major cinema markets of the world in 1938, based on the number of cinemas within each country. There were over 92,000 cinemas in the world in 1938.[3] The 30,000 cinemas of Russia rarely showed American films, but the remaining

Table 2 1938 – world theatres compared (countries with over one hundred cinemas)

English-speaking countries			
English-speaking		Latvia	100
countries	*25,044*	Other countries	229
United States	16,228		
Britain	5,300	*Latin America*	*5,239*
Australia	1,371	Brazil	1,450
Canada	1,224	Argentina	1,021
New Zealand	721	Mexico	823
Irish Free State	200	Cuba	375
		Colombia	276
Europe	*57,543*	Chile	243
Russia	30,000	Peru	205
Germany	6,500	Uruguay	150
France	4,600	Venezuela	147
Italy	4,049	Puerto Rico	121
Spain	3,500	Other countries	428
Sweden	1,907		
Czechoslovakia	1,305	*Far East*	*4,109*
Belgium	1,100	Japan	1,749
Poland	769	India	1,025
Hungary	524	China	275
Yugoslavia	383	Philippines	258
Romania	372	Netherlands East Indies	170
Denmark	370	Other countries	632
Switzerland	354		
Netherlands	333	*Africa and the Near East*	*881*
Finland	285	South Africa	300
Norway	247	Algeria	165
Portugal	215	Egypt	118
Greece	170	Other countries	298
Turkey	120		
Bulgaria	111	*Total*	*92,816*

Source: T. Ramsaye (ed.), *The 1939–1940 Motion Picture Almanac*, p. 944.

62,000 cinemas constituted markets that were – technically at least – open to American films in the 1930s. By 1941, nearly half of these cinemas had become out of bounds to Hollywood, as 26,000 cinemas in Europe and 2,500 cinemas in the Far East came under the control of hostile governments.

Remarkably, however, the loss of so many markets had no discernible effect upon the financial health of the American film industry. In fact, the war years were a period of unprecedented prosperity for the film industry. The predicted financial crisis never occurred, and Hollywood's foreign earnings rose in step with domestic earnings – swiftly and steeply – throughout the war years. The crucial factor in this good fortune was not Latin America, but the survival of Britain and the popularity of American films in the British market. If Britain had been lost to a German invasion, Hollywood would have been lost in red ink. Instead, the thriving British exhibition market compensated for the loss of many other markets. Although the industry's foreign network was much smaller, it was actually more prosperous than ever before. Subsequent chapters will explore the extent to which Hollywood's reliance upon Britain shaped the industry's policies and its films. In this chapter, the economic impetus that lay behind Hollywood's British concerns will be established.

Europe

The statistics in table 1 and table 2 were compiled by the US government's Department of Commerce. This agency offered the film industry such information as a means of aiding the exports of a business whose international high profile and cultural presence had an economic and political significance to the United States far beyond that of Hollywood's own rewards. By the measurements of cinema numbers and export footage, Europe was a vast conglomeration of markets, particularly when compared to Britain. When combined, the European markets had many more cinemas and imported far more film footage than Britain. Yet in the late 1930s, the whole of Europe supplied the American film industry with only $3 million in remittable earnings each year, whereas remittable British earnings ranged between $35 million and $50 million annually.[4] Clearly, the economic importance of a given foreign market cannot be gauged simply by counting its cinemas or measuring the amount of footage imported. In fact, each country represented a unique set of circumstances, including the strength of its own film industry, the value of its currency, the restrictions placed on imported films, the taxes aimed specifically at film imports, the frequency with which its citizens attended the cinema, and the extent to which they favoured foreign films. Throughout much of Europe, most of these factors worked against American films in the 1930s. In fact, the spread of fascism and German expansionism were only the last and final blows to be struck against the pre-eminence of American films in Europe. Hollywood's fortunes on the continent actually had been in a steep decline throughout the 1930s.

A key starting point for the decline of American films in Europe would be the late 1920s, when the introduction of 'talking pictures' placed a language barrier between American films and non-English-speaking audiences. Hollywood's attempts to overcome this barrier testify to the importance of European revenue at this time. Initially, the larger studios even made foreign-language versions of their films by substituting the English-speaking casts with casts that spoke French, German or Spanish. This proved uneconomical and the foreign-language production units did not last long into the 1930s. It is unclear whether they failed because the countries themselves were not lucrative enough to warrant such extra investment or because the audiences preferred to see the established Hollywood stars and not their foreign substitutes. But by the mid-1930s, dubbing and subtitling were left as the options for American films in Europe. Dubbing apparently was preferred by audiences, and in some countries it was required by law that foreign-language films were dubbed.[5] It was the more expensive option, though, and so this was another factor to affect Hollywood's European returns. Subtitling was far cheaper, but it was not popular with audiences.

The new language barrier was just one problem that worked in combination with others during the 1930s. The introduction of sound coincided with the growth of indigenous film industries across Europe as well as the spread of legislation that was punitive to Hollywood. Indeed, these three factors combined were a potent force in opposition to American films. 'Talking pictures' created demand for films in a variety of languages, and Europe's indigenous film industries undoubtedly were boosted by this new advantage. Many were assisted further by the introduction of quotas, tariffs and other restrictive measures placed on imported films. Between 1925 and 1938 no fewer than eleven European countries introduced such measures.[6] They aimed to ensure that indigenous films received some measure of protection in their home market, and in some cases to limit the amount of money the American film companies were able to remit. The argument behind such measures could be cultural or economic, depending on the country and the government; either way they worked to diminish the predominance of American films.

France provides clear evidence of why major European markets provided the American industry with such comparatively small returns. With over 4,500 cinemas, the French exhibition market was nearly as large as the British, and in the mid-1920s American films accounted for 80 per cent of all releases in France. But high exhibition taxes, a cumbersome distribution method and low attendance rates meant that France returned only 3 per cent of the American industry's foreign earnings.[7] Then, in 1931, the

French government imposed a quota on film imports. The quota fluctuated, but it was designed to ensure that French films outnumbered imports. The legislation also stipulated that only ten of the country's cinemas could show foreign-language films. In all other cinemas, foreign films had to be dubbed in French, and the dubbing had to be done in France.[8] By the end of the decade, the success of this legislation was overwhelmingly apparent. French films were said to be the most popular films in France, and the number produced each year had doubled over the decade. The American share of films released in France, meanwhile, had sunk to 45 per cent of all releases. Not only were there fewer American films in France, but the American film companies were required to pay the necessary dubbing costs out of their French earnings.[9]

It is clear that the French film industry benefited from the advent of 'talking pictures'. French films did well not only in France, but also in other francophone regions. For example, they had the leading market share in the French-speaking regions of Belgium and Switzerland. However, in the cinemas of the German-speaking regions of Switzerland, German films predominated in cinemas, and in much of Europe this pattern was repeated.[10] Wherever native-language films were available, either they had the highest market share, or they were reported to be the most popular type of film. Even the smaller film industries of Denmark, Finland, Norway, Poland and Sweden provided American films with significant competition in their home markets. In Finland, for example, Finnish films were said to earn six times more than any type of foreign film, while in Denmark a mere nine Danish films earned 50 per cent of the country's box-office revenues in 1938. These films apparently had little export value, but they consistently captured the highest box-office returns in their home markets.[11] American films remained the most numerous in many European markets and they were frequently ranked second in popularity behind the native-language films. In these respects, the international status of American films was still intact in the 1930s; no other film industry had such a strong presence. Yet this fact would be of little value to an industry which saw its European earnings steadily dwindling over the course of the decade.

The first European market to be lost completely was Spain. All of the American film companies withdrew from Spain when the Spanish Civil War began in 1936. Spain had not been a particularly lucrative market before the war: only 400 Spanish cinemas operated as full-time cinemas, and the remaining 3,100 venues that acted as cinemas did so only on one or two days of the week.[12] Even so, American films had predominated in Spain before the war and the industry was eager to re-establish itself when the war ended in 1939. Technically, this was made possible by a wider trade agreement between the United States and Spain which was established in 1940. The Franco regime, however, constructed an obstacle course for American companies wishing to show their films in Spain. For example, foreign films could be sold to Spanish distributors only on a flat rental basis, instead of the more lucrative percentage scales which Hollywood preferred. The government was also intent upon building Spain's own film industry, and so it issued few permits for foreign films and applied what were described as 'drastic import duties' on those that were given permits. Furthermore, all foreign films had to be dubbed in Spanish, and the dubbing had to be done in Spain. The result of these restrictions and expenses was that, although American companies were said to have gross earnings of $3 million in Spain in 1945, very little of this was returned to the USA as net earnings.[13]

Similar conditions were encountered in the Italian market in the 1930s. As Tino Balio has described the situation, the Mussolini government set out to 'bleed, antagonize and alienate' the American film industry in the 1930s.[14] There was a quota on imported films, a dubbing requirement for all foreign-language films, a regime of high taxes on both distribution and exhibition, a schedule of currency restrictions, and strictly enforced political and moral censorship. The Motion Picture Producers and Distributors of America (MPPDA), a trade organization which negotiated with foreign governments on behalf of the entire industry, found the Italians to be particularly difficult customers. When a new set of currency restrictions was imposed in 1936, the MPPDA retaliated with its ultimate negotiating weapon: it called upon its members – all of the major Hollywood studios – to boycott the Italian market. The boycott lasted only six weeks, at which time a compromise was reached which allowed the American companies to remit a total of $1,000,000 annually.[15] With American films having a 65 per cent share of the Italian exhibition market at that time, the fact that the paltry annual remittance allowance would have to be divided among at least eight studios indicates the limitations faced by Hollywood even in such a major film market. By 1938, the Italian government apparently felt more confident about its ability to satisfy audience demand without Hollywood, and so it pressed ahead with a plan to place the Italian film industry under its own monopoly control. This was opposed by the MPPDA, which claimed that the plan would remove any possibility of a profitable release for American films in Italy. Thus, after unfruitful negotiations, another boycott took effect on 31 January 1939. Some independent producers, who did not belong to the MPPDA, broke the ban in the period before the attack on Pearl Harbor (December 1941). This proved to be dis-advantageous in some cases. In March 1941, when it became known that *Intermezzo* (1939) and *Rebecca* (1940) had been released in Italy, producer David Selznick was accused in the press of 'trafficking with the enemy' and Selznick felt obliged to donate the films' Italian proceeds ($25,650) to the British War Relief Society.[16] Apart from such incidents, American films did not return to the Italian market *en masse* until they were brought in by American troops in 1943. In the meantime the growing Ital-ian industry, which had been nurtured by the government throughout the 1930s, was intent upon supplying its own cine-mas. Any additional films would come primarily from Germany rather than the United States.[17]

The German exhibition market was the largest in Europe, and during the 1920s individual American films could earn better grosses in Germany than in Britain. However, while 35 per cent of the American industry's foreign earnings came from Britain in the 1920s, only 10 per cent came from Germany. This was because Germany had a well-developed and successful film industry of its own, as well as an effective quota system. It was estimated that, due to the quota, it was possible to release only 40 per cent of Hollywood's output in Germany. Thus, in the 1920s the German market already had become 'a constant source of frustration for the American industry'. The introduction of sound brought a more severe quota in 1928, and a require-ment that all foreign films had to be dubbed in German and that the dubbing had to be done in Germany. As a result, the number of American films released in Germany dropped from 205 in 1928 to 80 in 1931. Thus, the American situation in Germany had deteriorated markedly before Nazi policies came into effect.[18]

Under the Nazi regime, all sectors of the German film industry were nationalized and placed under the control of the Minister of Propaganda, Joseph Goebbels. In 1934 Goebbels stated that the Nazi policy was to allow only high-prestige American films to be shown in Germany, while German films would make up the majority of releases. This, in fact, already had become the prac-tice, but the Nazis penalized the American industry in many other ways. Currency restrictions were imposed, and a tax of approxi-mately $8,000 was placed on each imported film. *The Motion Pic-*

ture Herald quoted one (unnamed) American foreign manager as saying that the new tax was 'the last straw'. It was seen as 'a deliberate attempt to crowd us out of that market. We can't get any money out of Berlin, so what's the difference?' Censorship provided a further problem. The Nazis proclaimed that all films shown in Germany must be of 'German character', and films with Jewish names among the credits were not allowed. Furthermore, the import tax had to be paid, and a film had to be dubbed in German, before it could be considered for censorship. Thus, a substantial financial outlay could be lost to the whims and prejudices of the censors.[19]

On the basis of the new import tax alone, the US Department of Commerce proclaimed in 1934 that the German market had become 'prohibitive' for the American industry, and the possibility of an MPPDA boycott of Germany was raised.[20] Remarkably, this never happened. Instead, it was left to the individual companies to decide their own policy toward Germany. Most withdrew in the mid-1930s, but the three largest – MGM, Paramount and Twentieth Century-Fox – maintained their Berlin offices until 1940.[21] Their continued presence in Germany, and the reluctance of the MPPDA to boycott the market, must have been based on hopes that conditions would improve. It certainly was not based on earnings derived from Germany in the late 1930s. By that time, only twenty-five American films were released in Germany each year. In the first six months of 1940, just three American films were released in Germany. Then the Germans banned American films altogether and the three remaining film companies were forced to leave.[22] Even at that point, Hollywood foreign managers had hopes that wartime conditions might force Germany to begin importing American films again.[23] A country that had once supplied 10 per cent of the industry's foreign revenue was, it seems, a difficult one to abandon.

The Nazi film policies benefited the German film industry, but the restrictions were also a means of political and cultural control. Goebbels was intent upon promoting the Nazis' formulation of the 'German character', while denying the German people access to foreign cultures and ideologies. These film policies were then extended to the countries invaded and occupied by the Nazis. By 1941, the 'Hitler circuit', as the trade papers described markets that came under Nazi control, included Austria, Belgium, Bulgaria, Czechoslovakia, Denmark, France, Greece, the Netherlands, Hungary, Luxembourg, Norway, Poland, Romania and Yugoslavia. It was announced that the only American films that could be shown in the occupied territories were those that had been passed by the German censors after 1937, and this of course amounted to very few films.[24]

With Spain, Italy, Germany and German-held territory off limits, few European countries remained open to American films during the war years. Moreover, some of those which remained open posed operational difficulties. In Finland, for example, German influence was said to restrict the number of American films that were given import permits.[25] In Sweden, American films reportedly benefited from the unpopularity of German films, although there were also reports that political censorship excluded some war films from Swedish screens.[26] Portugal and Switzerland also remained open, but theirs were small markets. Portugal's was so small that in 1940 MGM and RKO were the only American film companies to have offices in Lisbon.[27] And because Switzerland was landlocked and surrounded by Nazi-held territory, it was said to be difficult to reach. As one trade paper commented in 1940, it seemed that the European film market had 'ceased to exist virtually overnight'.[28] Its decline as a source of earnings, though, had been so long that, by the time war came, the abrupt loss of so many large markets actually had no effect on the industry's financial health.

The Far East

The Far East had never been as lucrative for the American industry as Britain, Europe or Latin America. In the 1930s the largest exhibition market in the region was Japan's, but Japan had a well-developed and highly successful film industry of its own. Approximately 600 Japanese films were produced each year. Although these had little export value (even within the Far East) they predominated in Japan, constituting 80 per cent of the films released in the country's 1,700 cinemas. American films came second in the Japanese market but accounted for only 12 per cent of all films shown.[29] Even this small share was lost in 1937, when the Japanese government included American films in a ban on foreign luxuries. This was part of a financial auster-ity programme that was initially set to last only twelve months, but in 1938 a new set of prohibitive regulations was applied. The number of American films was restricted severely and, more importantly, currency regulations were imposed. Thereafter, American film companies found it very difficult to remit their Japanese earnings. That these restrictions may have had a politi-cal or ideological purpose became evident when more favourable treatment was given to German and Italian film imports. German and Italian films soon took the place of American films as Japan's leading film imports, and in 1940 Japan was said to be a 'dead market' as far as American films were concerned.[30]

India was the second largest Far Eastern market, and its film industry developed rapidly during the war years. The number of cinemas grew from 1,025 in 1938 to 1,500 in 1945 and, more significantly, box-office revenues trebled over the same period. However, this growth was fuelled by the burgeoning Indian film industry, which produced culturally distinctive and highly popular films. Even in the early 1930s, when only thirty Indian films were produced each year, they were reported to be 'very popular with the native audience'.[31] Just ten years later, production had increased to approximately 180 films each year, and the American share of the market had fallen from 80 per cent to 45 per cent of all releases. By 1944, it was estimated that American films earned just 15 per cent of the country's box-office revenues.[32] Thus, while India was the only country in the Far East to remain open during the war, American films suffered in competition with indigenous films.

The remaining Far Eastern markets were small, but they were not inconsequential. China, Hong Kong, the Netherlands East Indies and British Malaya had fewer than 350 cinemas each, but as a group they returned a substantial share of Far Eastern earnings in the 1930s. American films predominated in all of these markets, with minor competition from Chinese and Indian films. Until, that is, Japan invaded and occupied these territories, and American films were banned. By January 1942, the Far Eastern region had been reduced to India and the thirty cinemas within 'Free China'. These losses received little attention in Hollywood's trade papers, particularly by comparison with the anxious headlines which had proclaimed the loss of European markets eighteen months earlier.[33] Of course, this can be attributed to the fact that the Far Eastern markets were less lucrative than the European markets. Equally, though, by 1942 the industry's fears for its financial health had passed. It had already become apparent that wartime conditions were the source of unprecedented prosperity, both at home and in the industry's remaining foreign markets.

Latin America

Latin America, as defined by the American film industry, encompassed all of the Americas south of the Rio Grande: Mexico, the Caribbean Islands, and Central and South America. This was a vast and populous region, but in the late 1930s it had only 5,200 cinemas and was estimated to provide Hollywood with only 10 per cent of its annual foreign earnings.[34] As conditions in Europe deteriorated, many in the American film industry hoped that increased returns from Latin America would compensate for the predicted shortfall in foreign earnings. The fact that the region was stable and peaceful, at least by comparison with Europe and the Far East, led many to believe it offered the industry a ray of hope amid the anxieties of the early war years. To a limited extent, such hopes were fulfilled. Much of Latin America enjoyed increased prosperity during the war years, and box-office revenues in the largest markets (those of Argentina, Brazil and Mexico) rose by between 50 per cent and 100 per cent. By 1945, another 1,000 cinemas had been built in the region as a result of growing demand. However, as in India, the increasing popularity of cinema-going was largely the result of indigenous film production.[35] As table 3 indicates, in the late 1930s the region's own film industries already had gained ground at the expense of Hollywood.[36]

The film industries of Argentina and Mexico were the most successful in the region, and they grew rapidly in the first decade of sound films. In the early 1930s production in each country was limited to three or four films annually, but a decade later both Argentina and Mexico were producing fifty films per year.[37] A shortage of film stock limited any further increase during the war years, but the quality of both countries' films was said to have improved, and it was these films that reaped the benefits of wartime prosperity. An American foreign manager reported in 1944 that, while box-office revenues had climbed during the war, 'a large part of the increase has been absorbed by Spanish language films', and that therefore the box-office gains would not benefit Hollywood. It was said that in the Spanish-speaking countries there was a marked preference for Mexican and Argentinian films. So much so that they received far longer engagements and

Table 3 American films in the largest Latin American markets (as a percentage of all films released in the countries listed)

Country	1931 (%)	1938 (%)
Argentina	90	66
Brazil	86	78
Cuba	98	80
Mexico	98	60

Source: *The Motion Picture Herald* (27 July 1940), p. 33.

earned three times more than American films. American films remained pre-eminent only in Brazil, where Spanish-language films had no special appeal.[38]

The language barrier was the most significant problem for American films in Latin America. Most American films were released with Spanish or Portuguese subtitles, and very few were dubbed in either language. The subtitles were a severe drawback in rural areas, where there was a high rate of illiteracy. Hence, American films were said to do best in the major cities and to suffer elsewhere.[39] In 1940, the prevailing view among American companies was that the region was not lucrative enough to warrant the expense of dubbing, estimated to be between $25,000 and $35,000 per film. Furthermore, dubbing was said to be problematic because of the wide range of dialects in the region. This view persisted until 1944, by which time it had become obvious that most American films were not sharing in the increased box-office returns of the war years. Then, in 1945, MGM scored a huge box-office success with a dubbed version of *Gaslight* (1944) which was said to have broken box-office records throughout the Spanish-speaking capitals of the region, including the records previously set by *Gone with the Wind* (1939). This led MGM to dub into Spanish all of its subsequent releases for 1945, and eventually it motivated other companies to follow MGM's lead.[40]

Cultural differences also limited the popularity of American films during the war years. Audiences in Latin America were said to loathe Hollywood's patriotic war films. These 'died the death of dogs' in the region, according to one American foreign manager. In fact, Argentina's neutral stance meant that many American war films were not released there until early in 1945, when Argentina belatedly declared war on Germany.[41] Overt attempts to appeal specifically to the region's audiences often failed, too. Beginning in 1940, Hollywood began making what perhaps can be described as 'Latin American' films; that is, films set in Latin American locales and featuring the region's own stars. Twentieth Century-Fox, for example, brought the singer and dancer Carmen Miranda (the 'Brazilian Bombshell') to Hollywood to star in such films as *Down Argentine Way* (1940), *That Night in Rio* (1941) and *Weekend in Havana* (1941). Other studios offered *Argentine Nights* (1940), *Rio Rita* (1941) and *They Met in Rio* (1941), to name but a few obvious examples. That 'Latin American' films are best remembered for Miranda's fruit-laden head-wear is only one indication of their excesses. Many of these films proved to be popular in the United States, which was in the midst of a Latin American music and dance craze, but they drew scathing responses in the region itself. *Variety* reported that the films were often 'laughed off the screen' in the region, and the US Department of Commerce reported that they were 'seldom successful' because they were seen as 'distasteful' by Latin American audiences.[42] The Office of the Co-Ordinator of Inter-American Affairs, a US government agency set up in 1940 to monitor and influence political opinion in the region, also warned of their harmful effect.[43] But 'Latin American' films represented only a very small percentage of Hollywood's output. The popularity of the region's own films and the language barrier to American films were more substantial problems. While the American industry may have been correct in predicting the potential of the Latin American exhibition markets, it was wrong to assume that it would be the sole or even the primary beneficiary.

Britain before the war

For Hollywood, the British market was the most lucrative foreign market in the world. This was already the case in the 1920s, when this one country was estimated to provide 35 per cent of Hollywood's foreign earnings, and in the 1930s the proportion rose to over 50 per cent.[44] The reasons for this were manifold. Britain was an easily and efficiently serviced market, in comparison with other countries and regions. For example, the 5,000 cinemas of Latin America were spread over a vast continent, necessitating distribution centres in numerous capital cities, where Hollywood's representatives had to deal with each country's different regulations on import matters, taxes and censorship. In sharp contrast, Britain's 5,000 cinemas were within one small but populous country and only one distribution centre (usually in London) was needed. Britain also had a comparatively strong currency, and the British were frequent cinema-goers. Furthermore, while some may believe that Britain and the United States are 'divided by a common language', the advent of talking pictures had no detrimental effect on the popularity of American films in Britain.[45]

One of the most important factors behind the industry's good fortune in Britain was the weak competition posed by the British film industry. While the American industry benefited from being 'vertically integrated' – that is, the major companies operated in the three key fields of production, distribution and exhibition – its British counterpart was a 'tripartite industry'. Its production, distribution and exhibition sectors were separate, and they often had conflicting interests.[46] A British exhibitor's primary concern was to show popular films, which were usually American films, and this meant that the box-office revenue from one of the world's most lucrative film markets often did not benefit its own production sector. This situation was remedied to an extent when J. Arthur Rank built a vertically integrated film empire in the 1940s, but in the 1920s and the 1930s the British production sector was plagued by funding crises. It reached its most dire state in the mid-1920s, when American films consistently captured 80 per cent of the British market. The remaining 20 per cent was divided almost equally among British, French and German films, indicating that indigenous films were no more numerous than foreign-language films.[47] At this point, the government was at last moved to support the country's film-makers. The Cinematograph Films Act of 1927 stipulated that a certain percentage of films distributed and exhibited within Britain had to be British films. The regulations required that 7.5 per cent of the films handled by distributors and 5 per cent of the films shown by exhibitors had to be British films in 1928, which was the first year of the 'quota' system, and then the percentage figures rose annually and in steps to a plateau of 20 per cent for distributors and exhibitors in 1936. While such figures may seem unambitious, particularly when compared to the German and French quota systems, they were realistic. The British film industry could not be revived instantly by legislation alone.

The major Hollywood studios distributed their own films in Britain, and so the new regulations made them liable to distribute British films as well. Most did so cheaply, by producing or financing films at very low prices, giving rise to the so-called 'quota quickies', the inexpensive and quickly made British films that were reportedly of poor quality and had little box-office value. It has been estimated that 50 per cent of all films produced in Britain during this first quota regime were 'quota quickies', and this has led many commentators to label the 1927 Films Act as a failure. However, this view overlooks the great strides made by the British film industry during the lifetime of this legislation. Even if one does accept that 'quota quickies' were numerous and dreadful, they can still be seen to have provided a training ground for British film-makers and technicians, and to have led the way to the British cinema's subsequent achievements. It is also evident that as early as 1932 British production had surpassed the level required by the quota figures, indicating that there was a demand for British films beyond the numbers required by the quota. Furthermore, while it always has been recognized that the films of Gracie Fields, George Formby and Jessie Matthews were popular in the 1930s, recent research has shown that a wider variety of British 'quality' films emerged, many of which were as popular as their American rivals. Thus, despite the 'quota quickies' – whose numbers and poor quality may have been exaggerated – it appears that the 1927 Films Act did far more good than harm.[48]

The growing popularity of British films in the 1930s must have set off alarm bells in Hollywood. With so many other markets fading away, Hollywood simply could not afford to lose further ground in Britain. The discussions surrounding the new Films Act, which was due in 1937, also signalled trouble. British producers were lobbying for a quota set as high as 50 per cent. They also wanted a 'films bank' to subsidize production and a 'quality test' as a means of eliminating 'quota quickies'. These proposals were seen as a means of bolstering the British industry and freeing it from American domination. The American industry, according to Dickinson and Street, was 'desperately anxious' about maintaining its presence in the British market, and used all of its lobbying powers to avoid such punitive measures. It was not just the MPPDA that argued on the industry's behalf, but also the US Secretary of State (Cordell Hull) and the US Ambassador to Britain (Joseph Kennedy). Eventually, a compromise was reached which would allow American films to continue to predominate on British screens, but would also require the American companies to make more substantial investments in the British industry.[49]

The Cinematograph Films Act of 1938 set a quota of 15 per cent for distributors and 12.5 per cent for exhibitors in 1938, which was less than the 20 per cent that had been required in 1936 and 1937. The quota figures were then set to double over the next ten years, but at that point only 25 per cent of the films shown in Britain would have to be British. This would safeguard the American share of the market, which had levelled off at approximately 75 per cent of all releases in the mid-1930s. In return for these modest figures, though, there were cost requirements. In order to be counted for quota purposes, a feature film had to have British labour costs of at least £7,500. A single film with British labour costs of £22,500 or more was counted twice under this system, and a single film with British labour costs of £37,500 or more was counted three times. Labour costs were estimated to be roughly half of a film's total costs, and so a film would have to cost approximately £15,000 (or $67,500) to count once under the quota rules; approximately £45,000 ($202,500) to count twice; and approximately £75,000 ($337,500) to be counted three times. These costs were at the lower end of Hollywood's own production costs, but they would still protect against the 'quota quickies'. Another allowance was offered in the 'reciprocity clause', which enabled distributors to garner quota credits when they purchased the foreign distribution rights for British films at a fee of at least £20,000.[50]

It was the American interests that pressed for a low quota, for triple quota credits and for the reciprocity clause. Of course, it is not surprising that Hollywood wanted a low quota, but it may seem surprising that the studios would want to spend more on their British quota films and release them abroad, particularly when it is remembered that they responded to the 1927 regulations by making their quota films as inexpensively as possible. The difference between 1927 and 1937 was that the British industry posed a threat to Hollywood in 1937. The threat existed only within Britain itself, but this was the industry's most important foreign market and it could not be lost to the emergent British industry. The studios would safeguard their interests only by moving into British production and placing Britain's top stars and its most noteworthy film-makers under contract. This was a tried and true method for Hollywood, which had a long history of dealing with foreign competition by moving into its backyard and appropriating its best talent. It is little wonder, then, that the American industry welcomed legislation that required it to invest more substantially in a threateningly competitive foreign film industry. In 1937 this must have appeared to be the most effective means of safeguarding a foreign market worth $35 million per year.

Britain during the war

The settlement of the new quota provided a brief period of relief for the American industry. Any sense that the British market was safe and sound, at least in regard to Hollywood's interests, collapsed in September 1939. This was a result not simply of the declaration of war, but of the government's closure of all cinemas. It was feared that cinemas made perfect bombing targets, and that a massive German bombing campaign would start in a matter of days. It was soon realized that this was not going to happen, and most cinemas reopened within the first month of war. By the time the bombings did begin, in the summer of 1940, the government had realized that the threat was not so great as to warrant closing such a vital means of sustaining morale. Cinemas not only remained open during the worst months of the Blitz, but did a thriving business.

In fact, the only real problem that Hollywood encountered in wartime Britain was that a portion of its earnings was 'frozen'. The British government faced a shortage of dollar reserves when war was declared in 1939, and dollars were needed to buy crucial war materials. Basing its approach on estimates that the American film industry had remitted $35 million annually before the war, the government at first proposed limiting American film remittances to $5 million per year. The industry's remaining earnings, some $30 million, would be 'blocked' or 'frozen' in Britain until the currency situation improved. The ensuing negotiations between the American industry and the British government were far more confrontational than the negotiations over the quota laws had been. The British government was dealing with a war issue rather than a trade matter, while the American industry faced losing access to a major part of its foreign earnings. During the first round of negotiations, Joseph Kennedy and representatives of the State Department were brought into the negotiations in the hopes that the dispute would be seen to have far-reaching ramifications. Kennedy warned that the proposals could devastate the film industry and damage Anglo-American relations. The Ambassador predicted that limiting the industry's remittances to $5 million per year would bring the American film companies 'very close to destruction'. The companies would be forced to close cinemas across the United States, and the resulting unemployment would create 'a focus of ill-will toward Great Britain' among Americans. This scenario was frightening enough to bring about a compromise. Between November 1939 and October 1940 the American film companies were allowed to remit $17.5 million (predicted to be 50 per cent of their earnings), while the remaining earnings would have to stay in Britain, where they could be spent or saved.[51]

When the first agreement was due to expire, the British currency crisis had worsened, and the British government again proposed allowing only $5 million to be remitted over the next twelve months. Kennedy termed the restrictions 'unfair, unreasonable and unrealistic' and warned that the MPPDA could boycott the British market. The government then seriously considered supplying its own film industry with enough money, manpower and resources to fill the gap left by an absence of American films. A subsidized British film industry, freed from the competition of American films, was contemplated for the first time. But this was not to be. It was not the time to alienate Americans, and particularly not those who controlled a powerful and influential medium. The government also recognized the propaganda value of the American industry's war films. Since the outbreak of war, Hollywood had produced numerous films with a pro-British and anti-Nazi bias. Of course, British films also put forth the British and anti-Nazi point of view, but American films reached a far wider international audience, particularly in neutral areas such as the United States and Latin America. Hollywood had taken up the British cause, and this not only meant that the American industry should not be alienated, but also reduced the need to have a strong and independent British industry.[52] Hence, a compromise was reached in which the American companies were allowed to remit $12 million between November 1940 and October 1941. When this agreement expired, the British currency crisis had lessened, and remittance of $20 million was allowed between November 1941 and October 1942. By the time the latter date was reached the United States had entered the war. The currency restrictions were lifted, and in 1943 all of the 'frozen' funds were released. The American industry then had full access to its British earnings, which had increased greatly since 1939.

Throughout the war, British cinemas enjoyed record attendance levels. Even at the height of the Blitz, when sirens frequently interrupted film showings, box-office revenues were 10 per cent higher than pre-war levels.[53] Weekly attendance figures steadily grew from 19.0 million in 1939 to an all-time high of 31.4 million in 1946. The British film industry benefited from this to some extent. For the first time, British films were consistently earning grosses on a par with Hollywood films. It came as some surprise to Hollywood, for example, when it was reported that the British film *The Wicked Lady* (1945) was likely to earn the highest gross ever on the Rank circuit of cinemas. Its earnings were predicted to reach £375,000, and two other films financed by Rank, *Madonna of the Seven Moons* (1945) and *Waterloo Road* (1945), were not far behind. These revelations led *Variety* to exclaim that 'the once farcical British motion picture industry is now a force to be reckoned with in the British Empire'.[54] But Hollywood's fears of an invigorated and prolific British film industry were focused on the post-war period. During the war, the competition was not so fierce simply because British production had fallen dramatically. The government had requisitioned studio space, placed studio workers in war-related work, and rationed the materials necessary to build sets and make costumes. Production fell from a pre-war average of 150 films per year to only 42 films in 1942. The problems related to film production were so acute that the quota requirements set out in the 1938 Films

Act were relaxed, and the American share of releases again climbed toward 80 per cent.[55] While British films were more popular in Britain than ever before, there were far fewer of them.

In this climate, Hollywood reaped the benefits of Britain's thriving box office. According to one contemporary estimate, American films earned 82 per cent of the country's total box-office takings, while British films earned the remaining 18 per cent.[56] Exact figures were seldom published, but a Twentieth Century-Fox memorandum, which lists 'actual and anticipated' earnings figures for twenty-one of the studio's wartime releases, provides evidence of the strength of British grosses in wartime (see table 4).[57] The figures indicate that earnings from prestige releases such as *Jane Eyre* (1944) and *The Song of Bernadette* (1943) were expected to reach £325,000 (approximately $1,400,000), while films featuring Twentieth Century-Fox's top stars – Betty Grable (*Coney Island, Sweet Rosie O'Grady, Springtime in the Rockies*), Tyrone Power (*The Black Swan*) and Alice Faye (*Hello Frisco Hello*) – were expected to earn between £250,000 and £280,000 (approximately $1,100,000). The strength of the studio's British earnings were cited when the company reported its best earnings ever in 1944. Twentieth Century-Fox's domestic earnings had risen sharply, and its foreign earnings had reached an all-time high. The studio was able to earn 40 per cent of its worldwide earnings in the foreign markets in 1944, and this was attributed by a spokesman to the fact that 'motion pictures are enjoying their greatest boom in history throughout Great Britain'.[58]

In fact, Britain had become central to the industry's good fortune, and many of the films produced by the Hollywood studios reflect this. Beginning in the 1930s, the studios had realized that 'British' films could bring extraordinary British earnings. The annual, year-end estimates of *Kinematograph Weekly* indicate that from the late 1930s (when *Kinematograph Weekly* began listing the top box-office successes of each year) through the war years, Hollywood's 'British' films were regularly among the most popular films of each year in Britain. *Mutiny on the Bounty* (1935), *A Tale of Two Cities* (1935), *The Dark Angel* (1935), *A Yank at Oxford* (1938), *The Citadel* (1938), *Rebecca* (1940), *Foreign Correspondent* (1940), *Lady Hamilton* (1941), *Mrs Miniver* (1942), *How Green Was My Valley* (1941), *Random Harvest* (1942), *Frenchman's Creek* (1944), *Jane Eyre* (1944), *The White Cliffs of Dover* (1944) and *National Velvet* (1945) were all at or near the top of *Kinematograph Weekly*'s annual lists, and many more 'British' films were singled out in the list of the monthly box-office hits.[59]

Table 4 British grosses in wartime: on 21 films released by Twentieth Century-Fox (in British pounds)

Film (year)	Actual earnings (£)	Anticipated earnings (£)
Jane Eyre (1944)	300,000	325,000
The Song of Bernadette (1943)	130,000	325,000
The Black Swan (1942)	275,000	280,000
Coney Island (1943)	260,000	275,000
Sweet Rosie O'Grady (1943)	250,000	260,000
Hello Frisco Hello (1943)	240,000	250,000
Springtime in the Rockies (1942)	240,000	250,000
The Sullivans (1944)	180,000	200,000
Buffalo Bill (1944)	150,000	200,000
The Lodger (1944)	150,000	200,000
Pin-Up Girl (1944)	110,000	200,000
Wintertime (1943)	165,000	175,000
Footlight Serenade (1942)	150,000	150,000
My Friend Flicka (1943)	150,000	150,000
Home in Indiana (1944)	30,000	150,000
Thunderbirds (1942)	120,000	130,000
Holy Matrimony (1943)	90,000	100,000
Lifeboat (1944)	80,000	95,000
A-Haunting We Will Go (1943)	80,000	85,000
Meanest Man in Town (1943)	40,000	50,000
Berlin Correspondent (1942)	32,000	35,000

Source: 'British Grosses in Wartime', Memorandum dated 15 December 1944, file 2, box 7, series 1F, United Artists Collection, Wisconsin State Historical Society.

Canada, Australia and New Zealand

Because Canada was usually considered to be part of a North American 'domestic' market, Canadian earnings were normally included in the domestic, rather than the foreign, earnings figures. Australia and New Zealand were grouped together as 'Australasia'. None of these countries was particularly large as an exhibition market. Canada had 1,200 cinemas, Australia 1,400 and New Zealand 700. Yet several important similarities with the British market gave them a collective importance. First, cinema audiences in these countries were predominantly English-speaking, and this meant that in the 1930s the advent of sound had no adverse effect on the appeal of American films. Second, none of these countries had a competitive feature film industry of its own. And third, American films predominated in these markets, accounting for between 75 per cent and 85 per cent of all films released in the 1930s. The minimal competition came mainly from British films or, in the French-speaking areas of Canada, French films. Hence, the problems that the industry faced in Europe and other non-English-speaking markets were not encountered in these British Commonwealth markets. Indeed, Hollywood's experience in these markets during the 1930s was quite the opposite to its experiences elsewhere. Consumer demand was high, and the increased returns from the English-speaking countries were said to have offset the declines in other foreign territories.[60] Then, during the war years, each of these markets remained open to American films, and the two largest, Australia and Canada, experienced rises in cinema admissions comparable to those in the United States and Britain. The decline in the number of British films, meanwhile, allowed the American share of these markets to climb to 90 per cent of all releases.[61]

The British Commonwealth markets were much smaller than the British market, but their collective importance was significant. One element of this was that these markets had similar tastes – tastes that were similar to those of the British market. When *Variety* conducted a survey of foreign market tastes in 1941, it was found that British tastes overwhelmingly predominated. This was attributed to the fact that Britain, together with Australia, Canada and New Zealand, constituted such a large portion of the remaining foreign market. The preference for British stars who worked in Hollywood, and the popularity of 'British' films were among the findings.[62] This has been reinforced more recently by the Australian film historian Mike Walsh, who has suggested that 'British' films drew a very favourable response in Australia, where the combination of Hollywood polish and British culture met a particularly sympathetic audience.[63] When American film-makers set out to appeal to the British market, then, they were also aiming at the wider British Commonwealth market.

The film sample

The Hollywood studios regularly reported domestic film grosses to the industry's trade papers in the 1930s and 1940s, but they seldom provided such information on their foreign earnings. Only in recent years, as film industry archives have opened, have foreign earnings figures become accessible to historians, thus making possible a greater understanding of Hollywood's world view. The film sample offered here is one example of this newly available information. The sample provides financial statistics on nineteen films released between 1937 and 1942, the years in which the greatest changes occurred in the foreign markets. The first seventeen films were released by United Artists in the years 1937 to 1941, and the last two films (*Eagle Squadron* and *Arabian Nights*) were released by Universal in 1942. All of the films were produced by Walter Wanger. Wanger is best described at this point in his career as a 'prestige' producer, which is reflected in the fact that the average production cost of these nineteen films was $750,000. Otherwise, it is difficult to generalize about his films. The nineteen films considered here, for example, encompass a wide variety of genres (romantic comedies, melodramas, a western and wartime action-adventure films), and include the work of a diverse array of directors (Frank Borzage, John Cromwell, John Ford, Tay Garnett, Henry Hathaway, Alfred Hitchcock, Fritz Lang) and stars (Jean Arthur, Joan Bennett, Joan Blondell, Charles Boyer, Henry Fonda, Leslie Howard, Hedy Lamarr, Fredric March, Joel McCrea, David Niven, Gene Tierney, John Wayne, Loretta Young). This diversity, albeit in a limited selection of films, enhances the credibility of what serves here as a representative sample of foreign market statistics. The statistics have been compiled from numerous financial documents found within Walter Wanger's collected papers and the United Artists Collection, and they are listed here in five tables (tables 5, 6, 7, 8 and 9).[64]

Table 5 lists the production cost, the domestic earnings and the foreign earnings of each film. On average, the films earned 66 per cent of their worldwide gross in the domestic market and the remaining 34 per cent in foreign markets, and these figures are very similar to those found at studios such as MGM, RKO and Warner Bros. And, as at these other studios, the foreign earnings actually rose, in both real terms and percentage terms, as Hollywood's foreign market contracted in the late 1930s and the early 1940s.[65] Indeed, three of the films released after the outbreak of war (*Foreign Correspondent*, *Eagle Squadron* and *Arabian Nights*) have the highest foreign earnings in the sample. Also, it is apparent that foreign earnings were crucial to profitability. Most of the films barely covered their production costs in the domestic market, and the costs of distribution, prints and advertising are not included in the table. Thus, it is likely that in most instances Wanger covered his costs in the domestic market and found profits in the foreign earnings.

Table 5 The film sample: a comparison of production costs, domestic revenue and foreign revenue (in US dollars)

Film (studio/year)	Production cost ($)	Domestic earnings ($)	Foreign earnings ($)
1. *You Only Live Once* (UA, 1937)	589,503	664,203 64.0%	373,000 36.0%
2. *History Is Made At Night* (UA, 1937)	821,790	1,000,304 62.7%	596,000 37.3%
3. *Vogues of 1938* (UA, 1937)	1,048,435	1,101,429 65.4%	583,000 34.6%
4. *Stand In* (UA, 1937)	523,123	589,768 69.1%	263,582 30.9%
5. *Fifty-Second Street* (UA, 1937)	523,868	619,040 76%	195,000 24%
6. *I Met My Love Again* (UA, 1938)	428,799	435,758 73.2%	159,560 26.8%
7. *Blockade* (UA, 1938)	692,086	704,300 60.7%	455,000 39.3%
8. *Algiers* (UA, 1938)	691,833	1,128,886 67.2%	551,100 32.8%
9. *Trade Winds* (UA, 1938)	738,733	1,022,792 72.4%	389,700 27.6%
10. *Stagecoach* (UA, 1939)	531,374	1,242,016 63.7%	708,600 36.3%
11. *Winter Carnival* (UA, 1939)	412,639	506,609 76.8%	153,000 23.2%
12. *Eternally Yours* (UA, 1939)	790,878	785,634 72.8%	292,800 27.2%
13. *Slightly Honorable* (UA, 1939)	434,873	464,073 73.1%	170,400 26.9%
14. *The House Across the Bay* (UA, 1940)	713,965	783,027 70.1%	333,600 29.9%
15. *Foreign Correspondent* (UA, 1940)	1,484,167	1,428,538 64.9%	772,700 35.1%
16. *The Long Voyage Home* (UA, 1940)	682,495	656,653 70.1%	280,300 29.9%
17. *Sundown* (UA, 1941)	1,257,779	1,285,330 67.5%	619,700 32.5%
18. *Eagle Squadron* (Uni, 1942)	908,768	1,736,753 65.4%	918,375 34.6%
19. *Arabian Nights* (Uni, 1942)	not indicated	1,645,892 59.4%	1,125,000 40.6%

Source for the UA films: file 3, box 38, series 3A, United Artists Collection, Wisconsin State Historical Society.

Source for the Universal Films: file 6, box 42, The Walter Wanger Collection, Wisconsin State Historical Society.

When Hollywood loved Britain

Table 6 offers a partial breakdown of the foreign grosses for these nineteen films. The total foreign gross is divided into three categories: British earnings, European earnings, and earnings from 'other foreign' markets. The figures demonstrate the extent to which British earnings predominated among Hollywood's foreign earnings, accounting for at least 53 per cent of the foreign gross and at most 73 per cent. Thus, in every instance British earnings were higher than earnings from all of the other markets combined. It is also noteworthy that British earnings increased over the time span of the sample, while earnings from Europe were in decline. European earnings provided close to 22 per cent of the total foreign gross on the earliest three films, released in 1937, but from that point they decline and then disappear. The 'other foreign' category would include the Far East and Latin America, as well as Australia and New Zealand. Earnings from these markets were greater than those from Europe even in 1937 and 1938, and despite the loss of the Far Eastern markets, they rose throughout the time period of the sample.

More detailed foreign earnings records are available for the first twelve United Artists films in the sample, those released between 1937 and 1939. These are the net earnings sheets compiled by United Artists for Walter Wanger, which show the earnings due to Wanger once the costs of distribution, prints and advertising had been deducted from the gross. While these reports do not show the gross figure, they are nonetheless valuable for showing which countries the films were released in, and for comparing the lucrativeness of different countries and regions. Table 7 offers an example of one of these earnings sheets, reporting Wanger's share of the earnings from *Stagecoach* (1939).

The net earnings reports indicate that each of the twelve films earned far more in Britain than in any other country. Net British earnings range from a low of $56,394 (from *I Met My Love Again*) to a peak of $217,570 (from *History is Made at Night*). Canadian earnings are listed for only four of these twelve films, but it is apparent that they were significantly higher than those from any foreign market other than Britain. Wanger's highest Canadian return was the $30,475 recorded for *Stagecoach*. When Canadian earnings were not listed, it was usually Australia that ranked second behind Britain. Australian returns reached as high as $12,995, which was recorded for *History is Made at Night*. The market of New Zealand was much smaller and did not figure so prominently: its highest return was the $2,984 earned by *Vogues of 1938*. However, when returns from these English-speaking markets are combined, they represent a prodigiously large

Table 6 The film sample: breakdown of foreign revenues (in US dollars)

Film (total foreign)	British earnings ($)	European earnings ($)	Other foreign earnings ($)
1. *You Only Live Once*	215,000	75,000	83,000
(373,000)	57.7%	20.1%	22.2%
2. *History is Made at Night*	318,000	128,000	150,000
(596,000)	53.3%	21.5%	25.2%
3. *Vogues of 1938*	307,000	123,000	153,000
(583,000)	52.7%	21.1%	26.2%
4. *Stand In*	180,639	22,195	60,748
(263,582)	68.5%	8.4%	23.1%
5. *Fifty-Second Street*	119,000	18,000	58,000
(195,000)	61.0%	9.2%	29.8%
6. *I Met My Love Again*	91,060	22,000	46,500
(159,560)	57.1%	13.8%	29.1%
7. *Blockade*	277,000	52,000	126,000
(455,000)	60.9%	11.4%	27.7%
8. *Algiers*	312,100	60,000	179,000
(551,100)	56.6%	10.9%	32.5%
9. *Trade Winds*	226,700	30,000	133,000
(389,700)	58.2%	7.7%	34.1%
10. *Stagecoach*	389,600	100,000	219,000
(708,600)	55.0%	14.1%	30.9%
11. *Winter Carnival*	90,000	12,000	51,000
(153,000)	58.8%	7.9%	33.3%
12. *Eternally Yours*	196,800	12,000	84,000
(292,800)	67.2%	4.1%	28.7%
13. *Slightly Honorable*	124,000	–	46,400
(170,400)	72.8%		27.2%
14. *The House Across the Bay*	229,100	–	104,500
(333,600)	68.7%		31.3%
15. *Foreign Correspondent*	480,000	–	292,700
(772,700)	62.1%		37.9%
16. *The Long Voyage Home*	180,000	–	100,300
(280,300)	64.2%		35.8%
17. *Sundown*	400,000	–	219,700
(619,700)	64.5%		35.5%
18. *Eagle Squadron*	585,828	–	332,547
(918,375)	63.8%		36.2%
19. *Arabian Nights*	665,000	50,000	410,000
(1,125,000)	59.1%	4.5%	36.4%

Source for the UA films: file 3, box 38, series 3A, United Artists Collection, Wisconsin State Historical Society.

Source for the Universal Films: file 6, Box 42, The Walter Wanger Collection, Wisconsin State Historical Society.

When Hollywood loved Britain

Table 7 *Stagecoach* (1939): producer's share of net foreign earnings to 3 April 1943 (in US dollars)

Region/Country	Earnings ($)	Percentage of total
British Commonwealth	*214,649.68*	*68.20*
Britain	170,308.34	54.11
Canada	30,474.92	9.68
Australia	12,515.63	3.98
New Zealand	1,350.79	0.43
Europe	*53,500.18*	*17.00*
Italy	19,144.00	6.08
France	9,625.90	3.06
Sweden	7,887.60	2.51
Denmark	4,522.71	1.44
Belgium	3,034.29	0.96
Switzerland	2,806.97	0.89
Hungary	2,445.00	0.78
Portugal	1,275.28	0.41
Norway	885.19	0.28
Romania	675.00	0.21
Yugoslavia	634.64	0.20
Greece	503.13	0.16
Czechoslovakia	60.47	0.02
Latin America	*26,230.65*	*8.33*
Argentina	6,941.55	2.20
Brazil	4,977.42	1.58
Mexico	4,365.77	1.39
Central America	3,418.55	1.09
Cuba	1,839.50	0.58
Chile	1,622.41	0.51
Puerto Rico	1,581.87	0.50
Colombia	809.97	0.26
Peru	647.66	0.21
Panama	19.93	0.01
Ecuador	6.02	–
The Far East	*11,327.97*	*3.60*
India	3,229.02	1.03
Philippines	2,758.71	0.88
Netherlands East Indies	1,989.42	0.63
British Malaya	1,855.85	0.59
China	821.55	0.26
Indo-China	540.55	0.17
Japan	132.87	0.04
Other foreign	*9,025.35*	*2.87*
South Africa	4,437.35	1.41
Egypt	2,639.32	0.84
Turkey	1,036.25	0.33
Iceland	332.50	0.10
Syria	176.19	0.06
Miscellaneous	145.12	0.05
Persia & Iraq	143.91	0.04
West Africa	114.71	0.04
Total	*314,733.83*	*100.00*

Source: file 3, box 38, series 3A, United Artists Collection, Wisconsin State Historical Society.

proportion of the foreign earnings. In the case of *Stagecoach*, 68 per cent of the net earnings came from English-speaking countries of the British Empire.

There were twenty-four European countries listed on United Artists' earnings sheets in 1937. These included Austria, Germany and Spain, but none of the twelve films was released in those countries, and by 1939, with the removal of most of the countries of Central Europe, the list had been cut down to eight. *Stagecoach* must have been released in Italy after the MPPDA boycott had become operative in January 1939. It is likely that this was a result of contractual obligations rather than indifference on the part of the producer, because it was the last of these films to reach Italy. The film's Italian earnings demonstrate the relative strength of this market and the appeal of this particular film. The return of $19,144 was the highest from any European country for all of the twelve films, and it was four times higher than any other sum received from Italy. Otherwise, net returns from most European markets were usually between $500 and $5,000, with the best returns coming from France, Italy and Sweden. However, they could be surprisingly low. *Algiers*, which was otherwise one of the most successful of these films, returned a mere 35 cents from its release in Poland.

Net earnings from Latin America were generally similar to those from Europe. Argentina, Brazil, Mexico and Cuba offered the largest returns from this region. The highest Latin American return was the $11,838 that *Algiers* earned in Argentina. By contrast, many of the smaller Latin American markets offered remarkably feeble returns. Bolivia, Chile, Colombia, Peru and Puerto Rico never returned more than $2,000 for a single film, and Ecuador never returned more than $7. It is thus not surprising that in the 1930s the Hollywood studios were reluctant to invest in dubbed versions for these countries.

In the Far East, India was by far the most lucrative market, returning as much as $7,613 for *Algiers*. The Philippines also offered four-figure sums, while other markets (China, Indo-China, the Netherlands East Indies, the Straits Settlements) offered three-figure sums at best. Seven of the films were released in Japan, but the best return was only $394 (for *Stand In*) and two of the films (*History is Made at Night*, *Vogues of 1938*) showed loss figures for their Japanese release. Other countries listed on the earnings sheets include British West Africa, Egypt, Iceland, Iraq, Lebanon, Palestine, Persia, South Africa and Syria, but not all of the films were released in each of these small markets, and only South Africa returned sums that occasionally reached four figures. The

Irish Free State, which had only 200 cinemas, was not listed at all, but its earnings were probably included in the category referred to as 'England', which also included Scotland and Wales. A 'miscellaneous' category existed and this presumably covered even more countries and territories, but the 'miscellaneous' earnings never exceeded $300.

Table 8 and Table 9 offer detail on the gross foreign earnings of *Eagle Squadron* and *Arabian Nights*, respectively. Their particular significance here is that they were released in 1942, and thus the figures offer evidence of how the level of foreign earnings was maintained later in the war. The figures on these films demonstrate that although the foreign market was much smaller in 1942 than it had been in 1937, it was far more lucrative for Hollywood. In fact, the foreign grosses earned by *Eagle Squadron* and *Arabian Nights* were nearly twice as high as the best foreign grosses from the 1937 films. A difference between the two films is that *Eagle Squadron*, a war film, was less successful in neutral countries than *Arabian Nights*, an escapist adventure film. Indeed, the figures for *Arabian Nights* indicate that returns from the Latin American markets could be substantial, at least in the case of non-war films. But Britain was still by far the most lucrative foreign market. In both cases, Britain provided over one-half of the gross foreign earnings, and the British Empire countries provided over two-thirds of the gross foreign earnings.

Table 8 *Eagle Squadron* (1942): gross foreign earnings to 1945 (in US dollars)

Region/ Country	Earnings ($)	Percentage of total
British Commonwealth	*712,726*	*77.61*
Britain	585,828	63.79
Australia	101,197	11.02
New Zealand	25,701	2.80
Other foreign (not itemized)	*205,689*	*22.39*
Total	*918,415*	*100.00*

Source: file 6, box 42, The Walter Wanger Collection, Wisconsin State Historical Society.

Table 9 *Arabian Nights* (1942): gross foreign earnings to November 1943 (in US dollars)

Region/ Country	Gross earnings ($)	Percentage of total earnings
British Commonwealth	*750,000*	*66.67*
Britain	665,000	59.11
Australia and New Zealand	85,000	7.56
Latin America	*295,000*	*26.22*
Mexico	67,500	6.00
Brazil	63,000	5.60
Argentina	55,000	4.89
Panama	26,500	2.36
Chile	22,000	1.95
Cuba	20,000	1.78
Puerto Rico	14,000	1.24
Uruguay	10,000	0.89
Peru	9,000	0.80
Trinidad	8,000	0.71
Europe	*50,000*	*4.44*
Sweden	35,000	3.11
Switzerland	15,000	1.33
Far East	*30,000*	*2.67*
India	30,000	2.67
Total	1,125,000	100.00

Source: file 6, box 42, The Walter Wanger Collection, Wisconsin State Historical Society.

Conclusion

When Hollywood's trade papers reported on the war events of 1939 and 1940, and warned of doom and gloom as events unfolded, they were careful not to be too specific about exactly how and where the industry would be hit the hardest. Hollywood's reliance upon Britain was not stated plainly, and the reports implied that the concern was for general losses throughout Europe rather than the loss of one key market. This caginess is understandable. It would not have benefited the industry to have its good fortune in Britain made public. The news would probably have raised calls for additional tariffs or protectionism within Britain itself, while in the USA it would have enabled isolationists to refer to Hollywood's selfish motives in making pro-British films. Hence, the trade papers reported the industry's despair without revealing its particular dependence on Britain, or its vulnerability in the case of invasion or defeat. But the information now available makes it plain that, while Hollywood still sought foreign earnings wherever possible in the 1930s – including even the most minor sums from the most faraway places – the majority of its foreign earnings came from Britain and the English-speaking countries of the British Commonwealth. This realignment of the industry's foreign markets can be seen, in retrospect, to have prepared the industry for the abrupt changes brought by the war. A war that formed an alliance among the English-speaking peoples did not damage Hollywood's interests. As subsequent chapters will explore, Hollywood's growing dependence on the British market had a profound effect on the feature films produced during this era.

2   Hollywood's foreign policy

Hollywood's foreign policy was shaped and administered by the film industry's trade organization, the Motion Picture Producers and Distributors of America (MPPDA), which was also known as the Hays Office. It is remembered now primarily for its censorship activities, but it also acted to safeguard the collective interests of its member studios in both the domestic and foreign markets. This included monitoring foreign-market conditions, negotiating with foreign governments on behalf of the industry, and advising film-makers on the tastes and prejudices of foreign censors and audiences. The most basic foreign policy was to avoid giving offence to any country which provided the industry with revenue. Paying customers were to be treated with care and respect, and so film-makers were warned against stories that had any relevance to contemporary international events and issues. When the foreign market began to disintegrate in the 1930s, however, this policy became difficult to maintain. Hollywood was divided between film-makers seeking timely and topical stories and those who sought a more conservative policy of 'pure entertainment'. The Hays Office favoured the latter position, and up until 1941 it attempted to maintain some semblance of neutrality for American films. Thus, the Hays Office was at the centre of the industry's foreign policy and played a key role in shaping the earliest American war films.

The Hays Office and the Production Code

By the early 1920s, the American film industry had become an oligopoly controlled by several vertically integrated film companies. In 1921, these companies formed the MPPDA. At its inception, the primary duty of the MPPDA was that of a public relations agency for the industry. A series of widely publicized scandals, involving drugs, sex and murder, had brought the film industry into disrepute. The tabloid press, civic organizations and religious groups focused their attentions on the immorality of Hollywood film-makers, and ever increasing attention was paid to the immorality of their films. Furthermore, in an attempt to lay the blame for this immorality beyond the borders of the United States, critics of the industry often alluded to the fact that the industry had been founded and was led by immigrant Jews.[1]

The film industry needed to improve its image, and so it hired Will Hays to head the MPPDA. Hays was from the Midwest, he was an elder in the Protestant Church, and he had served as a high-ranking official in the Republican Party. With these religious and political credentials, he was everything that Hollywood, as perceived by its critics, was not. Hence, Hays was sent out to act as the industry's spokesperson, talking to groups such as the National Council of Catholic Women and the Boy Scouts of America, and assuring them that Hollywood would reform under his guidance. Behind this facade of all-American respectability, however, the studios continued in a business-as-usual fashion.[2]

At this time, censorship of films was haphazard, inefficient and costly. Many states and foreign censorship agencies insisted that offensive scenes be cut out of a film before it could be granted a release within their territory. To circumvent these chop-and-splice tactics, and in an attempt to predict what sort of material was likely to be cut, the Hays Office began to advise the studios on their scripts. The Hays Office's Studio Relations Committee reviewed scripts with an eye toward cutting out offensive material before the studios went to the expense of filming it. Hays wrote a list of 'Don'ts and Be Carefuls', a precursor of the Production Code, which covered topics such as miscegenation, adultery and incest, and warned against 'unfavourable' portrayals of foreign institutions, customs and peoples. His list was sent to newspapers across the United States as proof that Hollywood was indeed reforming. Of course, it was also sent to the studios and to producers but, believing this to be another public relations exercise, many reportedly returned their copies unopened.[3]

Hays was in a difficult – if well-renumerated – position. His job involved representing an industry with a questionable reputation, and assuring the outside world that the industry was becoming ever cleaner, more wholesome and more responsible towards its youthful audience. The concern over 'movie-made children' in the mid-1920s necessitated this. But the studios' primary goal was profit, and the films that were deemed to be salacious and offensive often drew the best earnings. Hays could advise the studios that certain topics or storylines were likely to draw the wrath of moralists, but he could not stop the studios from using them in their films. He was employed by the studios, and everything related to the Hays Office – from the rent for its premises to the salaries of its employees – was paid for by them. So he could advise the studios, but he did not have power over them. In fact, one of the main purposes behind the establishment of the Hays Office was to avoid the introduction of external regulatory bodies (such as a federal censor) with statutory power to interfere with the industry and its pursuit of profits.

The Hays Office's position was improved considerably, though, when a Catholic Church group, the Legion of Decency, was formed in 1934 as a pressure group against the film industry. The Legion of Decency boasted of having eleven million followers, ready and willing to boycott films, and their initial exercises proved to be economically damaging to the studios. This new and far more tangible threat persuaded the members of the MPPDA to agree to a more elaborate code of practice. The Production Code, as it was known, had been written several years earlier by a Catholic priest, Father Daniel Lord, at the request of the owner of *The Motion Picture Herald*, Martin Quigley. Quigley was a prominent Catholic who was eager to lead a real reform movement in Hollywood. To this end, he wrote editorials that castigated producers and studios for their films' iniquity. He was also instrumental in establishing the Production Code Administration office (PCA) within the Hays Office, and having his associate and fellow Catholic, Joseph Breen, placed as its Director.[4]

It has been conjectured that Quigley and Breen were instrumental in prompting the Legion of Decency's assault on the industry as a means of enforcing the Production Code and establishing Breen's importance within the Hays Office. The Legion of Decency was certainly attuned to the language the film industry understood and responded to. The potential for a further loss of business – amid the ravages of the Depression – led to the studios' acceptance of the Code and Breen's interpretation of it. From 1934 onward, every script proposed for production was submitted to the Hays Office. Breen and his staff read the scripts and wrote reviews suggesting what changes, if any, were necessary to bring the scripts into compliance with the Code. Then, the finished film went through the same process. If a film did not comply with the Code, it would not receive the MPPDA 'Certificate of

Approval', and it could not be released in a cinema affiliated with the MPPDA. As the MPPDA members owned the majority of the most lucrative 'first-run' cinemas in the United States, a film without the certificate was consigned to the limbo of independent exhibition and financial perdition.[5]

The Hays Office's authority over the film industry should not be exaggerated, even when the Production Code Administration had Joseph Breen at the helm and the Legion of Decency as a zealous back-up. The MPPDA paid Breen's salary, and it would be wrong to suggest that Breen or anyone with the PCA gave orders to the producers who belonged to the MPPDA. Yet the actions of the Legion of Decency had brought to light the best means of protesting against the film industry, and Breen stood as a mediator between such pressure groups and the Hollywood studios. The Code would protect Hollywood from its detractors, and this meant that Breen's advice was best followed, and that the Hays Office's talk of reform was no longer simply a public relations exercise.

Foreign concerns of the Hays Office

Although the Hays Office and the Production Code are most often remembered for their moral preoccupations, and particularly the insistence that 'compensating moral values' should balance any script that dealt with sexual or criminal activity, a keen eye was fixed on the portrayal of domestic, foreign and international political issues. The Foreign Division of the Hays Office had been created in 1923, and was charged with protecting the industry's collective interests abroad. When foreign governments proposed tariffs, quotas and other restrictions on imported films, the Hays Office negotiated on behalf of the Hollywood studios, and was frequently successful in reaching compromises. It also liaised with foreign governments, foreign censorship agencies and the Hollywood studios' own foreign departments, attempting to prevent or iron out any conflicts that might arise. This often had ramifications for the PCA.[6]

Only one clause in the Production Code related directly to foreign considerations. The 'National Feelings' clause stated that: 'The history, institutions, prominent people and citizenry of other nations shall be represented fairly.'[7] While this may seem to have a lofty moral purpose, it was also a very practical measure and one based on the industry's experience in foreign markets. If a foreign government thought that a film represented its country or its people in an unfavourable light, that government might ban the offensive film. If the film was particularly insulting, it might threaten to ban all of the films released by the studio responsible for the offence. In the most extreme cases, it might ask other friendly governments also to ban the film. The 'diplomatic ban' was a strategy pioneered by France in reaction to *Beau Geste* (1926), but it was used thereafter throughout the world.[8] The perceived power of the medium, together with resentment against the power of the American film industry, ensured that such measures became commonplace amid the international tensions of the 1930s.

The practical nature of the 'National Feelings' clause can be seen in the manner in which it was applied. The clause was designed to protect the industry's foreign income and therefore it was applied only to countries that imported American films. Furthermore, the amount of consideration given to a country corresponded with the amount of earnings it provided. The British market was the most lucrative foreign market for American films, and so British sensibilities received by far the most attention from Breen and his staff. In fact, the regulations of the British Board of Film Censors (BBFC), which were in many respects more rigorous than those of the Production Code, became a *de facto* code at the Hays Office.[9] If Breen saw a scene in a script that was permissible by his own guidelines, but not by the British regulations, he would urge the studio involved either to alter the scene or to make 'protection shots' for the British market. If a script or sequence went against both the BBFC regulations and the Production Code, Breen often used the threat of British censorship to add weight to his own warnings. And, if Breen was uncertain about the suitability of a novel or play for screen adaptation, he often sought the BBFC's opinion.

The British censors do not appear to have been particularly sensitive to Hollywood's portrayal of Britain in feature films. Of course, film-makers knew that studio executives would not finance any film that could be construed as anti-British. This is why there were so few films made about the American Revolution during the studio era. Remarkably, there were films made about the more contemporary conflict between Britain and Ireland, but they were made in as careful a manner as possible and the BBFC passed them with only bits of dialogue cut out. The British release print of John Ford's *The Informer* (1935), for example, contains no mention of what the conflict was about, nor indeed the nationalities of anyone involved.[10] It is as vague, in fact, as Hollywood's earliest exposés of Fascism, which also avoided naming countries and places. In other instances both the

When Hollywood loved Britain

BBFC and the Hays Office seem to have been unconcerned by films that offered unflattering or even critical views of Britain. Warner Bros.' *Captain Blood* (1935), for example, begins with the wrongful conviction of an Irish doctor (Errol Flynn) by a tyrannical English judge (Leonard Mudie), and then follows the doctor's ordeal as a mistreated slave on an English plantation in the Caribbean. Yet the Hays Office's only concern about this film was that the female characters' plunging necklines would provoke a furore in the British press. On this acount alone, Breen was warned by the Hays Office's foreign division that 'they [Warner Bros.] ought to be watched because again I say we must keep our eyes on our money markets and the main money market is England outside of the U.S.'.[11]

Film historian James Robertson has suggested that historical dramas such as *Captain Blood* did not cause concern at the BBFC because they were set in the distant past. However, the BBFC also passed MGM's *The Citadel* (1938), a film that portrays contemporary Britain as having an appalling healthcare system, as well as extreme poverty and sharp class divisions. Breen consulted with the BBFC over this story, which was based on a recent and bestselling novel, even before MGM had submitted its script.[12] But the BBFC's response indicated their primary concern was that the film should avoid the implication that bad doctors 'are the rule and not the exception', and so MGM added a written prologue that makes this clear. When submitted to the BBFC, *The Citadel* was under consideration for longer than usual, and Robertson indicates that some (unspecified) cuts were made to the film.[13] Yet it was passed, and the British press greeted it with high praise rather than hurt pride.

Other countries were far more sensitive. Mexicans became so weary of seeing swarthy Mexican bandits in Hollywood films that the Mexican government banned all the films of the companies that perpetuated this stereotype. The Italian censors, meanwhile, were made indignant by comical Italian characters, such as the ridiculously overzealous and preening fashion designer in the musical *Top Hat* (1935). In the wake of that film, Italy decided to ban any Hollywood film with Italian characters unless they were 'completely sympathetic'.[14] Hollywood took heed of such criticisms, particularly as Italian and Mexican officials were clearly aware of how to deal with the industry. Threatening its earnings produced results. This left only the Russians, who imported few American films and had little influence with the industry's more lucrative customers, as the only foreigners available for ridicule and contempt. This is most apparent in MGM's *Ninotchka* (1939), a scathing satire on Communism that centres on the seduction of a humourless Russian official (Greta Garbo) by a Parisian playboy (Melvyn Douglas). Breen's comments on the script contain no references to the many insults and jokes aimed at the Russians. His only concerns were the 'illicit sex affair' between the two main characters and the 'general acceptability of this story, particularly from the standpoint of the French government and people'.[15] France, which had no reason to find offence in *Ninotchka*, was on the industry's foreign circuit, while the derided Russians were not.

Germany and the 'National Feelings' clause

Over the course of the 1930s, Germany's standing with the industry plunged nearly to the debased level of Russia. The fact that it did not sink any further may be attributed in part to the German Consul in Los Angeles, Dr Georg Gyssling. Indeed, the amount of attention Gyssling paid to the film industry provides testimony to Hollywood's standing in the world. Gyssling faithfully read trade papers such as the *Hollywood Reporter* and *Variety*, and when he found items that roused his suspicions, he immediately wrote directly to Joseph Breen. Invariably, he cited news reports of upcoming productions which would feature German characters or a German setting. Often, Gyssling was able to inform Breen of these projects before Breen had seen a script or treatment. Gyssling was determined to prevent films which cast a negative light on Germany, whether related to Nazi Germany or to Germany's past, and he was well versed in the means with which to deal with the industry. For example, even before Twentieth Century-Fox began filming the First World War spy drama *Lancer Spy* (1937), which centres on a British double agent, Gyssling informed Breen that he heard that there would be 'several scenes apparently objectionable from the German standpoint'. He also reminded Breen that 'many Fox films are being shown in Germany at this time'.[16] This was only one of many references made to the link between film content and the studios' ability to operate in Germany. There were also numerous references to the 'National Feelings' clause. Gyssling apparently had read the Production Code, and was determined to see that this clause was applied to Germany.

Difficulties arose, however, because by 1937 only the three largest studios – MGM, Paramount and Twentieth Century-Fox – continued to do business with Germany, and the very limited number of films they were able to release there did not warrant the careful consideration the German Consul demanded. Hence, the studios' concern over German sensibilities differed, and none was willing to bow to German demands completely. This is illustrated by the production of two films adapted from novels by the German author Erich Maria Remarque, *The Road Back* (1937) and *Three Comrades* (1938). The studios were aware that adaptations of Remarque's work would be troublesome. Universal had already filmed his classic anti-war novel *All Quiet on the Western Front* (1930), which is set in the German trenches during the First World War, and the film had been banned in both Austria and Germany. Remarque went into exile and his books were banned by the Nazis, who – as one Hays Office memorandum stated – 'very thoroughly disapprove of him'.[17] Not surprisingly, then, Universal's plans to adapt *The Road Back* and MGM's plans to adapt *Three Comrades* drew swift protests from Georg Gyssling. Had the BBFC objected as strongly to these two proposed films, the studios almost certainly would have cancelled their plans immediately, but German protests were of less concern and so *The Road Back* and *Three Comrades* proceeded.

Originally, Universal had planned to film *The Road Back* in 1931. The story follows the fortunes of German soldiers as they return home from the front, and so it was seen by the studio as a logical follow-up to *All Quiet on the Western Front*. But the German government warned that if the film was made all Universal films would be banned in Germany.[18] *The Road Back* was cancelled as a result, but by the mid-1930s Universal had withdrawn from the German market and the studio was ready to proceed again. Gyssling, as usual, heard about the renewed production plans before the Hays Office, and he warned Joseph Breen in September 1936 that the *The Road Back* should be stopped 'on behalf of correct relations between the American film industry and Germany'.[19] When Breen consulted with the studio's executives, he found that:

The company [Universal] was not very much concerned about German protests because it was impossible for the company to operate in Germany at the present time, and that any business worth worrying about was not being done by Universal in Germany now.[20]

Gyssling based his protest on the grounds that *The Road Back* gave an 'untrue and distorted picture of the German people', a clear appeal to the 'National Feelings' clause.[21] But Breen disagreed. He thought that the film showed good Germans as well as bad Germans, and therefore it could be considered a fair portrayal. Moreover, Universal had cooperated with Breen in making the script acceptable. This was done on behalf of members of the MPPDA who were still operating in Germany and as a means of avoiding the diplomatic bans that Germany was likely to seek in regard to this particular film.

Breen felt that the studio had played by the rules and that the German Consul was being unreasonable. When the final script was submitted, Universal was advised only to make sure that the BBFC would not object to the film.[22] And then Breen tried to avoid Gyssling, who continued to protest against *The Road Back* with letters and telephone calls. In November 1936 Breen's secretary was told that he would make no reply to Gyssling's letters, and that 'if he phones – I'm out of town'.[23] In February 1937, Gyssling actually visited the MPPDA's offices, but he was not seen and was told to direct his comments to the studio.[24] Gyssling's final protest indicates the extent to which the Germans considered Remarque's work to be damaging. In April 1937, he wrote to the director and to every cast member of *The Road Back*, warning them that under new German laws all of their future films could be banned in Germany.[25] Given the limitations of the German market, this was a dramatic but hollow threat. All that remained for the Germans was to seek 'diplomatic bans', and they were successful in preventing the film's release in China, Greece, Italy and Switzerland.[26]

MGM's *Three Comrades* promised to be even more troublesome than *The Road Back*. MGM, unlike Universal, was still operating in Germany, albeit on a very limited scale. Furthermore, while both stories centre on the aftermath of the First World War in Germany, *Three Comrades* comes further forward in time than *The Road Back*, and depicts the turbulence of the 1920s and the rise of Fascism. When Gyssling heard that MGM was considering *Three Comrades*, he again raised the spectre of the 'National Feelings' clause in a letter to Joseph Breen.[27] Breen apparently agreed this time. He wrote to MGM that the story was 'inescapably a serious indictment of the German nation and people', and warned MGM that *Three Comrades* would be banned in Germany and Italy, and that its production could also lead to 'enormous difficulties from the standpoint of your company's distribution business in Germany', as well as 'considerable difficulties in Europe for other American producing companies'.[28] In the heated political atmosphere of the late 1930s, a single film, it seemed, could threaten the entire film industry.

Having already paid for the screen rights to the novel, MGM was not about to abandon *Three Comrades*, but it was willing to undertake the 'careful re-write' that Breen advised. Breen met with studio head Louis B. Mayer and producer Joseph Mankiewicz to discuss the adaptation in May 1938. It was decided that the timescale of the story should be abbreviated to within two years of the Armistice, before the Nazi Party existed. The film would not identify any political parties or clubs, nor would it include the novel's references to book burning and anti-Semitism. As Breen's memorandum on the meeting clearly states, the adaptation would 'have nothing to indicate in any way that the story is a reflection on the Nazi government'.[29] Further details of the meeting emerged in the left-wing newspaper *The New Masses*. It was reported that Breen had proposed making Remarque's fascist thugs into communist thugs, and that Louis B. Mayer was enthusiastic about this idea. Only Russia could object to communist thugs, and Russian opinion, of course, was not an issue for the industry. Apparently, it was only Mankiewicz's strong disapproval of this alternative that prevented its adoption.[30] Instead, *Three Comrades* was stripped of all political references, and the film focuses on the romance of stars Robert Taylor and Margaret Sullavan. This ensured that the 'diplomatic bans' were limited to Italy and Romania.

Somewhere in Europe

Most of the industry's leading executives were conservative businessmen who sympathized with the frequent assertion by Martin Quigley and Joseph Breen, that Hollywood made films to entertain and not to educate the public on the state of world affairs.[31] They sought profits – not controversy that would endanger earnings. Even the fact that many of these executives were Jewish émigrés from Central Europe did not lead them to make anti-Nazi films. Hollywood's Jewish leaders wanted to be seen first and foremost as Americans, and not as foreigners with a special cause to plead.[32] There was also the matter of domestic opinion to consider. At a time when Congress was passing Neutrality Laws to ensure that America would not be led into another European war, Hollywood's leaders must have realized that films which attempted to alert Americans to the danger spreading in Europe were likely to draw the wrath of American pacifists and German-Americans.

Despite all of these apprehensions, the Hays Office frequently had to warn the studios away from controversial stories. This was because Hollywood relied upon the latest novels, plays and behind-the-headlines dramas for its source material, and in the late 1930s these sources were increasingly concerned with international political events. The studios seem to have bought such material out of habit, and were then forced to embark upon a process of stripping a story of its relevance and original purpose.[33] This was often achieved by setting the stories 'somewhere in Europe', rather than specifying a locale, and by remaining vague about the nationality of villains. In certain cases (and in expert hands) this form of subterfuge could be used effectively to put across anti-fascist themes. *The Lady Vanishes* (1938), directed in Britain by Alfred Hitchcock, provides an excellent example of this. The film's European villains are not given a specific nationality nor a political philosophy but, through implication and visual metaphors, *The Lady Vanishes* makes it clear that appeasement and isolationism are ineffective as a means of dealing with foreign aggressors. The implications must have been obvious to a contemporary audience. Nevertheless, they were unspoken and uncensorable, and when the film was submitted to the Hays Office prior to its American release, it was passed without objections.[34]

Most producers were eager to use the well-known title of a controversial novel or play as a selling point, and had few qualms about removing the politically contentious elements. A bidding war began among the studios for Robert Sherwood's play *Idiot's Delight* in 1936 when it proved to be a success on Broadway and won the Pulitzer Prize. On these merits alone, *Idiot's Delight* was the sort of property that Hollywood found irresistible. Yet the story concerns the outbreak of another world war, which begins with an Italian air raid on Paris, and it features a combative array of characters – including a pacifist, a munitions tycoon and a head-in-the-sand American isolationist – who debate the issues of the day while stranded in a remote hotel. The story was 'full of dynamite' according to the Hays Office's Foreign Division, and Breen attempted to warn the studios away from it. When MGM bought the rights, he then tried to figure a way in which a commercially viable film could be made from it.[35]

The industry's foreign policy is plain to see in the manner in which Breen went about this task. He wrote first to the BBFC, rather than to the Italian and French censorship agencies, to ensure that his proposed solution would not face difficulties in the all-important British market. The solution was that the belligerents in Sherwood's fictional war, Italy and France, would be replaced by 'two of the smaller European countries – say, two of the Balkan countries'.[36] That way the offensive situation would be displaced to smaller, less lucrative and less influential countries. But the BBFC insisted that the two countries must be completely unidentifiable, and, through Breen, this advice was relayed to and accepted by MGM.[37] It was not quite enough for the Italian Consul. Over lunch with Joseph Breen in May 1937, the Italian Consul told Breen that 'his government and his people had been seriously offended by this play' and that they would be 'violently opposed' to a film version. The only solution, the Consul insisted, was that Italy must never be mentioned in the film, and that neither the original title nor Robert Sherwood's name should appear in the credits.[38] The Consul knew that Breen would take his demands seriously. Italy was a fairly lucrative market by European standards, and the Hays Office was making a concerted effort to attain more favourable terms there for American films. But the Consul's demands went too far for MGM. As the producer Hunt Stromberg pointed out, without the story, the title or the author's name, MGM actually had nothing to show for the $125,000 it had paid for *Idiot's Delight*. Stromberg, and presumably his superiors at MGM, did agree that the Italian Consul could vet both the script and the completed film, and that MGM would remove anything that the Consul thought likely to 'offend or hurt' his country. In return, MGM would retain the title and give Sherwood credit in all prints except those used in Italy.[39]

Robert Sherwood was then set to work transforming his play into a screenplay that would secure the approval of the Italian government. This was achieved by setting the story in an unspecified country, by not naming the countries at war, and also by trimming the more contentious dialogue, such as comments concerning the munitions industry and fascism. In a final gesture toward complete anonymity, it was decided to use the international language of Esperanto whenever the characters spoke in another language. In this guise, *Idiot's Delight* became a romantic vehicle for stars Clark Gable and Norma Shearer. It is memorable now mainly because Shearer seems to be impersonating Greta Garbo, and because Gable, who plays a song and dance man, temporarily sheds his machismo and performs 'Puttin' on the Ritz'. The film was only a moderate box-office success in the United States, and despite all of the efforts made, it did not have a wide release in Europe. *Idiot's Delight* was banned in Estonia, France, Spain and Switzerland, and, ironically, by the time it was released in 1939, the Hays Office had ceased negotiations with the Italian government and initiated a boycott of the Italian market. Thus, the efforts made to appease Italy served no purpose in the end, and *Idiot's Delight* did not receive an Italian release.

Walter Wanger and 'industry policy'

A far more difficult situation arose when an independent and moderately liberal producer, Walter Wanger, proposed two films that were conceived as exposés on European fascism, *Blockade* and *Personal History*. As a producer for United Artists, a company dedicated at its inception to artistic freedom, Wanger had a rare degree of autonomy in choosing which films he would make. However, he was constrained by the fact that his films would have to be released in cinemas affiliated with the MPPDA, and thus they would have to conform with 'industry policy' as determined by the Hays Office. *Blockade* (1938) was to be set amid the Spanish Civil War, as a Republican village slowly starves as a result of a blockade by Franco's fascists. The Spanish Civil War was, perhaps, the most controversial topic Wanger could have chosen. The war between the Republican government of Spain and Franco's fascist insurgents had divided opinion throughout the world. Liberal and left-wing opinion in the Western democracies was behind the Republicans, who also had the support of the Soviet Union. Germany and Italy supported the fascists, along with others, such as conservatives and the Catholic Church, who saw the war as an active front against the spread of communism.

Joseph Breen was doubly alarmed by *Blockade*. The proposed film went against not only his own beliefs as a conservative and as a Catholic, but also the principle of 'pure entertainment'. He told Wanger that the film must 'not identify either side of the warring factions'. This meant that real military uniforms could not be used, that 'real incidents or locations' must be avoided and, in fact, there should be nothing in the film that 'could possibly be tied in with actual events that have occurred or are occurring in Spain'.[40] Hence, *Blockade* was made in the same style as Paramount's *The Last Train from Madrid* (1937). Paramount had been attracted to this Spanish Civil War story by the topicality and excitement of a love story set in wartime, and had no intention of taking sides or making political statements. From the beginning, the studio had reassured the Hays Office that the story would use the Spanish Civil War only as a 'background to personal narratives'.[41] To ensure that this was apparent to the audience, the film was prefaced with a statement of neutrality. *Blockade* also opened with a statement of neutrality, and then concentrated on the romance of a peasant farmer (Henry Fonda) and the daughter of a spy (Madeleine Carroll).

All that remained of Wanger's original scenario for *Blockade* were scenes of a starving, war-torn village and a final-reel speech, delivered by Fonda, calling for the 'conscience of the world' to awaken. These elements were not enough to warrant withholding the MPPDA Certificate of Approval, but the familiar alliance of the Hays Office and the Catholic Church united in an effort to sabotage the film's domestic release. The Catholic Church, through the efforts of the Knights of Columbus, led a boycott of *Blockade*, and it has been alleged that Will Hays himself urged a large cinema chain to drop the film. The resulting poor domestic gross was undoubtedly intended to serve notice to Wanger (and other producers) that political relevance was box-office poison.[42] In the foreign markets, *Blockade* was banned in twelve countries.[43]

Before *Blockade* was released, Wanger sent another troublesome script, *Personal History*, to the Hays Office. Based on a bestseller by journalist Vincent Sheean, *Personal History* follows a young American reporter into Europe's hot spots. He visits Spain to cover the Spanish Civil War, and then goes to Germany, where he assists in rescuing Jews from the Nazis and marries a Jewish woman. His exposure to the brutality of fascism transforms his political philosophy from a naive radicalism to a belief in all-American democracy. When Breen read the script in June 1938, he told Wanger that he considered it to be 'pro-Loyalist, pro-Jewish, anti-Nazi propaganda'. He warned that the film would have a difficult foreign release, and that it might run afoul of the BBFC. Breen then laid down guidelines similar to those used with *Three Comrades*, *Idiot's Delight* and *Blockade*. Appropriate military uniforms could not be used, German concentration camps should not be mentioned, and 'derogatory' portrayals of the German police must be avoided.[44] These restrictions, stipulated during the very month *Blockade* was failing in the domestic market, persuaded Wanger to abandon *Personal History*.

Challenging 'industry policy': *Confessions of a Nazi Spy*

The first effective challenge to 'industry policy' came with Warner Bros.' *Confessions of a Nazi Spy* (1939). Twenty-five years later, Jack Warner explained in his autobiography why he felt compelled to make this ground-breaking film. He told the story of Joe Kauffman, the company's German representative, who, 'like many another out-numbered Jew', was beaten to death by Nazi thugs on the streets of Berlin. When Warner heard this news, he recognized that 'terror was sweeping across the country' and 'immediately closed up our offices and exchanges in Germany'.[45] Recently, some doubt has been raised about the veracity of this anecdote. The shocking death of such a high-ranking executive would have been a major news item in, and beyond, the Hollywood trade press, but it seems that no record exists of the man in question.[46] Of course, Warner had undoubtedly heard of similar atrocities and his outrage at these may have fuelled the decision to make *Confessions of a Nazi Spy*. What is interesting about the story, if indeed it is a fiction, is that it is so similar to that of a depoliticized Hollywood film. The wider and more complex issues are reduced to a personal level, thereby enabling an individualistic resolution of such disturbing events and the avoidance of more substantive issues. By telling the story of Joe Kauffman, Warner effectively distracted his readers and avoided two difficult issues. Why did it take Hollywood so long to produce an anti-Nazi film? And how did he reconcile his own background and beliefs with his position as a prominent and highly successful purveyor of entertainment? Even if it is accepted that Hollywood's leaders wanted to be seen as thoroughly assimilated Americans, it is remarkable that, with the film capital of the world controlled largely by Jewish men of European origins or descent, a policy of 'pure entertainment' prevailed until 1939.

Whatever is the truth about his motivation, the fact is that Jack Warner was able to make *Confessions of a Nazi Spy* only because it was based on a true story. A Nazi spy ring, involving members of the German–American Bund, had been discovered in New York City. The spies were tried and convicted in 1938, and Warners used the courtroom testimony as the basis for the script. A film that was based on fact – revealed and confirmed in a US courtroom no less – could not be accused of breaking the 'National Feelings' clause of the Production Code. And the film itself makes its factual basis overwhelmingly apparent. It is narrated in the urgent, booming style of the *March of Time* newsreels, with inserts of documentary footage and explanatory graphics. These documentary elements punctuate a melodramatic detective story, in which Edward G. Robinson plays the FBI investigator who solved the case.

When news of Warner Bros.' plans to make the film became known in 1938, the reactions ranged from dismay to disapproval. Predictably, Georg Gyssling was the first to contact Joseph Breen. Gyssling asked Breen to inform him 'whether this firm [Warners] has really the intention to make a film like that'.[47] The studio was well aware of Gyssling's interest. When the script was submitted to the Hays Office, Breen was urged to 'keep it under lock and key – the German Bund and the German Consul are dying for it'.[48] There was also considerable hostility to the film within the industry itself. Paramount registered its disapproval when Luigi Luraschi, the studio's liaison with the Hays Office, informed Breen that Paramount's policy was to avoid any film 'that will be obviously uncomplimentary to any nation abroad'. He added that if Warners proceeded, they would 'have on their hands the blood of a great many Jews in Germany'.[49] An unsigned memo within the Hays Office's file on the film brings out the full extent of feeling against the film:

Are we ready to depart from the pleasant and profitable course of entertainment, to engage in propaganda, to produce screen portrayals arousing controversy, conflict, racial, religious and nationalistic antagonism, and outright, horrible human hatred? ... I fear it will be one of the most memorable, one of the most lamentable mistakes ever made by the industry.[50]

Before filming began, Joseph Breen asked Jack Warner, 'whether or not your studio, and the industry as a whole, should sponsor a motion picture dealing with so highly controversial a subject'. Yet he had to admit that *Confessions of a Nazi Spy* was 'technically within the provisions of the Production Code'.[51]

Because Warner Bros. owned its own cinemas, the film's domestic release would not be as troubled as that of *Blockade*. The foreign market was another matter, though, and *Confessions of a Nazi Spy* was banned in thirteen countries in Europe, the Far East and Latin America.[52] Crucially, the BBFC did pass the film in June 1939. Luigi Luraschi reported to Breen that this was because the film was based on fact and was not 'some author's personal idea or prejudice'. However, it took the British censors much longer than usual to reach their decision, and they did insist on cutting some of the dialogue.[53] That this happened just three months before Britain declared war on Germany indicates that the Hays Office – and a majority in the American industry – were not alone in their apprehensions.

The early war years

The policy of 'pure entertainment' was lost during the early war years. The rationale behind it had been the protection of foreign earnings, but the countries that were offended by such films contributed little to Hollywood's earnings by the late 1930s. So little, in fact, that even the most controversial films, which were banned in many countries, still managed to earn healthy foreign grosses. As the figures in table 10 indicate, even *Confessions of a Nazi Spy* earned a fairly high foreign gross and probably made a substantial profit.[54] The crucial market was Britain, and so long

Table 10 Financial statistics on films widely banned in foreign markets (in US dollars)

Title (year)	Production cost ($)	Domestic earnings ($)	Foreign earnings ($)	Total earnings ($)	Profit (loss)
Blockade (1938)	692,000	704,000	455,000	1,159,000	N/A
Three Comrades (1938)	839,000	1,193,000	850,000	2,043,000	472,000
Confessions of a Nazi Spy (1939)	681,000	797,000	734,000	1,531,000	N/A
Idiot's Delight (1939)	1,519,000	1,167,000	545,000	1,712,000	(374,000)
Escape (1940)	1,205,000	1,357,000	1,007,000	2,364,000	345,000
The Mortal Storm (1940)	1,045,000	1,159,000	643,000	1,802,000	108,000

Source for *Blockade*: file 3, box 38, series 3A, The United Artists Collection, Wisconsin State Historical Society.
Source for *Three Comrades, Idiot's Delight, Escape* and *The Mortal Storm*: The Eddie Mannix Ledger, Academy of Motion Picture Arts and Sciences Library.
Source for *Confessions of a Nazi Spy*: The William Schaefer Ledger, The William Schaefer Collection, The Doheny Library, University of Southern California.

as the BBFC passed such films, it did not seem to matter what happened in other parts of the world. In this light, it appears that 'industry policy' could be turned around completely. Hollywood was now dependent upon Britain's survival for its foreign earnings, and it was thus in the industry's interests to make films supporting the British war effort.

There were other reasons for the industry to remain cautious, however. The studios did not want to get ahead of public opinion or public interest, and the first test of this was not reassuring. While *Confessions of a Nazi Spy* had substantial foreign earnings, its domestic earnings were lacklustre, and the message to the studios was that American audiences did not welcome war films. As the war progressed, and Germany became more threatening, public opinion in the United States did come down decidedly on the side of the Allies.[55] Yet even in 1941 the Hays Office tried to maintain some semblance of neutrality in American films. This was done largely in deference to German-Americans and to the various pressure groups, collectively referred to as isolationists, that opposed American involvement in the war. Will Hays had domestic opinion in mind when, in November 1939, he issued a press release stating a policy of 'complete neutrality' for American films. The statement reportedly was made in response to complaints from 'church and peace groups', but it was completely disingenuous.[56] There were already several anti-fascist and pro-British films in production, and the Hays Office had not advised the studios against making such films.

In fact, the restraint evident in these early war films seems to have stemmed from the studios' own sense of caution. The war films of 1940 were neither as specific as *Confessions of a Nazi Spy*, nor as indeterminate as *Idiot's Delight*. MGM, for example, submitted the scripts for two anti-Nazi melodramas, *Escape* (1940) and *The Mortal Storm* (1940), within weeks of the declaration of war. *Escape* follows the 'somewhere in Europe' approach to the extent that the film's setting is stated as being 'in the Bavarian Alps', and the words 'Germany' and 'Nazi' are never spoken. Yet swastikas, accurate Nazi uniforms and other clear and meaningful signals make the unspoken obvious. Most remarkably, the plot centres on an American artist's attempt to rescue his foreign-born mother from a concentration camp, but there is no mention of the Jews. The mother has been imprisoned for other reasons. *The Mortal Storm* does state that it is set in Germany, but it also avoids any mention of the Jews. Instead, the characters repeatedly speak of the persecution of 'non-Aryans'. There is no evidence that such caution stemmed from advice given by the Hays Office, and both the scripts and the films were passed without any difficulties.[57] Two similar melodramas from TCF, *Four Sons* (1940) and *The Man I Married/I Married a Nazi* (1940), also passed easily through the Hays Office.[58] It later became apparent, however, that the Hays Office considered it to be crucial that each of these four films portrayed 'good Germans' alongside of the villainous Nazis. The stories all centre on the personal conflicts – either between lovers or within families – that ensue when one character becomes a Nazi and another does not. In the process, it makes it clear that all Germans are not Nazis. This distinction was the Hays Office's final, half-hearted attempt to uphold the 'National Feelings' clause. At this point, it is likely that it was made with isolationists and German-Americans in mind, rather than on behalf of Nazi Germany itself.

The industry's changed foreign policy is most apparent in the production history of Charlie Chaplin's *The Great Dictator* (1940). Chaplin's original inspiration for the film came from Alexander Korda, who – along with many others – commented on the resemblance between Chaplin's 'Little Tramp' character and Hitler.[59] Chaplin had his own production company and released his films through United Artists. Like Walter Wanger, then, he was able to develop his films without interference, but the finished product had to be approved by the Hays Office in order to reach cinemas affiliated with the MPPDA. When Chaplin began working on *The Great Dictator* in 1938, there was little chance that the film would be approved. Realizing this, Chaplin kept quiet about his plans and did not issue the usual advance publicity notices. The film was referred to only as 'production number six' (it was his sixth film for United Artists) until it was completed, and neither Chaplin nor United Artists consulted with the Hays Office until the film was ready for release in September 1940.

Joseph Breen, however, had been aware of Chaplin's plans from the beginning. As usual, Breen heard first from the German Consul. In a letter written in October 1938, Georg Gyssling outlined the plot of the secret film with remarkable accuracy, and warned Breen of the economic reprisals that would ensue if the film was not stopped. Noting that Chaplin's production company was not a member of the MPPDA, Gyssling stated that if *The Great Dictator* was released in MPPDA cinemas, all of the MPPDA members would 'thus become affected by the film'.[60] Six months later, in March 1939, the BBFC expressed its concerns. Brooke Wilkinson, the BBFC's president, wrote to Breen to enquire about Chaplin's plans, and warned that a 'delicate situation might arise in this country if personal attacks were made on any living European statesman'.[61] It was a BBFC regulation that living people could not be portrayed on screen without their consent and, six months before Britain went to war with Germany, the BBFC was preparing to enforce this rule against *The Great Dictator*.

In June 1939 it was the British Foreign Office that expressed concern to the BBFC. Chaplin and his film came under the domain of the Foreign Office because, although he had lived in the USA for over twenty years, Chaplin was still a British citizen. The Foreign Office informed the BBFC that its sources reported that Chaplin had entered into the project 'in a spirit of fanatical enthusiasm'. Chaplin, according to these sources, was aware that the Hays Office would not pass the film, and so he was planning to distribute *The Great Dictator* in independent cinemas, and in theatres and halls that were not affiliated with the MPPDA. This would be a highly unusual, costly and cumbersome method of distribution, but it was possible to release a film in this manner in the USA. The Foreign Office's purpose, though, was to ensure that the film did not slip by the BBFC. Wilkinson was asked to give the film 'the most careful scrutiny' if Chaplin attempted to release it in Britain.[62]

By the time *The Great Dictator* was ready for release, in September 1940, all of these concerns had vanished. Britain had been at war with Germany for twelve months and the Battle of Britain was at its height. Germany occupied virtually the whole of the European continent and, where German troops went in, the American industry's films were banned and its assets seized. Thus, neither the BBFC nor the Hays Office protested against Chaplin's brilliant parody of Adolf Hitler. In fact, when Joseph Breen viewed *The Great Dictator* on 6 September 1940, he wrote that it was 'superb entertainment' and that it 'marks Mr Chaplin, I think, as our greatest artist'.[63]

It is somewhat ironic that Breen was so pleased with *The Great Dictator* because, in addition to being a parody of Hitler, the film can also be seen as a parody of the industry's earlier 'somewhere in Europe' prescriptions. At the time Chaplin began making the film, direct references to the people, places and events involved in Europe's political upheavals were forbidden, no matter how obvious the implications may have been to contemporary audiences. Chaplin actually follows these rules in *The Great Dictator* by referring to Germany as 'Tomania', to Italy as 'Bacteria', by redesigning the swastika as the 'double cross', and referring to the Führer as 'The Phooey'. Adolf Hitler is 'Adenoid Hynkel', Benito Mussolini is 'Benzino Napoloni', Goebbels is 'Garbage' and Goering is 'Herring'. But rather than seeing this as a satire on his own policies, Breen may have taken some comfort in these thinly veiled allusions. There was also comfort to be found in the fact that the film attacked fascism through humour rather than melodramatic exposé. And, in keeping with the 'National Feelings' clause, good Germans are portrayed alongside the bad Nazis. The film's targets are nonetheless hit with precision, and *The Great Dictator* was truly ground-breaking in its portrayal of violent, state-sanctioned anti-Semitism.

'Industry policy' had come a long way in the two years that it took to make *The Great Dictator*, but even in 1941 there were still distinct limitations to how hostile or critical a film could be toward Nazi Germany. TCF's *Man Hunt* (1941) tested the new limits. The film centres on a British big-game hunter (Walter Pidgeon) who, before war is declared between Britain and Germany, stalks Hitler for sporting reasons alone. He does not intend to kill him, but only to prove to himself that he can. In the opening scene, the hunter has his rifle aimed at Hitler, who is seen in the distance, and he pulls the trigger. The gun is not loaded, though, and German guards apprehend the hunter, and interrogate and beat him. When the hunter escapes from them, and flees from Germany to Britain, he is pursued by German agents who continue to use the most ruthless methods to apprehend him. They even murder the heart-of-gold cockney prostitute (Joan Bennett) with whom he takes refuge. War is declared in the midst of this cat-and-mouse game, and the German agents are eventually defeated on British soil. Then the hunter heads back to Germany to finish the job he had so tentatively started. *Man Hunt* thus portrays a change in British attitude from appeasement, to the belated realization that Germany is ruthless and dangerous, and finally, to that of going on to the offensive. It also portrays the Nazis as brutal, and directs audience sympathies to a character who realizes that Hitler must be killed. As such, it became the first war film to cause concern at the Hays Office since the outbreak of hostilities in Europe.

Breen was troubled by the script. He read it in March 1941, when the Lend-Lease bill was passing through Congress and, as a result, the isolationist campaign was reaching a crescendo. Amid the fierce debate over the United States' role in the war, he did not want the film industry to be associated with such a blatantly biased film. Breen referred the matter to Will Hays as one that involved 'industry policy'. *Man Hunt*, he asserted, was a 'hate picture', in which 'the British are always the heroes and the Germans [are always] the heavies'. This, Breen felt certain, would be perceived as 'inflammatory propaganda' by 'great groups of our patrons'. For Breen, the difference between *Man Hunt* and Hollywood's earlier anti-Nazi films was that, whereas *Escape*, *The Mortal Storm*, *Four Sons* and *I Married a Nazi* provide a 'balance' between 'Nazi heavies' and 'sympathetic Nazi characters', *Man Hunt* does not. Breen told the studio that the film posed a 'great danger' to the industry, and insisted that the characterization of the Germans should not be so brutal. Their brutality could be 'indicated', but not shown in detail. As a compromise TCF agreed to cut away from the action of the most violent scenes. Thus, when the Germans beat and torture the British hunter in the film, the beatings are heard but not seen. Breen accepted this nominal gesture, and *Man Hunt* was approved in June 1941.[64]

British propaganda and 'British' entertainment

Britain's own war films also prompted consideration of 'industry policy'. When these films were proposed for release in the USA, the Hays Office referred to them as 'propaganda films' and worried that their release 'might cause a revulsion against such American-made pictures as *The Mortal Storm*, *Four Sons* and others, which have been produced with a definite entertainment objective, in addition to whatever political elements the stories may contain'.[65] The issue first arose when United Artists submitted Alexander Korda's *The Lion has Wings* (1939) for approval in

December 1939. This hastily compiled film, which mixes documentary footage with contemporary and historical drama, stands as Britain's first 'why we fight' film. The Hays Office did not want the American industry to be seen to be endorsing British propaganda, and so it approved the film only on the basis that a prologue would be added, stating that it 'represents the views of the British people' and that:

The management of this theater trust that after seeing the film its patrons will be better able to contrast life in neutral America with life in the belligerent countries of Europe.[66]

By reminding the audience that America was neutral, and by labelling Britain a 'belligerent' (a loaded term in relation to the Neutrality Laws), it was hoped that the industry could avoid charges of bias.

A similar prologue was added to the Powell and Pressburger spy thriller *Contraband* (1940), but Samuel Goldwyn was stopped from distributing the Boulting Brothers' *Pastor Hall* (1940).[67] Even the liberal Walter Wanger, who had argued against Hays Office policies just a few years earlier, thought that this film should not be shown in MPPDA cinemas. Wanger, who claimed to be wary of the 'avowedly British propaganda' in *Pastor Hall*, was most likely worried about a backlash that would affect his soon to be released *Foreign Correspondent*.[68] Yet *Pastor Hall* was based on the true story of a German pastor who had opposed the Nazis and was killed in a concentration camp, and given the precedent of *Confessions of a Nazi Spy*, the story's factual basis would seem to make it permissible. The PCA, however, worried that it was 'a purely British picture' which was 'strictly anti-Nazi in character'.[69] Its release was approved only when President Roosevelt's son, James Roosevelt, purchased the rights and agreed to cut scenes of 'concentration camp brutality' from the film and to add an explanatory prologue delivered by First Lady Eleanor Roosevelt. Only in this form, and with the backing of the First Family, did *Pastor Hall* gain the industry's reluctant approval in July 1940.[70]

By contrast, few reservations were expressed about Hollywood's own 'British' films. Whereas actual British war films were deemed to be foreign propaganda, 'British' films were seen as entertainment. Prior to the outbreak of war, films such as *Goodbye Mr Chips* (1939), *Lloyds of London* (1937) and *A Yank at Oxford* (1938) were passed without any mention of their strikingly pro-British sentiments.[71] In the early war years, Warners' *The Sea Hawk* (1940) and Alexander Korda's *That Hamilton*

Woman (1941) put forward a British view of world events. Ostensibly, these were the sort of British historical dramas that the Hollywood studios had filmed throughout the 1930s, but both films used episodes from Britain's past to make timely parallels about dictators, appeasement and neutrality. While these historical masquerades were well noted by contemporary film critics, the Hays Office did not comment upon them in its own reviews and correspondence.[72] Anglophilia was fine, it seems, so long as it did not lead to direct and derogatory references to Germany.

Walter Wanger took advantage of this new freedom by having the rejected *Personal History* script turned into the readily accepted *Foreign Correspondent* (1940). Wanger placed the story in the hands of Alfred Hitchcock, and the script was transformed from an exposé of Spain and Germany into one of Hollywood's finest 'British' films. All references to fascism and anti-Semitism were removed, and the film became a spy thriller set predominantly amid the smart addresses and famous landmarks of London. The only reference to the villains' nationality comes when their leader is designated as being 'Borovian'. Breen informed Hays, with evident relief, that *Foreign Correspondent* 'has not the remotest resemblance to the story [*Personal History*] that we were so concerned about two years back'.[73] Yet Hitchcock had simply taken out the direct references. The climactic final scene, for example, takes place during an air raid in London. As the bombs fall and the lights go out, there is little mystery as to where the film's sympathies lie. But it is never stated which country is bombing London, and the words 'Germany' and 'German' are used as seldom as possible and never in a negative context. Hitchcock knew that the audience did not need to be told that the Germans are the villains, and that, as in *The Lady Vanishes*, implication could be used to bend but not break the rules.

Wanger had learned his lesson. His next film, *Sundown* (1941), was another 'British' war film. Set in an unnamed African colony of the British Empire, *Sundown* shows that most of the natives respect and trust their wise British rulers, but a troublesome and violent faction is being armed by an unnamed European country which wants to incite a civil war and then invade the colony. The British administrators are all that stands between order and chaos, while the European enemy is a force of destruction. The only clue to the Europeans' nationality comes when it is revealed that the guns being supplied to the natives were manufactured in Czechoslovakia. Otherwise, the villains are referred to simply as 'they' throughout the film. Again, this pro-British stance was fine as far as the Hays Office was concerned, so long as it did not become explicitly anti-German.[74]

This policy remained in place through much of 1941, as witnessed in the correspondence between Joseph Breen and TCF over its latest celebration of the British war effort, *A Yank in the RAF* (1941). Breen praised the fact that 'no Axis power is mentioned by name and the Germans are identified only by helmet and uniform'.[75] Breen was correct, but his reading of the film was remarkably narrow. The 'Yank' goes on flying missions over what is identified as Berlin, he is seen fighting at Dunkirk, and, when captured, he is held at gunpoint by a German-speaking soldier. The illusion of neutrality that Breen apparently took comfort in was, of course, in sync with the neutrality of the United States itself. By the time *A Yank in the RAF* was released, in September 1941, the United States was supplying Britain with 'all aid short of war', and Roosevelt and Churchill had signed the Atlantic Charter of 'joint war aims'. Yet even at this time, when the United States was so close to declaring war, the supporters of isolationism in the US Congress still posed a threat to Hollywood.

Hollywood on trial: the Senate hearings of September 1941

Between the outbreak of war in September 1939 and the attack on Pearl Harbor in December 1941, Hollywood's war films had progressed steadily and each cautious evasion had been breached. Films that did not mention Germany by name, films that avoided any mention of German Jews, and films that made their statements against dictators in historical costume were followed by increasingly direct portrayals of the need to fight Germany and to support Britain. This process was not a linear one (*The Great Dictator* and *Foreign Correspondent*, for example, were released six months before *That Hamilton Woman*), but nonetheless the progress was unmistakable. The box-office success of these films indicates that the American public was ready for them. However, there was still a very vocal isolationist movement in the United States, and organizations such as 'America First' – which was reported to have 50,000 members in 1941 – found their last rallying cry in attacking Hollywood.

A leading isolationist in the United States Senate, Senator Burton K. Wheeler (Democrat, Montana), introduced Senate Resolution 152, which called for an inquiry into 'any propaganda disseminated by motion pictures ... to influence public sentiment in the direction of participation of the United States in the European war'.[76] Wheeler sat on the Senate Committee on Interstate

Commerce, and so the inquiry was directed toward investigating whether the film industry was under the monopoly control of propagandists seeking to involve the United States in the war. As the industry's official spokesman, Will Hays was set to lead the defence. Hays initially thought that the best strategy would be to deny the charges and claim that the policy of 'pure entertainment' was still intact. The isolationists, however, had a list of seventeen films to prove their assertion that Hollywood was undeniably on the side of intervention. Hays' strategy was abandoned, and instead the industry hired the prominent lawyer Wendell Willkie as its defender. Willkie's defence was straightforward: the industry had made anti-Nazi and pro-British films, and it had been right to do so. The fact this differed so obviously from the strategy planned by Hays provides some indication of the tensions which had developed within Hollywood over the preceding years.

Senator Wheeler chaired the subcommittee (of the Committee on Interstate Commerce) that was formed to investigate and hold hearings. Three of the four other seats on the committee were given to leading isolationists (D. Clark Worth, Democrat, Idaho; Wayland Brooks, Republican, Illinois; Charles Tobey, Republican, New Hampshire). This left Senator Ernest MacFarland (Democrat, Arizona) as the only committee member who supported the Roosevelt Administration's foreign policy. The committee's first witness, Gerald Nye (Republican, North Dakota) was also a staunch isolationist. When hearings began on 9 September 1941, Nye declared that Hollywood's anti-Nazi and pro-British films were 'the most vicious propaganda that has ever been unloosed upon a civilized people'. He then hit upon the industry's most sensitive points in his search for a solution. Federal censorship of films, a prospect Hollywood had fought for twenty years, was one solution. If that was not feasible, Nye indicated that the inquiry would have to focus on breaking up the monopoly control of an industry led by foreigners. The 17,000 cinemas of the United States had become, in Nye's words, '17,000 daily and nightly mass meetings for war'. This was not because the American public wanted war films, but because the industry was 'a monopoly controlled by half a dozen men' who had been 'born abroad'. The foreign-born film executives had 'inborn hatreds and prejudices ... which are quite foreign to America and her interests', and their control over the film industry made them 'the most dangerous fifth column in our country'. During the three subsequent weeks of hearings, the statement that the industry's leaders were 'foreign born' was made repeatedly as a way of drawing attention to the fact that most were Jewish.[77]

Hollywood's Jewish leaders had been wary of making interventionist films precisely because they did not want to be seen as foreign propagandists. Indeed, their readiness to make films that celebrated the British war effort, as well as British culture and institutions, may have stemmed partly from a strategy of subterfuge. Rather than drawing attention to their own origins by attacking Nazi Germany, they preferred to pay tribute to a country with close links to the United States. If this was their strategy, however, it did not pass undetected. To back the claims that the industry had purposefully set out 'to incite the American people to war', the list of seventeen films was produced. Anti-Nazi films such as *Escape* and *Four Sons* predominated on the list, but much attention was also focused on 'British' films and the British influence in Hollywood.[78]

The director of the New York chapter of 'America First', John T. Flynn, testified that *That Hamilton Woman* was 'a pure piece of propaganda' that presents a 'persistent and continuous glorification of the whole object and progress of British imperialism'. Hollywood's 'Empire epics', such as *Lives of a Bengal Lancer* (1935) and *Gunga Din* (1939), also came under consideration. Flynn described them as 'pictures glorifying the British Empire' and commented that it was 'an odd thing' that American films should have 'that kind of propaganda'.[79] These remarks fed into Nye's claim that the European war was being fought for 'Empire and Communism', and that the United States should have no part in it.[80] It was also pointed out by Senator Nye that the list of seventeen films would be far longer if the films that emphasize 'the brotherhood of the United States and Great Britain' had been included:

In this approach the British are portrayed as a nation of people suffering and standing courageously and with determination against violent bombardment by a hideous enemy. But we learn only of British suffering. That kind of propaganda never lets us see and feel that maybe the people of Germany or of Italy or of Finland are also suffering, that their blood is red, too ... that those people suffer under British fire just as the British suffer under theirs.[81]

Most remarkably, Senator Nye had recognized the economic impetus behind Hollywood's pro-British and interventionist stance. Nye introduced a report by a Wall Street investment company, Goodbody and Company, that highlighted the importance of British earnings to the American film industry. The report began by saying that:

The fate of England is of major importance to nearly all American companies. To few, however, is it as grave a matter as the motion picture producers. In many cases the loss of the English market would transform satisfactory profits into sizable deficits.

The report then went on to offer Loew's/MGM as an example. In the previous year, Loew's/MGM had remitted $8 million in earnings from 'England'. The studio's profits for the year were also $8 million, indicating that without its British earnings, the company would not have earned any profit. Most of the other studios, the report maintained, were even more dependent upon the British market for their profits, and they would be 'badly in the red' if British earnings were lost. This enabled Nye to proclaim that the film industry had 'a very selfish interest in this pending European war ... their interest lies in the success or failure of Great Britain'.[82]

The film industry was also accused of harbouring British spies. Senator Clark claimed that Hollywood's pro-British conspiracy emanated from United Artists, where Alexander Korda and Charlie Chaplin sat on the board of directors. Clark pointed out that Chaplin had 'never thought well enough of the United States to become a citizen', and he stated that Chaplin and Korda had made *The Great Dictator* and *That Hamilton Woman* 'to poison the minds of the American people' in favour of war.[83] Senator Nye, meanwhile, singled out the British producer Victor Saville, whose work for MGM included *Goodbye Mr Chips* and *The Mortal Storm*. Saville came to Hollywood on the orders of the British Ministry of Information, Nye alleged, and he was known 'to entertain lavishly' and to give each of his guests 'a full course of British propaganda'.[84]

The isolationists actually had a strong case against Hollywood. The film industry was, indeed, under monopoly control. It had produced many films that could be described as interventionist while not producing a single film that put forward the isolationist case or the German point of view. The industry was dependent upon its British earnings, and many of its films reflected this. The primary system of censorship, the Hays Office, was under the industry's control, and could be used to suit the industry's own interests. And, if recent claims are to be believed, producers Korda and Saville really were working with British intelligence agencies.[85]

The evidence available at the time, however, was undermined by the isolationist Senators' own racist tactics and weak performance. Their worst moment came when Senator MacFarland questioned Senator Nye on the seventeen films labelled as propaganda. It quickly became clear that Nye had not seen most of the films, and that he could not remember ('for the life of me', as he said) those he had seen. The latter point did not speak well for the claim that Hollywood was 'inciting' people through films.[86] The isolationists also suffered from the strong defence put forth by Wendell Willkie.

The day before the hearings began, Willkie issued a press release setting out the industry's frank and honest rebuttal. He began by saying that there need be no investigation into whether or not the industry was hostile to Nazi Germany, as he stated plainly that 'we abhor Hitler and everything he represents'. He then turned the isolationists' claims of foreign influence against them, stating that the industry 'despised the racial discrimina- tions of Nazism' and that its employees included a wide range of nationalities and religious groups. In regard to Hollywood's war films, Willkie pointed out that of the 1,100 films produced by the industry since the outbreak of war, only 50 had any relevance to the war; thus undermining the claim that the country's cinemas had been turned into 'daily and nightly mass meetings for war'. He also offered to provide witnesses from Germany who would 'prove that the motion picture industry pictures Nazi Germany as it is'. English witnesses would be provided to 'prove to you that the industry's portrayal of the magnificent courage of the English people is correct'. Finally, Willkie pointed out that many of the films in question had been adapted from best-selling novels and stories which had appeared in newspapers and popular maga- zines. The motion picture industry was not alone in offering these war stories and, if it was to be censored, censorship of the press would follow.[87]

This argument won the support of the press, which almost universally condemned the hearings and the attacks made on the film industry. *The New York Herald Tribune*, for example, com- mented on 'the note of hysteria which every day becomes more apparent' in the Senators' questioning, while *The New York Times* referred to the hearings as a 'savage assault' on the industry and described the treatment of Hollywood's executives as a series of 'vicious attacks'.[88] When the hearings were adjourned on 26 September 1941, it was generally agreed that the isolationists had not benefited from their pursuit of the film industry. While the industry's leading executives had been polite and cooperative during their testimony, the isolationist Senators came across as anti-Semitic, unconcerned about the threat Hitler posed to the United States and, conversely, paranoid about the film industry. Still, the hearings were set to resume in January 1942, and with

Charlie Chaplin and Alexander Korda among the first witnesses listed to appear, they promised to be even more confrontational. Only the Japanese attack on Pearl Harbor on 7 December 1941 saved the industry from further investigation.

Conclusion

The Senate investigation into Hollywood finally put an end to the policy of 'pure entertainment'. When forced to defend itself, the industry had to admit that its films were biased against the Nazis and in favour of the British. Even Will Hays accepted this argument. In a press release issued in the week before the hearings began, Hays was unequivocal in his defence of films that dramatized the issues of the day:

To yield to the demand that picture makers ignore the fact that we live in an era of destruction and tyranny that surpasses the blackest periods of barbarism, that all the principles upon which American life is based are being destroyed in a great part of the world, would best serve the purposes and interests of the most bitter enemies of our way of life. There can be no compromise by the industry with respect to this issue.[89]

Hays' argument may seem noble, but it is not substantiated by Hollywood's films, or by the Hays Office's policies over the previous decade. The industry had gone to great lengths to avoid giving offence to Europe's fascist powers for so long as they contributed to its foreign earnings. When those earnings ceased to exist, the earliest war films were diluted by the careful consideration given to isolationist sentiments. And it was the Hays Office which devised many of the evasions that characterize films of this period. Hollywood's policy toward Europe, and later toward anti-Nazi films, was at best a series of compromises. The policy toward Britain was far more consistent. The Hays Office's frequent consultations with the BBFC indicate that British considerations played a key role in Hollywood, and, remarkably, the Anglophilia that characterizes so many American films was accepted and even encouraged throughout this era. Yet this, too, was moulded to a large extent by market forces. Britain was the most lucrative foreign market in the world, and throughout the 1930s and the early war years, the industry's foreign policy was centred on this fact.

The 'whiter and cliffier cliffs' of MGM

3

MGM Studios produced many of the most successful and best remembered of Hollywood's 'British' films. In the mid-1930s, MGM produced a series of highly popular adaptations of British literature and history that included *David Copperfield* (1934), *Mutiny on the Bounty* (1935) and *A Tale of Two Cities* (1935). In the late 1930s, when new British quota regulations spurred the Hollywood studios to invest in British film production, three of the most successful 'British' films of the decade – *A Yank at Oxford* (1938), *The Citadel* (1938) and *Goodbye Mr Chips* (1939) – were made by MGM-British Studios. Then, during the war years, several 'British' films were produced at MGM each year, including four of the studio's most successful films: *Waterloo Bridge* (1940), *Mrs Miniver* (1942), *Random Harvest* (1942) and *The White Cliffs of Dover* (1944).

Mrs Miniver is, of course, the film that is cited most often as the prime example of the Anglophilia that appears to have run rampant at MGM during the 1930s and 1940s. In addition to winning six Academy Awards in 1942, including the 'best picture' award, *Mrs Miniver* was MGM's top-grossing film of the 1940s. In this case, though, the idyllic English setting served a propaganda purpose. The producer of *Mrs Miniver*, Sidney Franklin, has said that he conceived the film as a 'tribute' to the British at war, at a time (in 1940) when Britain was suffering through the Blitz and the United States remained a neutral country. As a propaganda piece, the film reportedly received praise from both President Roosevelt and Prime Minister Churchill.[1] *Mrs Miniver* is thus seen not only as an example of the work of

Anglophiles in Hollywood, but also as their crowning achievement: a film which has been credited with summoning American sympathy for the British, and boosting British morale, at a crucial time in world history.

Sidney Franklin added to the film's reputation as the work of dedicated and concerned Anglophiles when he recalled the film's beginnings. Franklin claims that when he was planning his 'tribute' he felt obliged to warn MGM executives that *Mrs Miniver* was not likely to be a money-maker. The loss, he predicted, could be as high as $100,000. He also recalled having to overcome the objections of MGM vice-president Eddie Mannix, an Irishman (and by implication an Anglophobe), who had no enthusiasm for this homage to the British war effort. Somehow, however, Franklin overcame these obstacles and film was made, and the public response to Greer Garson's portrayal of an 'average' English housewife bravely facing the Blitz has become legendary.[2]

Of course, Franklin's recollections are the stuff that memoirs are made of: an individual and altruistic effort leads to against-the-odds success. It seems highly unlikely, however, that *Mrs Miniver* was put into production as a potential money-loser, or that Mannix's feelings toward Britain, whatever they might have been, were voiced in any serious way when the film was proposed. In fact, *Mrs Miniver* was only one of numerous 'British' films produced by MGM between 1930 and 1945, many of which were among the studio's most expensive and successful releases. Furthermore, the Anglophilia that is so readily apparent in *Mrs Miniver* is also evident in the vast majority of MGM's 'British' films, albeit to varying degrees. *Mrs Miniver*, then, was neither an unlikely success, nor an entirely altruistic exercise in propaganda. It was yet another example of a formula that MGM had developed over the previous decade.

Ironically, it is due to the book-keeping efforts of Eddie Mannix that it is now possible to see beyond Franklin's recollections, and to see through the naive notion that 'British' films were simply the work of devoted Anglophiles. A ledger bearing Mannix's name has recently come to light, and it lists the financial statistics on every film produced by MGM between 1924 and 1964. Here, the profit motive behind 'British' films is plainly evident. 'British' films drew consistently high earnings in the domestic market, but they also earned exceptionally high foreign grosses, and the additional foreign revenue often resulted in substantial profits. It is not surprising, then, that MGM made so many 'British' films, or that it was willing to invest so heavily in them. These films had a particular appeal to the English-speaking markets of the world, and in the 1930s and the war years these were the most lucrative markets for American films. Hence, the highest budgets were allocated to 'British' costume dramas, the screen rights for the most recent best-selling British fiction were purchased, and the best British film-making talent was recruited to work at MGM's Culver City (California) production centre.[3]

MGM and the foreign markets

It has often been said that the Hollywood studios relied upon the domestic market to recoup their production costs, and then sought profits in the foreign markets. Mannix's ledger confirms that this was the case at MGM. Between 1924 and 1950 MGM released every film it produced, with one exception, in the foreign markets.[4] Between 1930 and 1945 MGM's films, on average, made 66 per cent of their total earnings from the domestic market and the remaining 34 per cent from the foreign markets, and only the final 19 per cent of earnings were realized as profit. The greatest earnings, then, came from the domestic market, but it was the foreign markets that supplied the studio's profits.

For the vast majority of MGM's films, the proportion of foreign earnings was close to the 34 per cent average: few films varied more than 5 per cent either way. However, there were exceptions to this. Most of the films that drew strong foreign earnings were 'prestige' films. These were not only among the most expensive films the studio produced, but they often had some claim to cultural value. The combination of costly production values and cultural status was important to MGM, which was often referred to as the 'Tiffany' of Hollywood studios. In order to recoup the costs of such films, though, the films had to earn both strong domestic and strong foreign grosses. Thus, MGM's expensive 'prestige' releases were produced with an unusual attention toward the tastes of the foreign market.

The studio was clearly adept at this strategy. It combined stars who had a strong foreign following with genres that had a particular appeal in the foreign markets. In the 1930s, for example, Greta Garbo and the costume drama formed an equation that led to much foreign success. So, too, did Jeanette MacDonald, Nelson Eddy and musical operetta. In some cases, the foreign element is particularly apparent. Garbo, for example, often made costume dramas that had a particular appeal to her European following (for example *Queen Christina*, 1933; *Anna Karenina*, 1935; *Camille*, 1936). The limitation of this strategy was that the tastes of the domestic market and the foreign markets did not always coincide.

The 'whiter and cliffier cliffs' of MGM

Table 11 Financial statistics on selected 'British' films made by MGM (in thousands of dollars)

Season/ film	Production cost ($000)	Domestic earnings ($000)	Foreign earnings ($000)	Total earnings ($000)	Profit (loss) ($000)
1931–32					
Smilin' Through	851	1,004 49%	1,029 51%	2,033	529
Tarzan the Ape Man	660	1,112 44%	1,428 56%	2,540	919
1933–34					
Treasure Island	825	1,164 51%	1,110 49%	2,274	565
1934–35					
The Barretts of Wimpole Street	820	1,258 54%	1,085 46%	2,343	668
David Copperfield	1,073	1,621 55%	1,348 45%	2,969	686
Mutiny on the Bounty	1,905	2,250 50%	2,210 50%	4,460	909
1935–36					
A Tale of Two Cities	1,232	1,111 48%	1,183 52%	2,294	133
1936-37					
Romeo and Juliet	2,066	962 46%	1,113 54%	2,075	(922)
1937-38					
A Yank at Oxford	1,374	1,291 47%	1,445 53%	2,736	513
1938-39					
The Citadel	1,012	987 38%	1,611 62%	2,598	938
Goodbye Mr Chips	1,051	1,717 53%	1,535 47%	3,252	1,305
1939-40					
The Earl of Chicago	559	453 59%	315 41%	768	(63)
Pride and Prejudice	1,437	1,001 54%	848 46%	1,849	(241)
Waterloo Bridge	1,164	1,250 51%	1,217 49%	2,467	491
1940–41					
Haunted Honeymoon	677	250 46%	298 54%	548	(27)

Table 11 (cont.)

Season/ film	Production cost ($000)	Domestic earnings ($000)	Foreign earnings ($000)	Total earnings ($000)	Profit (loss) ($000)
1941–42					
Dr Jekyll and Mr Hyde	1,140	1,279 54%	1,072 46%	2,351	350
Mrs Miniver	1,344	5,358 60%	3,520 40%	8,878	4,831
1942–43					
Journey for Margaret	484	779 50%	775 50%	1,554	561
Random Harvest	1,210	4,650 57%	3,497 43%	8,147	4,384
A Yank at Eton	751	1,542 58%	1,135 42%	2,677	1,101
1943–44					
The Canterville Ghost	1,433	1,243 68%	577 32%	1,820	(274)
Gaslight	2,068	2,263 49%	2,350 51%	4,613	941
Lassie Come Home	666	2,613 58%	1,904 42%	4,517	2,249
Tartu	1,029	608 33%	1,246 67%	1,854	254
The White Cliffs of Dover	2,342	4,045 64%	2,249 36%	6,294	1,784
1944–45					
National Velvet	2,770	3,678 63%	2,162 37%	5,840	785
The Picture of Dorian Gray	1,918	1,399 47%	1,576 53%	2,975	(26)
1945–46					
Vacation from Marriage	2,218	648 30%	1,522 70%	2,170	(760)

Source: The Eddie Mannix Ledger, The Academy of Motion Picture Arts and Sciences Library.

The films of Garbo, MacDonald and Eddy had consistently strong foreign grosses throughout the 1930s, but at the end of the decade their domestic popularity was in decline and their careers rapidly faded. However, as table 11 reveals, a more successful and enduring combination of high domestic and foreign earnings was found with MGM's adaptations of British history and literature in the 1930s.

Developing a 'British' formula

While the importance of British earnings was the impetus for MGM's 'British' films, it was also important that the films appealed to American audiences. Actual British films were seldom popular in the USA, and so Hollywood had to find it own unique approach to British stories. The search began shortly after the advent of sound, when all of the studios sought stories that would have a particular appeal in the increasingly important English-speaking markets. Warners found a solution to this by placing the veteran British stage actor George Arliss under contract and film-ing adaptations of his greatest stage successes, including *Disraeli* (1929), *The Green Goddess* (1930) and *Old English* (1930). Arliss had starred in silent films during the early 1920s but, unlike so many silent stars, his career was actually renewed by the 'talkies'. Ronald Colman made his talking debut as the British detective in *Bulldog Drummond* (1929) and soon after played the 'amateur cracksman' of *Raffles* (1930). There was a great interest in British horror stories, which resulted in screen classics such as Paramount's *Dr Jekyll and Mr Hyde* (1932), and Universal's *Dracula* (1931), *Frankenstein* (1931) and *The Old Dark House* (1932), as well as romances with supernatural elements, including MGM's *Smilin' Through* (1932) and Fox's *Berkeley Square* (1933). 'British' melodramas such as Universal's *Waterloo Bridge* (1931) and Samuel Goldwyn's *Cynara* (1933) used class as a source of romantic conflict. And MGM inaugurated one of its most suc-cessful series of films with the British Empire adventure story *Tarzan the Ape Man* (1932). Thus, Hollywood's taste for the most famous, traditional and antiquated aspects of Britain was already established at the beginning of the decade.

However, it was two other noteworthy films – one 'British' and the other British – that proved to be particularly influential for MGM and the other Hollywood studios. Noel Coward's *Cavalcade* was filmed by Fox in 1932, and was probably the most imitated of all 'British' films. The story follows an upper-class British family and their servants from the Boer War through the 1920s, using the developments and upheavals of the era as the backdrop to personal melodramas. With its class distinctions, patriotism and its romanticized view of upper-class life, *Cavalcade* was, in Sheridan Morley's words, 'everything that Hollywood and

America seemed to want to know about England'.[5] Fox gave the film the prestige 'British' treatment. West End playwright Reginald Berkeley was brought to Hollywood to adapt the play. The veteran silent-film director Frank Lloyd, who was British-born but had been in Hollywood for many years, initiated a new phase to his career by directing *Cavalcade*. The cast included Clive Brook, Diana Wynyard and Frank Lawton, as well as many British character actors. This array of talent, together with the elaborate sets and costumes, reportedly pushed the production cost up to an extraordinary $1,700,000. Film historians disagree over the box-office performance of *Cavalcade*, but it did win the film industry's most respected award, the Academy Award for 'best picture' of the year, as well as the 'best director' award.[6] Such a success, whether measured by box-office takings or awards, was crucial for a struggling studio such as Fox, and it was also the sort of success that MGM needed in order to maintain its 'Tiffany' status.

The other key influence on 'British' film-making was Alexander Korda's *The Private Life of Henry the Eighth* (1933). The American success of Korda's film is not in dispute. It has gone down in history as the first British film to achieve box-office success in the United States. Korda's biographer, Karol Kulik, asserts that it was Korda's belief in the 'international film' that made *Henry the Eighth* popular outside Britain. Kulik defines the international film as 'one which relied on stereotyped situations and characters peculiar to one country, but recognized immediately by audiences of other countries'.[7] Hence, with *Henry the Eighth*, the story of a well-known, almost mythical English character was dramatized in order to make a film of 'national subject matter' that would be immediately recognizable to international audiences. According to Korda, it was crucial that the story had been adapted by foreigners. Korda, a Hungarian who had worked as a film-maker in both France and Hollywood before settling in Britain, produced and directed the film. His brother, Vincent Korda, was the set designer. The Hungarian Lajos Biro wrote the script, and the cinematographer was the Frenchman Georges Périnal. The success of the film was attributed by Korda to its foreign perspective. As he put it, 'an outsider often makes the best job of a national film. He is not cumbered with excessively detailed knowledge and associations. He gets a fresh slant on things'.[8] Perhaps most importantly, *The Private Life of Henry the Eighth* had, as the title suggests, more concern for box-office values than historical accuracy. The film is not a staid history lesson, but revels in bawdy humour and the carnal appetites of its characters.

Costumes and classics at MGM

MGM drew upon these precedents when it embarked on a cycle of British historical dramas and literary adaptations in 1934. They would be prestige films, with the highest budgets, the best directors and top stars. As with *Cavalcade*, a wide array of British talent would be used, but it would be balanced by the 'fresh slant' of American screenwriters or directors. And only the most immediately recognizable British stories would be filmed. Indeed, within the space of three years, 1934 to 1936, MGM seems to have embarked on a programme of promoting British culture to international audiences. Classic literature (*Treasure Island*, *David Copperfield*, *A Tale of Two Cities*, *Romeo and Juliet*), a renowned episode in British history (*Mutiny on the Bounty*) and the romance of poets Elizabeth Barrett and Robert Browning (*The Barretts of Wimpole Street*) were filmed at this one studio and in these three years alone.

The 'costumes and classics' cycle began with *Treasure Island* (1934). Like Korda's *Henry the Eighth*, this was a well-known British story with strong box-office elements. The story of swashbuckling pirates and lost treasure was sure to overcome any doubts the cinema-going public would have about seeing a costume drama with a British setting. With Robert Louis Stevenson's classic story as its source material, a high production cost ($825,000) and two of MGM's top stars (Wallace Beery and Jackie Cooper) in the lead roles, *Treasure Island* was a prestige film by Hollywood standards. It was also a box-office success. At a time when 'blockbuster' status was signalled by a domestic gross over $1,000,000 and a foreign gross over $500,000, *Treasure Island* earned $1,164,000 and $1,110,000, respectively. For MGM, this confirmed the commercial viability of well-known British stories in the domestic market, as well as the superior foreign returns that such British stories could bring.

Treasure Island had been produced by one of MGM's foremost producers, Hunt Stromberg, but the British costume dramas that followed were produced by MGM's most powerful and creative producers, Irving Thalberg and David Selznick. These two producers had the studio's highest budgets and its best stars, writers and directors at their disposal. In 1933, however, both men also felt the need to prove their value to MGM. The young but frail Thalberg had recently suffered a near fatal heart attack, and Hollywood waited to see whether the 'boy wonder' could continue his long winning streak. Selznick, meanwhile, had a fine track record himself, but when he decided to join MGM as a producer in 1933 it did not go unnoticed that studio head Louis B. Mayer was his father-in-law. Indeed, one trade paper offered the news of his appointment with the headline, 'The Son-In-Law Also Rises'. Both producers, in need of strong box-office returns and critical recognition, turned to British stories.[9]

David Selznick initiated the move toward more ambitious 'British' films. The producer told MGM executives that Charles Dickens' *David Copperfield* was a story 'known and loved by millions' and one that had 'stood the test of time'. It was, in other words, a story that would draw an international audience. The executives were not entirely convinced. *David Copperfield* had none of the conventional box-office elements of *Treasure Island*, and the story's large cast of characters meant that the film would not have the usual focus on one or two prominent stars. Such a literary film might do well in London and New York City, the producer was told, but it would never play in the provinces.[10] Selznick had the standing at MGM to proceed with *David Copperfield*, and he did so in a manner that set the blueprint for MGM's approach to 'British' films. He justified the high production cost, necessary for the large ensemble cast and the period sets and costumes, with his predictions of an unusually high British gross from the film. He then set out to make a very British adaptation of *David Copperfield*. While *Treasure Island* had been written, directed and acted by Americans, Selznick intended to use British talent for *David Copperfield* and to film the story in Britain. This, he predicted, would give the film an authentic British quality, and the publicity garnered would 'add hundreds of thousands to the British gross'.[11]

For reasons that remain unclear, however, *David Copperfield* was filmed almost entirely in California. Selznick and the film's director, George Cukor, did go to Britain in May of 1934, but only to shoot background material. Cukor later recalled that few of these shots were actually used in the film. A 'charming shot of the young David walking [from London] to Canterbury' made the final edit, but Cukor remembered being disappointed with the British scenery. Even the shots of the white cliffs of Dover, atop which David's Aunt Betsey lives, were discarded. Instead, the cliffs at Malibu (in California) were used. 'Our cliffs', Cukor recalled, 'were better – whiter and cliffier'.[12] MGM's international approach to 'British' films centred on a romantic and idealized view of Britain. Film-makers sought to fulfil expectations rather than capture reality, and if the legendary white cliffs were not as bright and imposing as their reputation would suggest, better cliffs would have to be substituted.

1 A very 'British' film: Mr Murdstone (Basil Rathbone), Peggotty (Jessie Ralph), young David (Freddie Bartholomew) and David's mother (Elizabeth Allan) in *David Copperfield* (1934)

Selznick did seek some measure of authenticity by insisting upon a largely British cast. MGM wanted its top child-star, Jackie Cooper, to play the part of the young David. The thirteen-year-old Cooper had played Jim Hawkins in *Treasure Island*, but Selznick insisted that British audiences would reject an American David.[13] An extensive talent-scouting effort in Britain yielded Freddie Bartholomew, a ten-year-old whose crisp British accent would be heard in Hollywood's 'British' films for the next decade. The British actor Charles Laughton initially took the role of Micawber, but Laughton felt ill at ease and was replaced by the American comedian W.C. Fields. Frank Lawton, fresh from a leading role in *Cavalcade*, was the adult David, and a plethora of other British actors – Elizabeth Allan, Violet Kemble-Cooper, Elsa Lanchester, Herbert Mundin, Lennox Pawle, Basil Rathbone and

Roland Young – constituted a near perfect cast. Hugh Walpole, one of Britain's most prominent novelists of the 1930s, wrote the script (and also made an appearance in the film as the Vicar) along with MGM scriptwriter Howard Estabrook. The combination of British and American talent found in *David Copperfield* became a hallmark of future MGM 'British' films.

In the midst of the Great Depression, the story of the young David's fading fortunes and increasing hardships was a timely one for audiences, and it was also a reassuring one. Few could claim to be worse off than an orphan in Victorian England, and of course even David eventually finds a happy ending. *David Copperfield* also benefits from an array of vivid performances, including Basil Rathbone's chilling Mr Murdstone, Roland Young's creepy Uriah Heep and Edna May Oliver's wonderfully formidable Aunt Betsey. The result was a film that appealed far and wide, and certainly beyond London and New York City. The domestic earnings reached $1,621,000, which means that – given the average of 66 per cent of worldwide from the domestic market and 34 per cent from the foreign market – the foreign earnings would be expected to be approximately $800,000. But *David Copperfield* went on to earn $1,348,000 in the foreign markets, or 45 per cent of the worldwide total of $2,969,000. The strength of the foreign gross was a direct result of the film's popularity in Britain and the English-speaking markets of the British Empire, where it earned approximately $700,000 of its foreign gross.[14] The British gross was clearly exceptional, as many of MGM's top releases earned less than $700,000 in the entire foreign market, and the strong foreign earnings were particularly important in light of the film's high cost ($1,073,000). Selznick had shown that British stories, given the right treatment, could draw an American audience. He had also shown that by targeting the British market, the extra expense needed for such 'prestige' productions could be returned with a profit.

While Selznick was working on *David Copperfield*, Thalberg had cast his wife, MGM star Norma Shearer, as the ailing poet Elizabeth Barrett in *The Barretts of Wimpole Street* (1934). Her love affair with fellow poet Robert Browning (Fredric March) proceeds despite the intervention of her cruelly oppressive father (Charles Laughton). With its period setting (1845), its literary and historical pretensions and its lavish production values (the film cost $820,000), *The Barretts of Wimpole Street* had all the elements of MGM's prestige films of the 1930s. Few studios could have made a box-office success of such material, and fewer still would have tried. However, with an all-star cast enacting a story much more concerned with forbidden love than poetry, the film was made palatable for mainstream audiences. *The Barretts* became one of the most successful films of the 1934-35 season, earning $1,258,000 in the domestic market, $1,085,000 (46 per cent of the total) in the foreign markets and a profit of $668,000.

The Barretts of Wimpole Street is a 'British' film by any measure, but it is also one of several films Thalberg made as a showcase for Norma Shearer. Many of these films were adapted from Broadway or West End plays and, although they now seem stagebound and slow, and Shearer's performances sometimes seem mannered and false, they served to further Shearer's status as one of Hollywood's leading actresses.[15] Thalberg's next film, however, was neither a stage adaptation nor a vehicle for Shearer. *Mutiny on the Bounty* was, in fact, among the most memorable and exciting films of the decade.

It was the success of *David Copperfield* that inspired Thalberg to make *Mutiny on the Bounty*, and he clearly followed the newly established blueprint for 'British' films. The story of HMS *Bounty* certainly meets the 'international' standard. As the opening titles remind the viewer, it is 'famous in history and in legend'. Thalberg also made ample use of Hollywood's British talent, including director Frank Lloyd and actors Charles Laughton, Henry Stephenson, Herbert Mundin, Francis Lister and Ian Wolfe. As in *David Copperfield*, there is also an emphasis on lavish period sets and costumes, which in this case includes an exact replica of the *Bounty* and elaborate sets for the scenes set in eighteenth-century Portsmouth. But *Mutiny on the Bounty* is also a visually exciting film, with spectacular scenes of storms at sea, the arrival of the *Bounty* in Tahiti and crash of the *Pandora*.

Thalberg's casting decisions were inspired. Clark Gable plays the mutineer Fletcher Christian and Charles Laughton is the detested Captain Bligh. It has been said that Gable and Laughton loathed one another and that the tension between them enhanced their on-screen conflict.[16] But the decision to have an American actor play Fletcher Christian also adds an entirely new dimension to the story. The detested Captain Bligh, masterfully portrayed by Laughton as both a cruelly sadistic and tragic character, is clearly a representative of the old England, in which rank, tradition and regulations take precedence above all else. Pressganging, cruel and unusual punishments and corruption are the hallmarks of this harsh and unjust past. Fletcher Christian, though, is 'one man who would not endure tyranny' (as his friend Roger Byam tells the naval court). With his New World accent, his concern for the common man, and his ultimate search

2   Representatives of the new world and the old: Fletcher Christian (Clark Gable) and Captain Bligh (Charles Laughton) in *Mutiny on the Bounty* (1935)

for a new country, Gable/Christian appears to be as much a Yankee rebel as a naval mutineer. This is not to say that *Mutiny on the Bounty* is an example of American Anglophobia. Fletcher Christian's rebellion is seen to be justified and his search for a new world is seen to be admirable. Yet at the same time his actions are seen to have ushered in a kinder and gentler era in the British navy and, by extension, throughout Britain itself. The film's opening statement tells the viewer as much, and praises 'Britain's sea power' for maintaining 'security for all who pass upon the seas'. When Roger Byam is given the king's mercy, we also see that the most important of all British institutions is sound and compassionate. Thus, the film not only offers an American audience the opportunity to have its faith in the New World confirmed but also manages to celebrate British accomplishments and traditions. The latter point is made abundantly clear by the film's ending, in which a shot of the Union Jack proudly flying is accompanied by a rousing chorus of 'Rule Britannia'.

Thalberg spent nearly $2,000,000 on *Mutiny on the Bounty*, a sum so extraordinary in 1935 that MGM's executives must have dismissed the chance of ever seeing a profit from the film. But it became the most successful film MGM had released in ten years,

The 'whiter and cliffier cliffs' of MGM

earning over $2,000,000 in both the domestic and the foreign markets. The foreign gross was particularly noteworthy, as even Garbo's films had never reached such a pinnacle. The profit, at $909,000, surpassed even those earned by the less expensive *David Copperfield* and *The Barretts of Wimpole Street*. Each of these films was a critical success as well. All three were nominated for the 'best picture' Academy Award, and *Mutiny on the Bounty* won the award for 1935.

In Hollywood, then as now, success leads to repetition. However, among the plethora of expensive costume dramas, 'British' and otherwise, to emerge from MGM in the late 1930s, there were few outstanding successes and several costly failures.[17] Irving Thalberg's follow-up to *Mutiny on the Bounty* was particularly grandiose, both in terms of cost and of source material. His *Romeo and Juliet* (1936) was the last film he completed before his death in 1936, and unfortunately it was both a commercial and critical failure.[18] The most frequently cited problem with *Romeo and Juliet* is the age of its stars. Shakespeare's adolescent lovers are played by Norma Shearer, who was then thirty-six years old, and Leslie Howard, who was forty-six years old. However, this was only part of the problem. Director George Cukor recognized the film's primary fault when he attributed its failure to a lack of 'garlic and the Mediterranean'.[19] Shakespeare's story of Italian passion had been rendered at MGM as a 'British' film, and a very theatrical 'British' film, too. Indeed, by casting mainly British actors, and summoning vocal coaches and set designers from London's West End, Thalberg seems to have set out to film a stage production rather than create a cinematic adaptation.[20] This was one of the few instances in which the effort for British authenticity backfired.

David Selznick was not quite so ambitious with his follow-up to *David Copperfield*. He chose to make another lavish adaptation of a Dickens novel, in this case *A Tale of Two Cities*. As in *Mutiny on the Bounty*, the American perspective on the story is as pronounced as the careful treatment of British sensibilities. References to George Washington (a man likely to be better remembered than George the Third, according to Sydney Carton) make it clear that the American Revolution – alluded to but never discussed – was entirely sound and just. Yet the modern perspective on the old world order, which is seen to be a combination of heartless aristocrats and filthy rabble, is directed entirely at France rather than England. Indeed, London is seen to be eminently civilized and democratic, particularly when compared with Paris, where the evil of the aristocracy is matched by the monstrousness of those who gleefully watch the guillotine in action. The film's Anglo-American balancing act also extended to the credits: MGM's Jack Conway directed, the British playwright W.P. Lipscomb co-wrote the script with MGM's S.N. Behrman, and the cast (Ronald Colman, Elizabeth Allan, Reginald Owen, Basil Rathbone) was once again largely British and near perfect. This formula clearly worked, as *A Tale of Two Cities* provided MGM with another solid success in the United States and the British Empire.[21]

A Tale of Two Cities was David Selznick's last film for MGM. In 1936 he sought freedom from his father-in-law and the independence of his own production company. His greatest achievement as an independent producer would be *Gone with the Wind* (1939), but Selznick's interest in 'British' films was a defining characteristic of his career. At the time he was preparing *David Copperfield* and *A Tale of Two Cities*, he also proposed MGM productions of *A Christmas Carol*, *The Forsyte Saga* and *Beau Brummel*, all of which would be made eventually under the supervision of other producers. Selznick also continued to produce 'British' films after leaving MGM, including *Little Lord Fauntleroy* (1936), *The Prisoner of Zenda* (1937), *Rebecca* (1940) and *The Paradine Case* (1947). And he put together the 'package' for another British literary adaptation, *Jane Eyre* (1944), before selling it to Twentieth Century-Fox in his post-*Gone with the Wind* exhaustion. As Selznick undoubtedly expected, *Jane Eyre* broke box-office records in Britain.[22] MGM also continued to produce 'British' films, but in the late 1930s the studio turned to more contemporary source material.

The MGM-British films

MGM's foray into British production in the late 1930s was long overdue. Louis B. Mayer and other MGM executives had been planning to set up a British production base for several years.[23] The most obvious reason that this was done in 1937 was to meet the requirements of the new British quota legislation. The 1938 Films Act offered multiple quota credits for a single, moderately expensive British-made film. Under this new system, MGM could make its 'British' films on location and at the same time satisfy quota obligations. It was equally important to the studio, however, that a British production base enabled it to recruit British actors, directors, producers and writers. It was a long-standing practice in Hollywood to deal with foreign competitors by recruiting their best talent. Buying up the stars and film-makers of a

3   Hollywood in Britain: MGM director Jack Conway, producer Michael Balcon and star Robert Taylor during the filming of *A Yank at Oxford* (1938)

foreign film industry not only disarmed that industry, but was also a strategy toward winning over its audience.

British films were becoming increasingly popular within Britain in the mid-1930s, and this was very much against Hollywood's own interests. Hence, the move into British production was meant to bring the country's leading film-making talent into the Hollywood fold. Robert Donat, already a star of international standing, was signed to MGM-British for six films and £150,000. There was also the opportunity to develop new stars, and Vivien Leigh, Greer Garson and Deborah Kerr were among those who gained early film roles at MGM-British before taking up Hollywood contracts. Britain's best-known director, Alfred Hitchcock, was offered a deal of £40,000 for four films, but Hitchcock took up a better offer from David Selznick in Hollywood. Producer Michael Balcon, one of Britain's most successful film executives, became the unit's head of production. Balcon, however, soon found the parent studio's interference intolerable, and left after the first film. That film, ironically, was the paean to Anglo-American cooperation, *A Yank at Oxford*. Victor Saville, who had directed the most successful musicals of Jessie Matthews and other popular British films, then became the new head of production. Leading British

When Hollywood loved Britain

screenwriters, including Ian Dalrymple, Sidney Gilliat, Frank Launder, R.C. Sherriff and Emlyn Williams also worked for MGM-British.[24]

MGM's plans for British production were delayed in part by the trouble the studio had developing the script for *A Yank at Oxford*. The scenario for the film had been written in 1934 by John Monk Saunders, an American writer who had attended Oxford, and it had been thought that Saunders' scenario could be expanded and then filmed in Britain later that year. However, it took another three years and no fewer than thirty-five scriptwriters to complete the script.[25] Throughout the writing process Saunders' basic story remained intact. A brash American student (Robert Taylor) wins an athletic scholarship to an Oxford college. There, the enthusiastic American finds the cultured British students to be haughty and distant, while they find him to be a braggart. Although the Yank is an excellent athlete, he has no sense of sportsmanship and is ostracized for this shortcoming in his character. Gradually, however, his romance with a British student (Maureen O'Sullivan) and his exposure to the superior British character lead him to mature, and his athletic abilities propel his college to victory. The energy and individualism of the American meet with the British sense of fairness and form, to the benefit of all concerned.

A Yank at Oxford is, as one scriptwriter noted, the story of an American's 'regeneration through Oxford and environment', in which the American 'learns that there is such a thing as playing cricket'.[26] The difficulty that the scriptwriters had with this transformation, and what kept the script from completion for three years, was getting the balance of sympathies correct. It was feared that American audiences would find the Oxford students to be 'namby pamby' and that 'the flower of the British aristocracy is likely to come across as a pansy'. The other problem was that the American character seemed to be a 'heel', and that his transformation indicates that American values are somehow inferior. 'Can't we pay tribute to English tradition without kicking America into the gutter?', one writer asked.[27] A solution to this problem was never found. Instead, the writers emphasized the respect that the Yank develops for British history and culture.

The film shows just how easily Americans are seduced by romantic and antiquated images of Britain's past. Upon his arrival in Oxford, the Yank quickly realizes that his fellow students view him with disdain. He is disappointed and disillusioned, and with the help of the kind and elderly college porter, 'Scatters' (Edward Rigby), he begins to pack his bags and leave. But Scatters points out the numerous cathedral spires, ancient buildings and lovely scenery that can be seen from the window, and when the cathedral bells begin to sound, he adds that Sir Walter Raleigh 'and many other great gentleman' heard the very same bells during their years at Oxford. This is enough to convince the 'Yank' to stop packing and stay, and throughout the film the pattern is repeated. The 'Yank' repeatedly comes into conflict with British manners and customs, but each time his discomfort is overcome by the traditions and ambience of the 'Oxford environment'.

In subsequent years, *A Yank at Oxford* would inspire an entire sub-genre of films based on 'Yanks' in Britain during the war. The film's ending makes it clear how easily this plot was adapted to suit wartime concerns. Rather than ending with a traditional romantic 'clinch' shot of the newly formed couple (the 'Yank' and his British girlfriend), *A Yank at Oxford* ends with the 'Yank' and the girl's brother winning a race together for their college. Having fully displayed Anglo-American differences, the film ends with this overt statement of Anglo-American unity. The two sides have overcome their differences and joined in the pursuit of a common goal.

Goodbye Mr Chips celebrates another British institution, the public school, and presents a similarly idealized and romantic view of British society and traditions. The story, based on a novella by James Hilton, centres on the sixty-year career of a Latin Master at the Brookfield School, which is described in Hilton's story as an undistinguished public school. As a young man, Mr Chipping is fastidious and unpopular, but in middle-age he meets a loving and vivacious younger woman, Kathy, who bolsters his confidence and brings out his sense of humour. She dies after only one year of marriage, but in that time she has turned his life around. She renames him 'Chips' and, through her belief in him, enables him to become a beloved figure at the school. Her death, followed by the death of Chips' students in the Boer War and then in the First World War, and finally the death of Chips himself, form the melodrama of this bittersweet and nostalgic story.

MGM purchased the rights to *Goodbye Mr Chips* shortly after its publication in 1934, and Irving Thalberg was overseeing its adaptation at the time of his death in 1936, with Charles Laughton and Myrna Loy set to play the lead roles. The notes that remain from Thalberg's conferences with the scriptwriters indicate that he wanted the story developed as that of a man who 'started his career as a failure and was bound to mediocrity. He never really improved, but he met a woman who ... turned his mediocrity into success.[28] In this light, *Goodbye Mr Chips* appears to have been seen as an ideal vehicle for Laughton, who had developed a speciality for playing emotionally repressed and tender-hearted misfits. When the film was put back into production in 1938 as an MGM-British production, though, the emphasis of the story was very different.

Goodbye Mr Chips was assigned to the MGM director Sidney Franklin in 1938. Franklin was, according to his colleagues, a devout Anglophile, and he had already developed a speciality for romantic melodramas with British settings (*Smilin' Through*, *The Barretts of Wimpole Street*, *The Dark Angel*).[29] Along with a team of British writers that included R.C. Sherriff, Claudine West, Eric Maschwitz, Monkton Hoffe and Ian Dalrymple, Franklin set out to transform *Goodbye Mr Chips* into another paean to Britain's age-old virtues.[30] By the time the script was finished, MGM had convinced Franklin to give up directing and take up a production post at the studio, and so it was MGM director Sam Wood who went to Britain to direct the film under the guidance of producer Victor Saville. Franklin, however, maintained a close watch on the film. He told Saville that *Goodbye Mr Chips* was his 'favorite child' and that he should not change 'a comma or a period' in the script. When filming was complete, the footage was sent back to Culver City, where Franklin presided over the editing process.[31]

Under Franklin's firm guidance, *Goodbye Mr Chips* was no longer the character study of Mr Chipping that Thalberg had imagined. Instead, the film captured an American Anglophile's preferred view of Britain. The Brookfield School is not the undistinguished school of Hilton's story but is one of the greatest of all public schools. The school's long history and its role in forming the minds of Britain's historical figures are established in the first five minutes of the film. The opening shot of the ancient profile of Brookfield closes in on two teachers who are reading a plaque that commemorates the school's founding. One teacher comments, '1492, the year Columbus discovered America!' To which the other replies, 'We're in the heart of England, a heart with a very gentle beat.' Chips (Robert Donat) is then seen reassuring a new boy. He points out the inscription of the boy's ancestor – 'The Duke of Dorset: 1650' – in the chapel alcove, and also points to an inscription that reads 'Sir Francis Drake: 1552'. Again, and as with Scatters in *A Yank at Oxford*, the newcomer (and, of course, the audience) is being sold on a British institution by allusions to its illustrious history and heritage.

The revised approach to *Goodbye Mr Chips* also eschewed what Thalberg had described as Chips' mediocrity. Indeed, Chips is the embodiment of what the film presents as the virtues of Britain: its history, traditions and heritage. His sixty-year career (1870 to 1930) covers an array of historical events, which are presented with both humour (the arrival of the telephone and the automobile) and apprehension (the Boer War, the First World War). It is the values Chips holds dear, those of a nineteenth-century gentleman, that will see Britain through change and crisis. When Chips is told by a new headmaster to update his teaching methods, he decries the modern age and states his ethos (and that of the public school), 'Give a boy a sense of humour and a sense of proportion and he'll stand up to anything!'

The film's endorsement of the public school ethos is, by extension, an endorsement of the British class system. In both the novel and the film, class is presented as a benevolent force in British society. Some class discord is evident when a Brookfield student, Colley, is seen fighting with a 'town cheese'. Later, however, we see Colley going off to the First World War as an officer with the very same 'town cheese' as his trusted batman. When Colley is killed in action, it is only through his efforts to save the life of his batman. The social order works well, we are given to believe, because the upper classes look after the lower classes. This notion would became a cornerstone of MGM's wartime 'British' films.

The publicity packet MGM released for *Goodbye Mr Chips* makes the film's patriotic nature fully evident: 'All that England is, and stands for, was brought with gracious dignity to the screen in this film version of James Hilton's novel. Truly *Goodbye Mr Chips* is this England ... set on the silver screen.[32] The studio had its view of the film confirmed when *Goodbye Mr Chips* was cited by the British Ministry of Information as an 'obvious example' of how feature films could best embody 'British life and character' during wartime.[33] An editorial in *The Listener* also praised the propaganda value of *Goodbye Mr Chips*, when it stated that 'there must be few Englishmen who can see the film without having their faith in the English ideal strengthened'.[34]

The Citadel is a far more contemporary and realistic film. MGM's decision to make such a film undoubtedly stemmed from the fact that it was based on a recent best-selling novel, and that Victor Saville had purchased the screen rights. *The Citadel* was also well suited to the American director King Vidor, who was known for pursuing social themes within the acceptable limits. However, Vidor and his wife, the screenwriter Elizabeth Hill, travelled through Wales before filming began. The director later recalled that they were shocked by the dismal poverty and appalling living conditions they saw in the Welsh valleys, and that the journey convinced them that the film should not avoid this reality. Hence, *The Citadel* did not improve upon Britain and seek the romantic and more appealing aspects of the country, but had a considerable measure of bleak realism.[35]

This is immediately apparent in the first scene, when a young doctor, Andrew Manson (Robert Donat) arrives in the Welsh village of Blaenelly. A montage seen through the train window establishes the squalor of the village, with its row upon row of dismal terraced houses dominated by a smoking industrial plant. Manson is at first idealistic and genuinely concerned with helping the people of the village. They are ill nourished and suffer from chronic bad health. The miners have lung disease, and a faulty sewer system causes a typhoid epidemic. But he soon realizes that he cannot help, that he alone cannot overcome poverty and ignorance. In his frustration, he loses his idealism and moves to London. There, he joins a lucrative Harley Street practice and the wealthy social set that surrounds it. He soon finds that the doctors are interested only in making money, and that the patients are wealthy socialites with imagined illnesses. When he eventually rediscovers his ideals, he walks the streets of London and sees that it too has a dark and impoverished underside. He becomes a crusader for medical reforms, and in doing so wins back the affections of his wife (Rosalind Russell).

The Citadel exposes all that MGM's other 'British' films seek to repress. They never hide the fact that there are sharp class divisions in British society, but class is usually portrayed as a matter of accents and dispositions rather than harsh economic inequalities. Crusty but lovable aristocrats and quaint working-class caricatures populate most 'British' films, but in *The Citadel* the wealthy are seen as haughty and over-privileged, while the poor are ignorant and suffer from malnutrition, bad housing and an inferior social welfare system. It is little wonder, then, that the BBFC hesitated before passing the film. Britain's censors maintained a tight control over the portrayal of social issues and they did not like to see professionals criticized. At the same time, though, the BBFC was unlikely to be obstructive with a studio such as MGM, which was investing so heavily in Britain's film industry. *The Citadel* was passed by the censors and this precedent (as well as the film's popularity) undoubtedly helped to usher in an era of greater realism in British films.

Each of the three pre-war MGM-British films was highly profitable, but it is interesting to note the differences in their financial profile. *The Citadel* drew the highest foreign gross of the three films. It was particularly popular in Britain, where it was reported to have been the second most popular film of 1939, and its earnings were expected to reach $1,000,000.[36] British audiences, it seems, were more than ready for a dose of social realism. American audiences, however, preferred the more nostalgic Britain to be found in *A Yank at Oxford* and *Goodbye Mr Chips*. Both films were hugely successful in the domestic market. Thus, the MGM-British enterprise was an unqualified success, but the war interrupted plans for further productions. Shortly after *Goodbye Mr Chips* was completed, in March 1939, the production unit was closed. With war looming in Europe, MGM was wary of sending its stars and directors overseas, and, in fact, Victor Saville and Greer Garson were summoned quickly to Culver City. Two further films were made by MGM-British during the war years, but *Haunted Honeymoon* (1940) and *Tartu* (1943) were comparatively modest films and neither was successful in the United States. In 1944 it was announced that Alexander Korda was taking on the role of head of production at MGM-British, and ambitious production plans were announced. These plans fell apart when Korda's extravagance and the delays on the first film, *Vacation from Marriage* (1945), sent its budget skyward.[37] In the meantime, the production of MGM's 'British' films had reverted to California.

Wartime 'British' films

Between 1940 and 1945, no fewer than fourteen 'British' films were produced at MGM's Culver City studios, most of which closely followed the formulas established in the 1930s. While Britain was threatened with invasion and bombings, MGM created the most idealized portrayals of Britain and the British. One facet of this was a continuing line of costume dramas. An adaptation of Jane Austen's *Pride and Prejudice* (1940) had been initiated by Irving Thalberg in 1935, after *The Barretts of Wimpole Street*. Norma Shearer had been set to play Elizabeth Bennett but the project was cancelled when Thalberg died and Shearer took a two-year hiatus from acting.[38] It re-emerged, with a script co-written by Aldous Huxley, when Greer Garson arrived at MGM in California, fresh from her success at MGM-British in *Goodbye Mr Chips*. *Pride and Prejudice* offered Garson a last opportunity to play a girlish and flirtatious role before her screen persona became fixed as the mature and maternal Mrs Miniver. Laurence Olivier co-starred, and both the stars and the film received critical praise. The 'Merrie England' setting, as the film's opening titles describe it, was mounted at great expense, and when the film was only moderately successful a loss of $241,000 was incurred. Following *Pride and Prejudice*, the only 'British' costume dramas produced at MGM would be those that have the added box-office attraction of some element of the macabre. *Dr Jekyll and Mr Hyde* (1941), *Gaslight* (1944) and *The Picture of Dorian Gray* (1945) were modestly successful, but had domestic returns below those of more contemporary 'British' films.

The numerous wartime reworkings of *A Yank at Oxford* also drew mixed returns. The most successful was also the most obvious imitation of the original. *A Yank at Eton* (1942), starring Mickey Rooney, may have been an uninspired repetition of the original, but it nonetheless earned a profit of over $1,000,000. Anglo-American differences were also highlighted in *The Earl of Chicago* (1940), in which a Chicago gangster (Robert Montgomery) inherits a seat in the House of Lords. This was an inexpensive production with a fading star, and it made a slight loss. *The Canterville Ghost* (1944) is an even more improbable 'Yank' film. MGM originally intended to adapt Oscar Wilde's ghost story in a straightforward manner, but then the scriptwriters had the idea of updating the story and renaming it 'Thirty-Six Yanks and a Ghost'. That title was dropped, but the new story remained. The ghost of Sir Simon De Canterville (Charles Laughton) is confronted, and eventually befriended, by a platoon of American soldiers who have been stationed at his ancestral home. This was another box-office flop and loss-maker.

The Franklin melodramas

The 'British' melodramas produced by Sidney Franklin were the source of MGM's greatest earnings and profits during the war years. *Waterloo Bridge*, *Mrs Miniver*, *Random Harvest* and *The White Cliffs of Dover* follow closely in the footsteps of Franklin's 'favorite child', *Goodbye Mr Chips*. Franklin had never been to Britain at the time he made these films, but he was drawn to what he referred to as the 'quaintness and charm' of the country. His antiquated conception of Britain is apparent in his instructions to the scriptwriters of *Mrs Miniver*. When describing the village setting, Franklin told them that there should be 'a beautiful composition of the Norman tower of the old village church', with the 'landscape of the English countryside in the background'. The church bells would sound, tentatively at first, so that the 'well known pigeons' could fly away before the bells began in earnest. Then there would be 'shots of the village reacting to the bells', including the 'village smith, shoeing a horse' and the 'exterior of the old village pub'.[39] Franklin eventually would face a less idyllic reality. After the war, when he visited Britain for the first time, he was disappointed by the 'grey drabness' he found there.[40] During the war, however, his storybook image of Britain clearly suited the needs of wartime audiences on both sides of the Atlantic.

Each of the Franklin melodramas centres on the pain and anxiety caused by wartime separation or loss, and each offers a strong, maternal and caring woman as a source of safety and serenity amid the heartaches of war. In *Waterloo Bridge*, a newly wed couple are separated when he goes off to battle during the First World War. The young, frail bride (Vivien Leigh) mistakenly believes that her husband (Robert Taylor) has died and, when she is destitute and starving, she is forced into prostitution in order to save herself. Had she maintained contact with her husband's kind and wealthy mother (Lucile Watson), however, her troubles would not have arisen. In the end, the mother can only offer wise words and sympathy. The maternal heroine of *Mrs Miniver* (Greer Garson) comforts her younger children during the Blitz, sees her husband and elder son off to Dunkirk, and creates goodwill throughout her war-torn village. In *Random Harvest*, a shell-shocked veteran of the First World War (Ronald Colman) has amnesia, and is nursed back to health by a music-hall entertainer (Greer Garson) who abandons her career to care for him. When he regains his memory, though, he forgets her and she spends years at his side, hoping he will remember their romantic involvement. And in *The White Cliffs of Dover*, an American woman (Irene Dunne) marries into the British aristocracy, but loses her husband (Alan Marshal) in the First World War, and then faces the loss of her son (Peter Lawford) in the Second World War with stoic patriotism.

The films' depiction of strong, maternal women as a source of consistency and comfort is paralleled by their depiction of Britain, the 'mother country' of the United States, as a timeless haven of peace and serenity. The war, or some aspect of war, always intrudes upon the serenity, but the overwhelming impression in each of the films is one of rural charms and maternal fortitude. There is a brief scene in *Random Harvest* in which the connection between the two is made plain. The First World War has left Smithy with shell-shock and amnesia, but Paula, the music-hall performer who nurses him back to health, takes him to the country to recuperate. When they arrive by train at their rural destination, they stand on the station platform and gaze at the landscape. The rolling green hills, dotted with tiny hamlets and

4 Paula (Greer Garson) and Smithy (Ronald Colman) are finally reunited in the ending of *Random Harvest* (1942)

church spires, lead her to exclaim, 'we'll be safe here'. And they are safe there. Danger only arrives in these films in the form of modernity, whether it comes from bombs or the characters' rare ventures into the city. The blissful happiness of Smithy and Paula, for example, is shattered when he leaves their isolated cottage to visit Liverpool, where he is hit by a car and loses all knowledge of Paula.

Class distinctions are overwhelmingly apparent in these idyllic rural settings, but they are a source of order and harmony rather than conflict. Everyone knows their place and is happy with it. The servants and shopkeepers are salt-of-the-earth types, who are comically simple-minded and have a reverential respect for the upper classes. The wealthy and titled are stoic and unemotional, and they bear a strong sense of responsibility toward their inferiors. The latter point is most evident in *Random Harvest* and *The White Cliffs of Dover*. In *Random Harvest*, Smithy takes on his birthright as the 'industrial prince of England' when he has forgotten Paula. He assumes the management of the family's business empire not for personal gain, but because its businesses 'keep other families going too – little families in little homes all over England'. When a strike occurs at one of his factories, he immediately settles it by giving in to all of the workers' demands. The grateful workers respond by singing 'For He's A Jolly Good Fellow' to him, as he looks down upon them from the height of a balcony. In a similar vein, when the American mother of *The White Cliffs of Dover* intends to return to the United States, her British son stops her, declaring the family's responsibility to look after the tenants of their estate.

Sharp class distinctions had been integral to 'British' films long before these war films. The entertainment value of the class system – to be found in the grand homes and manners of the upper class, the comic simplicity of the working class, and the drama of cross-class romances – had fuelled 'British' films for many years. In the war films, class differences are still fore-grounded, but a small measure of the egalitarian wartime spirit is also evident. Cross-class romances still occur, for example, but they are not the primary dramatic issue and they are seldom opposed. In *Waterloo Bridge* and *Random Harvest*, the central female characters are of undefined class origin yet they marry aris-tocratic men. In *The White Cliffs of Dover*, the American woman also marries into the aristocracy, and her son becomes romanti-cally involved with the daughter of a tenant on the family's estate. And *Mrs Miniver* introduces a class previously unseen in 'British' films: the middle-class. The middle class Miniver family is still sur-rounded by upper-class and working-class characters, but the romance of Vin Miniver (Richard Ney) and the upper class Carol Beldon (Teresa Wright) brings only the briefest and most half-hearted protests from Lady Beldon (Dame May Whitty).

The first of Franklin's wartime melodramas, *Waterloo Bridge*, was not a film that either he or MGM had originated. Robert Sherwood's play had been filmed once before, by Universal Stu-dios in 1931, and the story of a prostitute on the streets of London was not the sort that attracted Franklin. David Selznick, however, thought that the story was perfect for Vivien Leigh, whom he had under contract, and MGM was eager to use Leigh in the wake of *Gone with the Wind*. Hence, *Waterloo Bridge* and Vivien Leigh came to MGM as a package deal.[41] In Franklin's hands, the remake was lush and gentle by comparison with Uni-versal's film, and it included key elements of his idealized Britain. Most significantly, the enlisted man of the play was upgraded to an officer, his mother was made into a stronger and kinder char-acter, and the family home became a palatial Scottish estate. The young couple's carriage ride through the estate grounds, the greetings of the humble servants and the formalities of upper-class life place the viewer firmly within the never-never land of MGM's Britain. The contemporary threat to this never-never land was also included by having the story told in flashback. The film opens with the announcement 'Sunday, September Third, 1939 – a date long to be remembered', and shows a long line of children walking gloomily with their gas masks to an air-raid shelter.

Franklin was adamant that a British actor should co-star with Vivien Leigh, but Louis B. Mayer rejected Franklin's choices (Laurence Olivier or Michael Redgrave) and insisted that the MGM contract star Robert Taylor play the part of the aristocratic Scotsman. Franklin recalled that he 'made such a fuss that had I gone much further I would have been thrown off the lot'.[42] Robert Taylor got the part, but the cast otherwise included British actors such as C. Aubrey Smith, Virginia Field and Leo G. Carroll. And although the script was credited to the non-British ensemble of S.N. Behrman, George Froeschel and Hans Rameau, the British writers Cyril Hume and Dodie Smith were also contributors.[43] In Britain, *Kinematograph Weekly* listed *Waterloo Bridge* as the most popular film of December 1940, and its foreign earnings ($1,217,000 or 49 per cent of the total) were particularly strong.[44] The film's domestic earnings ($1,250,000) and profit ($491,000) were also strong, but all of these figures would appear slight when compared with those of the 'British' melodramas that followed.

Mrs Miniver, *Random Harvest* and *The White Cliffs of Dover* were based on sources far closer to Franklin's own preferred view of Britain. Jan Struther's *Mrs Miniver* stories had appeared first on the pages of the London *Times*, and centred on the heroine's leisurely observations about life amid the upper-middle class. *Random Harvest* was based on a novel by James Hilton, author of *Goodbye Mr Chips*, and was another story steeped in nostalgia. And *The White Cliffs of Dover*, written as a narrative poem by Alice Duer Miller, was basically the Cinderella story of a plain American girl marrying into a titled British family. Each of these sources was adapted by an ensemble of predominantly British screenwriters, all of whom contributed to *Goodbye Mr Chips* (see table 12). Franklin assigned British writers such as James Hilton, R.C. Sherriff, Arthur Wimperis, and the Austrian refugee George Froeschel, to write individual scenes for the films, and often sent comments back to the writers on how to improve their scenes. The full script was then assembled by the British writer Claudine West, who was Franklin's close friend and frequent collaborator.

Table 12 Screenwriters on MGM's 'British' melodramas

Writers	Goodbye Mr Chips	Mrs Miniver	Random Harvest	White Cliffs of Dover
George Froeschel	X	X		X
James Hilton	*	X	*	
R.C. Sherriff	X	X		
Claudine West	X	X	X	X
Arthur Wimperis	X	X		

* Hilton wrote the novels upon which these films are based

The casts of Franklin's melodramas were also predominantly British. The leading roles went to British actors such as Vivien Leigh, Greer Garson and Ronald Colman, although in some cases a Canadian such as Walter Pidgeon or an Australian such as Alan Marshal was cast in lieu of British stars. In at least one instance the studio had the British market in mind when making a crucial casting decision. The issue was whether Ronald Colman or Walter Pidgeon should be Greer Garson's co-star in *Random Harvest*. British exhibitors were surveyed, and when they answered that Colman would offer the greater box-office draw in Britain, Colman got the part.[45] The smaller parts were given to Hollywood's British featured players, who made a consistent living playing the aunts, uncles, dinner guests, nannies, butlers and shopkeepers of 'British' films. As Jeffrey Richards has noted, these recurring 'familiar faces' contributed to the 'idealized dream world' of Hollywood's Britain. Like Shangri-La, the dream world of James Hilton's *Lost Horizon*, the British setting in these films seems to exist, with the same people and settings, peacefully and outside of time.[46] Table 13 indicates just how familiar these faces became in wartime 'British' films.

The overwhelming appeal of Franklin's 'British' melodramas can be seen in the films' earnings figures. *Mrs Miniver* was a phenomenon. It was the most popular film of the year (from any studio) in both North America and Britain,[47] and its foreign earnings ($3,520,000) were three times higher than those of any other MGM film released in the 1941–42 season. The production cost ($1,344,000) was one of the highest of the season, indicating that the studio had never thought of the film as a potential loss-maker. When the film earned a worldwide gross of $8,878,000, MGM had the highest profit ($4,831,000) in its history. *Random Harvest* nearly matched the success of *Mrs Miniver*, with worldwide earnings of $8,147,000 yeilding the second-

Table 13 MGM's British featured players: the 'familar faces' of Hollywood's Britain

Actor's name	Mrs Miniver	Random Harvest	Lassie Come Home	Gaslight	White Cliffs	National Velvet	Picture of Dorian Gray
Jill Esmond		X			X		
Brenda Forbes	X				X		
Angela Lansbury				X		X	X
Peter Lawford	X	X			X		X
Aubrey Mather	X	X					
Roddy McDowall			X		X		
Reginald Owen	X	X				X	
Arthur Shields		X	X		X	X	
Elizabeth Taylor			X		X	X	
Henry Travers	X	X					
Norma Varden		X			X	X	
Dame May Whitty	X		X	X	X		
Rhys Williams	X	X					

highest profit in MGM's history ($4,384,000). *Random Harvest* was also the most popular film of the year in Britain, where it proved to be even more popular than Britain's most acclaimed war film, *In Which We Serve*.[48] By the time *The White Cliffs of Dover* went into production, the success of *Mrs Miniver* and *Random Harvest* was fully apparent. *The White Cliffs of Dover* was thus mounted on an epic scale and at a production cost ($2,342,000) nearly double that of the previous films. In North America, it was MGM's top-earning film of the 1943–44 season, and in Britain it ranked ninth among the most popular films of 1944.[49] The world-wide earnings, $6,294,000, were very strong, if not quite as spectacular as those from the two previous wartime films. The same can be said of the $1,784,000 profit.

It was a common practice in Hollywood to create inexpensive imitations of box-office successes, and MGM followed *Mrs Miniver* with the 'B' films *Journey for Margaret* (1942) and *Lassie Come Home* (1943). In *Journey for Margaret* five-year-old Margaret O'Brien made her film debut as the waif whose parents are killed during an air raid, and Robert Young and Laraine Day co-starred as the Americans-in-London who adopt her. Produced at a cost of just $484,000, *Journey for Margaret* earned $1,554,000 and a profit of $561,000. *Lassie Come Home* had higher costs ($666,000), which provided for Technicolor views of its York-shire moors setting (filmed in California). Set in the 1930s, the story centres on the troubles that ensue when Lassie's unemployed owner is forced to sell the beloved collie to a wealthy duke. All is solved when the kind duke employs the former owner as

Lassie's trainer, providing another example of the benevolent feudalism to be found in MGM's Britain. This was the first ever Lassie film, and it had an entirely British cast, including newcomers Roddy McDowall and Elizabeth Taylor and veterans Nigel Bruce, Donald Crisp, Elsa Lanchester and Dame May Whitty. The earnings ($4,517,000) and profit ($2,249,000) ensured that this was not Lassie's last starring role. Thirteen-year-old Elizabeth Taylor had only co-starring roles in *Lassie Come Home* and *The White Cliffs of Dover*, but she was soon given the starring role in *National Velvet* (1945). The setting was another picturesque English village before the war, and once again the cast was filled with the familiar faces of Hollywood's British players, including Donald Crisp, Reginald Owen, Arthur Treacher and Norma Varden. Technicolor was used to capture the dramatic scenery of the Sussex coast (again, filmed in California), where Taylor rides her beloved horse. The earnings ($5,840,000) mark this as one of the most successful of all 'British' films.

Conclusion

Between 1933 and 1945, MGM produced two or three 'British' films each year. The number of 'British' films is not particularly significant, given that MGM's annual output amounted to approximately thirty-five films. Rather, the significance of 'British' films lies in their expense and their popularity. High returns from the key markets, those of the United States and Britain, were needed to recoup the production costs of prestige films, and 'British' films were consistently successful in providing them. Most remarkably, the American success of these films suggests that during this era Americans were particularly interested in Britain. Of course, the films were designed to appeal both to Americans and to the British. The 'Yank' films are the most obvious example of this, as the British setting was viewed with an American perspective. However, it also is apparent that films centred on Britain's literature and history, its culture and heritage, and later its war effort, found favour on both sides of the Atlantic.

In the post-war period this was not the case. Some 'British' films continued to draw unusually high foreign returns, but American interest fell off rapidly.[50] *If Winter Comes* (1947), a wartime melodrama modelled on *Mrs Miniver*, failed miserably in both the domestic and foreign markets. Even when Mrs Miniver herself returned, in *The Miniver Story* (1950), few were interested. In fact, Greer Garson's post-war career was an unmitigated disaster, and, after a succession of films which incurred huge losses, she finally left MGM in 1955. Sidney Franklin's career sank with *The Miniver Story*, *Young Bess* (1954) and a remake of *The Barretts of Wimpole Street* (1957). In this climate, younger British stars such as Elizabeth Taylor, Peter Lawford and Roddy McDowall quickly took on American accents and roles. Even Lassie soon became an American dog. Hollywood's Britain no longer captured the American imagination, and the return of a larger foreign market after the war meant that the importance of British earnings steadily declined. With these key factors no longer in place, and after a long and surprisingly successful run, MGM's conspicuous Anglophilia came to an end.

4   Early 'British' war films

From the outset of the Second World War, Hollywood's 'British' films were given wartime themes and relevance. In fact, 'British' films were rejuvenated by the war and the dramatic situations it offered. Even historical dramas could be made relevant and timely, by dramatizing earlier conflicts in which Britain fought to defend itself from invasion. It was the current conflict that excited film-makers and audiences the most, though, and films set amid the Battle of Britain and the London Blitz soon outnumbered forays into the past. Films such as *The Sea Hawk* (1940), *That Hamilton Woman* (1941), *Foreign Correspondent* (1940), *A Yank in the RAF* (1941) and the long-delayed *Eagle Squadron* (1942) are an integral part of Hollywood's reputation as an industry of Anglophiles. While the United States remained, technically at least, a neutral country until December 1941, Hollywood made its sympathies abundantly clear. Closer scrutiny of the films and their production histories, however, reveals the many different motives that lay behind Hollywood's support for the British cause.

The Sea Hawk: 'Merrie England' at war

The Sea Hawk provides a prime example of just how quickly and easily 'British' films were given patriotic war themes. It was the sixth in a series of costume dramas from Warners, referred to by Nick Roddick as Warners' 'Merrie England' films.[1] These were made on a lavish scale similar to that of the 'British' films produced by David Selznick and Irving Thalberg at MGM, but with a greater emphasis on action and adventure. The series began in

1935 with *Captain Blood*, which launched the career of Errol Flynn, and it continued with one film each year: *The Charge of the Light Brigade* (1936), *The Prince and the Pauper* (1936), *The Adventures of Robin Hood* (1938), *The Private Lives of Elizabeth and Essex* (1939) and, finally, *The Sea Hawk* in 1940. All of the films have Flynn in a leading role, and the casts include many of the best-known Hollywood 'British' actors, including Olivia De Havilland, Claude Rains, Basil Rathbone, Donald Crisp, Henry Stephenson, Henry Daniell and Una O'Connor.

Like MGM, Warners discovered that the high costs of prestige could be recouped with 'British' films. The average production cost at Warners during the late 1930s hovered around the $400,000 mark, and many of the studio's top stars – James Cagney, Bette Davis, Dick Powell and Edward G. Robinson – made films that cost little more than this average figure. The 'Merrie England' films, however, were far more expensive. *The Adventures of Robin Hood*, which cost $2,033,000, was by far the most expensive film produced at that studio in the 1930s, and the others were among the most expensive films produced in their respective years. As Table Fourteen indicates, the costs were amply returned by the combination of high domestic and particularly high foreign returns. *Captain Blood*, *The Charge of the Light Brigade* and *The Adventures of Robin Hood* were the only Warner Bros. films to earn foreign grosses of more than one million dollars in the 1930s, and *Robin Hood* – by far the most successful of all the films – earned twice that amount.[2]

The 'Merrie England' films bear strong similarities to one another in plot, theme and characterization. They are action-adventure films, with Flynn typically cast as a swashbuckling 'gentleman pirate' or a daring soldier. Roddick notes that each of Flynn's characters is engaged in a heroic struggle for justice and against corruption, a struggle which inevitably leads to climactic sword-fights and epic battles. In all but one of the films (*The Charge of the Light Brigade*), his efforts are centred on the defence of the most famous and celebrated of all British institutions, the monarchy. *The Sea Hawk* clearly fits within these established parameters; Roddick labels this last 'Merrie England' film as 'almost entirely formulary'.[3] The film's generic basis is apparent in its production history. Initially, *The Sea Hawk* was seen only as a means of capitalising on the success of *Captain Blood*, and certainly not as a vehicle for timely political statements. When the Warner Bros. producer Hal Wallis first began to consider the story in December 1935, it was as 'a possible follow-up to *Captain Blood*' and as 'a big sea picture for next year's program'.[4] Like

Table 14 Costs and earnings of Warner Brothers' 'Merrie England' films (in thousands of dollars)

Film (year)	Production cost ($000)	Domestic earnings ($000)	Foreign earnings ($000)	Total earnings ($000)
Captain Blood (1935)	995	1,087 44%	1,388 56%	2,475
The Charge of the Light Brigade (1936)	1,076	1,176 43%	1,560 57%	2,736
The Prince and the Pauper (1936)	858	1,026 61%	665 39%	1,691
The Adventures of Robin Hood (1938)	2,033	1,928 48%	2,053 52%	3,981
The Private Lives of Elizabeth and Essex (1939)	1,073	955 59%	658 41%	1,613
The Sea Hawk (1940)	1,701	1,631 61%	1,047 39%	2,678

Source: The William Schaefer Ledger, The William Schaefer Collection, The Doheny Library, University of Southern California.

Captain Blood, the original story for *The Sea Hawk* was based on a novel by Rafael Sabatini, which had been the basis of a hugely successful silent film in 1922. All of these factors seemed to Hal Wallis to add up to another box-office success and to a perfect vehicle for the studio's newest star, Errol Flynn.

Wallis assigned the screenwriter Seton Miller to develop *The Sea Hawk*, but Miller soon informed his superiors that he considered Sabatini's original story to be 'an out-dated piece of junk'.[5] Miller was then set to work on *The Adventures of Robin Hood*, and returned to *The Sea Hawk* only when he was allowed to abandon Sabatini's story and develop one centred on Sir Francis Drake, Queen Elizabeth I and the threat posed to England by the Spanish Armada. This was in August 1938, and the script was written and rewritten by Miller and his fellow Warner Bros. screenwriter Howard Koch until filming began in January 1940. During this period, Britain moved from a policy of appeasement, which reached its climax at Munich in September 1938, to its declaration of war against Germany in September 1939. With each draft Miller and Koch strengthened the story's parallels with the present, so that by the time the director Michael Curtiz began filming *The Sea Hawk* in January 1940, it served as an explanation of British foreign policy over the previous years.[6]

The new story takes place in the late sixteenth century and centres on England's confrontation with Spain and its tyrannical King Philip II. Geoffrey Thorpe (Errol Flynn), a character based upon Sir Francis Drake, plunders Spanish ships not for his own gain, but to enable Queen Elizabeth I (Flora Robson) to build a fleet to fight the Armada. The Queen is not convinced of the threat posed by Spain, and is encouraged to use diplomacy rather than force by the traitorous Lord Wolfingham (Henry Daniell). Wolfingham is acting on behalf of Philip II (Montagu Love), and hopes to take the throne when Spain defeats England. Thorpe obtains evidence of Wolfingham's deceit, kills him in a climactic sword-fight, and is knighted by the Queen. The film ends as the Queen sends her new fleet to defeat the Armada.

The parallels are not difficult to discern. Sixteenth-century Spain, under Philip, is seen to have expansionist aims akin to those of Germany under Hitler. In the first scene of the film, the sinister Philip sits before a map of the world and states his designs on Europe and the New World. He tells his advisers that the Armada must be built as quickly as possible because the only thing that prevents his ambitions is 'a puny rock-bound island':

We cannot keep Northern Europe in submission until we have a reckoning with England. With England conquered nothing can stand in our way. Northern Africa, Europe as far east as the Urals, then the New World, to the North and the South, west to the Pacific, over the Pacific ... [the scene fades out].

England is thus held to be the only bulwark against such European tyrants, and the English fight not only for themselves, but for the protection of all those threatened by tyranny, including those in the 'new world'.

The Sea Hawk also attempts to cast the British reluctance to go to war, in the sixteenth century and by extension in the late 1930s, in the best possible light. Queen Elizabeth believes in appeasement, but her reluctance to confront Spain is seen to be characteristic of a kind and civilized monarch. Elizabeth dislikes war, and does not want to burden her countrymen with the high taxes necessary to finance a new fleet. Philip, by contrast, is a ruthless tyrant. The galleys of his ships are filled with brutally treated slaves, the victims of the Spanish Inquisition, and he is thirsty for war and world domination. Thus, the benevolent and peaceful Elizabeth is contrasted with the tyrannical and war-mongering Philip. However, having established that England is not eager for war, the ending makes it clear that England will rise to defend itself when its territory and principles are threatened.

Warners apparently was not troubled about making a film so supportive of Britain's reasons for attempting to avoid war, but the studio was very careful with the ending of the film, which portrays the beginning of the war itself. Two versions of the ending were made. In the first version, Thorpe is knighted by Queen Elizabeth and then Elizabeth gives a rousing speech to her troops:

And now my loyal subjects a grave duty confronts us all, to prepare our nation for a war that none of us wants – least of all your Queen. We have tried by all means in our power to avert this war. We have no quarrel with the people of Spain nor of any other country. But when the ruthless ambitions of one man threaten to engulf the world, it becomes the solemn obligation of all free men to affirm that the earth belongs not to any one man but to all men, and that freedom is the deed and title to the soil on which we exist. Firm in this faith, we shall now make ready to meet the great Armada that Philip sends against us. To this end I pledge you ships. Ships worthy of our seamen, a mighty fleet hewn out of the forests of England, a navy foremost in the world, not only in our time but for generations to come.

The speech makes it clear that the English fight for the noble cause of freedom, in England as well as wherever else it is threatened. Additionally, it is implied that the new fleet, and the defeat of the Armada (taken for granted rather than shown), herald a turning point in history. 'For generations to come', England will be ready and able to assume its role in the defence of world freedom. This point is then furthered by a montage of shots which shows the wooden masts of the sixteenth-century fleet transforming into a fleet of modern battleships.[7]

This first ending was written in August 1939 and it remained in the shooting script that was filmed between January and April of 1940. At some point, however, it was decided that it should be used only in the prints made for the film's British release. In the prints made for the American market and all other neutral countries, a different ending was used. In this more equivocal ending, Thorpe is knighted and then the film fades out as the fleet sets off to defeat the Armada. Elizabeth's call to arms – not just for Englishman but for 'all free men' – was omitted, and the montage showing a wooden fleet becoming a modern fleet of battleships was also cut.

Unfortunately, no record remains in the production files indicating why this change was made. It was not the Hays Office that

5 The last of the 'Merrie England' films: Geoffrey Thorpe (Errol Flynn) and Elizabeth I (Flora Robson) in *The Sea Hawk* (1940)

objected to the longer version. In fact, when Joseph Breen read the full script in January 1940 he did not even comment on the story's timely parallels.[8] The decision to use the abbreviated version, then, must have come from within Warners itself. Writer Howard Koch recalled many years later that the studio was very cautious toward the film's 'message':

People don't like message pictures, so whatever we were saying in *The Sea Hawk* was said by implication. Except in the last speech I think it was pretty much put into words. We would say our theme was tyranny must be faced, whether it was in Spain in that time or Germany in that time.[9]

The theme of the film and the similarities between the historical situation and the present situation are certainly evident in both versions of the film. Audiences in the United States and Latin America, where the shorter ending was used, could hardly fail to recognize the similarities between Spain under Philip and Germany under Hitler, and they would also have seen Britain portrayed as the bulwark against such aggressors. As Koch noted, though, it was the longer ending that brought the theme and the parallels out of the realm of 'implications' and into the realm of a more direct 'message'. The Queen's speech, and particularly the final transformation shots, had removed the mask of the costume allegory.

Early 'British' war films

Warner Bros. clearly benefited from using both endings. The shorter ending was used in neutral countries such as the United States and the countries of Latin America, where overtly pro-British messages were likely to lead to trouble. This proved to be wise. *The Sea Hawk* was the studio's top earning film of the year in the domestic market, and it escaped the bans that were routinely placed on war films in Latin America. Its political implications also seem to have escaped the attention of isolationists in the United States. *The Sea Hawk* was never mentioned in the Congressional inquiry into 'war propaganda' that was held in 1941. The British version, meanwhile, was used to build goodwill for Warners in Britain. There, *The Daily Mail* heralded *The Sea Hawk* as 'the film with which Hollywood abandons its neutrality'. The review in *The Evening Standard* was entitled 'Hollywood Fires a Shot for Britain'. And *The Daily Express* reported that Harry Warner had contacted Duff Cooper, the Minister of Information, to inform him that 'a good pro-British photoplay was on its way', and that Cooper was 'so impressed' with the film, he urged the studio to hasten its release.[10] When it went into general release in Britain in December 1940, *The Sea Hawk* was second only to MGM's *Waterloo Bridge* at the British box office.[11] It also had the highest foreign earnings of any Warners' film released in the 1939–40 season.

Warner Bros. was not alone in tailoring its political commitment to suit particular markets. When Paramount filmed *Arise My Love* (1940) and *One Night in Lisbon* (1941), which were both stories of Americans caught in the midst of wartime European intrigue, the studio filmed two versions of any scene that contained either statements of support for Britain or criticism of Germany. One print retained the comments, the other omitted them. That way, the films could be released in every market that remained open to American films, with their political convictions tailored to suit each country's sensibilities and its censors.[12] Warners went a step further than this, however, when it proposed that it should be given an economic incentive to continue making films in the 'Merrie England' series.

The proposal was made in response to the currency restrictions that the British government had set in place in October 1939, which allowed the studios to remit only a portion of their British earnings to the United States. In November 1939 Warner Bros. contacted the British Ministry of Information (MoI) to indicate that it was ready and willing to make further anti-Nazi and pro-British films. At this stage, it appeared that the studio merely wanted the Ministry's guidance with such films. Warners looked set to fulfil its promise when, in January 1940, it hired the British novelist C.S. Forester to adapt his own *Horatio Hornblower* stories for the screen. These seafaring adventures, set during the Napoleonic wars, were undoubtedly seen as further vehicles for Errol Flynn, and as a means of continuing the 'Merrie England' series. They were also seen as vehicles for British propaganda, and Forester was instructed by his studio supervisors to emphasize the films' pro-British message.[13] It soon became apparent, however, that Warners was seeking an economic reward for its pro-British films. In May 1940, the studio proposed to the MoI that, in return for making the *Hornblower* films, it should be allowed to remit the full amount of the films' British earnings rather than the portion allowed under the wartime currency agreement. Remarkably, the MoI actually approved of this scheme, but the more practical British Treasury – still in the grip of a dollar crisis – rejected it. Warners then shelved the plans for the *Horatio Hornblower* series.[14] Errol Flynn moved on to star in Westerns and war films, and the 'Merrie England' series came to an abrupt end. In Hollywood, it seems, Anglophilia was seldom completely separate from the pursuit of British earnings

That Hamilton Woman: propaganda with a 'sugar coating'

Alexander Korda's *That Hamilton Woman* was not made in an attempt to maximize the producer's earnings or free 'blocked' funds. Rather, the film provides a prime example of what isolationists in the US Congress protested against: a British film-maker in Hollywood making a film designed to counter American neutrality. In recent years, it has even been said that Korda made the film at the request of Winston Churchill himself, and that Korda actually worked as a spy for British intelligence agencies during the war. However, the evidence presented for this claim is flimsy. Churchill did love the film, and even after repeated viewings he was apparently reduced to tears by it, but this does not necessarily mean that it was made on his orders, and it certainly does not qualify Korda as a spy. Furthermore, while Korda did receive a knighthood in 1942, his achievements went far beyond the making of this one film. The screenwriter R.C. Sherriff, who travelled from Britain to Hollywood in 1940 in order to collaborate on the screenplay, recalled its origins in less dramatic terms. In his autobiography, Sherriff remembered that 'the government ... recognized the propaganda value of good British pictures' in Britain and neutral countries. Korda was 'consulted' over this, and when he suggested a film based on Lord Nelson's defeat of Napoleon at Trafalgar, 'the authorities ... wholeheartedly agreed'.[15]

The Hungarian-born producer and director was the natural choice to make such a film. Korda, who became a British citizen in 1936, had a well-established record as a patriotic film-maker on behalf of his adopted country. In 1933, he had provided the British film industry with its first internationally successful film, *The Private Life of Henry the Eighth* (1933), and then became known as its leading producer. Korda's films often projected patriotic themes. His 'trilogy' of British Empire films – *Sanders of the River* (1935), *The Drum* (1938) and *The Four Feathers* (1939) – are definitive examples of what Jeffrey Richards has termed the 'cinema of Empire'; that is, feature films which wholeheartedly endorse the British Empire.[16] Then, just after the outbreak of war in 1939, Korda quickly assembled *The Lion has Wings* (1939), a semidocumentary feature film which put forth the British view of the war. These films managed to combine their patriotic nature with the traditional elements of commercial cinema: stars, action and adventure, elaborate period settings and, in some cases, exotic location filming.

Korda was also well established in Hollywood. He was on the board of directors at United Artists, and had an ongoing distribution deal with that company. This meant that *That Hamilton Woman* would be guaranteed a wide American release, which was far from certain for most British films, and that it would be comparatively simple for Korda to make the film in Hollywood. The delays and shortages that plagued British film production during the war would be avoided, and the film's timely message would be circulated as quickly as possible. Furthermore, Korda would be able to use the wealth of British talent in Hollywood at this time, including stars Laurence Olivier and Vivien Leigh. Olivier, fresh from leading roles in *Wuthering Heights* (1939), *Rebecca* (1940) and *Pride and Prejudice* (1940), had become a major star in the United States on the strength of these films, and Leigh, of course, was the star of the phenomenally successful *Gone with the Wind* (1939). The fact that these two stars had only recently divorced their respective spouses in order to marry could only add to audience interest in this story of forbidden romance.

Most importantly, perhaps, the British government recognized that Korda could deliver an entertaining and commercially successful film. When Korda asked Laurence Olivier to portray Lord Nelson, he explained his approach to propaganda by saying that 'propaganda can be bitter medicine. It needs a sugar-coating – and *Lady Hamilton* is a very thick sugar-coating indeed.'[17] The elements of 'sugar-coating' in *That Hamilton Woman*, the title by which the film was known in the United States, are reminiscent of those in *The Private Life of Henry the Eighth*. Although the comic-burlesque approach to history taken in the earlier film is not present in *That Hamilton Woman*, both films are through-the-keyhole treatments of historical subjects. Nelson's crusade against Napoleon, culminating in victory off Cape Trafalgar in 1805, is given far less screen time than his adulterous affair with Emma Hamilton (Vivien Leigh). Indeed, the film focuses primarily on the rise of the young Emma, who begins as a courtesan and becomes Lady Hamilton, wife of the ageing British Ambassador to Naples. When she meets Nelson, she falls in love with him, and uses her position in Naples to aid and abet Nelson's campaign against Napoleon. The spouses, Lady Nelson (Gladys Cooper) and Sir William Hamilton (Alan Mowbray), are portrayed as cold and unsympathetic, providing all the more sympathy for the lovers. This 'propaganda' film had the conventional box-office elements of stars, romance and melodrama amid all of the historical trappings.

Korda was eager to make his timely film as quickly as possible, and *That Hamilton Woman* was filmed hurriedly over six weeks in the autumn of 1940. There was not even time to finish a full script before filming began, with the result that the writers struggled to stay ahead of the filming, finishing some scenes only on the day before they were to be filmed.[18] The story concocted by Korda, R.C. Sherriff and Walter Reisch had timely parallels similar to those of *The Sea Hawk*. Once again, England is threatened with invasion by a European country led by a single malevolent figure. Napoleon is never actually seen, but his ambitions for world domination are repeatedly stated. In *That Hamilton Woman* the parallel to the present is made even more clear by referring to Napoleon as a 'dictator' (a word not in use in the early nineteenth century, as many American critics pointed out), and also by referring to Napoleon's ambitions to be 'master of the world', a reference that echoes Hitler's claims of a German 'master race'.

Furthermore, the historical story once again focuses on a charismatic individual, who tries to alert his country to the threat of a ruthless European 'dictator'. The British authorities' reluctance to heed the warnings parallels Britain's appeasement of Germany in the 1930s, and Nelson serves as the Churchillian figure who attempts to awaken his country's establishment to the danger. The British Admiralty is eager to avoid war, but Nelson scoffs at the peace treaties and warns that Napoleon 'just wants to gain a little time, to re-arm himself and make new alliances with Italy and Spain'. This, of course, proves to be correct, and Nelson takes on the responsibility of defending the world from the European aggressor.

However, while *The Sea Hawk* provides an elaborate explanation for appeasement, *That Hamilton Woman* focuses also on the issue of other countries' neutrality. The difference is due to the time in which the films were produced. *The Sea Hawk* was written and filmed during the period of the 'phoney war', and so its only concern was to cast British war aims, and the policies that led Britain to war, in a favourable light. *That Hamilton Woman*, though, was written and filmed when the Nazis occupied virtually the whole of Europe and while Britain was being bombed on a nightly basis. The invasion and defeat of Britain was a distinct possibility in the autumn of 1940, and American support for Britain was now actively sought. Hence, *That Hamilton Woman* argues far more directly that it is the duty of neutral countries to 'stir themselves' and join the effort to defeat European tyranny.

This is most evident in two scenes that come after Nelson has already scored significant victories over Napoleon. Napoleon is still a threat and Nelson's efforts to thwart him are hindered by a lack of supplies. In the first scene, Nelson's second-in-command, Hardy, speaks angrily of countries that are 'neutral against England', which are 'so scared of Bonaparte they daren't lift a finger for the people brave enough to fight him'. Similarly, when Nelson is trying to convince the King of Naples that he must aid the fight against Napoleon, he tells him, 'if you value your freedom stir yourselves ... either advance sword in hand or stay here and be kicked out of your kingdom!' The message to the neutral United States was clear: neutrality is a form of cowardice, and it will eventually bring the danger to your own doorstep. In this respect, *That Hamilton Woman* was more daring, and its parallels were more direct, than had been the case with *The Sea Hawk*.

The prospect of invasion is also portrayed in stronger terms in Korda's film. Just before the climactic battle at Trafalgar, Lady Hamilton finds a document that Nelson has written entitled 'Plans for the defence of London in the event of invasion', and Hardy tells her that:

Bonaparte has made himself Emperor of France. His next move will be the invasion of England ... He has raked together a new fleet from goodness knows where, and he's building transports and barges as fast as he can turn them out. From Boulogne to Brest every single Channel port is chock full of them. He has got a whole army behind him waiting to embark. A few weeks from now all he will need is a fair wind.

6   'Propaganda with a sugar-coating': Lord Nelson (Laurence Olivier) and Lady Hamilton (Vivien Leigh) in *That Hamilton Woman* (1941)

Nelson's eventual triumph at Trafalgar signals Britain's historic ability to defend itself from even the most powerful and ruthless of aggressors. The British may need the aid and support of their allies, the film suggests, but given that support Britain ultimately will triumph.

Korda's production seems to have caused little concern in Hollywood or within United Artists itself. While filming proceeded in the autumn of 1940, there were no protests or complaints made in the name of American neutrality. *That Hamilton Woman* seems to have been accepted as simply another 'British' film. Miklos Rozsa, the film's musical director, later recalled that a United Artists' executive did object to the song 'Rule Britannia' being sung during the battle scenes. This one element of the film, the executive argued, would reveal that the whole was 'British propaganda'. Rozsa and Korda got around this by leaving the less recognizable verses in the film, and having the more familiar chorus heard in instrumental form only. But this, apparently, was United Artists' only instance of caution over *That Hamilton Woman*.[19]

More substantial problems were expected when the script was submitted to the Hays Office. In October 1940 R.C. Sherriff was summoned to see Joseph Breen, and he was flatly told that the film could not be approved for release in the United States. Breen was not at all concerned with the film's historical parallels, though; his only concern was that the script seemed to advocate the adulterous relationship of Lord Nelson and Lady Hamilton. The film lacked what Breen routinely referred to as 'compensating moral values'. That is, the lovers had to be punished for committing adultery. The writers then set to work on scenes that would show the couple suffering for their sins. Nelson was given a pious father (Halliwell Hobbes) who admonishes his heroic son for his scandalous private life. It was Emma Hamilton, however, who bore the brunt of the hastily assembled moral condemnation. The story was placed within a flashback structure so that it could begin by showing an elderly and destitute Emma, who has been exiled from England and now wanders the streets of Calais wearing rags. She is caught stealing a bottle of wine, and then she recounts her story from a grimy prison cell. To make it clear that she is a moral outcast, the film's original title, *Lady Hamilton*, was changed to *That Hamilton Woman* in the United States. These changes placated Breen, although Korda did retain his preferred title in prints made for all other countries.[20]

The film's historical parallels did not escape the scrutiny of American film critics. *The New Republic* referred to *That Hamilton Woman* as 'a bundle for Britain'. *The New York Times* commented that the film 'has some especially timely opinions about dictators who would desire to invade England', and *The New Yorker* complained that it 'falls over backward in drawing the analogy between England's trial today and its crisis and ultimate triumph in the Napoleonic wars'.[21] Karol Kulik has suggested that such criticisms and a subsequent awareness of the film's politics hindered the film's popularity in the United States.[22] However, *That Hamilton Woman* earned $1,147,000 in North America, which was a healthy if not spectacular gross. Furthermore, this figure is slightly higher than the grosses of contemporaneous 'British' costume dramas such as *Wuthering Heights* and *Pride and Prejudice*, which have no political subtext.[23] Meanwhile, *Lady Hamilton*, as the film was known to British audiences, became the fifth most popular film of 1941 in Britain.[24]

When *That Hamilton Woman* was released in April 1941, the US Congress had just passed the Lend-Lease bill, which provided war materials for Britain. Korda's film provided an explanation and an endorsement of this act, and so it was undoubtedly a success in his own eyes. However, it was no longer necessary to express pro-British sentiments within costume dramas. The release of *The Great Dictator* and *Foreign Correspondent* in the autumn of 1940 had signalled that the American film industry's foreign policy, as administered by the Hays Office, did not prohibit contemporary war films. Furthermore, the box-office success of these films indicated that American audiences were ready and willing to see war films. The Nazi occupation of Europe and the Battle of Britain, in fact, had turned both US government policy and American public opinion in favour of the British war effort. American producers no longer needed to look to British history for a means to approach war themes, nor did they need to look to the past or to literary classics for stories that would be recognized by and interest American audiences. Such stories filled newspapers, magazines and newsreels. From 1941 onward, contemporary 'British' war films proliferated, and 'British' costume dramas became increasingly scarce.

Yanks in the British war

It's funny about England and the way Americans feel about you. It's sort of like being related in a way. You know the way you feel about relatives. They do a lot of things that irritate you, but when it comes right down to it, you are related. You have the same ideas, speak the same language and have the same plans for the future.

This dialogue is spoken by Fred MacMurray, an American actor playing a Yank in the RAF in Paramount's *One Night in Lisbon* (1941). Similar sentiments were expressed in the numerous Yank films released between 1940 and 1942. Indeed, the dialogue can serve as a plot synopsis of these films. The American arrives in Britain to find that, superficially at least, he has little in common with the British. He finds them peculiar, reserved and snobbish. Through the course of the story, though, he finds that on a more basic and important level he is related to the British. He shares with them a common history, heritage, language and political ideology, and that is enough to convince him that he must fight for Britain.

It is little wonder that the Hollywood studios liked this formula so much. It not only offered an American perspective on the British setting, but it also allowed the presence of a major American star in a 'British' film. The formula originated with MGM's *A Yank at Oxford* in 1938, in which Robert Taylor plays a brash American at odds with the refined Oxford environment. Anglo-American differences of speech and manners are used for comedy, but it is also a transformation story. The self-centred 'Yank' matures by complementing his American individualism with the British values of fairness and team spirit. *A Yank at Oxford* was a huge success in the markets that mattered most in the late 1930s and early 1940s: North America and Britain; and it quickly became Hollywood's means of dramatizing the Battle of Britain. Between 1940 and 1942, cinema audiences saw Yanks learning to appreciate the spirit and meaning of the British war effort in Walter Wanger's *Foreign Correspondent* (1940) and *Eagle Squadron* (1942), TCF's *A Yank in the RAF* (1941) and *Confirm or Deny* (1941), Paramount's *One Night in Lisbon* (1941) and Warner Bros.' *International Squadron* (1941).

The conflicts of *A Yank at Oxford* and the means by which they are resolved served as a blueprint for the wartime Yank films. In *A Yank at Oxford* the brash and boastful Yank is an excellent athlete, but he has no sense of sportsmanship; the British, by contrast, put team spirit and honour before personal glory. The Yank eventually recognizes the superiority of the British values, and takes them on. In the wartime films, the Yank is again portrayed as brash and boastful. He is sent to Britain as either a journalist or an aviator, and he is excellent in his work. However, he goes to Britain for selfish reasons alone, either to get a big story or to make money ferrying planes. Through his exposure to the collective British war effort, he realizes that he must take on the higher cause and fight for Britain and democracy. Thus, the films transform the Yank from an immature, self-centred isolationist to a mature, committed ally of Britain. No doubts are cast as to whether or not the American should make this transformation. His initial indifference to the war is the problem the narrative works through and solves, and American involvement in the British war is endorsed.

The similarities between *A Yank at Oxford* and the wartime Yank films extend to the romantic sub-plot. In *A Yank at Oxford*, the Yank's main rival is the captain of his rowing and track teams, who is also the brother of his British girlfriend. The Yank reconciles with the rival/brother and wins the affections of the girl once he has matured and taken on the British values of sportsmanship. In the wartime films, a male British authority figure once again stands in the way of the romance between the Yank and a British girl. The British man can be the girl's father or brother, or a rival lover, but his maturity is always contrasted with the immaturity of the Yank. By the ending of the film, however, the Yank has matured and this enables his romance with the British girl. His new-found maturity also enables him to reconcile with the British authority figure. In *A Yank at Oxford*, the ending shows the Yank and his British rival winning a race together, while the wartime films often end with the Yank and his British rival successfully completing a wartime mission.

Walter Wanger's *Foreign Correspondent*, released in September 1940, was the first of these films to reach the screen after the outbreak of war. *Foreign Correspondent* did not originate as a reworking of *A Yank at Oxford*, but evolved from Wanger's attempted adaptation of Vincent Sheean's *Personal History*. The Hays Office had convinced Wanger to abandon Sheean's story in 1938, but as soon as war was declared Wanger hired Alfred Hitchcock and a team of British screenwriters to transform *Personal History* into *Foreign Correspondent*.[25] The story, now a spy thriller set in London and Amsterdam just before the outbreak of war, follows 'industry policy' as it stood in 1940. John Jones (Joel McCrea) is a New York crime reporter who has no interest in international affairs. His editor sends him to London in August 1939, hoping that his investigative skills and his lack of bias will yield fresh news about the impending war. In London, and under the new name of Huntley Haverstock, the reporter meets Stephen Fisher (Herbert Marshall), the wealthy leader of the 'Universal Peace Party', and Fisher's daughter, Carol (Laraine Day). Although they are initially at odds, Haverstock and Carol eventually fall in love. Haverstock, meanwhile, discovers that Stephen Fisher is behind the kidnapping of a Dutch diplomat, Van Meer (Albert Basserman). Van Meer is tortured by his villainous captors until he reveals the secret clause of a European peace treaty. The revelation pushes Europe into war, as Stephen Fisher had hoped, but by then Haverstock and both of the Fishers are on a plane bound for America. The plane is shot down by a German battleship, and Stephen Fisher drowns himself as a means of saving others. Carol and Haverstock survive, and Haverstock finally has his big story. In the film's final scene, set in London, he gives a dramatic radio address during an air raid. While the bombs fall around him, Haverstock tells his American audience that what they hear is 'death coming to London', and he urges Americans to rearm.

The story and film contain all of Hitchcock's trademarks.

Jones/Haverstock is the innocent protagonist, unsure of his identity, who becomes involved in a complex web of intrigue and a long chase to capture the truth and to recapture his identity. There are visually dramatic and intricately staged sequences involving an assassination attempt and a plane crash. The romance, as ever, is a source of suspense and tension. The couple are suspicious of one another, and must work through their doubts before coming together in the ending. Most importantly, the finer points of the intrigue are deliberately kept vague. Which European country are the spies working for? Why do they want war? What information is in the secret clause? Why will knowledge of the clause lead to war? None of these questions is answered, and that, of course, suited the Hays Office. But it also fitted well within Hitchcock's standard mode of storytelling. Hitchcock referred to the finer points and details of his stories as the 'MacGuffin' of the plot. The 'MacGuffin' sets the story in motion, but it is not in itself important. The audience is meant to become overwhelmed by the larger story: the romance, the chase and the intrigue. The smaller details are forgotten, and Hitchcock maintained that if they were explained it would detract from the dramatic tension.[26] This was his belief and his practice over decades of film-making, but in *Foreign Correspondent* it clearly suits a particular purpose.

In fact, the story – as scripted – maintains a carefully contrived neutral stance. The villains are identified only as being 'Borovian', and one must strain to catch even this one reference. Before he dies Stephen Fisher does admit to his daughter that he is not English (he has 'only a coating of Englishness'), but he does not reveal his true nationality. And when the plane is shot down by the Germans, it is stated that the Germans fired by mistake, and that they will rescue the plane's passengers. (Conveniently, however, an American ship arrives first.) Clearly, the film-makers went out of their way to avoid making censorable statements. Yet audiences in 1940 would have had no problem in decoding the story, and they may not have noticed that they had to decode it. Indeed, as the reviewer for *Variety* noted, 'it is hardly necessary to have the Nazi implications clarified'.[27]

The final scene offers a perfect example of how skilfully Hitchcock used every available element – except the scripted words – to overcome the script's cautious neutrality. Haverstock, now an acclaimed war correspondent, speaks directly to America from London in a live radio address, and calls upon the American audience for action:

7   A carefully contrived neutral stance: the Borovian, Krug (Eduardo Ciannelli), with Stephen Fisher (Herbert Marshall), Carol Fisher (Laraine Day) and Huntley Haverstock (Joel McCrea) in *Foreign Correspondent* (1940)

I'm speaking to you from a part of the world as nice as Vermont and Ohio, Virginia, California, and Illinois ... You can hear the bombs falling on the streets and the homes. Don't tune me out. This is a big story and you're part of it. It's too late to do anything here now except stand in the dark and wait for them to come. It's as if the lights are all out everywhere, except in America. Keep those lights burning. Cover them with steel. Ring them with guns. Build a canopy of battleships and bombing planes around them. Hello America, hang on to your lights! They are the only lights left in the world.

On paper this statement could not be faulted. It is a warning to Americans that they had better prepare to defend themselves, and even the 'America First' isolationists were in favour of patriotic self-defence. (They called upon resources to be reserved for the United States rather than given to Britain.) But the effect on screen is quite different. Having the words spoken by a once-neutral American, who now equates the streets and homes of London with America itself, is part of the strategy. But much more importantly, as Haverstock speaks, the lights go down around him, and the sounds of the bombing fade away as 'The Star-Spangled Banner' begins to play in the background. It is heard quietly and only as an instrumental at first, but as soon as Haverstock finishes saying 'they are the only lights left in the world', the vocals come in loudly and triumphantly, and a brightly lit screen displays 'The End'. Hitchcock thus manages to link the United States, its national anthem, the Battle of Britain, and lightness itself, and he shows that together these elements overcome the forces of darkness. The emotional impact is overwhelming, and it is not at all neutral. Indeed, it can be taken as a subtle, filmic representation of Winston Churchill's widely quoted words that 'in God's good time', the New World, 'with all of its power and might', would step forth to rescue the Old.

This appears to have been Hitchcock's exact intention. Churchill made this dramatic statement in June 1940, the very same month in which this final scene was rewritten and filmed. Originally, the scene was to be set in Paris, but by the time it was due to be filmed France had been overrun by the Germans and the intensive bombing of London was expected to begin soon. Thus, the setting was changed to London.[28] By the time the film was released in September 1940, the Blitz had begun in London. American radio audiences listened with awe as actual foreign correspondents such as Edward R. Murrow described the intensive bombing as it occurred around them. Audiences were said to have been riveted by the broadcasts, which brought the war across the ocean and into their living rooms.[29] *Foreign Correspondent*, the first 'British' war film, could not have been more timely. It was a resounding success in North America, where it earned $1,429,000, and in Britain *Foreign Correspondent* was the second most popular film of the year (behind Hitchcock's *Rebecca*), and it earned a rentals gross of $480,000.[30] It drew generally favourable reviews, including one from *The Documentary News Letter*. Yet this, in turn, brought a remarkable spate of criticism. The British documentary film-maker Paul Rotha wrote a hostile letter to the editor of *The Documentary News Letter* that was signed by some of Britain's most prominent filmmakers and critics, including Michael Balcon, Cavalcanti and Dilys Powell. Their main objection centred on the final scene of the film, which, they said, was 'an insult' to the people of Britain at a time when Britain's own lights 'have never burned so brightly and more proudly than they do now'.[31] One can assume that they had no idea of the parameters that Hitchcock was working within, or that they resented the flagship journal of the British documentary movement giving praise to a commercial American film. Either way, they demonstrated a remarkable prejudice against both Hitchcock and Hollywood. Even Joseph Goebbels, the German Minister of Propaganda, was able to admire *Foreign Correspondent* as a 'masterpiece of propaganda'.[32]

The 'Eagle Squadron' films

As *Foreign Correspondent* enjoyed a successful box-office run in the autumn of 1940, numerous 'British' war films went into production, including *A Yank in the RAF, International Squadron* and *Eagle Squadron*. These three films were all inspired by press reports of the real-life Eagle Squadron, a squadron of the British Royal Air Force made up of approximately forty American fliers who volunteered for service in Britain. The American press devoted much attention to the newly formed Eagle Squadron in the autumn of 1940. Newspaper reports portrayed the pilots both as adventurous young daredevils, in the war just for the thrills, and as the solemn defenders of democracy, the United States' only contributors to the fight against fascism. Such disparate motivations were often attributed to a single individual within the same newspaper article.[33] The films based upon the Eagle Squadron would also apply these diverse characteristics to their American fliers. However, the characteristics were ordered in a linear fashion, and formed the progression of the 'Yank' from self-interested immaturity to a mature belief in the higher cause.

The first story outline of TCF's *A Yank in the RAF*, written in October 1940 by studio head Darryl Zanuck, was initially entitled 'Eagle Squadron'. Zanuck's outline suggests that his writers should 'pattern' the film on the experiences of Billy Fiske, an American who volunteered for the RAF before the Eagle Squadron was formed. Fiske had become America's first war hero when, after downing three German planes over southern England, he was himself shot down and killed in August 1940.[34] Darryl Zanuck thought that the film should also show the American character dying in battle after a heroic performance. Then, in an epilogue, the forty-three members of the actual Eagle Squadron would be shown, and the film would end with them flying off on a mission. Zanuck added that, if the Eagle Squadron 'should do some big spectacular thing in the next four or five months', it should be incorporated into the story.[35] Timeliness, he realized, would add immeasurably to the box-office takings.

Zanuck's story outline may have been inspired by Billy Fiske and the Eagle Squadron but, as the title change indicates, he was in fact re-making *A Yank at Oxford*. Zanuck described the American flier to his writers as 'a cock-sure know-it-all' who 'never knew how to take orders ... [and] doesn't know how to play team ball'. He comes to England to work as a test pilot, and has no particular interest in the war. He thinks that 'all this talk about England, *esprit de corps*, the cause, the team play, etc., is just so much baloney ... All he cares about is being paid-off'. However, toward the end of the story:

> He learns that England is a spirit; they are fighting for more than personal gain; they are fighting for freedom, for liberty, for a cause they believe in. He realizes it and it is proven to him. He becomes a part of the *esprit de corps*, willing, if necessary, like the English themselves, to die for it, and eventually he does die for it.[36]

MGM's Yank had learned to play 'team ball' at Oxford, while Zanuck's Yank would learn his lesson in *esprit de corps* in the RAF.

This storyline clearly served Zanuck's purposes as propaganda. The American audience was meant to undergo the same conversion as the protagonist. Zanuck, however, was also acutely aware of the commercial prospects of *A Yank in the RAF*. He wanted the writers to 'convey the idea of England at war in comedy fashion whenever possible'. This, too, was to be copied from *A Yank at Oxford*. The writers were told to screen MGM's film as 'an example of an American in England and his relationships with Englishmen'; to copy the 'running gag' between the Yank and his Oxford don; and to write 'breezy dialogue ... loaded with the typical U.S. versus Great Britain arguments ... that scored so heavily for comedy in *A Yank at Oxford*'.[37]

The British characters that Zanuck's Yank would encounter were, as ever in 'British' films, members of the upper class. The American's British squadron leader was to be '... well-born, public school trained and ... the type of man to whom Wellington referred when he said "Waterloo was won on the playing fields of Eton"'. The British woman was to be 'the daughter of a duke', but one who is also a volunteer nurse 'doing her bit in the emergency'. The first scripts place these two characters in a familiar triangular situation with the American. The woman is romantically involved with the British squadron leader, and she is repelled by the American's initial indifference to the war. Once the Yank has realized the higher cause, however, he wins her affection.[38]

With a few notable exceptions, *A Yank in the RAF* emerged in October 1941 much as Zanuck had planned it one year earlier. The film opens with a shot of planes being towed across the border from the United States to Canada. A narrator explains that, 'in the early days of the present war', US neutrality laws

8 The cocksure know-it-all: Tyrone Power as
A Yank in the RAF (1941)

required such 'democratic ingenuity'.[39] The American Tim Baker
(Tyrone Power) breaks the rules by flying his plane directly to
Canada. He is reprimanded by British officials, but then is offered
work ferrying the planes on to Britain. The salary of $1,000 per
plane causes him to exclaim, happily, 'boy, what a war!' Once in
London, he finds his ex-girlfriend, Carol (now an American rather
than a British character, and played by Betty Grable), doing
volunteer work by day and singing and dancing on stage by
night. Intent upon winning her back, Tim joins the RAF to be
near her. However, she is now involved with his aristocratic
squadron leader, Morley (John Sutton). Tim discovers his commitment to the war when his fellow flyer and friend, Roger (Reginald Gardiner), is killed in action. At Dunkirk, Tim downs
numerous German planes (saying, 'that's for Roger') and, with

Morley's help, he eventually makes it back to London, where Carol is waiting for him.

No reference is made in the film to the real Eagle Squadron. Walter Wanger had copyrighted the much sought-after film title before Zanuck, and Wanger had already arranged to film the real Eagle Squadron in action.[40] Nor does the Yank die for England in the end, as Zanuck originally intended. This change was made at the request of the British Air Ministry. Zanuck had asked the Ministry to provide technical advice and assistance in filming the aerial scenes. The Ministry agreed, provided it was given script approval, and it did not believe that having Americans die for Britain would be good propaganda. Furthermore, they wanted the film's deaths and injuries kept to a minimum.[41] Hence, the death toll in *A Yank in the RAF* is limited to Tim's friend, Roger, who is British. The other major difference between Zanuck's story and the finished film was the change from a British to an American woman. This enabled Betty Grable, Zanuck's newly signed and fastest-rising star, to play the part of Carol. It also enabled Carol to be a nightclub singer, and the film contains two scenes of her singing and dancing on stage. This was the 'sugar-coating' of *A Yank in the RAF*.

A Yank in the RAF has, in fact, many elements of 'sugar-coating'. Zanuck used his other top star, Tyrone Power, as the lead, and much of the film is devoted to the romantic banter between Power and Grable. The part of Roger, a rather droll and sophisticated aviator, is played entirely for comedy (until his death). The film also contains the familiar Anglo-American humour that Zanuck ordered. And the transformation of the Yank is handled without a final reel speech, such as that in *Foreign Correspondent*. Furthermore, the film avoids direct references to Germany, the Nazis and their ideology. Its propaganda value lay partly in its portrait of the collective British war effort, but mainly in the presence of stars Power and Grable as part of it.

While *A Yank in the RAF* was in production, Zanuck learned that Warner Bros. was also planning a film entitled 'Eagle Squadron', and that the plot had many similarities to that of *A Yank in the RAF*. Zanuck wrote a hostile letter to Hal B. Wallis at Warners in March 1941, protesting that Warners was 'hastily concocting' their 'minor budget film to beat [Zanuck's] major production to the punch'. Zanuck also stressed the importance of *A Yank in the RAF*, and exaggerated official British interest in the film:

It is one of the biggest budgeted pictures that I have attempted in a year and the British Air Ministry themselves are so anxious for us to produce it that they are even here in Los Angeles extending extraordinary cooperation direct on orders from abroad. You can readily see why I was so shocked to learn that practically all of the elements in our picture – including the characterisation, the central theme and many incidental sequences are also included in a minor-budget picture from another studio.[42]

Zanuck warned Wallis of a 'legal fight' unless Warners either abandoned its film or agreed to release it at least sixty days after the release of *A Yank in the RAF*. Wallis, however, ignored Zanuck's protests. Both studios had been inspired by press reports on the Eagle Squadron. More importantly, both studios were reworking MGM's *A Yank at Oxford*, which made Zanuck's claims on the story rather spurious.

Warner Bros. re-named its film *International Squadron* but, as Zanuck suspected, it is a strikingly similar story. Ronald Reagan plays the irresponsible playboy and aviator, who becomes interested in ferrying planes to Britain when he learns that he will be paid $2,000 per plane. He decides to stay in Britain and to join the RAF only when he is named in a divorce suit back home. The romantic triangle consists of the Yank, his British squadron leader, Charlie Wyatt (James Stephenson), and the squadron leader's wife (Julie Bishop). The transformation occurs after the Yank's first mission. He is assigned to protect the rear of the squadron, but he breaks the rules by flying ahead in heroic fashion. The pilot left unprotected at the rear, French, is shot down and killed, and the Yank is (unofficially) blamed. Attempting to ease his conscience, the Yank tells his squadron leader that, 'it's every man for himself', but the squadron leader replies, 'not over here it isn't'. The Yank demonstrates his remorse when the squadron draws straws for a dangerous mission. The Yank does not draw the unlucky straw, but he knocks unconscious the man who did and then goes on the mission himself. He shoots down many German planes on the mission (saying 'this one's for French!'), before being killed himself. In the final scene, Charlie toasts his bravery. Once again, the Yank has learned to put Britain before himself, although in this case he was also able to die for Britain.

Warner Bros. succeeded in beating *A Yank in the RAF* to the box office. *International Squadron* was released two months before Zanuck's film, in August 1941, and it apparently benefited as a result. Made at a cost of just $384,000, *International Squadron* earned $831,000 in the domestic market and $671,000 in foreign markets. Zanuck's only recourse was to make his own inexpensive variation on the Yank theme. This time, Zanuck borrowed from *Foreign Correspondent*. In TCF's *Confirm or Deny*, released in December 1941, an American journalist (Don Ameche) in London eventually puts aside his selfish pursuit of a story in order to aid the war effort and win the affections of his British secretary (Joan Bennett). But the star pairings of both *International Squadron* and *Confirm or Deny* could not compete with Tyrone Power and Betty Grable in *A Yank in the RAF*. The latter became the fourth most popular film of 1941 and earned an estimated $2,500,000 in North America. In Britain, *Kinematograph Weekly* listed it as the second most popular film of February 1942.[43]

Walter Wanger's 'Eagle Squadron' film

Producer Walter Wanger, meanwhile, was having far greater difficulties with his *Eagle Squadron* film. Wanger was inspired to make *Eagle Squadron* in November 1940, when he saw the Crown Film Unit's acclaimed documentary, *London Can Take It* (1940). His idea was to make a documentary about the British war effort using the actual Eagle Squadron as the necessary American angle to the story. Wanger was a personal friend of Sidney Bernstein, who was a highly placed adviser within the MoI, and Bernstein was able to obtain initial approval and support for Wanger's film. Bernstein arranged for Ian Dalrymple and Harry Watt, who were key members of Britain's Crown Film Unit, to be seconded to Wanger and the *Eagle Squadron* project. Quentin Reynolds, the American journalist who narrated *London Can Take It*, agreed to serve as the narrator for Wanger's film; and Merian Cooper, an acclaimed American documentarist, agreed to direct *Eagle Squadron*.[44]

Wanger's enthusiasm for this project appears to have had many facets. As one of Hollywood's noted interventionists and as the producer of many 'British' films, including *Foreign Correspondent*, Wanger undoubtedly wished to build sympathy for Britain and to valorize the men of the Eagle Squadron. His desire to make the film as a truly innovative feature-length documentary is also evident in his correspondence with Bernstein and with Cooper. There were, however, other aspects of this venture that seem plainly opportunistic. One was that making the film in Britain would enable Wanger to utilize the British earnings that were 'frozen' by the wartime currency regulations; funds that could not be remitted to the United States could be spent in Britain. Wanger's 'frozen' funds stood at no less than $470,000 by the spring of 1941, and his production company was suffering from a shortfall of funds. Hence, the making of *Eagle Squadron* in Britain offered the cash-strapped producer a means of utilizing production funds that otherwise would be untouchable.[45] Wanger also hoped that he would find himself the owner of priceless footage showing an actual invasion attempt. Since he had members of the Crown Film Unit on his payroll, he proposed to the Ministry of Information that any footage of 'the invasion of England' should be exclusively his and not released to the newsreels. The Ministry responded that it was 'utterly opposed' to this, and Wanger, perhaps realizing his instincts as a showman had overcome him, let the matter drop.[46]

The showman's instincts were also at work when Wanger decided to keep his options open regarding the documentary approach. If the documentary footage was dramatic and entertaining, he hoped to release a documentary feature film, but if it was 'disappointing' or 'uncommercial' the footage would be used only as part of a fictional film shot within a British studio. What made sense to a showman, however, made no sense to the Air Ministry, which demanded to read a script or at least a treatment before it would grant any permission for the filming of its operations. The Air Ministry, in fact, seems to have been opposed to *Eagle Squadron* from the beginning, not least because the film had been conceived before the actual Eagle Squadron was operational. Indeed, Wanger's proposed film must have appeared to the Air Ministry as American boastfulness at its worst – a film that would pay tribute to a military unit even before it had entered battle – and the Ministry treated the project with some apparent contempt.[47]

When Ian Dalrymple completed a story outline in February 1941, Merian Cooper reported to Wanger that it was 'pedestrian' and 'too much like something that would be made in Hollywood'.[48] Dalrymple resigned, and Cooper persuaded Wanger to make the film entirely a documentary. He also persuaded him that it was 'essential not to be bound down by treatments' and for three months he pressed the Air Ministry for 'a free hand' to film the Eagle Squadron at their base and on missions, but the Air Ministry continued to insist that it must see a script before any further permissions were granted. Finally, in May 1941 a treatment was hastily put on paper. It closely followed the by now familiar storyline:

Some emphasis will be given to fact that many of the [American] boys joined up for adventure's sake and therefore are not too deeply committed to the values England defends, through youthful thoughtlessness, principally – and therefore in a pardonable way. These elements of friction ... will be eliminated as the boys come to understand the scene better and to acquire a different feeling for their job. Having succeeded here we should, in effect, have acknowledged the presence of the little barriers there are to intimacy between Americans and Englishmen – and have swept them away.

Having swept away the barriers, the ending would show the Eagle Squadron and other units of the RAF executing a successful mission over Germany.[49]

The Air Ministry was not impressed. Wanger's proposed documentary appeared to be no different from the feature films produced on the Eagle Squadron in Hollywood. Furthermore, despite Darryl Zanuck's claims to the contrary, the Air Ministry had little regard for the propaganda value of this storyline. In a letter written to Jack Beddington at the MoI, Commander Williams of the Air Ministry expressed his disapproval:

The only suggestion of a story-line follows the same idea expressed in *A Yank in the RAF*, i.e., that Americans have so far come into the war for purely trivial and selfish motives and that, once embroiled, they gradually come to learn what it is all about. That may or may not be good propaganda and I suppose one cannot complain if an American company expresses such a low view of their national character. However, there can be no 'free hand' for shooting RAF material.[50]

Further discussions were held regarding the value of the project and the permissions needed, but in August 1941 the Air Ministry finally made it clear that it considered the propaganda value of the film 'very doubtful' and flatly refused all involvement or assistance.[51]

Harry Watt then resigned from the film, and explained to Wanger the difficulties that he had encountered over the previous six months. Ironically, his account has strong parallels with the Yank storyline itself. Watt found the young American men of the Eagle Squadron to be 'unanimously resistant' to the film from the beginning. The fliers refused to be filmed unless they were paid for their involvement, and such payment was forbidden by RAF regulations. Another problem was that the Air Ministry was uncooperative and overtly hostile to the very idea of the film. Watt explained that this was because the Eagle Squadron had received so much publicity, even before it was operational, that it was widely resented within the RAF. The Air Ministry, Watt claimed, 'would now very much like to see and hear as little as possible of the Eagle Squadron'. Finally, when Watt was able to convince nine of the 'better class of boys' in the squadron to be filmed, six were killed in action within three weeks. His letter ended with the advice that the only way forward was to make a fictional film in Hollywood.[52]

Wanger was reluctant to take Harry Watt's advice, but then the board of directors of United Artists, which provided Wanger's production funds, intervened. Wanger's last few films had been over budget, and the board was not willing to let costs on the seemingly ill-fated *Eagle Squadron* continue to spiral. The board insisted that Wanger abandon the film, and he resigned from United Artists in protest.[53] With the rights to *Eagle Squadron* in hand, Wanger then signed a contract with Universal Studios. It was decided that *Eagle Squadron* would be made as a fictional film in Hollywood, and that any documentary footage that could be salvaged would be interspersed with the fictional sequences. Hollywood screenwriter Norman Reilly Raine was hired to write the script, and Arthur Lubin, a contract director at Universal, was assigned to direct the film. Finally, *Eagle Squadron* was filmed, at Universal Studios in Hollywood, between February and April 1942.[54]

When Wanger received the footage that had been filmed in England, which had cost £13,500 to acquire, he found most of it 'unsuitable'.[55] The only shots he was able to use were of the Eagle Squadron members themselves. *Eagle Squadron* opens with Quentin Reynolds speaking in praise of the Eagle Squadron members. As the camera pans across a line-up of the actual fliers, Reynolds identifies each by name, tells of their achievements, and in some cases of their subsequent deaths. It is by far the most moving sequence in the film, and it offers some indication of what Wanger had hoped to achieve with a documentary. Much of the film centres on two missions the Eagle Squadron executes over Germany, and, interspersed with these sequences, is documentary footage that Wanger purchased from the MoI. For example, when the American flyer, Chuck Brewer (Robert Stack), is shot down over the English Channel, scenes taken from the British documentary *The Pilot is Safe* show a pilot bailing out of his plane, parachuting into the water and being rescued by the Coast Guard.[56]

The fictional story closely follows the 'Yank' storyline. When Chuck Brewer is asked why he joined the RAF, he replies 'I joined for a bet'. His antagonism toward the British members of the RAF comes to a head when his friend and fellow American, Johnny (Leif Erickson), defies orders by flying outside the squadron's formation to take one more shot at a German base. Johnny is killed, and Chuck is appalled by the British flyers' indifference to Johnny's death. The British tell Chuck that, 'in this game it's teamwork or the kiss of death'. The romantic triangle centres on Chuck's relationship with Anne Partridge (Diana Barrymore), an

9   A troubled Yank in the Eagle Squadron: Chuck Brewer (Robert Stack) and
Sir John Patridge (Paul Cavanagh) in *Eagle Squadron* (1942)

aristocrat who has volunteered for the Women's Auxiliary Air
Force (WAAF), and Chuck's superior officer, Paddy (John Loder).
Anne refuses Chuck's marriage proposal by saying, 'You and me
aren't important, nothing is important but the job we've got to
do for England.' Chuck resents this until, on a mission with
Paddy, Paddy gives his life to save Chuck. Then, Chuck realizes
the higher cause, saying:

When this war started England didn't mean a thing to me. When
Johnny died, I went sort of haywire. Well now I know. Johnny
showed me, and Anne. I asked her to marry me and she turned me
down, said there was something bigger than just us. I didn't get that,
but now ... Anne was right!

When Chuck returns, Anne agrees to marry him, and they both
receive medals for bravery. During the ceremony an air raid
begins and the Eagle Squadron run to their planes. As they fly off,
a list of the German cities that are their destinations appears in
the titles, ending with 'Berlin!'

By the time *Eagle Squadron* was released in July 1942,
audiences already had seen many self-centred Yanks realizing the
higher British cause. This storyline, however, seems to have had

When Hollywood loved Britain

an appeal that endured throughout the earlier 'Yank' films and beyond the United States' entry into the war seven months earlier. At this late juncture, and with no major stars in its cast, *Eagle Squadron* did remarkably well at the box office. It earned a healthy domestic gross of $1,737,000, and in Britain it earned $586,000 of its $1,004,000 foreign gross. From the worldwide gross of $2,731,000, Wanger and Universal were able to split a profit of just over $1,000,000.[57] Wanger's prolonged efforts, and his Anglophile sentiments, paid off handsomely in the end.

Variations on a familiar theme

The production of Yank films gradually diminished after the United States entered the war, but not before every conceivable variation had been offered. *One Night in Lisbon* follows the standard storyline (set in London) throughout the first half of the film, before the Yank becomes embroiled in a spy plot that leads him to Lisbon. *International Lady* (1941) centres on the competitive relationship of an FBI investigator (George Brent) and a Scotland Yard detective (Basil Rathbone) as they pursue the same spy ring and the same woman (Ilona Massey). Warner Bros.' *Captains of the Clouds* (1942) stars James Cagney as a Canadian training for the RAF. Warner Bros.' British production company produced the low-budget *Flying Fortress* (1942), another film centred on a Canadian (Richard Greene) in the RAF. Republic Studios released one of the more original variations in *Thumbs Up* (1943). This low-budget film follows an American nightclub singer (Brenda Joyce) who begins working in a British munitions factory as a publicity stunt but then decides to stay on and work for the higher cause. In MGM's *The White Cliffs of Dover* (1944) an American woman (Irene Dunne) marries into an aristocratic British family and comes to terms with their odd customs and reserved manners. And the final variations on the theme emerged late in the war from British studios. *Johnny in the Clouds/The Way to the Stars* (1945) and *A Yank in London/I Live in Grosvenor Square* (1945) were produced at a time when 1,750,000 American soldiers were, as the British described them, 'over-paid, over-fed, over-sexed and over here'.

The persistence of the theme was remarkable, and if the net is cast wider it is an even more prominent feature of wartime films. For example, two of the most popular films of the war years, *Sergeant York* (1941) and *Casablanca* (1943), play out this transformation scenario in different settings and contexts. Indeed, the appeal of such stories is a sign of just how belatedly and reluctantly Americans entered the Second World War. The 'British' versions, however, focus not only upon the necessary transformation from isolationism to interventionism, but also upon the American ambivalence to Britain. The perceived propaganda value of the Yank films was that they portrayed Anglo-American differences as superficial and showed that such differences were resolved through contact. As we have seen, though, the Air Ministry had little regard for the storyline, and later in the war its views were echoed by the British MoI and the United States Office of War Information (OWI). To the OWI, the Yank films revealed more – about indifferent Americans and Anglo-American antagonisms – than they could possibly resolve in their final reels. American film-makers were profit-minded propagandists, though, and the expression of interventionist and pro-British sympathies always occurred within the 'British' genres or formulas that had an established box-office record. *A Yank at Oxford* had established a formula that, for better or worse, ran and ran throughout the war years.

Conclusion

It is hardly surprising that American isolationists accused Hollywood of attempting to lead the American public into the war. By the Autumn of 1941, Hollywood's pro-British sympathies had been made abundantly clear. Not only were British film-makers such as Korda and Hitchcock working within the Hollywood studio system, but they were successfully subverting the pretence of neutrality that the industry itself attempted to maintain. Even American producers such as Walter Wanger, Warner Bros. and Darryl Zanuck were eager to convince audiences that Britain was a cause worth fighting for, and they used all the tools of their trade to do so. What is remarkable is the extent to which these film-makers were concerned with commercial considerations. Of course, there was no purpose in making 'message' films with a limited box-office appeal. Korda himself spoke of the 'sugar-coating' necessary to draw in an audience. However, the profit-motive often seems to have overridden the apparent good intentions. Without a financial inducement, Warners stopped its key series of 'British' films. Wanger saw *Eagle Squadron* as a means of using his frozen funds, and he was eager to obtain the film rights to the invasion of Britain. Zanuck, meanwhile, seemed most intent upon remaking *A Yank at Oxford* in a timely fashion. Indeed, as the films themselves reveal, the desire for both propaganda and profit was inextricably mixed in 'British' war films.

A new England

In *Movie-Made America*, Robert Sklar discusses the rise of stars such as Rudolph Valentino and Greta Garbo in Hollywood during the 1920s. According to Sklar, these European stars fulfilled a key role for American film-makers and audiences. American stars and the young heroes and heroines they portrayed had to be wholesome and naive; to be otherwise would cast aspersions on the moral character of the nation. However, this did not preclude the American audience's desire to 'experience vicariously the sweet succumbing to temptation, and the guilt and retribution of those who step beyond the boundaries of the social code'. Hence, Valentino, Garbo and other European-born stars were allowed to do 'so many things forbidden to Americans'. They could be 'more sensual, decadent, emotional, [and] sinful than Americans'. In Sklar's words, American film-makers adopted an equation of 'Europe = passion' that previously had been used by nineteenth-century novelists such as Henry James.[1]

If 'Europe = passion' in the American cinema of the 1920s, 'Britain = class' can be used as a way of describing the Hollywood 'British' films of the 1930s. This is particularly evident in the 'British' films set in contemporary times. American film-makers chose to adapt the works of British authors such as Noel Coward (*Private Lives*, 1931; *Cavalcade*, 1932), Frederick Lonsdale (*The Last of Mrs Cheyney*, 1937), John Galsworthy (*One More River*, 1934) and Somerset Maugham (*Of Human Bondage*, 1934); writers who focused almost exclusively upon drawing-room comedies and melodramas of upper-class life. The lower classes are not ignored altogether in these films. Melodramas such as *Cavalcade*,

Of Human Bondage and *Cynara* (1933) portray the disruption that occurs when an upper-class gentleman succumbs to a working-class woman. Usually, however, working-class characters are relegated to minor roles, as faithful and contented servants, or comical shopkeepers and pub landlords. The focus of these films remains fixed upon the upper-class milieu. The main characters live in grand houses, they attend elaborate balls and weekend parties given by titled hosts, and they visit London's elite clubs and formal restaurants. Urban and working-class settings are rarely if ever shown, and one could be forgiven for concluding, on the basis of these films alone, that Mayfair is the only urban area that exists in Britain.

For American audiences the entertainment value of the British upper classes can be seen as a somewhat 'forbidden' and 'vicarious' pleasure. The United States had been conceived, and had defined itself, in opposition to Britain, and more particularly in opposition to the Britain of monarchy, titles and the class system. Furthermore, as David Reynolds notes in his analysis of Anglo-American relations between 1937 and 1941, Americans of this era maintained 'a deep conviction that Britain was not a genuine democracy':

Americans were ever alert to evidence of the 'class system' – the divide between what one commentator called 'cap-in-hand England' and 'old-school-tie England' – usually contrasting it with the supposed 'classlessness' of their own country. And they tended to attribute most of Britain's failings, at home and abroad, to the machinations or ineptitude of the 'ruling class'.[2]

The paradox here, between Americans' taste for class-ridden 'British' films and their distaste for class-ridden Britain, can be attributed partly to the escapist manner in which class is presented in 'British' films. Class antagonism is seldom evident; indeed, class is seen as a divide between people with different accents and dispositions, rather than a matter of economic inequality. The upper classes live glamorous and privileged lives, restrained only by their restrictive social code. While the servants are, as the maid in *Cavalcade* states, 'so happy in service'. The paradox can also be explained by Reynolds' assertion that it is overly simplistic to categorize Americans of this era as either Anglophiles or Anglophobes; they were, for the most part, 'Anglophile culturally and Anglophobe politically'.[3] Hence, American audiences could appreciate a 1930s 'British' film such as *David Copperfield* or *Cavalcade*, as entertainment or as an example of British culture, while at the same time maintaining their political disdain for the British class system, and having their notion of the superiority of American classlessness reinforced.

During the early war years, 'British' films became more self-conscious in their depiction of British class relations. To an extent, Hollywood was eager to follow the lead of British news-reels and documentaries, as well as American news correspondents in Britain, by stressing the shared sacrifice of all classes during wartime, and the levelling effect that this had on class barriers. But Hollywood was always preoccupied with the upper classes, and so most 'British' war films seemed concerned primarily to show that the aristocracy was sacrificing and suffering just as much as their social inferiors. This was already apparent in the earliest 'British' war films. When Darryl Zanuck was writing *A Yank in the RAF*, he wanted the British girlfriend of the Yank to be 'the daughter of a duke ... doing her bit in an emergency'.[4] The part was changed to accommodate the American star Betty Grable, but the film still shows a character addressed as 'Lady Fitzhugh' leading a team of volunteer nurses (including Grable) through a practice drill. Similarly, in *Eagle Squadron* the aristocratic British girlfriend of the classless Yank has joined the Women's Auxiliary Air Force (WAAF), and the family's palatial rural home, Ashton Court, has been given over to housing children of London's East End for the duration of the war. The girl's father (Paul Cavanagh), a former MP, has joined the services in an attempt to diminish his guilt for having backed the policy of appeasement in the 1930s. These incidents were only minor sub-plots, and Britain's changing class system was explored more fully in two films released in the summer of 1942, *This Above All* and *Mrs Miniver*. These two films were produced by different studios and they were adapted from very different sources, yet they have striking similarities. Both films foreground class issues in a manner that is quite unusual for 'British' films, and both address the American disdain for the 'old school tie' England with assurances that a new and more egalitarian England is emerging from the rubble of the Blitz. Even while portraying the new England, however, the films do not stray very far from the characters and settings of the old England.

This Above All: Anglophilia versus Anglophobia

Twentieth Century-Fox's *This Above All* was adapted from a novel by Eric Knight, a Yorkshire-born journalist who spent most of his adult life in the United States.[5] The novel was published in April 1941, eight months prior to the United States' entry into the war, and it offers a full range of arguments for and against Britain. The character of Clive Briggs, a working-class deserter from the

British army, offers an outpouring of anti-British arguments that echo the US isolationist movement's criticisms of Britain. The character of Prudence Cathaway, meanwhile, rebuts his arguments with an Anglophile's view of Britain that would be familiar to any patron of Hollywood's 'British' films. Prudence cites Britain's historical and literary achievements, and the beauty of the British countryside, in defence of her country.

In the novel, Clive and Prudence meet in a black-out during the summer of 1940. They soon sleep together, and later go on holiday to a south-coast resort town. There, while the town is being bombed, they argue over the war. Clive had volunteered for the army on the first day of the war and had been decorated for bravery at Dunkirk, but the debacle at Dunkirk has now made him question whether Britain is worth fighting for. He blames Britain's military and government leaders for being ill prepared and inept in the fight against Germany, and decides to desert because he does not want to fight to keep Britain's ruling class in power. In his arguments with Prudence, he recalls that he was an illegitimate child, shunned by both his upper-class father and his mother's working-class neighbours. He remembers having to go hungry, being unable to afford a dentist or doctor, being forced to leave school at fourteen and, afterwards, taking a series of menial and poorly paid jobs. The England he is asked to fight for, in his opinion, has made life a misery for him and for the working class. He blames the Church of England for focusing on moral rather than social issues, and he sees the British Empire as an exercise in economic exploitation akin to the exploitation of Britain's workers.

Prudence, by contrast, has led a sheltered life in a wealthy family, and she has a more sentimental view of England. Her commitment to the war effort, though, has led her to join the WAAF as a private. She assures Clive that a new and more democratic England will emerge after the war, but insists that the first priority must be to defeat Germany. Clive eventually decides to go back to the army; not because he has changed his mind, but because he hates life on the run and misses Prudence. In the meantime, Prudence has discovered that she is pregnant. The two agree to marry, but before they do so Clive is injured in an air raid. It is then discovered that Clive is suffering from a brain disease, resulting from the pneumonia he contracted at Dunkirk. Clive dies, and on the last page Prudence vows that their illegitimate child will grow up in a better England.

The revelation that Clive has a 'diseased brain' indicates that his political and moral quandaries occurred at a time when his mental facilities were impaired. This is a rather strong qualification to what is otherwise a highly contentious book: a book by a British author that airs a wide range of criticisms toward Britain while the country is fighting for its survival. *This Above All* was published within a year of the events that are described in its pages. Critics in the United States hailed it as the first important novel of the Second World War. In Britain, the critic for *The Times Literary Supplement* agreed with this judgement but, in an echo of Prudence's view, questioned 'the wisdom of writing in this way just now'.[6]

Eric Knight was, however, firmly on the side of Prudence. The novel's promise of a 'new England' after the war was also stated in his private correspondence with the critic and film-maker Paul Rotha. In July 1941 he echoed Prudence's views in a letter to Rotha:

I am fully aware of all the social adjustments that cry out for execution in England, and no less aware of the need for them when the time comes, but now the first job is to beat the hell out of Hitler. It's facing the bigger of the two evils first. When it's over, then we must fight for a new England – for an end to stricken areas, to the drug of workless dole, to the scandal of over-privilege and utter want.[7]

In *This Above All*, Knight allows Clive to state the social changes needed in Britain; but, by portraying the Nazi campaign in Europe and the Blitz in England as cruel and barbaric, and showing that the disparate classes of British society are pulling together in the war effort, the novel makes it clear that the first priority for England is the defeat of Germany. To think otherwise was, in fact, symptomatic of a diseased brain.

Darryl Zanuck and 'British' films

Darryl Zanuck purchased the screen rights to *This Above All* on behalf of Twentieth Century-Fox. Zanuck was a veteran at 'British' film-making. During his reign as head of production, TCF produced British historical dramas such as *Lloyds of London* (1937) and *Stanley and Livingstone* (1939); adaptations of British literature such as Robert Louis Stevenson's *Kidnapped* (1938) and Charlotte Brontë's *Jane Eyre* (1944); and, in 1939, the first films to pair Basil Rathbone and Nigel Bruce as Sherlock Holmes and Dr Watson (*The Hound of the Baskervilles* and *The Adventures of Sherlock Holmes*). These, and the wartime films *A Yank in the RAF* (1941) and *Confirm or Deny* (1941), were all fairly formulaic 'British' films, but Zanuck also had a taste for more unusual 'British' films.

The Rains Came (1939) is an early example of the wartime films that showed the reformation of the British aristocracy. The film is based on a novel by Louis Bromfield that was considered to be highly critical of the British administration in India. Zanuck sought the consent of the British Consul in Los Angeles before proceeding with his adaptation, and proved willing to exclude its criticisms of the British government from the screenplay. However, the climactic disaster of the story – a dam bursts during monsoon season – is still blamed on a greedy British aristocrat, Lord Esketh (Nigel Bruce), who financed the dam's construction. Zanuck believed that the central plot of the story, concerning two decadent British aristocrats (George Brent and Myrna Loy) who redeem themselves through hard work and sacrifice after the tragedy, overcame the more critical elements.[8]

Man Hunt (1941), the film the Hays Office termed a 'hate picture', also takes a less than flattering view of the British aristocracy. The criticism is not aimed at the big-game hunter (Walter Pidgeon) who stalks Hitler purely for sport; he reforms and eventually goes back to finish the job. His brother, however, is typical of the aristocrats American films poured scorn upon during the war years: Lord Risborough (Frederick Worlock), a wealthy government official, is appalled by the controversy stirred by his brother's attempt on the life of Hitler, and he is eager to appease the Nazis. The heroine of the film, by contrast, is a cockney prostitute (Joan Bennett) who gives her life to save the hunter.

How Green Was My Valley (1941), based on Richard Llewellyn's novel, centres on a prolonged miners' strike in a Welsh village that leaves the miners and their families poor and hungry. Zanuck insisted that much of the novel's depiction of rural poverty and troubled labour relations be diminished in the script. He advised his writers in April 1940 that to depict troubled British labour relations would be 'in bad taste at this time'. And one month later that, 'In view of what is happening today, we certainly don't want to attack the English [sic] manner of things, right or wrong'.[9] The resulting film was gentle and nostalgic, but it remains one of the few 'British' films to venture beyond Mayfair and the Home Counties, and into the home of a Welsh mining family.

Thus, Zanuck had dealt with good, bad and reformed aristocrats before *This Above All*, and he clearly had a predilection for 'British' films that went beyond the drawing-room glamour that typified Hollywood's Britain. However, this should not be attributed to any political agenda. Indeed, Zanuck toned down the more contentious elements in these films while highlighting what made them attractive box-office propositions. *The Rains*

Came has an epic disaster sequence, similar to that seen in MGM's hugely successful *San Francisco* (1936) three years earlier. *Man Hunt* is a thrilling chase film laced with wartime topicality; and *How Green Was My Valley* follows closely in the footsteps of Fox's highly praised *The Grapes of Wrath* (1939), an earlier family drama set amid (American) rural poverty.

This Above All: two people in England

The primary attraction of *This Above All* for Zanuck was the story's romantic and sexual dimension. R.C. Sherriff was hired to write the script; and Sherriff, whose previous films included *Goodbye Mr Chips* and *That Hamilton Woman*, was clearly chosen as a means of ensuring that the novel's more acerbic elements would be smoothed over in an appropriate manner. However, Zanuck did not want *This Above All* to focus on either anti-British or pro-British arguments. He repeatedly told Sherriff to tone down the propaganda and to focus on the love story and the physical attraction between Clive and Prudence.

Sherriff's first treatment of *This Above All*, completed in July of 1941, reveals the two central themes of his propaganda efforts. For the opening scene, Sherriff proposed that Clive should witness the preparations being made in a south-coast resort town for a German invasion. Clive would comment that this was 'an unusual experience for a holiday resort'. An air-raid warden would then explain, in a long-winded speech, that the town had previously prepared for the invading armies of Julius Caesar, Saxon pirates, the Spanish Armada, Napoleon, and 'Kaiser Bill'. Sherriff was evidently still in the historical mode of *That Hamilton Woman*. He also proposed sub-plots that would reveal the wartime dissolution of class barriers in a similar fashion to that of *Goodbye Mr Chips*. Prudence's aristocratic relatives are present in the novel, but they are largely unsympathetic and selfish characters. To soften this aspect, Sherriff proposed scenes that would show Prudence's grandfather, a Colonel Blimp type in the novel, opening the family estate to house children from London's East End. Then, Prudence's Aunt Iris, a haughty snob who flees to the United States in the novel, would lose her snobbery through exposure to the charming East Enders. In the ending, Clive would convalesce happily at the family's estate, which he had previously vowed never to enter.[10]

This was all cast aside by Zanuck and the director Anatole Litvak, who were disappointed with Sherriff's 'preachy' approach. In story conferences, it was made clear that the story's conventional box-office elements were to be emphasized, and that the propaganda was to be kept to a minimum:

> Mr Zanuck emphasized that this story is first and foremost a LOVE STORY, in which the story of wartime England is combined but is not our focal point. Or, as Mr Litvak put it, it is a story about two people in England, and not England with two people in it. This must be kept in mind throughout. Mr Zanuck fears that if this element gets out of hand and we try to be impressive or preachy ... the result will be a 'colored' picture rather than a fascinating love story, which is what it should be – and in addition we risk the danger that it will not be commercially successful.[11]

Even the debates between Clive and Prudence, which form the bulk of the novel, were to be abbreviated and treated lightly. For example, in one conference Sherriff was advised to 'avoid dullness and/or propaganda' by the following means:

> We should maintain a sense of comedy in [Clive and Prudence's] quarrels, except, of course, in the few really serious moments. In other words, try to express the issues in humorous terms ... When an argument seems to be getting too deep, Clive should take [Prudence] in his arms, put his hands over her mouth and say: 'Don't say any more' and then he kisses her.[12]

As these notes indicate, the political aspects of *This Above All* were secondary, in Zanuck's plan, to the love story. Indeed, Zanuck was adamant that Sherriff include the sex scenes from the novel, particularly a seduction that takes place in a haystack. In successive story conferences, Zanuck repeatedly urged Sherriff to include more sex and to get to the sex scenes more quickly. In a meeting with the writer in July 1941, Zanuck 'emphasized the importance of our finding ways and means of getting the sex attraction of the novel into our story without offending the Hays Office'. Nine days later, and having read Sherriff's latest efforts, Zanuck again 'stressed the importance of injecting as much of the sex element of the book into the script as we can get away with ... as much as decency will allow'. And after another month and another rewritten script, he still complained to Sherriff that 'we take twice as much time as we should to get to the haystack scene'.[13]

Zanuck and Litvak constructed much of the film. They described both individual scenes and the overall plotting of the film to Sherriff, and left him to fill in the dialogue. They even conceived the means through which Clive's harsh views would be abbreviated and undermined, which was done by reorientating the story towards Prudence, and making her a much stronger character. This is apparent in the opening of the film which, as the conference notes indicate, was written entirely by Zanuck and

Litvak.[14] The first few scenes, which are not in the novel, take place in the grand 'Cathaway Manor House', and the setting and characters seem to have been inspired by one of Noel Coward's drawing-room dramas. An elegantly attired butler named Parsons attends the middle-aged Cathaways, who sit in the parlour in formal evening wear, sipping sherry before dinner. After a dinner served by several maids, the family passes the port around the table, speaking in clipped tones about 'Lord Evesham's charity party'. The difference in this drawing-room drama is that the characters are almost entirely unsympathetic. They are stuffy and snobbish, and view the war only as a threat to their comfort. For example, when the family listens to the war news on the radio they hear that France has fallen and an invasion of England seems imminent. Yet General Cathaway (Henry Stephenson) merely complains that the news reader 'talks as if he had a mouthful of golf balls', and the vain Aunt Iris (Gladys Cooper) insists that they 'talk about something cheerful' as she adjusts her hair in a mirror.

These complacent and idle aristocrats are soon contrasted with young Prudence (Joan Fontaine), who arrives late and announces that she has joined the ranks of the WAAF. Aunt Iris is horrified, and asks her if she is aware that 'Annie Smith, who scrubs the schoolhouse floors, joined the ranks of the WAAFs'. Uncle Wilfred (Melville Cooper) explains that Prudence should have asked him to arrange a commission, that the Cathaways have 'a tradition of leadership'. Prudence, the progressive aristocrat, lashes out at them:

You and people like you are a worse danger to us than Hitler is. Yes, I mean it! One day we may look back and thank Hitler for some of the things he's done to wake us up, but we'll never look back and thank you. You believe that forty million people exist in England to make you comfortable. You hate this war because you knock your shins in a black-out. You grumble about it because it deprives you of your favourite German bath-salts; and what's more you fear it, because the common men who are doing the fighting may suddenly begin to doubt the importance of risking their lives to keep the Uncle Wilfreds and Aunt Irises an immortal part of England.

None of this is in Knight's novel: Prudence never argues with her relatives, and she certainly never imagines thanking Hitler for his effect on English society. Criticisms of the class system come solely from Clive. In the film, however, Prudence's first speech shows that she already has a reformer's zeal, before she meets Clive (Tyrone Power). This makes Prudence the moderator between the old and the new England. She defends certain aspects of the aristocracy in her arguments with Clive, but agrees that some change is needed. Also, as Zanuck told Sherriff in a story conference, Prudence's acceptance of the need for change makes Clive's arguments seem 'just as extreme in their way as her family's beliefs are in theirs'.[15]

In fact, the entire emphasis of the story was shifted away from Clive and toward Prudence. Much of the novel is narrated from Clive's point of view, and his bitter memories of childhood and his war experience form the bulk of his conversations with Prudence. Yet the film opens at the Cathaway home, and then shows Prudence's first days at the WAAF camp. Her meeting with Clive and their initial dates and their holiday together are also seen from her point of view. This enables the film to veer away from Clive and his unpleasant memories, and it also enables it to focus on Prudence's perceptions of Clive. The film is thus made strikingly similar to Joan Fontaine's most recent films, *Rebecca* (1940) and *Suspicion* (1941), in which her character is in love with a man she does not understand or trust. In *This Above All*, Clive seems to be in love with her, but he is troubled and mysterious. He sneers at her privileged background, he refuses to answer when she asks why he is not in uniform; and, when he cries out in his sleep, he won't tell her that he has nightmares about Dunkirk. His unstated background and beliefs are the obstacle to their romance, and the melodrama centres on the question of what is wrong with Clive.

This was Zanuck's design. He repeatedly told Sherriff that Clive was 'too talkative' in the first drafts of the script. Zanuck wanted him to be 'a man of mystery – dark, brooding, strange ... like Laurence Olivier [as Heathcliff] in *Wuthering Heights*'.[16] Zanuck also thought that Clive should 'come from a slightly higher class than is indicated in the novel ... his father was a doctor, or whatever you want to make him'.[17] In the film, Clive's background is never explained and his childhood memories are not recalled. The mystery of Clive is furthered by having the American star Tyrone Power play him. Power does not even attempt a British accent and, rather than seeming working class, he comes across as being classless. He certainly bears no resemblance to the films' other working-class characters, who are presented in the familiar comical cockney fashion.

The climactic debate between Clive and Prudence finally occurs sixty minutes into the film. Zanuck's concern for the entertainment value of *This Above All* is evident even in this ten-minute scene. Just in case audiences became bored by the arguments for and against 'England', Prudence is seen undressing in silhouette

10 What is wrong with Clive?: Monty (Thomas Mitchell), Clive Briggs (Tyrone Power) and Prudence Cathaway (Joan Fontaine) in *This Above All* (1942)

and shadow throughout. The scene solves the mystery of Clive but, because he has not yet told Prudence of his background and beliefs, Clive pretends that he is reporting the views of 'a friend' rather than his own feelings. Clive's views on the Church of England and the British Empire are not included; these were judged to be too harsh for the film. Furthermore, his war memories and his bitterness toward Britain's government and military leaders is reduced to a few lines of dialogue:

He found his leaders stupid, complacent and out-of-date. There's no claim to leadership but birth and class and privilege. They weren't leading him in a struggle for a better England. They were leading him in a struggle to preserve the same rotten worn-out conditions that kept their class in comfort and his in poverty. They were asking him to give his life for something he hated and despised.

Clive's impoverished childhood, and his reasons for deserting, are also abbreviated to a few lines of dialogue:

He keeps asking himself, if England were to lose, could we be worse-off, or weaker or more shameful? Do you know what England means to this man? It means poverty, hunger, begging for work no matter how cruel and humiliating. And if our armies did win this war, what share will this man have in the England he has helped to save? They'll give him nothing! It will return to the men who have owned

A new England

139

it and disgraced it, so that they can go on disgracing it until the next war comes.

His criticisms are not only abbreviated, but they are offered in the third person, and in an American accent devoid of class connotations. This greatly diminishes the anger and class resentment present in Knight's novel, but it also adds a new dimension to *This Above All*. In the previous year Tyrone Power had played the lead role in *A Yank in the RAF*, as the Yank who must learn the meaning of the war, and does so at Dunkirk. In *This Above All*, though, Power's character deserts after his experiences at Dunkirk. Furthermore, his reasons for doing so are offered in his American accent, and his grievances sound as though they are those of an American Anglophobe or isolationist rather than a working-class British soldier. It is as though the Yank, rather than taking on British values, has instead developed the point-of-view of an Anglophobe.

This Above All can thus be seen to place a maverick element into the Hollywood 'British' film, American Anglophobia. It is quickly contained by Prudence's rebuttal. Her words represent not only the Anglophile's point of view, but a definitive view of Hollywood's England. Prudence, now dressed in a bathrobe, begins by saying that 'England is not perfect', but that 'it's too late to doubt or question'. She tells Clive to listen to what his heart says about England, and launches into a two-minute speech on what England means to her. Speaking with great emotion and reverence, she tells him that 'England' is the land of:

Shakespeare and thatched roofs ... speakers in Hyde Park, free to say what they wish ... polite bobbies at the corner ... Drake alive in memory ... the New Forest deep in ferns ... the ancient dignity of our cities ... May blossoms rich in spring and bluebells like a God-sent carpet ... and knowing that we'll never be beaten, knowing that we won't give in, we won't, we just won't!

The scene ends as Prudence bursts into tears and Clive comforts her. The final word and the greatest emotion, then, is given to Prudence, and her vision of an England seen so many times before in 'British' films. The few scenes that follow contain many departures from the novel. Clive is injured in an air raid, but no mention is made of brain disease. Clive and Prudence marry while he is in hospital and there is hope that he may survive. In the most important departure from the novel, though, Clive admits that his views are wrong and Prudence is right. In his hospital bed he tells her, 'It's going to be a different world when all of this is over ... Some day, we're going to fight for what I believe in, but first, we've got to fight for what you believe in. You were right. We've got to win this war, we've got to!' Thus, Tyrone Power has learned once again (as he does in *A Yank in the RAF*) that he must give up his own selfish preoccupations and fight for England.

Eric Knight had little hope that Hollywood would render a faithful adaptation of *This Above All*. Before the film was made, he wrote to Paul Rotha that:

If you think I'm going to try to make Hollywood do anything sensible with *This Above All* you're batty ... I expect it to come out as a Don Ameche special with Tyrone Power backing, and a musical comedy translation with Horace Heidt's orchestra and a Busby Berkeley chorus.[18]

And, after seeing *Mrs Miniver* and *This Above All*, Knight was apparently contemptuous of both films. In another letter to Rotha, he wrote: 'Just saw *Mrs Miniver* ... My wife says it's a picture she's glad she saw, because now she thinks even *This Above All* wasn't really so putrid.'[19] Knight had his reasons to be disillusioned with Fox's adaptation of *This Above All*. While he, too, favoured Prudence's arguments, he had given Clive an opportunity to state his grievances in full. Furthermore, Knight's novel presents a full array of British characters and settings, ranging from the upper-class Cathaways and their manor house to many working-class characters and their more humble homes. In the film, however, the characters and settings form a much smaller sample – a sample that typifies the class bias of 'British' films. The Cathaways are seen in their palatial home. Then, after a brief glimpse of the WAAF camp, Clive and Prudence stay at a grand and formal hotel, and then decide to move to a romantic village inn. The working-class characters, meanwhile, are reduced to Violet (Queenie Leonard), the skittish WAAF; Monty (Thomas Mitchell), Clive's hard-drinking and salt-of-the-earth fellow soldier; and the Dickensian innkeeper, Mr Ramsbottom (Nigel Bruce). There is also Clive, of course, but he bears no resemblance to these heavily accented and simple-minded folk.

Knight was too dismissive of the film. Granted, it is formulaic: Zanuck managed to combine elements of *Rebecca*, *Suspicion*, *Wuthering Heights* and *A Yank in the RAF* – all recent and successful 'British' films – into *This Above All*. And the film does present Hollywood's favoured view of Britain, not least in Prudence's speech. Yet *This Above All* also offers, however briefly, Clive's contradictory view. When Clive finally does speak out he offers views on Britain previously unheard in 'British' films. His statements indicate that the class system is not matter of accents and dispositions, but a matter of economic inequality. And though Clive eventually comes round to Prudence's view, to expect otherwise from a film released in 1942 would be to expect the impossible. Furthermore, the film does not compromise Clive's views with the revelation that he has a diseased brain, as Knight's novel does. Clive contradicted Hollywood's view of Britain, and did so within a Hollywood 'British' film, while he was completely sane.

Mrs Miniver: the top drawer but one

MGM's *Mrs Miniver* offers a kinder and gentler view of wartime England and the changing class system. There is no angry young man akin to Clive Briggs crying out for social change, and the working-class characters are a humble and contented lot. Instead, *Mrs Miniver* defines its main characters, the Miniver family, as middle class. Whereas this category was virtually unknown in previous 'British' films, it is the cornerstone of the new England offered here. The Minivers act as a bridge between the two disparate classes who intermingle harmoniously as the war brings about a gradual and mild diminution of class barriers. Otherwise, the characteristics of MGM's England remain firmly in place.

The film-makers drew their conception of the English middle class from a series of stories that began appearing on the Court page of the London *Times* in October 1937. The stories, written by journalist Jan Struther, offer the anecdotes, opinions and impressions of the fictional character Mrs Miniver. E.M. Forster described the class standing of Jan Struther's Mrs Miniver as 'the top drawer but one'.[20] She is not an aristocrat, but she is married to a prosperous architect, and the Minivers do have two homes (one in London and one in Kent), several servants, a son at Eton, and a nanny to look after their two younger children. Mrs Miniver spends much of her time shopping or attending concerts and parties. Her home life, amid endearing children and a loving husband, is a happy one, and many of the stories concern the small pleasures and sweet sorrows she encounters in her cosy world. For example, she confides her bliss in returning home to find that, as ever, the maid already has laid her tea in the upstairs drawing-room, and she becomes nostalgic for the family's old car when her husband buys a new one.[21]

The stories took on a more serious tone in the last few instalments of the series, which were published in the autumn of 1939. In the story 'From Needing Danger', Mrs Miniver comments that:

It oughtn't to need a war to make a nation ... give its slum children a holiday in the country ... However, it has needed one: and that is about the severest criticism our civilization could have.[22]

'From Needing Danger' is one of the few *Mrs Miniver* stories to mention the war. The series ended in December 1939 when Jan Struther moved to the United States. The stories were published in one volume in July 1940, and the book became a best-seller in the United States. The screen rights were purchased by MGM at the request of producer Sidney Franklin, who recalled that he came upon Struther's book at a time when he was contemplating making a 'tribute' to the British war effort:

Having made so many pictures with English backgrounds, I was in love with the atmosphere, the quaintness and the charm ... I had a notion that someone should pay a tribute, a salute to England and the Few. Suddenly I realized that I should be that someone.[23]

Struther's stories were ostensibly an odd choice for such a film. The three stories set in wartime were written at the time of the 'phoney war', and none concerns the RAF ('the Few'). Franklin, however, was drawn to the 'charming atmosphere' of the stories, in which he saw the opportunity to update his favourite film, *Goodbye Mr Chips*. On 7 October 1940 he set himself the task of deciding whether the novel's author, James Hilton, or the screenplay's author, R.C. Sherriff, should be assigned to *Mrs Miniver*. On 8 October he decided they should collaborate, and in order to get them into the new wartime spirit, he arranged for them to have a screening of the British documentary *London Can Take It* a few weeks later.[24] Sherriff, however, did not stay with *Mrs Miniver* for long. His most notable contribution to the script is the scene in which the Minivers read *Alice in Wonderland* during an air raid, which is rather close to a scene from his play *Journey's End*.[25] He then went on to TCF and *This Above All*. James Hilton was then joined on *Mrs Miniver* by the Austrian refugee George Froeschel and by Arthur Wimperis, who had co-authored *The Private Life of Henry the Eighth* and other Korda scripts. The most obvious influence on the script, however, does not come from any of these authors or their previous works. Instead, it was Noel Coward's *Cavalcade* that clearly served as a blueprint for *Mrs Miniver*.

Both *Cavalcade* and *Mrs Miniver* focus upon the traumas of an affluent family during wartime, and particularly upon the heartaches of the wife/mother when her husband and son are in battle. Furthermore, both films portray the lowering of class barriers, and a cross-class romance is an integral element of the changing class order. However, *Mrs Miniver* is in many respects an updating of *Cavalcade*. The wife/mother of *Cavalcade* is far from the battlefield, and suffers only emotional traumas during the Boer War and the First World War. *Mrs Miniver*, though, is a home-front story set amid 'total war', in which women and children face dangers similar to those of the battlefield. Furthermore, MGM's film takes a more progressive view of the class system than *Cavalcade*. The lowering of class barriers is seen as one of the ill effects of a confused age (the 1920s) in *Cavalcade*. The cross-class romance, for example, is a source of conflict and melodrama. In *Mrs Miniver*, by contrast, the gradual and mild reduction of class barriers is heralded as a sign of social progress and of social cohesion in wartime. The cross-class romance, in fact, is accepted without qualms.

The structure of *Cavalcade* was also borrowed for *Mrs Miniver*, as it had been by James Hilton for *Goodbye Mr Chips*; decades of British history are seen in well-punctuated time segments. When Hilton and R.C. Sherriff began work on *Mrs Miniver* in October 1940, Franklin imposed a similar structure, albeit in a compressed time span. The writers were told to construct the story in three distinct time segments. The script was written and rewritten over twelve months, and many writers – including Claudine West, Arthur Wimperis, George Froeschel and Paul Osborn – contributed to it.[26] However, the basic structure imposed from the beginning remained. The first, pre-war segment portrays Jan Struther's affluent and contented Minivers. The second segment shows the Minivers' reaction to the outbreak of war. And the third segment dramatizes their hardships and sacrifices during the Blitz.

The early treatments and even the first scripts reveal that Franklin and his writers intended to portray the Minivers as too contented and too complacent in the pre-war segment. They drew upon Struther's stories for scenes in this segment, such as Mrs Miniver's shopping trip in London and Mr Miniver's purchase of a new car. These scenes were placed in the context of Struther's 'From Needing Danger', a story in which Mrs Miniver comments on 'the hundreds of ways the war has brought us to our senses'.[27] This aspect of the script – that the Minivers needed danger to shake off their complacency – is reminiscent of the opening of *This Above All*, in which the elderly Cathaways represent an England that needs awakening. Remarkably, Franklin's 'salute' to the British war effort was originally intended to open with a German spy dictating a report on the British class system. The German refers to the upper class as 'still clinging tenaciously to its ancient privileges'; and the 'proletariat' as 'only kept from actual revolt by an ample provision of sport, amusement and drink'. Then, his commentary turns to the middle class:

Despite their appearance of prosperity, the cars they are so proud to own and the fashionable clothes they contrive to afford, these people are morally and spiritually bankrupt. Once the bulwark of England's greatness, they are now its weakest element because of their craving for pleasure – their lack of wholesome discipline. Supine, comfort-loving, materialistic, this class in its decadence foreshadows the death of a once mighty nation – it will offer no resistance to the world domination of a Master Race.[28]

The German spy then looks out of his window on a London street and sees Mrs Miniver shopping. The camera was to follow her as she went into the hat shop, and the next scene would show Mr Miniver purchasing an expensive car.

Further evidence of the Minivers' complacency would come when Mr Miniver praises the infamous Munich Agreement because it had restored business confidence and he had received new contracts.[29] The writers also intended to dramatize the village flower show as a 'juxtaposition' between the importance the villagers attach to their flowers and 'their blindness to Hitler's dangers'.[30] The Minivers' eldest son, Vin, was to arrive home from Oxford 'full of communistic ideas' and 'dressed like a laborer', before 'sitting by the river with a pipe and a volume of Marx'.[31] Then, in the episode set on the day war is declared, Mrs Miniver becomes upset when Vin announces he intends to join the RAF. Mr Miniver attempts to comfort her by saying, 'you wouldn't care to have a son who didn't want to fight for his country'. To which she replies, 'his country! What has Poland got to do with us?'[32] Mrs Miniver would finally have an awakening later in the film. Franklin told the writers that Mrs Miniver should, at some point, say to Mr Miniver, 'Maybe we are at fault ... maybe we, as a family, have something to do with this war.' Franklin clarified the meaning of this statement by saying, 'In the sense that they are sentries of civilization and fell asleep at their posts, and that their crime is not one of Commission but Omission'.[33]

As Franklin's comment indicates, it was never intended that the Minivers were to be seen as wholly to blame for Britain's plight in 1940. Rather, their pre-war complacency would provide the background to Britain's appeasement of Germany ('their blindness to Hitler's dangers'), and then the German commentator would be proven entirely wrong. The German, for example, makes a case for class antagonism in Britain, but this was to be undermined by a scene in which Vin speaks of communism to the 'workers in the pub'. Vin would be surprised to find that the workers weren't interested, and in fact 'they liked everything and seemed quite contented'.[34] Thus, the espousal of communism merely serves to show that, as usual in 'British' films, the working class is content. The earliest scripts also show that, as in the film, the Minivers would prove their mettle and offer considerable resistance to the 'master race'. Vin would abandon communism in favour of the RAF, and the disparate classes would unite in the war effort. Furthermore, the villagers were to replace their roses with potatoes and cabbages after the Blitz.[35]

The script for *Mrs Miniver* was written and rewritten between October 1940 and September 1941, with a variety of different plot twists and endings. The most remarkable of these was one in which only Mrs Miniver and her son Vin survived at the end; all others would be killed by a direct hit on Lady Beldon's cellar after the village flower show.[36] The writing process was slowed by Franklin's problems with another production, *The Yearling*, which was shelved for several years and eventually filmed in 1946. *Mrs Miniver* finally went into production in the autumn of 1941. William Wyler arrived at MGM, on loan from the independent producer Samuel Goldwyn, to direct the film on 29 September 1941.[37] Wyler worked with the writers on the script until filming began on 6 November 1941. The most significant change made concerned the Minivers' complacency; this aspect of the script was all but abandoned during the filming. The change served a dramatic purpose. Wyler remembered that he thought that *Mrs Miniver* was 'perfect as propaganda for the British because it was a story about a family, about the kind of people audiences would care about'.[38] Audiences certainly would care more for the Minivers if they weren't seen to be 'at fault'. However, the United States' entry into the war on 7 December 1941 undoubtedly played a part in this change. For example, Mrs Miniver's comment on Poland and the German spy's commentary are still included in the script dated 18 October 1941, which was after Wyler's arrival but before the US entered the war. The next surviving script is dated 9 February 1942, at which point the German spy's commentary had been cut and the Minivers had lost their faults and weaknesses.[39]

Other changes made to *Mrs Miniver* also reflect wartime developments. When Germany attacked the Soviet Union in June 1941, the Soviet Union became an ally of Britain. Suddenly, Franklin had second thoughts about what he called 'the running gag on Communism'. In July 1941 he wrote to Paul Osborn that, 'the word "Communism" seems to frighten me in the present circumstances'. He instructed Osborn to rewrite the scenes concerning Vin's communism, with Vin saying 'social reform' rather

11   They don't take tea: A German flier (Helmut Dantine) confronts
Mrs Miniver (Greer Garson) in *Mrs Miniver* (1942)

than 'Communism'. Vin's work clothes and his volume of Marx
were abandoned in favour of a formal suit and hat, and much of
the dialogue on this issue was eliminated.[40]

The United States' entry into the war also had a dramatic
effect on the scene in which Mrs Miniver confronts a downed
and wounded German flyer in her kitchen. When it was first
written in October 1940, this scene had little drama or danger.
The German points a gun at Mrs Miniver initially, but she
'understands at once that the German is much more frightened
than she'. She says 'you must be hungry, my boy, come and let
me feed you'. Then she talks him into giving himself up to the
police so that he can have medical attention. Meanwhile, Mr
Miniver joins them in the kitchen. The German introduces himself as Emil Wagner and says that he is from Cologne. Mrs
Miniver knows a family in Cologne and asks if Emil knows them.
She offers tea and they all have a cup. The only awkward
moment comes when Mr Miniver says that he was stationed in
Cologne during the last war, and the German replies, 'this time

A new England

there will be no British army in Cologne – we will defeat you'. Then the police arrive.[41]

That was how the scene stood in the first script Wyler received in September 1941. Wyler insisted that the scene be made more confrontational. MGM's Louis B. Mayer reminded Wyler that the United States was not at war with Germany and, while *Mrs Miniver* could be a pro-British film, it could not be an anti-German 'hate picture'. This was merely a statement of Hays Office policy, and the Hays Office had, in fact, already approved this script without reservation.[42] Wyler's copy of the September 1941 script reveals his discomfort with this scene. In the margins, alongside Mrs Miniver's dialogue, he has scribbled 'one can't talk these fellows out of their ideas!', and then at the end of the scene he has written, 'it's too easy'.[43] With Mayer's permission, Wyler rewrote the scene in October 1941, making the German more menacing and the situation more threatening. Wyler suspected that Mayer was merely humouring him, though, and that as soon as he was off the studio lot another director would film the gentler version.[44]

In Wyler's new version of the scene, Mr Miniver is away at Dunkirk when the German flyer confronts Mrs Miniver, making the situation much more threatening for her. She is frightened and the German is very menacing. There are no offers of food or tea, and no mention of Cologne. Instead, the German takes food from her refrigerator and 'bolts it down'. Then he launches into a fanatical speech about the death and destruction German bombers have brought to European cities, and says, 'and we will do the same here!'[45] This version of the scene was filmed, but after all other filming had finished, in March 1942, it was decided to go back and film this scene one more time. Only one change was made in the final version. When the German says 'we will do the same here!', Mrs Miniver loses control and, as the revised script describes it, 'slaps him across the mouth – hard – her eyes blazing'. Thus, four months after the United States declared war on Germany, Mrs Miniver was allowed at last to hate – and to slap – the German flyer.[46]

All post-production work on *Mrs Miniver* was finally completed on 5 May 1942.[47] The finished film portrays the Minivers much more favourably than the original treatments and scripts. Most notably, the Minivers' pre-war complacency barely registers. Instead, their contented pre-war lives serve as a preamble, making their wartime hardships and tragedies all the more poignant. The film's opening statement reveals this strategy:

This story of an average English middle-class family begins with the summer of 1939; when the sun shone down on a happy, careless people, who worked and played, reared their children and tended their gardens in the happy, easy-going England that was so soon to be fighting desperately for her way of life and for life itself.

The word 'careless' is the only indication here that the Minivers may be, in a minor way, at fault. The only sign of complacency is that the Minivers' prominently displayed grandfather clock needs repeated forwarding; evidence that in 1939 they are happily behind the times. And the pre-war segment does include scenes in which Mrs Miniver (Greer Garson) buys a rather ridiculous and expensive hat and Mr Miniver (Walter Pidgeon) buys a new convertible car, but no judgement is passed upon them. Indeed, the Minivers comment in the first episode on 'how lucky we are'. Not, they make clear, because they have a new hat and car, but because of their children and love for one another.

The opening titles also define the Minivers as 'average' and 'middle-class', but the Minivers are a conspicuously affluent sort of middle class. In Struther's stories the Minivers had two homes, one in London and one in Kent. In the film, they have only the one house in the Kent village of Belham. This change made the Minivers' class standing more plausible, and it also eschewed an urban setting for the green and pleasant 'easy-going' England indicated in the prologue. Still, the house is large and spacious, and it fronts a river on which the Minivers keep a large pleasure boat. They have a cook and a maid, and, after purchasing their hat and car, they attend a black-tie dinner-dance at their country club. This ends with a rendition of 'God Save the King', for which everyone stands. In choosing a family whose class standing is 'the top drawer but one', the film-makers did not stray far from the upper-class settings and values of so many 'British' films. Nor does the film stray, at all, from the quaint and charming setting that Franklin found so pleasing.

The Minivers' middle-class status, however odd it might appear, is central to the film's view of a more egalitarian England. Aristocratic and working-class characters are present in *Mrs Miniver*, but the focus of the story is placed squarely on the middle-class Minivers. They are classless in that they have none of the exaggerated mannerisms, dispositions and accents of the other classes; but they are also affluent, church-going, wholesome consumers. Thus, the Minivers represent an idealized and American conception of the middle class; a family American audiences could respect and identify with much more readily than they would identify with either extreme of the British class strata.

Then, when this identification has been established, the war arrives to threaten all that the family represents.

It is made clear that the affluent Minivers are not aristocrats when Mrs Miniver, returning from her London shopping trip, meets the haughty Lady Beldon (Dame May Whitty) on the train. Lady Beldon calls Mrs Miniver 'Mrs Mannering – the lawyer's wife', and when Mrs Miniver politely tells her that her husband is an architect, Lady Beldon says dismissively, 'well I knew he was something of that sort'. She also tells Mrs Miniver that: 'I spent the entire afternoon being pushed around by middle-class females buying things they can't possibly afford ... Everyone trying to be better than their betters: mink coats and no manners. No wonder Germany is arming!' When the train reaches Belham station, Mrs Miniver is then contrasted with the humble station master, Mr Ballard (Henry Travers). He shows Mrs Miniver the beautiful rose he has grown, and he asks her permission to name it the 'Mrs Miniver Rose', since she has always taken the time to speak to him. He plans to enter the rose into competition against Lady Beldon's 'Beldon Rose' at the village flower show. In past years, no one has ever dared to compete with Lady Beldon.

The working class may be taking liberties, and the middle class may be taking on the prestige and titles once reserved for the aristocracy, but there is no revolution in the air. This is made clear when the Minivers' eldest son, Vin (Richard Ney), arrives home from Oxford speaking of the 'social consciousness' he has developed. He complains, while being served tea by the maid, of the plight of the working man, and says that England is a 'feudalistic state' just as it was in 'the ninth to the fifteenth centuries'. As in *This Above All*, then, class antagonism is not voiced by an authentic working-class character, but is displaced and made unauthentic. In *Mrs Miniver*, it is also undermined by Vin's fatuous delivery. His views are undermined even further by the reactions of a representative of each class. Gladys (Brenda Forbes), the simple-minded maid, listens to Vin with a look of bewilderment on her face. Such thoughts clearly have never troubled her. Mr and Mrs Miniver dismiss Vin's views as part of yet another 'phase' that he is going through. Last year, it seems, he was a vegetarian. Carol Beldon (Teresa Wright), granddaughter of Lady Beldon, assures Vin that 'big words' will not solve any problems. Carol, by contrast, is an aristocrat with a real social conscience. She does 'settlement work in the slums of London'.

The film-makers' preferred view of the British class system is one which admits to the existence of class differences, but not to class antagonism. There is no need for communism; the most the working man wants is to be able to enter his rose in the flower show. The film merely shows that the classes are mixing more, with the new middle class providing a point of intersection. The 'Mrs Miniver Rose', for example, becomes the catalyst for more friendly class relations. Mr Ballard's comment to Mrs Miniver, that his perfect rose is the product of 'breeding, budding and horse manure – if you'll pardon the expression ma'am', is particularly revealing. The class equivalent of the formula – upper-class breeding, the emergent middle class and the humble working class – will also combine, and the result will be a more unified society and war effort.

The film's second episode takes place on the day war is declared. The first indications of wartime hardship and the levelling of class barriers are seen. The village flower show is cancelled on account of 'conditions'. Vin no longer speaks of his social consciousness but, much to Mrs Miniver's concern, he decides to enlist in the RAF. An air-raid warning is sounded and the Minivers take cover in their cellar. At Lady Beldon's ancestral home, Beldon Hall, the butler announces 'sirens m'lady', but Lady Beldon is horrified at the indignity of having to go down to the cellar, particularly because she has been instructed to do so by the village Air Raid Warden, Mr Foley (Reginald Owen), a mere shopkeeper. Lady Beldon resents his new authority, and says, 'the worst thing about this war is the chance it gives to little people to make themselves important!' The portrayal of Lady Beldon is at this point similar to that of Iris Cathaway in *This Above All*. She sees the war as an inconvenience, and fears for her place in society when the class order begins to change. However, in the kinder and gentler England of *Mrs Miniver*, the aristocrat eventually accepts and even condones the changes.

This is revealed in the third segment, when the war descends upon the Minivers and the village of Belham. Vin and Carol become engaged, and Lady Beldon arrives at the Minivers' home to protest. It emerges, though, that Lady Beldon is more concerned about her granddaughter's youth than the class of her fiancé, and Mrs Miniver's charm allays even that point of contention. Then, when the village proceeds with the flower show, the judges decide to award Lady Beldon's rose the first prize. But Mrs Miniver leads Lady Beldon to recognize that Mr Ballard's rose is superior to the Beldon entry, and that the judges were too timid to go against her. When Lady Beldon announces the winners, she awards first prize to the 'Mrs Miniver Rose'. She calls Mr Ballard 'a man of spirit', and Ballard takes the prize with humility, saying 'thank you m'lady – pardon the liberty'. Thus, Mrs Miniver and the rose named after her bring about a mild change in class relations. The haughty aristocrat is not quite so haughty, and the working man, while remaining humble, has his efforts rewarded.

The village flower show takes place despite the heightening war, but this is portrayed as fortitude rather than complacency. Prior to the flower show, the Minivers have already displayed their courage. Mrs Miniver confronts the German flyer in her kitchen while Vin and Mr Miniver are at Dunkirk. Also, when Mr Miniver returns, the family is seen in its tiny bomb shelter at night. As the bombs draw closer and closer, the Minivers stoically read lines from *Alice in Wonderland* ('those carefree summer days of long ago'). Finally, the bombers are directly overhead, and as the bombs descend with menacingly high whistles and earth-shaking impact, the Minivers clutch their terrified and screaming children. The next day, the flower show ends with another air-raid warning. Lady Beldon, now reformed, invites the entire village to take shelter in the cellar of Beldon Hall. However, Mrs Miniver and Carol drive Vin to the RAF base and, while they are driving home, the bombers arrive. The village is in flames, Carol is wounded by stray bullets and later dies, and Mr Ballard dies in the village. Thus, the war results in the deaths of both an upper-class and a working-class character.

In the final scene, at a service in what remains of the village church, the Vicar (Henry Wilcoxon) questions why the village and its civilians have paid such a high price in the war. He answers that this is 'a war of the people':

of all the people; and it must be fought not only in the battlefield, but in the cities and the villages, in the factories and on the farms, in the home and in the heart of every man, woman and child who loves freedom ... Fight it, then! Fight it with all that is in us! And may God defend the right!

The speech draws together the two strands of *Mrs Miniver*; the effect of 'total war' on an 'average' family, and the lowering of class barriers in the 'people's war'. Vin, once the class antagonist, joins Lady Beldon in her church pew when the vicar is finished, sharing her grief for Carol. The film then ends on a triumphant note. The camera tilts upward through a gaping hole in the church roof and, as the congregation sings 'Onward Christian Soldiers', fighter planes are seen heading off to battle.

Much of the tension felt in *Mrs Miniver*, and the sympathy the film engenders for its characters, can be attributed to director William Wyler. Through his repetition of camera angles, Wyler links scenes of happiness and tragedy in a manner that heightens

12   From a spacious house to a cramped bomb shelter: Mr and Mrs Miniver
(Walter Pidgeon and Greer Garson) outside their Anderson shelter in
Mrs Miniver (1942)

the film's emotional impact. For example, when Vin first becomes
interested in Carol, she is seen from his point of view, across the
church aisle in a pew with her grandmother. Then in the final
scene, when Carol is dead, the pew is again seen from Vin's same
point of view, but he sees only a sad and frail Lady Beldon. Similarly, the staircase of the Minivers' home is at first the site of
light-hearted family moments, then apprehensive moments and
finally tragedy. Wyler also contrasts the spaciousness of the
Minivers' house with their cramped and tiny bomb shelter. The
Miniver's descent from pre-war contentment to wartime hardship
is emphasized when they crouch in the claustrophobic shelter,
while bombs destroy their once happy home. Wyler strengthened
the German flyer scene and, together with actor Henry Wilcoxon,
wrote the final version of the vicar's speech.[48] It was also Wyler
who conceived the film's final shot. In his shooting script, next to
the original version of the vicar's speech, he has written, 'through
the roof – a squadron of British bombers going to Germany?'.[49]
This shot, of British bombers seen through the remains of the
church roof, provides a visual coda to the film's depiction of a
down, but not out, British people.

Another key change was made to *Mrs Miniver* after Wyler's

arrival. The September 1941 script includes scenes of Mr Miniver fighting at Dunkirk. However, in the film Mr Miniver is only seen leaving for Dunkirk, and when he returns he is exhausted and never tells the story of what happened there. Similarly, Vin is never seen flying and does not speak at any length on the subject. Thus, we do not even hear of what happens to men at war, but stay fixed on the women and children. And although expectations of Vin's death are built up, ultimately it is Carol who dies. The importance the film attaches to its female characters is also evident in the cast choices. Greer Garson and Teresa Wright give powerful performances, particularly by comparison with the affable but vacuous Walter Pidgeon and Richard Ney.

Reception

Mrs Miniver made its debut at New York City's 6,000-seat Radio City Music Hall on 4 June 1942, and it remained at Radio City for a record-breaking ten weeks, surpassing the previous record of six weeks. At this one venue alone, the box-office gross exceeded $1,000,000 and attendance reached 1,500,000 people. By March 1943, it was estimated that thirty-three million Americans had seen the film.[50] President Roosevelt reportedly urged MGM to put the film into general release quickly and without advanced admission prices. MGM did so, and Sidney Franklin estimated that this reduced the rentals gross by $4,000,000.[51] Still, *Mrs Miniver* earned MGM's highest-ever domestic gross, $5,358,000 and the foreign gross, at $3,520,000, was second only to that of the epic *Ben Hur* (1925) in MGM's eighteen-year history. In Britain, *Mrs Miniver* was named as the top box-office attraction of 1942, indicating that it was more popular than Britain's own war films.[52]

The United States had been in the war only seven months when *Mrs Miniver* was released, and the Minivers' hardships and tragedies seem to have a struck a chord with Americans. American critics heralded the film's dramatic portrayal of an 'average' family besieged by total war.[53] In *Film Daily's* annual critics' poll, 555 of the 592 critics polled named *Mrs Miniver* as the best film of 1942.[54] In *The New York Times*, critic Bosley Crowther went so far as to say that 'it is too soon to call this one of the greatest motion pictures ever made ... But certainly, it is the finest film yet made about the present war, and a most exalting tribute to the British.[55] *Mrs Miniver* also swept the 1942 Academy Awards, winning 'best picture', 'best actress' (Greer Garson), 'best supporting actress' (Teresa Wright), 'best direction' (William Wyler), 'best written screenplay' (Froeschel, Hilton, West and Wimperis were credited) and 'best cinematography' (Joseph Ruttenberg).

Despite its overwhelming popularity in Britain, *Mrs Miniver* drew mixed reviews from British critics. In *The Monthly Film Bulletin*, the critic commented that 'in spite of the obvious criticism that can be made', *Mrs Miniver* 'is a most moving film'.[56] In *The Spectator*, Edgar Anstey referred to it as 'unconsciously pro-fascist propaganda' because it portrayed Britain's war effort as 'the defence of bourgeois privilege'.[57] *The Documentary News Letter* found that 'in a lot of ways [*Mrs Miniver*] is just repulsive', and the writer took 'grave exception' to the depiction of the middle-class Minivers as 'the backbone of Britain'.[58] The most scathing criticism came in a *Sunday Pictorial* editorial, entitled 'She's a Disgrace to the Women of Britain' and written by Harry Ashbrook. Ashbrook complained that Mrs Miniver's maid is 'a giggling half-wit', the maid's boyfriend 'an imbecile' and the station master an 'amiable fool':

Do these ghastly caricatures honestly represent the workers of Britain? ... Why resurrect this useless baggage, Mrs Miniver, from the comfortable Court page of the *Times* to represent the nation at war? What sort of people do Hollywood directors think we are?[59]

Such criticism was later echoed by the Office of War Information, which was particularly uneasy with the portrayal of class in *Mrs Miniver*, but MGM preferred to focus more upon the praise the film received and, of course, its extraordinary popularity.

This Above All was released three weeks before *Mrs Miniver*, on 12 May 1942, but nonetheless it was overshadowed by this rival portrait of Britain during the Blitz. *Variety* estimated that the domestic gross reached $2,400,000, making it one of thirty-three films to earn more than $2,000,000 in 1942.[60] However, this was less than half the domestic gross of *Mrs Miniver*. In Britain, *This Above All* was named by *Kinematograph Weekly* as the most popular film of September 1942, but it was not among the top ten films of the year.[61] It is tempting to attribute the greater success of *Mrs Miniver* to its more idyllic portrayal of England and the class system. However, it is equally likely that the troubled wartime romance of *This Above All* did not move audiences as greatly as *Mrs Miniver's* portrayal of women and children in the midst of 'total war'.

American critics praised *This Above All*. *The Motion Picture Daily* called it 'moving dramatic material'. *The Hollywood Reporter* referred to it as 'a strong and thoughtful film', and *Variety* termed it 'a splendid example of film entertainment'.[62] But when *This*

Above All was released in Britain (one month after *Mrs Miniver*), the British critics once again found much to criticize. Dilys Powell commented in *The Sunday Times* that, 'I begin to find myself, when I am in an American film about the brave British, reaching for my hat. *This Above All* (the novel) has been boiled down to another piece about pulling together and taking it.'[63] Powell also pointed out that the film displays a 'conviction' that 'the working classes consist largely of comics'. Similarly, William Whitebait of *The New Statesman* complained that the issues discussed in the novel were reduced in the ending to the notion that 'sex can solve everything' and that 'the glimpses of the upper classes aren't very credible'.[64] The new England of *This Above All* and *Mrs Miniver*, and their views of the 'brave British', drew decidedly mixed reactions from British critics.

Conclusion

This Above All and *Mrs Miniver* provide further evidence of Hollywood's Anglophile tendencies. Both films went into production before the United States entered the war, and both attempt to portray a new and more egalitarian Britain. This was clearly designed to counter isolationist criticisms that Britain was not worthy of American aid. However, the films also exemplify the mixture of good intentions and commercial concerns that characterize 'British' war films. They set out to show that the class system is changing in wartime and that England is becoming more democratic, but the portrayal of average Britons is handled in a most peculiar manner. Clive Briggs is meant to be working class, but he is played by the American Tyrone Power, and the Minivers are meant to be middle class but they are far too affluent to be 'average'. The film-makers could not resist settings such as Cathaway Manor House and Beldon Hall. Neither film, in fact, strays very far from the upper-class milieu that characterizes 'British' films. Rather than championing the role of the working class in Britain's wartime survival, though, the films instead portray youthful and progressive aristocrats, who are committed to the war effort as well as to a new and more egalitarian England. Working-class characters, meanwhile, are presented in the familiar manner, as contented and comical simpletons. The films hold out the promise of a new and more egalitarian England, then, without reforming the 'British' film itself, and Hollywood's fascination with Britain's upper classes continued unabated throughout the war years.

The Hollywood British at war

During the early years of the war, the British presence in Hollywood reached an all-time high. 'British' film-making was at its peak – no fewer than twenty-eight 'British' films were made in 1939 and 1940 – and the Hollywood studios recruited the leading British writers, stars, directors and producers to make them. Of course, the promise of higher salaries, greater fame and a more stable film industry had lured British film-makers to Hollywood for many years before the war, and many of those who went between 1938 and 1940 were only a part of this long-running trend. Stars such as Leslie Howard, Charles Laughton, Merle Oberon and Laurence Olivier had been back and forth between Britain and Hollywood earlier in the decade, and the fresh recruits of 1939, such as Alfred Hitchcock and Vivien Leigh, were taking up contracts that no ambitious director or star was likely to resist.

By 1940, however, the migration from Britain to Hollywood seemed to have become an exodus. It was hastened by the 1938 Films Act and by the uncertainty caused by the war itself. The Hollywood-friendly provisions of the Films Act had ensured that many British stars and directors came under transatlantic contracts, and, when the war was looming in 1939, the Hollywood studios were eager to bring their prized British talent to the safety and stability of California. The situation was compounded further by the British government's own indifference to the film industry during the first year of war, when studio space was requisitioned for war production, materials for sets and costumes were rationed, and technicians and other key personnel were called up for service. It appeared, initially at least, that the British film industry was out of action for the duration of the war. It is hardly surprising, then, that many of the industry's most successful directors (Hitchcock, Alexander Korda, Victor Saville, Robert Stevenson, Herbert Wilcox), its top stars (Gracie Fields, Greer Garson, Anna Neagle) and its leading writers (C.S. Forester, Aldous Huxley, Christopher Isherwood, R.C. Sherriff and Arthur Wimperis) joined the growing Hollywood British community in this period.

In Britain, however, the Hollywood British soon became the targets of a campaign of spiteful criticism and accusations. They were accused of being cowards and deserters, who had fled from their country in its hour of need. The attacks, made mostly in the press, were aimed not only at those who had left most recently, but also at the British colony as a whole. For a group of expatriates who saw themselves as flying the British flag in a key outpost, and at a pivotal point in history, the attacks were devastating. Their response came in the form of a film, *Forever and a Day* (1943), which was made as a collective effort over the first three years of the war. Seven directors, twenty-one writers and seventy-eight actors worked without pay on the film so that the proceeds could be contributed to wartime charities. The production was lengthy and troubled, and when the film finally emerged it was long overdue. Yet it stands as a remarkable showcase for the community's talents. An episodic structure enables the film to offer an example of nearly all of the 'British' genres that had been developed in Hollywood over the previous ten years, and it enables the film's directors and stars to reprise their most noteworthy films and roles. Thus, while setting out to cleanse their names and to raise money for charity, the makers of *Forever and a Day* paid tribute to the British talent in Hollywood, and to the Hollywood 'British' film itself.

The Hollywood British community

The Britons who arrived in Hollywood in the late 1930s found themselves within a well-established community of expatriate writers, directors and stars. Sheridan Morley has traced the British presence in Hollywood back to the earliest days of filmmaking in Southern California.[1] Silent comedians Charlie Chaplin and Stan Laurel made their first films in Hollywood in the 1910s. West End stage stars occasionally visited Hollywood in the silent era, often to appear in adaptations of Shakespeare and Dickens. British actors Ronald Colman, Clive Brook and Basil Rathbone achieved varying degrees of stardom in silent films in the 1920s, and directors Frank Lloyd and Edmund Goulding made many successful silent films. But being a Briton in Hollywood at that time did not confer an automatic advantage. The muteness of silent films meant that, firstly, the likelihood of success in the industry was not skewed toward the speakers of any one language, and, secondly, the local language of a production centre was not important, because intertitles could be translated into the language of any export market.

The advent of 'talking pictures' in the late 1920s destroyed this taken-for-granted universality. Immediately, the language of a production centre became important not only in terms of its domestic market, but also in relation to export markets. Under these abruptly changed conditions of trade, things British suddenly looked especially attractive to Hollywood. Thus it was that, in the early 1930s, the British presence in Hollywood became so marked that one could speak of a British community. The studios needed writers accustomed to writing dialogue, and these were found in both American and British novelists and playwrights. John Galsworthy, James Hilton, Aldous Huxley, Christopher Isherwood, W.P. Lipscomb, Frederick Lonsdale, J.B. Priestley, R.C. Sherriff, Hugh Walpole and P.G. Wodehouse were among the British writers lured to Hollywood in the 1930s by the incomparable financial rewards and the chance to spend some time in the sun.[2] Actors also benefited from the advent of sound. When the technology was in its infancy, the clear diction of a British accent became an asset, and silent stars such as Ronald Colman, Clive Brook and Basil Rathbone made the transition to 'talking pictures' with far more success than many of the American and European stars in Hollywood.

While the transition to 'talking pictures' provided a boost to the British colony in Hollywood in the early 1930s, it was the growing number of 'British' films that hastened and sustained the colony's phenomenal growth. British writers were thought to be essential for 'British' films. Even if they only contributed dialogue or wrote scripts in tandem with veteran American screenwriters, they were seen to provide the necessary British perspective to the films. British directors were also called upon to lend their expertise to 'British' films. Frank Lloyd made a wide variety of films in the silent era, but in the 1930s he was placed at the helm of high-profile films such as *Cavalcade* (1932), *Berkeley Square* (1933) and *Mutiny on the Bounty* (1935). Similarly, Edmund Goulding was given assignments such as *Riptide* (1934), *The Dawn Patrol* (1938) and *We Are Not Alone* (1939). Newcomers to Hollywood also found that they were wanted, at least initially, to direct 'British' films. Within Alfred Hitchcock's first three years in Hollywood, he directed *Rebecca* (1940), *Foreign Correspondent* (1940) and *Suspicion* (1941). Two of Robert Stevenson's earliest Hollywood films were *Tom Brown's Schooldays* (1940) and *Jane Eyre* (1944), and Victor Saville began with *The Earl of Chicago* (1940). The British in Hollywood were not limited to 'British' films alone, of course, but 'British' films often offered their earliest and, in some cases, their best assignments.

British actors provided the most immediately recognizable British qualities to 'British' films, and throughout the 1930s their numbers grew most quickly. David Selznick was a particular exponent of the need for British actors to play British parts, and he expressed his disdain for films which featured American actors in British roles. For Selznick, this meant not only 'a loss of both quality and reality', but it was also 'one reason why so many pictures with English backgrounds, made in Hollywood, don't do better in the very big English markets'.[3] Selznick recruited stars such as Freddie Bartholomew, Vivien Leigh and Joan Fontaine to make sure that his films did not suffer the same fate.

The most prominent of all British actors in the 1930s, however, was not a recent recruit from Britain, nor one who owed his early success to the British film industry. Ronald Colman, like many of the most popular British stars in Hollywood, had come to Hollywood at an early stage in his career. By the mid-1920s, he was one of the leading screen idols of the late silent era. His 'talking' debut came when he played the eponymous hero of *Bulldog Drummond* (1929), an urbane detective who is first seen – and heard to speak – in a stuffy London gentleman's club. Thereafter, Colman's career was sustained far longer than most in Hollywood, as he starred in many of the most successful 'British' films of the 1930s. Through films such as *Raffles* (1930), *Cynara* (1933), *Bulldog Drummond Strikes Back* (1934), *Clive of India* (1934), *A Tale of Two Cities* (1935), *The Prisoner of Zenda* (1937) and *The Light That Failed* (1939) he became the standard-bearer for a type of role that was particularly British. While the leading American stars of the decade often embodied the traits of the 'common man', whether they were naively idealistic or gruff and masculine, Colman was uniquely well spoken. His characters had grace, dignity and a worldly charm. If this seems to be a rather old-fashioned ideal of an English gentleman, Colman's virtue was that he brought a warmth and romanticism to this persona that ensured its enduring appeal.

Numerous young British actors followed in Colman's footsteps. In his earliest Hollywood films, Laurence Olivier had a darker and more brooding quality than Colman, but he was nonetheless dashing and dignified. Olivier, in fact, received the part of Maxim De Winter in *Rebecca* only when Colman, who was David Selznick's first choice, turned it down.[4] David Niven was another of Hollywood's debonair English gentlemen. Niven arrived in Hollywood a complete unknown in 1934, but he proceeded to become a younger version of Colman, with officer-and-a-gentleman roles in *Thank You, Jeeves* (1936), *The Charge of the Light Brigade* (1936), *The Prisoner of Zenda* (1937), *Four Men and a Prayer* (1938) and *The Dawn Patrol*. Indeed, the peak of his early Hollywood career came when he received top billing in *Raffles* (1940), playing the part previously taken by Colman. If Niven's early career seems almost uncannily 'British', it is important to note that he was aided by Colman, Edmund Goulding and C. Aubrey Smith, who took it upon themselves to introduce him to the right people and to make sure that he was seen in the right places. The Hollywood British looked after their own, and Niven was wise enough to join their social set as soon as he arrived.[5]

Sheridan Morley has pointed out that many of Hollywood's leading British actors came from affluent backgrounds and were educated at public schools. The 'respectables', as he calls them, fitted easily into roles which called for upper-class gentlemen.[6] But such a narrow screen persona could be very limiting in a long-term career. C. Aubrey Smith was the very personification of this type, and he soon became a character actor with a seemingly endless series of small roles as regal and authoritative old colonels. Clive Brook belonged firmly in the clipped-accent-and-stiff-upper-lip category, and while this enabled him to play leading roles in films such as *Cavalcade* and *Sherlock Holmes* (1932), it was also a limitation. Perhaps fearing a descent into character parts, Brook returned to Britain in the mid-1930s. Basil Rathbone and George Sanders were also 'respectables' by background, but they found their own niche in Hollywood by playing the opposite of Colman. In fact, they were often the most ungentlemanly gentlemen. Rathbone took on the most loathsome parts available to a British actor (Mr Murdstone in *David Copperfield* (1934), Sir Guy Gisbourne in *The Adventures of Robin Hood* (1938)) before he gained the more noble role of Sherlock Holmes. George Sanders quickly became identified on screen as the sophisticated cad. He played such parts so convincingly and with such zest that when he occasionally took a benign and innocuous role, such as the friendly Herbert ffolliott in *Foreign Correspondent*, it was hard to believe that he would not be revealed as a treacherous villain in the final reel.

No matter how many 'British' films were made, there was not an unlimited supply of roles for well-heeled gentlemen, and so many of the other leading British stars developed wider screen personas. Most importantly, they avoided being associated solely with the old-fashioned and somewhat stuffy notions of Englishness that persisted in Hollywood. Charles Laughton's most stereotypical 'British' role was that of the butler in *Ruggles of Red Gap* (1935), who finds himself working for an American family on a ranch in the Wild West. But Laughton often played tortured misfits rather than dignified gentlemen. While the father in *The Barretts of Wimpole Street* (1934) and Captain Bligh in *Mutiny on the Bounty* (1935) were repressed characters, they had none of the stiff upper lip that marked Hollywood's gentleman, and Laughton was particularly masterful at conveying inner turmoil and angst. Furthermore, a tortured misfit need not be British, and Laughton scored two of his greatest successes in *Les Miserables* (1935) and *The Hunchback of Notre Dame* (1939).

Errol Flynn was an Australian, but when he came under contract at Warner Bros. in 1935, the studio decided to give him a different nationality. Rather than making him British, which would have placed him in the category of the gentleman, he was remade as an Irishman. The publicity was so convincing that no one would believe Flynn when he spoke in private about his real background in Tasmania. 'They wanted me to be Flynn of Ireland', he recalled in his autobiography, 'and they would not accept a less romantic background.'[7] Despite Flynn's apparent misgivings, it was undoubtedly a wise strategy on the part of the studio. An Irish star was likely to appeal to the many Irish-Americans in the domestic audience. It was also an appropriate background for the star of the 'Merrie England' films, in which Flynn played rebellious men of action and adventure. His characters may have fought for Queen and country, but they were seldom seen in a well-upholstered drawing-room.

Cary Grant was British, but his working-class background gave him a distinctive status among the Hollywood British. Born Archibald ('Archie') Leach in Bristol, he left school in his early teens and travelled with a theatre troupe to New York City. Gradually, he made his way from vaudeville to the Broadway stage and then on to Hollywood in 1931. There, he reinvented himself as Cary Grant, a man of charm and grace to be sure, but not one living in an elitist old world past. Both his accent and his mannerisms were 'mid-Atlantic', sufficiently polished to suggest a

13   'Not our class, dear'" Cary Grant as the down and out Ernie
              Mott in *None but the Lonely Heart* (1944)

gentleman, yet retaining enough vigour and spontaneity to convey modern American classlessness. Even the name Cary Grant, as his biographer Graham McCann has pointed out, positioned him in this way, with 'Cary' conveying refinement and 'Grant' suggesting solid masculinity.[8] For the most part, he played American roles, and these were often in screwball comedies that tapped into the tension between Grant's polish and his vitality. In the few 'British' films that he did make, Grant's characters were outsiders and mavericks rather than the well-heeled and respectable. He is a cockney performer and petty thief in *Sylvia Scarlett* (1935). In *Gunga Din* (1939) he is not a responsible officer and gentleman but a highly excitable cockney sergeant. In *Suspicion* (1941) he plays Johnny Aysgarth, a man who is on the make and eager to marry into an upper-class family. As his co-star Joan Fontaine later recalled, his character could be summed up in the family's reaction to him: 'not our class, dear'.[9] And, most notably for his biographers, Grant was the driving force behind the production of *None but the Lonely Heart* (1944). The bleak story of a cockney drifter who returns home to the back-streets of London's East End, this was unusual territory for a 'British' film, but it was not too far removed from Grant's own background.

No British actresses reached the status of Colman, Laughton, Flynn and Grant in the 1930s. Most of the prominent female roles in 'British' films called for the qualities of elegance and grace that were associated with Britain's upper classes, but in many instances this required the actresses to do little more than look poised and serenely beautiful. Madeleine Carroll and Elizabeth Allan, for example, had the leading female roles in several of the decade's high-profile 'British' films, yet they did not establish a unique identity and they seldom received top billing. Merle Oberon had prominent roles in films such as *The Dark Angel* (1935) and *Wuthering Heights*, but she never enjoyed a consistent run of box-office hits. There were also stars such as Olivia De Havilland and Maureen O'Sullivan, who passed for 'English roses', although the former was raised by her British parents in Tokyo and California, and the latter was Irish. Their roles – as the love interest, the younger sister or the lady-in-waiting – were at any rate secondary and limiting. In the absence of a genuinely British female star with the clout to match the marquee value of the top British male stars, the vacancy was often filled by Norma Shearer, one of MGM's top stars and also a Canadian citizen. Shearer had leading roles in prestige 'British' productions such as *Private Lives* (1931), *Smilin' Through* (1932), *The Barretts of Wimpole Street* and *Romeo and Juliet* (1936).

It was not until the turn of the decade, when Joan Fontaine and Greer Garson emerged, that British actresses received stronger roles and unique identities. Fontaine was the younger sister of Olivia De Havilland, and she too had little contact with her parent's native country. However, Fontaine maintained a British accent and was under contract to David Selznick, who guided her through a succession of very English roles. In *Rebecca*, *Suspicion*, *This Above All*, *Jane Eyre* and *Frenchman's Creek* (1944), Fontaine plays a waif so gentle that she seems at first to be almost simple-minded, and in each of these films she falls in love with a darker and somehow dangerous man. Garson, meanwhile, was actually named Eileen Garson, and she was raised in Ilford, a lower-middle-class suburb of London. She had already become known as Greer Garson by the time Louis B. Mayer spotted her on the London stage in 1937, yet MGM went one step further by promoting her as Greer Garson of County Down, Ireland. For good measure, she was also said to be a descendant of Rob Roy MacGregor.[10] This suited a red-haired beauty, and it suited a star who played women who were not born to the manor but earned their status as great ladies. Her characters always had impeccable manners and a benevolent personality, but these were not the airs and graces of an aristocrat. Rather, they were part of the democratic ideal of class mobility. Garson's characters were seen to be moving up in the world on the basis of their virtue and integrity. This careful class positioning is most obvious in *Mrs Miniver* (1942), but it also runs throughout Garson's other roles in highly popular (non-'British') films such as *Blossoms in the Dust* (1941), *Mrs Parkington* (1944) and *The Valley of Decision* (1945).

For the top stars, being British was an advantage, particularly in their early days, but it was not an end in itself. Stars needed greater breadth to guarantee a consistent run of good roles and a wide appeal, and they needed to appeal to Americans. MGM's casting director gave advice along these lines to Ray Milland when he first arrived in Hollywood. Milland was told to 'lose his limey accent'. Unlike the Ronald Colmans and Clive Brooks of Hollywood, who already were established and had cornered the market for the best British roles, he would have to play a variety of parts.[11] Ironically, Milland then found himself cast as C. Aubrey Smith's son in *Bachelor Father* (1931) and later as Bulldog Drummond (*Bulldog Drummond Escapes*, 1937). But in most of his 1930s films Milland served as a second-string Cary Grant: sophisticated but of indeterminate origins. Claude Rains and Herbert Marshall played older versions of the sauve leading man, and although their key early roles were in British parts, their careers were maintained by playing a range of American, British and European characters. The common factor was that they could be more convincingly worldly and debonair than most American actors.

The only actors to benefit from being identified first and foremost as British were, in fact, the character actors. Some of these, including Gladys Cooper, Sir Cedric Hardwicke and Dame May Whitty, had enjoyed distinguished stage careers in London, while others, such as Donald Crisp, had meatier film roles in their younger years. However, the vast majority were middle-aged or elderly actors at the end of undistinguished stage careers. In Britain, they would have faced modestly paid stage work, long tours through the provinces and retirement in a cold and wet climate.[12] In Hollywood, they found ample work in undemanding roles, extraordinary salaries and a more hospitable climate. Their key asset was that they could offer the required Britishness of 'British' films. The most successful character actors portrayed, over and over again, the same familiar British stereotypes. C. Aubrey Smith was, as previously noted, an elderly but still commanding and vigorous authority figure. Cedric Hardwicke and Henry Stephenson played similar roles, but did not have quite the same stature as Smith. Donald Crisp was a patriarch whose hard Yorkshire demeanour concealed a heart of gold. Nigel Bruce was the harmless upper-class buffoon, and Arthur Treacher and Eric Blore were very eccentric, very 'English' butlers. Dame May Whitty and Gladys Cooper played matriarchs with either kind or cranky dispositions, while Una O'Connor played innumerable shrill spinsters and maids.

It would be difficult to find a single 'British' film of the 1930s and 1940s that did not have the names of at least two or three of these character actors toward the lower end of the credits. They were as essential to conveying the British setting as the opening, establishing shots of Big Ben or Tower Bridge. Being British was their livelihood, and their Britishness had to be sustained in the rather unlikely environment of Southern California. Hence, the British community maintained strong bonds and seemingly eccentric rituals off the screen. The only newspaper that C. Aubrey Smith would read was *The Times* of London, and he was said to do this – somewhat ostentatiously – on the set while waiting for his next scene.[13] Smith was also the captain of a Hollywood cricket team that was a focal point for the community. And the community was known to congregate to hear Big Ben ring in the New Year over the radio, for its tea parties, and for socializing with one another almost exclusively. According to Joan Fontaine, they were 'a cliquey lot' who would 'sit in one another's dressing rooms, swapping theatre stories, and recalling old chums from their Mayfair days'.[14]

The cosiness of this community was thrown into turmoil by the outbreak of war. When R.C. Sherriff arrived in June 1940, he found that he was fêted as a hero by the Hollywood British simply for having been so recently in Britain, and for having had a taste of wartime Britain. He recalled that 'everybody wanted an up-to-date report' on what was happening.[15] The problem for the Hollywood British was not simply the distance or a lack of news from their native country. It was that so many in the community had become identified with a particularly old-fashioned and patriotic idea of Britain. Now their country was fighting for its life, and they carried on living out a mock British existence amid the sunshine and wealth of a neutral country. It seemed somehow unpatriotic and hypocritical, and this was, of course, the idea that was picked up by a number of commentators in the British press.

Gallantly facing the footlights in Hollywood

The criticisms began in January 1940, when an article in the leading fan magazine *Picturegoer and Film Weekly* sarcastically ('my heart aches for our exiles in far-off California') called for the British in Hollywood to be forced to return, so that they could be enlisted to make pro-British feature films on a military salary.[16] The producer Michael Balcon then took up the argument, using moral indignation rather than sarcasm to put across his message. He began by offering an interview to *Picturegoer* in May 1940. Speaking with 'a sincerity that was almost violent', he told his interviewer that he was 'disgusted' by the flight of British filmmakers to Hollywood. Balcon himself had once been under contract to MGM-British, but he had not lasted long and apparently was still harbouring a bitter resentment toward Hollywood and anyone who would go there. He implied that the Hollywood British were cowards and tax-evaders, and he claimed that they had no excuse for their absence. Those who were under contract could defy their studios and return. Those who were too old for active service could do some other sort of war work. Nor was he willing to admit that the depressed state of British film production was reason enough for working in Hollywood. According to Balcon the British industry's depression was due to the fact that so many of its leading producers and directors had fled to Hollywood. Even the community's fund-raising activities were derided as 'drinking champagne in aid of relief funds for Finland'. Apart from praising David Niven and Leslie Howard for having returned to Britain already, Balcon mentioned no names. But there was a thinly veiled reference to Alexander Korda and his brothers, the art director Vincent Korda and the director Zoltan Korda. They clearly were the 'Central Europeans', who had 'gained the benefits of British naturalisation' yet had 'no intention of repaying Britain'.[17]

A few weeks later, the prominent actor-manager and Equity official Sir Seymour Hicks offered his own criticisms of the Hollywood British. In a letter to *The Times*, Hicks used memorable puns rather than vitriol to make his point, but the message was the same. He joked that his colleagues were 'gone with the wind up' and 'gallantly facing the footlights in Hollywood', and then suggested that the government should 'explain quite plainly when they arrive in Britain on Armistice Day whether they are to be fined, imprisoned or welcomed back as charming prodigal sons'.[18] This was too much for the British community, many of whom were or had been Equity members. They sought support from the British Consul in Los Angeles, Eric Cleugh. From the outset of the war, Cleugh had told those who were above the age of conscription to stay in Hollywood, where they could do more for their country than they could at home.[19] Now, the Hollywood British wanted Cleugh to come to their defence publicly. The Consul, however, could not publicize the fact that the British government wanted to maintain a British presence in Hollywood. Such a disclosure would have been a gift to American isolationists. As the criticisms seemed to be growing rather than diminishing, however, Cleugh sought the advice of the British Ambassador in Washington DC, Lord Lothian. Lothian asked to meet with representatives of the community, and in July 1940 a delegation consisting of Cary Grant, Laurence Olivier, Cedric Hardwicke and Herbert Wilcox went to Washington DC to meet him.[20]

Publicly, Lothian could do little more than Eric Cleugh. The British Embassy issued a press release on 9 July 1940, stating that from the beginning of the war the British actors in Hollywood had 'repeatedly offered their services to the British government'. These offers had not been taken up because 'there is no shortage of manpower in the United Kingdom'. It was also stressed that only those between the ages of eighteen and thirty-one were required for military service.[21] Privately, Lothian did agree to write to Lord Halifax, the British Foreign Secretary, and express his concern over the attacks. Referring to the 'very undesirable' accusations which would 'do our cause no good', Lothian also pointed out what was at stake:

The maintenance of a powerful nucleus of older British actors in Hollywood is of great importance to our interests, partly because they are continually championing the British cause in a very volatile community which would otherwise be left to the mercies of German propaganda, and because the production of films with a strong British tone is one of the best and subtlest forms of British propaganda.[22]

If this was a request for official pressure to end the criticisms of the Hollywood British, it did not yield results. On 25 August 1940 Balcon gave an interview to *The Sunday Dispatch* in which he referred to the 'cowards' and 'deserters' in Hollywood, who were 'making fortunes' while their country was 'making sacrifices'.

This time Hitchcock (the 'plump young technician' whose career Balcon had fostered fifteen years earlier) was singled out for scorn.[23] Later in the same week, J.B. Priestley used his weekly radio slot to express his agreement with Balcon.[24]

The attacks seemed to dismay the American press, which came to the defence of the community. *The New York Daily News* listed the charitable activities of the community and the considerable sums of money that they had raised for British causes.[25] In a front-page article *Variety* also backed the Hollywood British by detailing their extensive work for war causes and pointing out that many – Nigel Bruce, Ronald Colman, Herbert Marshall, Claude Rains and Basil Rathbone – had served in the First World War. C. Aubrey Smith, it was pointed out, was 'old enough to have drawn a longbow at Hastings', while younger stars such as Errol Flynn, Cary Grant and Laurence Olivier were just beyond the age of conscription.[26]

In fact the community's efforts had been under way for many months. A committee, comprising actors Brian Aherne, Ronald Colman, Cedric Hardwicke, Herbert Marshall and Basil Rathbone, met weekly with Eric Cleugh to coordinate and plan the community's contributions to the cause. These included a wide range of activities. The Los Angeles headquarters of Bundles for Britain, for example, had a 'sewing unit' whose members included Gladys Cooper, Joan Fontaine and Dame May Whitty. Cooper and Whitty also organized an effort that would bring sixty children from the British Actors Orphanage in London to safety in the United States. Basil Rathbone organized efforts on behalf of the British War Relief Association, which sent stars such as Brian Aherne, Joan Fontaine, Charles Laughton, Anna Neagle, Laurence Olivier and Rathbone himself on tours throughout the United States and Canada for paid personal appearances. Aherne later remembered that he 'crossed and re-crossed the continent' with Joan Fontaine, raising money, while Anna Neagle recalled appearing everywhere from race tracks to aircraft factories in forty-seven states. Her efforts were said to have brought in $700,000. Charles Laughton contributed his salary for a weekly radio address, and made personal appearances in which he recited the Gettysburg Address to receptive American audiences. Cary Grant donated the $150,000 he received for his role in *The Philadelphia Story* (1940). Another $100,000 was raised from a stage production in Los Angeles of Noel Coward's *Tonight at 8:30* plays: Herbert Marshall and Rosalind Russell appeared in *Brief Encounter*, Brian Aherne and Greer Garson in *Ways and Means*, Reginald Gardiner and Binnie Barnes in *Red Peppers*, and Gladys Cooper, C. Aubrey

Smith and Joan Fontaine in *Family Album*. The community's most elaborate and prolonged effort, however, would be the production of *Forever and a Day*.[27]

Production of *Forever and a Day*

In March 1940, just two months after the first criticisms were made in *Picturegoer*, a meeting was held to explore the idea of a charity film. Cedric Hardwicke, Alfred Hitchcock, Victor Saville and Herbert Wilcox attended, and they decided that their first step should be to invite stars, writers and directors to participate. This was a clever strategy. As they undoubtedly expected, the response was outstanding and the resulting publicity generated attention and enthusiasm for the project. Promises of support came from stars Ronald Colman, Errol Flynn, Greer Garson, Cary Grant, Charles Laughton, Vivien Leigh, Herbert Marshall, Ray Milland, Anna Neagle, Merle Oberon, Laurence Olivier, Basil Rathbone, George Sanders and C. Aubrey Smith.[28] Even Charlie Chaplin, who had been in Hollywood for twenty-five years and had little connection with the community, indicated that there was 'a good chance' he would take part.[29] In addition to Hitchcock, Saville and Wilcox, directors Edmund Goulding, Frank Lloyd and Robert Stevenson were set to direct portions of the film; and writers A.J. Cronin, James Hilton, Aldous Huxley, Christopher Isherwood, W.P. Lipscomb and Alma Reville agreed to contribute to the script.[30] It was reported that producers all over Hollywood were spending their lunch hours tabulating the cost of the film if the participants were not donating their services free of charge. The agreed sum – said to have been figured on tablecloths and menus across Hollywood – was six million dollars.[31]

The film also needed financial backing, and the tide of interest ensured that MGM, RKO and the independent producer Samuel Goldwyn offered their services.[32] RKO offered the best terms. The new head of production, George Schaefer, was trying to lead RKO out of its financial difficulties by signing up high-profile, independent producers, and the all-star line-up of *Forever and a Day* made it just the sort of project that Schaefer was seeking. Schaefer and his colleagues at RKO repeatedly linked *Forever and a Day* to *Cavalcade*, which had raised the status of Fox Films a decade earlier, and they predicted that the new film would do the same for RKO. They also predicted that 'the grosses will be enormous'.[33] Of course, the grosses would go to charitable causes, but RKO's name would be attached to a timely and popular film, and the studio would have a strong product to market.

RKO's terms were generous. It was agreed that the studio would provide $300,000 in production funds, which was all that was deemed necessary for a film with such limited labour costs. In return, the production costs were to be repaid from the film's North American and British earnings, and the studio would also take 30 per cent of the worldwide earnings to pay for prints, publicity and distribution. Hardwicke, Hitchcock, Saville and Wilcox then became the board of governors for Charitable Productions, which would produce the film and distribute the proceeds to charities. As a means of counteracting those in the United States who might see the film as an exercise in British self-interest, it was decided that the earnings would be donated to causes within each country the film played. Thus, only the British earnings would benefit Britain, and the American earnings would go to American causes.[34]

With the financial matters settled, the producers faced the daunting task of assembling a script that could be filmed by several different directors, and one that would contain parts for a dozen of Hollywood's leading British stars as well as lesser parts for dozens of character actors. The segments and the characters of the story also would have to be of equal importance in order to avoid clashes of ego. This took some time. In fact, the producers originally promised to complete the film by June 1941, but it took until April 1941 to get an acceptable story outline.[35] This was written by W.P. Lipscomb and Robert Stevenson, who cast aside all the other ideas under consideration and used the most obvious source, *Cavalcade*, as their model. *Cavalcade* had been the first high-prestige 'British' film, and its story, concerning two families (masters and servants) living in one house, took a patriotic perspective on thirty years (1899–1929) of recent British history. It also called for a large cast. Thus, the story outlined by Lipscomb and Stevenson follows the history of a house and the two families who live in it, and it also uses particular moments in history to chronicle Britain's history. In order to allow an even larger cast, though, the time frame was expanded to 136 years (1804–1940).

Each episode was written with particular stars and a director in mind, so that each would serve as an echo of well-known films and characters. The first episode, set in 1804, was therefore taken by Herbert Wilcox, who had directed numerous patriotic historical dramas in Britain, including *Victoria the Great* (1937) and *Sixty Glorious Years* (1938). Like so many of Wilcox's films, these starred Anna Neagle, who also appears in this episode. More importantly, however, the film places C. Aubrey Smith at the centre of the entire film and at the top of the family tree which extends as the story unfolds. Smith was the grandest and the oldest of all of Hollywood's British gentlemen, and he appeared in innumerable 'British' films throughout the 1930s and the war years. In 1937, the film critic Bosley Crowther paid tribute to him in *The New York Times* by saying that Smith 'is Great Britain personified in the eyes of millions of people. Whenever he appears on screen – his elderly figure erect, his chin up and his eyes flashing out from under those beetling brows – it is as though an invisible band were playing Rule Britannia.'[36] It is only fitting then, that Smith's character serves as the patriarch of the film's families, and that his portrait is situated prominently in the house throughout much of the film.

The first episode begins as Admiral Eustace Trimble (Smith) and his wife (Dame May Whitty) choose the land on which the house will be built. The site that is chosen for the house is on the far outskirts of London and contains the remains of an ancient fortification. The old Admiral speculates that the fort was built to ward off invaders from Rome. He then alludes to the current threat of invasion by Napoleon Bonaparte 'if our Parliament doesn't stir itself'. If these lines were not written by R.C. Sherriff himself, they were certainly borrowed from his script for *That Hamilton Woman*. Once the house is built Susan Trenchard (Anna Neagle) is found unconscious on the doorstep one stormy night. Having run away from her malevolent guardian, Ambrose Pomfret (Claude Rains), she is saved from his clutches when young Bill Trimble (Ray Milland) agrees to marry her. Susan then gives birth to a son on the day that Napoleon is defeated at Trafalgar. Admiral Trimble exclaims that 'we're free from invasion forever!' and proudly quotes from Wordsworth ('We must be free or die, who speak the tongue/That Shakespeare spake'), again betraying the hand of Sherriff. The episode ends as news comes that Bill has died in the battle.

Wilcox finished filming the first episode within two weeks in May 1941. The second episode was then filmed by Robert Stevenson in June 1941.[37] Stevenson used the same cast as Wilcox, but in this brief episode Claude Rains' character, Mr Pomfret, plays a more significant role. Indeed, the film temporarily slips into the gothic horror mode so closely associated with the 'British' films made at Universal Studios. These included Rains' Hollywood debut, in *The Invisible Man* (1933), and here Rains once again plays the menacing and malevolent role. Following the death of Admiral Trimble and his wife, Mr Pomfret has used deceitful means to buy the house from an unsuspecting Susan. It is only

14 The portrait will survive: Mr Pomfret (Claude Rains) attempts to destroy the portrait of Admiral Trimble (C. Aubrey Smith) in *Forever and a Day* (1943)

when she and her son (Clifford Severn) are leaving that she discovers the true identity of the new owner. She tells Mr Pomfret that he will never be happy in the house, and indeed he is not. He is haunted by the portrait of Admiral Trimble, which taunts him, and when he climbs up a ladder to destroy it, he slips and falls to his death.

Filming then lapsed for several months. Alfred Hitchcock and Cary Grant had planned to work together on an episode as soon as they finished filming *Suspicion*, but delays on that film disrupted their schedules.[38] Victor Saville was also due to film an episode, but his commitments at MGM prevented him from beginning work until September 1941. It was hoped that this episode would centre upon Greer Garson and Ronald Colman, who were soon to appear together in *Random Harvest* (1942), and that Charlie Chaplin would appear in a non-speaking and comic role. But MGM apparently would not agree to the idea of an early teaming of Garson and Colman, and Chaplin refused to take part. In the place of Colman, MGM sent one of its featured players, Ian Hunter, and to replace Greer Garson, Victor Saville summoned the musical star Jessie Matthews from Britain. The star of numerous 1930s' musicals, many of which were directed by Saville himself, Matthews had been off screen for several years and welcomed the opportunity of making her Hollywood debut. The silent comedian Buster Keaton was also brought in to fill a role

15   An all-star cast that did not quite live up to expectations: the butler
(Charles Laughton), Dexter Pomfret (Ian Hunter) and Mildred Trimble (Jessie
Matthews) in *Forever and a Day* (1943)

that was intended for Chaplin. Saville finally had his cast and
directed the episode in September 1941.[39]

The only major Hollywood star to fulfil a promise to appear in
this third episode was Charles Laughton, who reprises his *Ruggles
of Red Gap* routine as an eccentric and haughty butler. Set in
1847, the episode begins as Mildred Trimble (Matthews) arrives
at the house to claim the portrait of Admiral Trimble. She is met
by the butler, upon whom the camera lingers for every long-suf-
fering gesture. The flighty and talkative Mildred does not take the
portrait, but marries her scholarly cousin, Dexter Pomfret
(Hunter), thereby uniting the once estranged Trimble and Pomfret families. Much to Dexter's consternation, Mildred insists on
having the modern luxury of a bathtub installed in the house.
This is done in a comically inept fashion by a pair of bumbling
plumbers (Cedric Hardwicke and Keaton). Dexter fears modernity,
but his troubled business, Pomfret Ironworks, is saved when it
begins making 'Pomfretware' bathtubs.

The fourth episode was prepared by Alfred Hitchcock with
Cary Grant and Ida Lupino in mind as the leads. The idea was to
provide an echo of a scene from *Cavalcade*, in which Queen Victoria's funeral procession passes the house, but to focus upon the

When Hollywood loved Britain

servants rather than the masters. Lupino, like Grant, seldom played the upper-class and genteel parts taken by so many of the Hollywood British. She was, in her own words, a 'poor man's Bette Davis', and when she occasionally played a British part, such as in *The Light That Failed*, she was a cockney rather than a lady.[40] Grant, of course, also avoided playing British gentlemen and preferred cockneys. Hence, they were to be Jenny the house-maid and Jim the handyman, who leave behind the snobbish Trimble-Pomfret family and depart for a better life in America. In October 1941, Hitchcock and Grant were still sending their regrets, and so the producers asked the French director René Clair to replace Hitchcock and Brian Aherne to take the place of Grant.[41]

Clair was not as out of place as one might assume. He later recalled that he was considered an 'honorary member' of the Hollywood British community because he had directed films in Britain during the 1930s.[42] The episode begins by showing the wealthy Trimble-Pomfrets assembling on their upstairs balcony to view Queen Victoria's funeral procession, but then departs from *Cavalcade* by following the skittish maid Jenny (Lupino), down the stairs and into the kitchen as she searches to find a vantage point for herself. Indeed, all sympathies in this episode are reserved for the servants. The family, led by Sir Anthony (Edward Everett Horton) and Lady Trimble-Pomfret (Isobel Elsom), have become the decadent and spoilt rich. When her husband dies, Lady Trimble-Pomfret even lets the house, and has the portrait of Admiral Trimble placed in the attic 'with the rest of the junk'. By that time, Jenny and Jim (Aherne) have departed for America, and because Jim is a distant cousin of the Trimbles, the family has branched out to become Anglo-American.

The fifth episode was filmed by Edmund Goulding over two weeks in November and December 1941. Goulding, the director of *The Dawn Patrol* (1938), was the appropriate choice for this First World War episode. While *The Dawn Patrol* centred on the waste of lives at the front, this episode portrays the heartaches back at home. It begins in 1917, when the young and exuberant American soldier Ned Trimble (Robert Cummings) – the son of Jenny and Jim – arrives in London on his way to France. The house is no longer on the outskirts of London but is part of the city's great sprawl. It is also a 'high-class boarding house', as Ned describes it, and he soon falls in love with its shy receptionist, Marjorie (Merle Oberon). The drama of the episode, however, cen-tres on an elderly couple, the Barringers (Gladys Cooper and Roland Young), who are waiting for news of their son. As dinner is served in the dining room, and with the staff and other guests surrounding them, the Barringers receive news that he has been killed, and they react with restraint and stoicism. Then Cooper gives the film's most affecting performance by quietly retiring to her room to weep. The boarding-house setting also enabled a number of the more prominent character actors – Nigel Bruce, Donald Crisp, Robert Coote, Reginald Gardiner, Elsa Lanchester and Una O'Connor – to make brief appearances. It was the character actors, in fact, who consistently supported the production from the beginning.

The first five episodes, filmed in forty-eight shooting days over an eight-month period, were finally completed in December 1941. They had been filmed in chronological order, and were set between 1804 and 1917. All that remained was to film a contemporary episode. Remarkably, at this late date the producers had difficulty deciding just how this might be done. They were eager to involve the United States' entry into the war, but it was a full six months before the script for this fifteen-minute sequence was complete. As late as April 1942 the producers were still meeting to 'discuss the beginning and end [of the film] and definitely decide upon the theme and purpose of this story'.[43] Frank Lloyd, the director of *Cavalcade*, agreed to direct the sixth and final episode, and also to make the final edit of the entire film. The producers decided that he should 'take up an arbitrary attitude and become the skipper of the ship in order to cut out further discussions and committee delays'.[44] As the director of *Cavalcade*, Lloyd was deemed the best choice to bring coherence to the sprawling narrative of *Forever and a Day*.

RKO and the producers were eager to bolster the film's star value in the final episode, but, in the event, it actually proved to be the most difficult to cast. The leading man was to be an American, who visits the house during a bombing raid in 1940, and the producers still were hoping to get Cary Grant. Frank Lloyd sent the script to Grant 'in the hope that his heart would be moved', but apparently it was not.[45] The British Consul was given the task of persuading Joan Fontaine, who was known to be on vacation, but she too refused.[46] Meanwhile, a frustrated Frank Lloyd threatened to quit the project in July 1942 if he wasn't given a cast within four weeks.[47] RKO was also impatient. In August 1942 the new head of production, Charles Koerner, wrote to the producers, pointing out that the film was not only fourteen months overdue but was also $150,000 over its original budget. He indicated that RKO would take control of the production if a cast list was not submitted by 7 September 1942, if filming hadn't

16   A high-class boarding house: The American Ned Trimble (Robert Cummings) at his ancestors' home, where he finds Marjorie (Merle Oberon), a nervous waitress (Elsa Lanchester) and Mr Barringer (Ronald Young) (1943)

begun by 15 September and been completed by 15 October.[48] Thus, when Frank Lloyd directed the sixth and final episode in September 1942, after nine months' delay, it was with American leads that RKO loaned to the production. In the place of Cary Grant there is Kent Smith, who had starred in two of RKO's recent low-budget hits, *Cat People* (1942) and *Hitler's Children* (1942). And in the part intended for Joan Fontaine there is Ruth Warrick, an American who had played Charles Foster Kane's first wife in *Citizen Kane* (1941).

Lloyd found to his dismay that the previous directors had not planned any devices to link the episodes. It was far too late to bring back the principal actors for such minor yet very necessary scenes. Lloyd decided that the only way around this was to set the first five episodes in flashback, and to have them linked by the sixth episode, which would open, close and punctuate the film.[49] Thus, the film begins in 1940 as the American Gates Pomfret (Kent Smith) arrives at the house and hears its story from the latest owner, his distant cousin Leslie Trimble-Pomfret (Ruth Warrick). The scenes are set during an air raid, and as she begins speaking the camera backs away from the house. Slowly, the blacked-out urban neighbourhood of 1940 is transformed into the bright and rural fields of 1804. The past episodes are linked together by shots of Gates and Leslie walking through the house, and by transition shots of the portrait of Admiral Trimble.

Initially, Gates Pomfret has no interest in his ancestors' home. His American family owns the house, and now that it is threatened by bombing, they want him to sell it at any price. Gates himself is eager to get back to America, where there is still 'meat seven days a week and sugar in my coffee'. He is thus the self-centred Yank, a staple of so many 'British' films made at this time. Even the sight of the local residents taking shelter in the cellar of the house (where a war poster of Churchill with the caption 'Let Us Go Forward Together' can be seen), and being led in song by the local vicar (Herbert Marshall), has little effect on Gates. But as Leslie speaks, and their shared heritage unfolds, his attitude gradually changes. In the ending, the house is hit by a bomb and falls to ruin. All that remains intact is the cellar archway, which bears the inscription that Admiral Trimble placed there shortly before Trafalgar, welcoming 'all who shelter here'. Like so many Yanks in 'British' films, Gates has been transformed by his exposure to the brave British, and declares that they will rebuild. The film ends with his overt statement of Anglo-American unity: 'that's our job – yours and mine'.

Release and reception

RKO and the film's producers must have been heartened when they tested the film on a preview audience. The preview took place at RKO's Pantages Theater in Los Angeles on 23 December 1942, and the responses were overwhelmingly favourable. The film was descibed on comment cards as 'a cinema masterpiece', 'marvelous', 'a great picture', 'the most interesting picture I have seen this year'. There were many references to the 'masterful portrayals' and 'splendid acting of the superlative cast'. The audience also seems to have welcomed the film's message and design: comments noted the 'interesting story promoting unity between the two nations' and that 'each player took a part they knew how to do best'. Only a comment which said 'an interesting subject for British audiences' struck a negative note.[50]

Critical responses were more varied. In *The New York Times*, Bosley Crowther applauded the film's 'amusing and affecting passages', but also commented that it was 'pleasant entertainment, particularly for those who dote on the past'. In Britain the populist *Evening Standard* praised the film's 'charm and comedy and emotion', but the loftier critics were hostile as ever to Hollywood's

Britain. The *Observer*'s C.A. Lejeune complained that 'the subject is seen mainly through the nostalgic eyes of the British colony in Hollywood' before condemning the film as 'monumentally and homogeneously dull', while in *The Sunday Times* Dilys Powell was 'somewhat embarrased by *Forever and A Day* because it is so obviously well meant'.[51]

The trade papers were more enthusiastic, and both *Variety* and *Kinematatograph Weekly* predicted box-office success.[52] The American public, however, clearly had little interest in the film. The North American gross reached only $862,745, and this was a particularly poor showing for a film released in 1943.[53] Nearly one hundred films earned over $1,000,000 in North America that year, and forty films passed the $2,000,000 mark.[54] In Britain, *Forever and a Day* earned $768,271, which was proportionately far better. Another $266,030 was derived from the remaining foreign markets, which included Australia, New Zealand, China, India, Egypt, Portugal, Sweden, Switzerland and a wide release throughout Latin America. While the film was not quite the blockbuster that it was intended to be, it did achieve the stated goal of raising money for charity. After deducting the production cost ($520,515) and RKO's fees ($572,849), there was $803,682 left for charitable causes. Donations were made in each country the film played, and the Red Cross was the most frequent recipient.[55]

By 1943, the film's other purpose – to show the Hollywood British community's commitment to the war – was no longer necessary. The press attacks had ceased when the United States entered the war, and many of those who had borne the brunt of the accusations had returned to Britain. Madeleine Carroll, Vivien Leigh and Laurence Olivier did not appear in the film because they departed as soon as they had freed themselves from other commitments. Herbert Wilcox and Anna Neagle waited until after they had filmed their episode, but they too felt obliged to return. Alexander Korda went back to work for MGM-British, and Alfred Hitchcock, anxious to be seen to have done his bit, returned to make two short films for the MoI. The other prominent members of the Hollywood British community devoted themselves to American causes. As Brian Aherne recalled, 'America's entry into the war changed the focus of our activities in Hollywood'. The committee that organized the British community's activities was disbanded and activities became focused on the Hollywood Victory Committee.[56] Hollywood, in fact, was taken over by a patriotic fever that resulted in numerous all-star and charity films. Films such as *Hollywood Canteen* (1944), *Stage*

Door Canteen (1943), *Star-Spangled Rhythm* (1942), *Thank Your Lucky Stars* (1943), *This is the Army* (1943) and *Thousands Cheer* (1943) were made to boost morale as much as to raise money, and they seem to have captured the public mood in the United States.

The American charity films were among the most popular films of the war years.[57] Some, of course, offered greater star value than *Forever and a Day*. More importantly, perhaps, each of the films is an energetic and flag-waving celebration of the American war effort, and this points toward the commercial weakness of *Forever and a Day* in the United States. As originally conceived in 1940, it was meant to be one of the first 'British' war films, thus capitalizing on American interest in Britain's heroic stance against the Nazis. By 1943, however, Hollywood had paid tribute to the British war effort in many different films, and the cycle of 'British' war films was near its end. Indeed, many of the leading stars may have backed out of the film simply because they (or their studios) feared over-exposure in such films. *Forever and a Day* emerged as an affectionate collection of reference points, but by 1943 it was neither timely nor relevant. The film refers to an era in which the American fascination with Britain was at its peak. That era was coming to an end, and whether the Hollywood British realized it or not, *Forever and a Day* was one sign of its passing.

'British' films and the Office of War Information

7

When the United States entered the Second World War in December 1941, Hollywood's careful and cautious approach to war films finally came to an end. The Hays Office no longer concerned itself with 'hate pictures', and producers making war films were not asked to skirt around the issues of who, what, where and how. The isolationist cause was dead, and the Senate investigation of Hollywood's anti-Nazi and pro-British bias, which had been due to resume in January 1942, was cancelled. Suddenly, the studios were able to make as many war films as they wanted, and to make them as specific and biased as they wished. During the war years, Hollywood could in fact present itself as an all-purpose morale booster, educator and entertainer, as the studios poured forth a stream of films celebrating the war effort, exploring war themes and issues, or simply offering escapism.

In Britain, some 'British' films had already received praise for the values and ideas that they projected. *Goodbye Mr Chips* (1939), for example, was cited in an MoI document as an ideal example of how feature films should portray Britain in wartime. The MoI was also reported to have urged the swift release of *The Sea Hawk* (1940). And a wider range of 'British' films received implicit praise when Lord Lothian told Hollywood's Britons that they would best serve their country by continuing to make patriotic 'British' films in Hollywood. Such positive comments were made before the United States entered the war, though, and at a time when British officials undoubtedly welcomed any support they received from the neutral United States. Once the USA had entered the war, 'British' films received far more scrutiny and criticism. In the opinion of both the OWI and the MoI, many 'British' films emphasized the wrong aspects of Britain, particularly in regard to American audiences. Both agencies stressed notions of 'the people's war', a war fought not only against fascism but for egalitarian and democratic principles. Thus, while Hollywood's nostalgic brand of 'British' patriotism may have seemed laudable between September 1939 and December 1941, by 1942 it was considered to be distinctly backward, and 'British' films became a major source of contention between the propagandists and the Hollywood studios.

The OWI in Hollywood

Cinema-going was a regular, weekly habit for most Americans in the 1940s, and its capacity to influence and persuade was thought to be powerful. The Roosevelt Administration saw its potential as a means of communicating what came to be known as the 'war information program', but at the same time realized that the idea of a propaganda agency with official power, or government control of the film industry, would go against the grain of American ideals. Propaganda and government censorship were associated with the fascist enemy, not a democracy such as the United States. Hence, a compromise was found in which the newly created OWI would 'advise' the Hollywood studios on how to portray war issues in feature films, but it would not have any statutory power or control over film-makers.

The OWI's duties were far-reaching: to monitor public opinion toward war issues and to disseminate information about the war and its related issues to all forms of the media. Films were one part of its duties, but the OWI's Bureau of Motion Pictures (BMP) was just one branch of a much larger organization, which dealt mainly with the journalists of radio, newspapers and magazines. Key posts at the OWI and even the BMP were filled with men from backgrounds in these other media. Elmer Davis, the director of the OWI, was a former journalist and radio commentator. The director of the BMP was Lowell Mellett, a former editor of *The Washington Daily News*. Mellett worked at the OWI's main offices in Washington DC, and his west-coast liaison was Nelson Poynter, the publisher of *The St Petersburg Times*. These appointments bewildered many in Hollywood, who thought that the posts should have gone to prominent Hollywood executives. Neither Mellett nor Poynter had any experience of the film industry or any form of show business. But the OWI was the creation of the Roosevelt Administration, and so the appointments were made on the basis of political beliefs. Mellett and Poynter were known as supporters of Roosevelt's New Deal policies and as ardent, pre-war interventionists.[1]

In keeping with the larger OWI philosophy, the BMP encouraged film-makers to portray the Second World War as a 'people's war'. The war was to be seen as a struggle for the 'common man', and for a more democratic and egalitarian post-war world, in which the 'four freedoms' (freedom of speech and religion, freedom from want and fear) would flourish. It was hoped by the OWI that this philosophy would be seen not only in war films, but in films of all kinds. For example, when TCF submitted a script for *Jane Eyre*, the OWI reviewer expressed disappointment that an opportunity to make a timely statement had been missed. The reviewer suggested *Jane Eyre* should become the story of Jane's 'fight for freedom', which could parallel 'the fight for freedom which is raging today'. It was further suggested that the scriptwriters could be informed on this by reading a recent speech given by Vice-President Henry Wallace 'on the struggle of the common man against the people and things that would enslave him'.[2]

Of course, the film industry had many liberal and left-wing writers and directors who would have welcomed such advice and sentiments, but most were not in positions of power. Those who did wield power were the studio executives and producers, and for the most part they were remarkably conservative men. Furthermore, the industry's leaders were deeply suspicious of outsiders and particularly suspicious of the federal government. They had been fighting various forms of federal intervention in the industry's affairs for many years. They were not likely, then, to welcome into their businesses a group of New Deal bureaucrats, and especially New Deal bureaucrats without any experience of film-making. This is not to say that all of Hollywood's studios and producers refused to cooperate with the OWI. The level of cooperation differed from studio to studio, and even differed among individual producers within a single studio. The OWI found that its advice was most welcome when the studios were dealing with war topics that they had not encountered previously, such as portraying Russia and China as sympathetic allies. When film-makers were on more familiar ground, as they were with 'British' films, they would take or disregard advice as it suited them. This limited cooperation became the source of much frustration for Mellett and Poynter.

When the OWI began reviewing scripts and completed films in June 1942, the reviewers were struck by Hollywood's frequently simple-minded approach to war stories. The studios were eager to make use of topical wartime subjects – spy stories, villainous Japanese and German characters, service comedies – but most often they did so only within the confines of their own generic formulae.[3] By the end of 1942, having seen such films for six months, and with little improvement visible on the horizon, Lowell Mellett began to seek a measure of power over the studios. The first attempt did not go well. Mellett made a public request for the studios not only to submit all of their scripts and films for review, but asked that this be done more promptly. That way, he declared, if there were problems, the studios would not have to go through the costly procedures of rewriting and reshooting. This sounded too much like a set of demands and threats to the industry, which became united in opposition to the OWI. Industry representatives as far apart as the conservative Martin Quigley and the liberal Walter Wanger found a common cause in rejecting these 'directives from amateurs'. Mellett was soon backtracking, and admitted that he had no right to make 'demands' but had merely 'suggested' the new procedures.[4]

His conciliatory tone masked the OWI's true intentions. When it became clear that the film industry was not willing to cooperate voluntarily, the OWI looked to the Office of Censorship for powers of coercion. This was the only censorship agency that had any legal power, and in fact every film that was exported from the United States had to receive an export license from the Office of Censorship. Its power initially was limited to censoring military secrets, but nevertheless Mellett and Poynter began to urge the official censors to consult with the OWI before granting an export license to a film. That way, the studios would have a financial incentive to the follow the OWI's advice. The OWI was, in effect, seeking an authority similar to that obtained by the Hays Office in the early 1930s. As the Hays Office's interaction with the Legion of Decency had made clear, a realizable threat of punitive economic measures was the most effective means of gaining influence in Hollywood.[5]

There were two key problems in convincing the Office of Censorship to cooperate. The first was that the BMP was within the OWI's domestic division, meaning that it was concerned with film content in regard to American audiences. The Office of Censorship, on the other hand, dealt only with material leaving or entering the United States: the two bodies therefore had distinct, non-overlapping remits. The second problem was that the Office of Censorship could deny export licenses only to films that showed the locations of military bases, war-related production factories or other information valuable to the enemy. The latter point was overcome in December 1942 when the code was strengthened to include films that portrayed 'labor, class or other disturbances since 1917 which might be distorted into enemy propaganda'. The new clause was not far-reaching enough to cover all of the BMP's concerns, but it did widen the powers of censorship to include unsuitable stories and scenes, where previously its concerns were limited to military secrets. At the same time, Mellett arranged to have an executive from the OWI's overseas branch join the BMP, thereby widening its own responsibilities from domestic to global concerns, and arriving at common ground with the Office of Censorship. The newcomer to the BMP was Ulric Bell, formerly the editor of *The Louisville Courier* and a leader of the 'Fight for Freedom' interventionist group before the war. Bell set out on a campaign to convince the Office of Censorship that its interests were very similar to those of the OWI. Part of this effort lay in angling the film reviews away from domestic concerns and instead emphasizing how American films would be perceived abroad.[6]

The key event in bringing together the OWI and the Office of Censorship was the Allies' liberation of territory previously occupied by the enemy. Where the troops went, films soon followed, and it was the duty of the Office of Censorship to decide which films the troops should take to the newly liberated peoples of North Africa, Europe and the Far East.[7] The Office of Censorship was eager to share with the OWI this new responsibility of deciding which films should be shown in liberated areas. It was an enormous task, as Hollywood made hundreds of features films each year, and many occupied territories had not seen any since 1939. The OWI rated the films as 'recommended', 'suitable but not recommended' or 'unsuitable', and in some instances the ratings would differ on a country by country basis. *Mrs Miniver*, for example, was 'suitable' for every country except Germany, presumably because of its stereotyped Nazi character.[8]

Thus, beginning with the Allies' success in North Africa during the autumn of 1942, the OWI had the power to permit or to deny a film entry into previously closed foreign markets. This was, of course, an incentive for the studios to seek and follow OWI advice. It was not always strong enough to sway producers, but it did lead them to consider more carefully the issues raised by the OWI. Most importantly, the increased responsibility came at a time when the agency was under fierce attack from a newly elected Congress. The 1942 elections had brought a Republican resurgence in Congress, and the Republicans were eager to silence the OWI, which had been termed a 'mouthpiece for the New Deal'. They did so in July 1943, by reducing the agency's budget to a fraction of its former standing. The resulting cuts were so deep that the domestic branch was closed altogether, and Lowell Mellett and Nelson Poynter lost their jobs. In the midst of a world war, the overseas division was considered more necessary, and so the portion of the BMP that fell within the overseas division survived the cuts. Ulric Bell, along with a staff of reviewers, continued to consider scripts and films until the entire OWI was disbanded at the end of August 1945.[9]

American attitudes toward the British

The OWI's *Government Information Manual for the Motion Picture Industry*, which was distributed throughout the industry in the summer of 1942, offered guidelines and pointers for film-makers. It covers the 'five aspects of the war that need to be better understood': why we fight, the nature of the enemy, the Allies, the home front and the fighting forces. The section on Britain draws attention to American criticisms of the British:

Public opinion polls show that even among staunch supporters of the United Nations, there is a tendency to be critical of the British, their past Imperialistic policies, and the purposes of certain elements in Britain. But, the British people are putting up a magnificent battle. Where would we be today if Britain had not continued to resist in the critical year when she stood alone, unprepared, and without allies, against the Axis?[10]

Thus, the OWI policy would be to emphasize British heroism and commitment to the war effort, while avoiding the Britain of empire and class ('certain elements'). This baffled many in Hollywood, who knew that the Britain of empire and class was the only Britain that Americans were interested in, at least so far as films were concerned. But the OWI did not draw its policies from box-office takings. Rather, they were formed on the basis of its frequent surveys of public opinion throughout the United States, and these gave a very different impression from that of the box office.

One of the most substantial OWI surveys on American attitudes toward the British was conducted in April 1943. The survey had a representative sample of 3,600 people, made up of people from diverse geographical regions and income groups, as well as different levels of educational achievement. The survey's results confirmed what several earlier surveys, with smaller samples, had already shown. Few Americans proclaimed an outright and complete dislike of Britain and the British people, but they did have strong criticisms on a number of different national characteristics and institutions. Most prominent among these were snobbery, Imperialism, the class system and the political system. There was also little regard for the British war effort. The fact that a considerable number of these negative traits were emphasized in many 'British' films could only have alarmed the OWI.[11]

One of the most striking findings of the surveys was that the American public did not rate the British war effort very highly. The question posed was, 'Considering what each country could do, which one do you think is trying hardest to win the war?' Britain came in a very distant last place, ranking far behind the other principal Allies.[12] The responses were:

Russia	31%
The United States	27%
China	19%
Britain	5%

Nor did Americans rank Britain's war motives very highly. While 70 per cent of Americans thought the United States was fighting for 'freedom, democracy and the defeat of totalitarianism', only 40 per cent of Americans attributed these 'idealistic motives' to Britain. The remaining 60 per cent thought that Britain was fighting for 'selfish reasons'. The most frequently cited selfish reasons were 'self-defence/survival' (37 per cent), 'the defence of her Empire' (22 per cent) and 'Imperialism/world power' (15 per cent).[13] Clearly, the opinions and accusations voiced by isolationists prior to the attack on Pearl Harbor had not been forgotten.

The survey also found that Americans had little knowledge of the British Empire, yet the subject brought out strongly negative opinions. When asked, 'have the British treated the people in their colonies and possessions fairly or unfairly in recent years?', 31 per cent of those polled fell into the 'don't know' category, and, in nearly equal percentage scores, the others indicated that they thought the British treated their colonies 'fairly' (38 per cent) and 'unfairly' (31 per cent). However, it was also noted that of those who replied 'unfairly', 80 per cent cited India as 'the chief example'; and 66 per cent of all respondents stated that India should be granted independence either immediately or as soon as the war ended.[14]

Other questions revealed that only a minority of Americans could be termed outright Anglophiles or Anglophobes. On the favourable side, 25 per cent of those polled 'found nothing to dislike about the British'. At the opposite end of the spectrum, only

10 per cent stated that they 'like nothing about the British'. The remaining 65 per cent had a mixture of likes and dislikes. Among the qualities Americans liked most about the British were 'sportsmanship and patriotism' (32 per cent), their 'democratic ideals and love of freedom' (21 per cent) and their 'culture and intelligence' (6 per cent). The commentary on the survey notes, though, that the findings reveal 'darker features that should not be minimalized'. Americans were very clear in what they disliked about the British:

Turning to dislikes, the poll brings one fact into all the prominence of a sore thumb. East and West, North and South, among educated and uneducated, the objections to the British center far more largely in their superiority, self-complacency, snobbery and love of class distinction than in anything else.[15]

The commentator grouped these traits together to conclude that 43 per cent of those polled agreed on this 'single group of undesirable qualities'.

In tandem with this dislike of British snobbery and the class system came the belief that Britain was not as democratic a country as the United States. In fact, some Americans believed that Britain was not a democracy at all. When asked, 'Which do you think have more say about the way their government is run, the British people or the American people?', the replies were:

The American people	66%
Don't know	14%
The two countries are equal	11%
The British people	9%

The commentator noted that among the majority who believed that democracy was stronger in the United States, there was 'a widespread belief that the British people are under personal rule of the sovereign'. 'Typical comments' included:

They're under a king and we're not.
The British are still under a king.
We vote for the man we want in.
We can write to our Congressmen and refuse to re-elect them; the House of Lords is not elected and is not as free as the elected Congress.
England is more like a dictatorship.
The English Government is more or less composed of royalty – a group of people who automatically come into office upon the death of a father or nearest relative; they're not elected to represent the people. In this country if we don't like a man after four years we can always get him out.

Thus, the commentator stated that Americans were 'extremely uninformed' about the British governmental system and were 'misled by external features, notably the Crown and the House of Lords'.[16] In a summary of the entire survey, it was concluded that:

It is evident that there is a widespread tendency to think of British folk, their characteristics, war aims, social and political system, and Empire, in stereotyped terms. Symbols or crude images have taken the place of precise ideas. This is strikingly demonstrated, for example, in the general emphasis on snobbery, smugness, and arrogance as British traits. It is also shown in the numerous comments on the aristocracy and nobility as an unwholesome British excrescence, the speakers obviously having an exaggerated idea of the part that titles and wealth play in present-day British life.[17]

It is plain to see how such attitudes and opinions could be formed or reinforced by 'British' films. A sense of sportsmanship is held to be the overriding national characteristic in *A Yank at Oxford* (1938), while British culture and patriotism are celebrated in nearly every 'British' film of the 1930s. But it is not only the positive aspects of the British that are seen in 'British' films. They also served as reminders of British Imperialism, the class system, snobbery and arrogance. Whether the films reflected or projected these views was not a point that the OWI pondered. Its purpose was to ensure that the negative aspects were not furthered in films or in any other medium. To this end, survey findings such as these were shared with Hollywood's leading executives.[18] Nevertheless, the OWI found it very difficult to steer producers away from the established 'British' film genres, which now had the added attraction of wartime topicality and relevance.

British Empire films

Hollywood had been making British Empire films for many years, and films such as *The Green Goddess* (1930), *Clive of India* (1934), *Lives of a Bengal Lancer* (1934), *Wee Willie Winkie* (1937), *Gunga Din* (1939) and *Stanley and Livingstone* (1939) were typical of the proud and patriotic approach to all things British in the 1930s. Some film-makers undoubtedly thought that they were making a valuable contribution to the British war effort when, in the early war years, they updated the genre to the present conflict. Like the earlier British Empire films, films such as *Safari* (1940), *The Sun Never Sets* (1939) and *Sundown* (1941) portray the good and civilizing influence of the British in their Empire. The novelty in these films is that, rather than fighting the uncivilized natives, the

British are now protecting the natives from fascists. The Hays Office's cautious policies ensured that the nationality of the fascists is never revealed, but American film-makers were by this time adept at implication. This trend toward more topical British Empire films was set to continue in 1942, with of course much more explicit information about the enemy, but the OWI was adamant that the genre should be abandoned altogether.

The OWI disapproved of the Empire films on several grounds. First, the films were a reminder to American audiences of British Imperialism. As the OWI's surveys indicate, many Americans not only thought that Britain treated its colonies unfairly, but also thought that the British were fighting only to defend the Empire. OWI policy was to avoid such negative issues rather than engage with them. Second, the portrayal of the superior British and the inferior natives did not accord with the OWI's view of a 'people's war' that was being fought for democratic and egalitarian principles. Third, the films were known to cause offence within the Empire itself. When *Lives of a Bengal Lancer* (1935) was released in India, for example, the reviewer for the *Times of India* could not contain his scorn. The film, the reviewer warned, was 'a strong incitement to sedition' which was likely to arouse 'violent and deeply subversive feelings' in Indian viewers.[19] The OWI was adamant that India, a country of great strategic importance during the war, should not be offended by further Empire films.

The issue arose in the BMP's first month of operations, June 1942, when Lowell Mellett heard that RKO was planning to re-release *Gunga Din* (1939), one of the most popular films ever produced at that studio.[20] Loosely adapted from a story by Rudyard Kipling, this light-hearted film is a boy's own adventure story concerning three British soldiers in India. Amid their brawls, high jinks and practical jokes, the three thwart a plot to massacre the British army. The film identifies Britain's enemies in India as the members of a cult which worships the evil and bloodthirsty goddess Kali, and – unfortunately from the perspective of 1942 – it makes it appear as though all Indians indulge in such savagery and that all Indians hate the British, who appear to be no more than an unwelcome occupying force. The exception is the character Gunga Din, the water boy of the soldiers' unit, who is a faithful servant of the British but also a mistreated one. The soldiers are callous and patronizing toward him. Nonetheless, his overriding ambition is to join the British Army, and he eventually gives his life to save the unit from the evil cult. For his heroism, Gunga Din is posthumously appointed a Corporal.

Lowell Mellett's first concern was the offence that *Gunga Din* could cause if the re-release reached India or became known to Indian leaders:

I am told that at the time of its first release there was a great deal of criticism from Indian leaders who resented the manner in which the people of India were presented. If that is true, the resentment at this time doubtless would be much greater and the consequences of such resentment might be serious.[21]

RKO was asked to withdraw the film, but studio head Ned Depinet complained that much had been spent already on prints and advertising for the re-release. He sent word to Mellett that 'as a patriotic American', he would comply with Mellett's request, but only if the OWI actually viewed *Gunga Din* and declared it to be harmful.[22] If Depinet hoped that the film would charm the OWI, he was entirely mistaken. The reviewer declared that *Gunga Din* 'can only aggravate the very delicate Anglo-Indian situation', and widened the critique to include the values that the film projects:

The picture glorifies British Imperialism. The assumption of the picture is that it is right for Britain to hold an alien country by force of arms. At a time when we are stressing that the current war is a people's war, this is an obviously inopportune comment.

The film was so 'hotly prejudiced' that it seemed to generate a nascent Anglophobia within the reviewer. The leader of the evil Indian cult was said to 'sound a distinctly sympathetic note' because he was willing to fight for the independence of his country. The reviewer was also perturbed by the racist manner in which Gunga Din is treated, and warned that this 'hardly squares with the notion that Britain is fighting the battle of all democratic peoples'.[23] In the midst of a 'people's war', it seems, there was no place for Kipling and his view of the British Empire, and so *Gunga Din* was put on the shelf for the duration of the war.

In the same month that *Gunga Din* was withdrawn, September 1942, Victor Saville announced plans that he would produce an adaptation of Kipling's *Kim* for MGM. Without realizing that he would alarm rather than reassure the OWI, Saville informed the agency that *Kim* was sure to demonstrate the protective role that Britain had played in India.[24] In the script prepared in 1942, the character Kim would be a British orphan, raised in India by Indians, who in adulthood is torn between life as a Buddhist and life in the British Secret Service. If he joins the Secret Service, Kim is told, he will protect India from tribal warfare, 'Tokyo's reaching hand' and 'Berlin's dream of domination'. After becoming involved in wartime espionage, Kim duly chooses the Secret Service and a life of fighting against the Axis powers.[25] For the OWI, it was not simply that making *Kim* would be impolitic, but – in Nelson Poynter's words – that *Kim* was 'an apology for British imperialism'. Kipling's views on the 'white man's burden', he asserted, were 'offensive to approximately one billion of our fellow citizens of the earth'.[26]

Kim was planned as a major production, with stars Mickey Rooney, Basil Rathbone and Conrad Veidt, and the studio was reluctant to abandon the heavy investment that it had already put into developing the script. Victor Saville tried to work out a compromise, proposing that Kipling's 'simple story of faith' could be restored and the wartime setting dropped, and that even the emphasis upon 'the advantages India enjoyed under British rule' could be lessened.[27] But Kipling under any guise was unacceptable to the OWI, and this view received the backing of the British government. Lowell Mellett presented Saville with ten pages of commentary 'prepared by experts of your own government' that detailed the 'myriad of opportunities ... for giving offense' with *Kim*.[28] This convinced MGM and Saville to postpone the production until after the war.

It is unlikely that MGM, if it had chosen to, could have hidden a major production such as *Kim* from the OWI. The trade papers and gossip columns would have reported on the film long before filming was completed. Warner Bros., however, was able to complete a low-budget 'B' film, *Adventure in Iraq* (1943), and also to obtain an export license for the film, before the OWI heard anything about it. Much to the OWI's dismay, this had become the trick of smaller studios and even large studios when dealing with 'B' films. The OWI would have to explain to the Office of Censorship why it had been wrong to grant a film an export license, and the censors could not always be convinced.[29] *Adventure in Iraq*, however, proved to be an exception to this. A remake of *The Green Goddess* (filmed in 1924 and 1930), the new and updated *Adventure in Iraq* begins when a plane carrying three Americans crashes in the Iraqi desert. The plane's radio is broken, and the three Americans are at the mercy of a tribe of 'devil-worshippers' who offer human sacrifices to their gods. Then they are 'rescued' by a wealthy and cosmopolitan sheik, who, it emerges, intends to execute them. The sheik is played by the British actor Paul Cavanagh, yet he tells the Americans that he is negotiating a treaty with Hitler and that he hates the British, who covet his oil-rich land. The Americans hope that the sheik's British butler will help them escape, but the butler is filled with resentment for Britain and, having declared his support for Germany, he asks, 'what did the British ever do for me but put me into a reformatory?' In the end, the US Air Force threatens to bomb the sheik's village if the Americans are not released. The sheik calls their bluff, but when the bombing begins he releases the Americans.

The BMP first encountered *Adventure in Iraq* when the film was finished and ready for release in December 1942. Its many objections included the portrayal of Iraq, a neutral country, as pro-Axis; the portrayal of Iraqis as 'devil-worshippers'; and the ending, which shows the US Air Force bombing the village of a neutral country. *Adventure in Iraq* was also held to be 'definitely anti-British'. The 'cut-throat and renegade' butler would cause offence to British audiences and mislead American audiences. Furthermore, the Sheik states that the British cannot be trusted in business deals, and that he prefers to do business with the Germans. The latter point was seen by the OWI to be particularly objectionable:

There has been a great deal of Nazi propaganda on the subject of British imperialism already. To add to it, no matter how innocently, is simply to play into Axis hands.[30]

Nelson Poynter asked Warner Bros. not to release the film until 'very serious consideration' had been given to the review, but the studio already had its export license and intended to proceed. Only the intervention of the US State Department stopped the film from being released abroad. Thus, *Adventure in Iraq* became the one and only film produced by Warners in the 1940s to be confined to the domestic market alone.[31]

By 1943 it had become clear to all of the studios that Empire films were forbidden, and the genre remained dormant for the duration of the war. This was a significant achievement for the OWI, although undoubtedly it was helped by the intervention of the MoI (in the case of *Kim*) and the US State Department (with *Adventure in Iraq*). It also is apparent that the issue at stake was not simply a matter of the OWI's war information programme, or of American attitudes toward Britain. Rather, the concern over Empire films involved the strategic importance of India. Hollywood's film-makers would give way in a matter of war strategy, but they were not so easily swayed by the OWI's ideological views and criticisms.

Horror films and spy films

In the 1930s Britain had often served as the setting for some of Hollywood's best horror films, including *Dracula* (1931), *The Old*

Dark House (1932), *Dr Jekyll and Mr Hyde* (1932) and *The Invisible Man* (1933). And the studios' predilection for remaking films and updating them to wartime settings did not exclude the horror genre. In fact, the Blitz and the blackout served as the starting point for numerous ghoulish scenarios. In *The Return of the Vampire* (1943) Dracula is freed when a bomb hits the crypt in which he has been held captive. In *The Brighton Strangler* (1943), an actor receives a head injury during the Blitz, causing him to assume the identity of the crazed murderer he portrays on stage. And *The London Blackout Murders* (1942) pays homage to London's macabre history by using Jack the Ripper's former home as its setting. Only the latter film caused difficulties. This was because the victims of the 'blackout murders' are a group of British and Swedish industrialists who are trying to arrange a negotiated peace with Germany. The film raised a number of uncomfortable points for the OWI, but the implication that the British government would consider a negotiated peace was considered intolerable. Ulric Bell thought that it should be denied an export license, or at the very least banned in Britain. But this was another instance in which the studio, Republic, had the cunning to acquire its export license before showing the film to the OWI, and the Office of Censorship was not willing to withdraw the license.[32]

Spy stories, meanwhile, were viewed with equal disdain. This was not a complaint reserved for 'British' films alone. The OWI held that Hollywood generally had exaggerated the activities of spies and saboteurs. The particular problem with 'British' spy stories was that they would do little to enhance American confidence in the British war effort. Universal remade *The Great Impersonation* (1935), for example, by updating the First World War story to the Second World War. In the later film, the spies are identified as a group of British fascists working to turn their country over to the Nazis. The OWI objected to this, and also to the film's portrayal of the British war effort, which centres on wealthy and titled officials who seem to spend much of their time engaged in a whirl of social events. As the reviewer commented, *The Great Impersonation* (1942) 'gives the impression that the war is somehow being decorously fought over a tea table in a very handsomely furnished British drawing room'.[33] At a time when Americans apparently had little respect for the British war effort, this was seen as an unfortunate scenario.

Sherlock Holmes and the Voice of Terror (1942) provided another view of official incompetence. Scotland Yard is unable to stop a Nazi saboteur who is wreaking havoc throughout the country, and so Sherlock Holmes is called to the rescue as the only man

17   Sherlock Holmes saves the day: Dr Watson (Nigel Bruce) looks on as Sherlock Holmes (Basil Rathbone) contemplates the saboteur problem in *Sherlock Holmes and the Voice of Terror* (1942)

who can save Britain from chaos. Holmes, of course, finds the saboteur and exposes a complicit government official. Hence, the British government is seen to be inept and also to harbour German spies.[34] Doubts about the British government were also seen in other spy films. In *Secrets of Scotland Yard* (1943), another Republic 'B' film, a Nazi spy is working within the British government's code deciphering unit.[35] In Paramount's *Ministry of Fear* (1944) there is also a Nazi spy ring operating in Britain, but it is much more widespread and the leader is a government official who has access to the allies' plans for the invasion of Europe. Furthermore, the spy ring's operations are masked behind a wartime charity innocently entitled the 'Mothers of Free Nations', and the most menacing and mysterious character is finally revealed to be a Scotland Yard detective. This is the paranoid world of *film noir*, but to the OWI *Ministry of Fear* was also 'an unfortunate picture of one of our allies'.[36] At this later point in the war, the OWI was able to give the film an 'unsuitable' rating for the liberated territories.

MGM: 'as pro-British as any Britisher'

MGM's 'British' films proved to be the most troublesome for the

OWI, not least because of the popularity and high profile of films such as *Mrs Miniver* (1942), *Random Harvest* (1942) and *The White Cliffs of Dover* (1944). Indeed, by the time *Mrs Miniver* made its premiere in Washington DC in July 1942, it had already become noteworthy enough for the British Ambassador, Lord Halifax, to attend the event in his official capacity. Halifax seemed to approve of the film, at least initially. He sent telegrams to director William Wyler and producer Sidney Franklin, congratulating them on the film's 'excellence' and adding that he considered it 'such an accurate and moving record of the way the normal English family carries on under war conditions'.[37] But the Ambassador's opinion apparently changed once he had discussed the film with his staff at the British Embassy. Lord Halifax told Sidney Bernstein that the embassy staff were 'appalled' by *Mrs Miniver* and considered the film 'a shocking and distorted picture of Britain'. Bernstein was the recipient of these comments because he had acted as a technical adviser on *Mrs Miniver*. He was so shaken by the criticisms that he commissioned a Gallup poll to prove that this film, together with two others he had advised upon, *Eagle Squadron* (1942) and *This Above All* (1942), actually had inspired support for Britain among Americans. Gallup reportedly indicated that Americans who had seen the films were 'seventeen percent more favourable toward Britain than those who had not', but no further details of the survey are available.[38]

Mrs Miniver continues to inspire reactions ranging from love to loathing whenever and wherever it is shown, but the most divergent reactions occurred in Britain during wartime. It was, for example, acclaimed as 'the best film on English wartime life' in *The Daily Herald*, and condemned as 'unconsciously pro-Fascist propaganda' in *The Spectator*.[39] *The Times* offered a somewhat condescending appraisal on its review page, but then found reasons to praise the film on its news pages in several instances when it was reported to have created a favourable impression abroad. Reports from neutral countries such as Argentina, Sweden and Switzerland told of its box-office success and its success in swaying public opinion toward Britain and against Germany. The film's impact in the USA was also considered newsworthy by *The Times*:

Mrs Miniver, whatever criticism may be made of it as a picture of English life, is generally accounted here as one of the most effective pieces of propaganda for Great Britain since the war began.[40]

This backhanded compliment is typical of the confusion the film engendered. There was no denying that *Mrs Miniver* seemed able to seduce a majority of the audience wherever it played, and to have people of many different countries weeping on behalf of Britain. Yet it was also said to be an inaccurate portrait of Britain at war, and, with its emphasis on a rural, affluent and unrepresentative way of life, an ill-judged approach to portraying the 'people's war'. This was particularly the attitude of propagandists, such as those at the OWI, who probably thought a great deal more about the 'people's war' than anyone else. And it was certainly the stance of Britain's highbrow film critics, who favoured realism above all else and resisted sentimentality.

In fact, *Mrs Miniver* provoked differing responses even within the OWI itself. When the film was reviewed in August 1942 the reviewer found it to be a 'thoughtful, moving and handsomely mounted picture', and praised its portrayal of the people's war and its depiction of the 'crumbling of the ancient, crusty prejudices of class and pedigree'. Only a final sentence admitted that the portrayal of class relations was 'patronizing' and questioned whether 'this sort of thing is going to sell Americans on British democracy'.[41] It was a brief and hasty review, like those given to other films (including *Eagle Squadron* and *This Above All*) which had already been released when the OWI arrived in Hollywood.[42] Then, three weeks later a longer and much more negative review was written on *Mrs Miniver*. This second review criticized at length the portrayal of the servants as simpletons, the manner in which the classes interact, and the Minivers' inappropriately lavish lifestyle.[43] Second reviews were unusual at the OWI, which had literally dozens of scripts and films to review each week, and thus little time for second thoughts. In this case, the additional attention is likely to have stemmed from the hostile reviews the film received in Britain. The *Spectator* review was sent to the BMP by Ferdinand Kuhn, the deputy director of the OWI's British division in Washington DC. It was the duty of the British division to monitor and influence American information about Britain and British information about America. Kuhn, who previously had been the London correspondent for *The New York Times*, was convinced that films such as *Mrs Miniver* and *Random Harvest* were bad from both points of view. He insisted that the films reinforced Americans' negative perceptions of Britain, and that the British resented Hollywood's portrayal of their country. The latter point in particular was stressed once the BMP had moved to the OWI's overseas branch, and overseas concerns superseded domestic concerns.[44]

Kuhn was by far the most vehement of those at the OWI who considered MGM's 'British' films to be harmful. His objection to

Random Harvest, for example, rested entirely upon a single scene in the House of Commons, in which Ronald Colman and Greer Garson have tea on the terrace. Around them are many MPs, and Kuhn's criticism was that these MPs seem 'snobbish and stuffy', whereas a true picture, he insisted, would include 'actual workers and trade union officials'. This was his constant concern: that films set in the present should portray a more modern and egalitarian country. This was not a part of MGM's vision of Britain, but in this instance the studio had a rather simple excuse for not changing the scene. When asked to reshoot it, with 'less immaculate clothing and more of the good Yorkshire or Lancashire accent in evidence', the studio declined on the grounds that the sets had been dismantled and the cast disbanded months earlier.[45]

If Kuhn was overzealous, however, it should be noted also that MGM was remarkably unconcerned by criticisms made of its 'British' films, including criticisms far more substantial than those made of *Random Harvest*. The studio's dismissal of such concerns is particularly apparent in its decision to produce *A Yank at Eton* in 1942. The script for *A Yank at Eton* had been on the shelf and gathering dust since the summer of 1939, when it had been planned as an MGM-British film and then abandoned because of the war. MGM-British had sent the script to Eton College and sought its approval in 1939 because they hoped to film on and around the campus. Eton had never responded to the request and heard no more about the matter until January 1942, when college officials received reports that the film was going to be made by MGM in California. The Provost of Eton then reread the script, and found that, whereas in 1939 it may have been possible 'to treat all of this foolishness with indifferent contempt', in 1942 the film seemed ill advised. Nazi propaganda had emphasized the elitism of Britain's public schools, and Hitler himself had cited Eton as a symbol of decadence in a recent speech on the British class system.[46] The script, it was thought, all but illustrated the Nazi argument. Its key departure from *A Yank at Oxford* is that the young American schoolboy (played in the film by Mickey Rooney) is forced to attend the great English institution against his will and he hates it. Of course, he too eventually learns to love all things English, but not before he has uncovered the snobbery and scandals of his fellow students.

Both the Provost of Eton and the British Minister of Information, Brendan Bracken, asked MGM not to film this story. Yet even when Eton threatened the studio with a lawsuit, the studio insisted that it would proceed.[47] At a meeting in March 1942, Brendan Bracken presented the objections to the script to MGM's

British representative, Sam Eckman. But Eckman had postponed the meeting for several weeks, so that by the time it took place he was able to tell the Minister that filming had already begun and far too much had been spent on the production to abandon it now. Eckman also listed MGM's previous 'British' films as proof of the studio's good intentions, and he delivered a 'personal message' from studio head Louis B. Mayer to 'my good friend Brendan Bracken', in which Mayer declared, 'I am as pro-British as any Britisher and love everything British second only to my adopted country'. Mayer promised that if the finished film was not 'a grand and pro-British picture', he would make it so before its release.[48] Remarkably, not only was Mayer insisting upon paying tribute to an institution which wanted no part of his efforts, but also he seemed to be telling Britain's Minister of Information that he was a better judge of what constituted a pro-British film than the Minister himself.

Neither Bracken nor the board of governors at Eton was convinced by Mayer's proclamations, and so the dispute continued. The threatened lawsuit prompted MGM to set its research department to the task of reading the memoirs of Eton alumni. The idea was to find some factual basis for the portrayal of life at Eton, thereby undermining any claims of slander. However, the researchers reported that their search for 'escapades, pranks, rule infractions or even mild moral laxity among the students at Eton' was unsuccessful, and that during their research they had realized 'the tremendous social and political importance attached to Eton by Englishmen'. They could only warn their superiors at MGM that it would be 'hazardous' to make the film.[49] Still, the filming continued according to the original script. In June, Bracken informed Eckman that 'Eton is still kicking up quite a fuss about the film', and he proposed a compromise: Lord Halifax, an Eton alumnus, would be given a screening before the film was released, and MGM would make whatever changes Halifax required. Both MGM and Eton agreed.[50] After the screening, in July 1942, Halifax asked for two scenes to be cut, and MGM complied with this.[51]

The OWI seized upon *A Yank at Eton* as the prime example of Hollywood's misguided approach to British stories. The OWI was willing to admit that the film tries to cast certain British traditions in the most democratic light. (The fagging system, for example, is said to uphold egalitarian principles because all boys go through it.) But they also pointed out that the setting itself is not 'the most ideal means of proving British democracy'. Eton, the reviewers complained, is 'a school into which a boy literally must be born

18   A 'false representation of England', the callous Yank (Mickey Rooney) in
A Yank at Eton (1942)

to be acceptable'. It was also regretted that the film focuses almost exclusively on the upper classes, and that little indication is given that a 'lower or middle-class England exists at all'. When servants do appear, they seem to be far too humble and deferential to the young aristocrats of Eton. Another significant problem for the OWI was that Rooney is too callous as the 'Yank'. At one point within the film, the headmaster of Eton tells him, 'you are not American, you are a barbarian', and the OWI reviewer noted that this seems to be a fair judgement.[52]

In the OWI's British division, meanwhile, Ferdinand Kuhn put *A Yank at Eton* at the centre of a campaign he launched against Hollywood's 'false representations of Great Britain'. He wrote a memorandum on the subject which was circulated within the OWI itself, and then was used as the basis for advice and criticism given to studios and film-makers. *A Yank at Eton* was said to be 'poisonous from start to finish' and all too typical of Hollywood's predilection for portraying snobbery, stuffiness and class distinctions as being the definitive characteristics of Britain. Kuhn also provided his own view of British society:

The caste system is a diminishing survival rather than an all pervasive condition of present-day English life. I don't deny the existence of the caste system or of its evils; nobody can deny it who seeks to write truthfully about England. But I do say that we have no business to perpetuate a stereotype in which the caste system is England, and England is the caste system in American minds.[53]

'Caste' refers to a greater separation of social groups than 'class', and so Kuhn was able to point toward Noel Coward's *In Which We Serve* (1942) as an appropriate portrayal of British society during the war. *In Which We Serve* shows that, while a very marked class system still exists in Britain, the classes mix more freely and they are united in the war effort. Perhaps more importantly, the lower classes are given more screen time and more dignity in *In Which We Serve* than in the majority of 'British' films. But this was not explained in the memorandum and the reference to *In Which We Serve* was a fleeting one. 'False representations of Britain' had far more to say on what should not be done than it had in the way of positive advice.

The Hollywood British

Ironically, the campaign against 'false representations' began in the same week that *Forever and a Day* was previewed for the BMP. For Kuhn, this was a typical 'British' film, with the focus upon a titled family, their ancestral home and their faithful servants. Yet the film had been made almost entirely by British film-makers, and so its British pedigree would seem to undermine Kuhn's view that such films gave a 'false' and American view of Britain. Kuhn, however, recognized the film as 'British' rather than truly British, and as a result he suggested that many of the writers and directors involved had been away from their home country for too long. They could portray only 'the England of castles and caste', whereas an appropriate wartime film would focus upon: 'the real people of England, the workers and shop-keepers and miners, those who live in the great provincial cities that Americans know so little about, and those who were the backbone of England in its darkest days'.[54] This was the most definitive statement by the OWI on how Britain should be portrayed: modern, urban, provincial settings with brave yet ordinary characters. It was a perfectly valid request, but one that was unlikely to be fulfilled by Hollywood's Britons or approved by the studio executives who were so impressed with the box-office returns from *Mrs Miniver* and *Random Harvest*.

Nonetheless, Kuhn pressed ahead with the idea of re-educating the Hollywood British. He contacted British Information Services in Washington DC and found that its director, Harold Butler, was equally concerned by the impression given by such films. Butler agreed to go to Los Angeles and add weight to the OWI's views.[55] In March 1943, and at the home of Eric Cleugh, the British Consul in Los Angeles, Butler met 'a gathering of British film writers, artists and directors'. He reportedly 'gave them a piece of his mind' and 'a stiff talking to'. His main point was that the writers should endeavour to portray Britain 'as it really has become during the war', while avoiding the Britain of 'palaces and peers'. To enable this, it was said that the writers would be sent home periodically, to update their views, but in the meantime Butler was happy to leave a representative of British Information Services, Marjorie Russell, at the British Consulate in Los Angeles, where she could advise on scripts related to Britain.[56]

It was thought to be highly impolitic to give the impression that the British government was exercising censorship in Hollywood, even in regard to films about Britain.[57] So while Russell's arrival in Los Angeles was well publicized, it was made clear that all opinions and advice would be offered only 'on a request basis'.[58] In practice, however, the OWI forwarded scripts dealing with British subjects to Russell, and her views were used as the basis of their opinions and advice. When the OWI received MGM's scripts for *If Winter Comes* and *The White Cliffs of Dover*, for example, they referred MGM's producers to Russell, and they sought out Russell's views on their own. MGM had planned these films as follow-ups to *Mrs Miniver*; films which would portray both the war effort and the dramatic changes war had brought to British society.[59] Yet neither Russell nor the OWI thought that the scripts offered convincing or even complimentary portraits of the new England.

Like its predecessor, *If Winter Comes* is set in an idyllic English village ('Penny Green') and it portrays the emergence of a more democratic community.[60] However, whereas *Mrs Miniver* stressed unity and the class system's gentle evolution, *If Winter Comes* would have its protagonist, a progressive aristocrat, clash with both his wife and his business partners on issues such as appeasement and class. The arguments for and against a new England would be angrily debated, and parallel to this conflict would be a more personal melodrama involving adultery, divorce, teenage pregnancy and suicide. The script reads as though it was intended to reveal the darker side of *Mrs Miniver's* England. In fact, it was based on a best-selling novel of the 1920s, and Marjorie Russell pointed out that this dated story was hardly the best vehicle to convey the new England. She and Harold Butler were said to be 'dismayed' by it, and Russell wanted no more to do with it. To try to advise MGM on ways of making it better would be 'a hopeless task'. This scorn apparently convinced MGM to shelve *If Winter Comes* until the war had ended.[61]

Butler and Russell also had a low opinion of *The White Cliffs of Dover* (1944). They informed the OWI that it was 'just the sort of thing that shouldn't be done', and the OWI agreed.[62] However, *The White Cliffs of Dover* was the project of producer Sidney Franklin, who had achieved 'prima donna status' at MGM because of the phenomenal success of both *Mrs Miniver* and *Random Harvest*.[63] Franklin now considered himself to be on a mission to improve Anglo-American relations, and his previous successes had convinced him that he was the right man for this mission.[64] He could only react with shock, then, when he read the OWI's lengthy critique of the script, detailing numerous objections and criticisms, and warning that this film – designed to further Anglo-American relations – could 'actually raise resentments on both sides of the Atlantic'.[65]

Based on a narrative poem by British writer Alice Duer Miller, *The White Cliffs of Dover* centres on Susan Dunn, an American woman who visits England with her father on the eve of the First World War. The father, Hiram Dunn, is an Anglophobe, who argues with the English over the Boston Tea Party and the War of 1812, and makes snide comments about the British Empire. Susan falls in love with Sir John Ashwood, marries him and moves into the family's ancestral home in Devon, where initially she encounters the snobbery of her husband's family and friends. Sir John is killed in the First World War, and Susan raises her son at Ashwood Manor. In the 1930s, when she sees that war is again imminent, she intends to take him to the United States, but the young aristocrat has developed a sense of responsibility toward the tenants of the family's estate and insists upon staying in England. They, of course, are grateful for the attentions of the young Sir John. Later, he goes to war and, in the ending, dies in hospital with his mother at his side.

The story's combination of elements from *A Yank at Oxford* and *Mrs Miniver* made *The White Cliffs of Dover* everything that MGM could wish for in a 'British' film. Its portrayal of a benevolent aristocracy, a humble working class, and British and American characters who always seem to be bickering, also meant that it encapsulated all that the OWI opposed. The reviewer pointed out that having characters argue over the War of 1812 was not the best means of cementing Anglo-American relations. There also seemed to be far too much that divided the American and British characters. Why did so many American characters have to be 'boorish' and so many British characters 'arrogant snobs'? The reviewers complained that the film was centred on the landed gentry, and warned that 'playing up the myth of snobbery [and] class consciousness' in Britain would only encourage American Anglophobes. The scene in which a young Sir John rides through the family's estate, and the tenants greet him by bowing, tugging their forelocks and referring to the twelve-year-old boy as 'sir', was particularly galling to the OWI. 'Noblesse oblige is not democracy', the review stated, 'and the American public knows it.' Hiram Dunn's reference to the British Empire ('a people who have managed to collar one-third of the earth') was also regretted.[66]

Sidney Franklin and screenwriter Claudine West considered these comments, and from West's notes it is apparent that neither took them very seriously. In response to the OWI's complaint that the tenant farmer should not say that economic conditions 'are worse for gentry than they are for us', West indicated that 'this is a true line', and that she would change it only to 'as bad for gentry as they are for us'. Criticisms of the script's Anglo-American antagonisms were cast aside, too. West felt that Hiram Dunn's arguments with the British characters were 'really typical of relationships of reasonable Americans and English people – good-natured kidding is the order of the day on both sides'.[67] Franklin and West were impervious even to the criticisms of the British technical adviser hired for the film, which echoed those of the OWI.[68] Thus, few changes were made to *The White Cliffs of Dover*. None of the dialogue the OWI found most objectionable was deleted, but two new scenes were added to the film. In one, the younger Sir John becomes romantically involved with one of the tenant's daughters; as in *Mrs Miniver*, the cross-class romance is used as a sign of a new egalitarian spirit. In the other, Susan launches into a speech upon seeing the white cliffs of Dover for the first time, mentioning the *Mayflower*, the Magna Carta and other points of Anglo-American heritage.

The changes were limited and did little to address the OWI's most basic criticisms of the script. Yet the agency made no further efforts against *The White Cliffs of Dover*. The review of the finished film was negative, but it was also restrained and brief. The restraint had been urged by Lowell Mellett himself, who had instructed Nelson Poynter in March 1943 not to take a stand against this particular film. He had no praise for the film, but he reassured Poynter that 'the common sense of American audiences is pretty certain to discard much of it'.[69] Mellett must have realized that criticizing the pet project of the top producer at Hollywood's most powerful studio was not the way forward for the

19 Crossing the class divide: The young Sir John (Roddy McDowall) and Betsy (Elizabeth Taylor), the daughter of one of the tenants on his family's estate, in *The White Cliffs of Dover* (1944)

OWI in Hollywood. This was in the spring of 1943, when the OWI was under attack from all sides.[70] Accordingly, the OWI even gave *The White Cliffs of Dover* a 'suitable' rating for release in liberated territories, although it was noted in correspondence that 'there was some disagreement about this' when the matter was debated at the BMP in Hollywood.[71]

Costume and period dramas

The presence of British Information Services in Hollywood proved to have a profound impact on 'British' films for the remainder of the war. Ulric Bell signalled the change in a letter to Ferdinand Kuhn that was written in May 1943. Bell indicated that Marjorie Russell was working closely with the OWI, and seeking the support of George Archibald, the head of British Information Services in New York City, on crucial matters. Bell also thought that Kuhn's memorandum on 'false representations' had been 'enormously helpful', and told him that even 'the MGM people' admitted that they were 'not qualified' to make a film about wartime Britain and that 'their British writers need very much to be sent home and brought up-to-date'. Bell predicted that all of these efforts would result in 'a new cycle of good pictures'.[72] However, he was not quite right. Rather, Hollywood became very wary of contemporary 'British' films. It was costly to rewrite films and abandon planned productions, and word undoubtedly had spread that MGM had been pressured to rewrite *The White Cliffs of Dover* and to stop production of *If Winter Comes*. It also appears that TCF was planning an adaptation of Terence Rattigan's *Flare Path* in mid-1943, and that this too was abandoned. According to Kuhn, this story of RAF officers during the Battle of Britain was likely to give another 'stereotyped picture of present day England'.[73]

In fact, the studios only dared to venture into what had become known as 'the new England' with relatively minor productions. Universal continued with its series of modern-day *Sherlock Holmes* films, but the master detective now worked only on civilian cases and war topics were avoided. Universal also included timely and approved messages in the films. In the final scene of *Sherlock Holmes Faces Death* (1943), for example, Holmes tells Watson that: 'There is a new spirit abroad in the land. Grab and greed are on the way out. We've begun to think of the other fellow', and Watson replies, 'I hope so, Holmes, I hope so.' The OWI could only applaud such sentiments.[74] It also applauded Republic Studio's *Thumbs Up* (1943), a wartime drama made in consultation with Marjorie Russell, which centred on workers in a provincial aircraft factory.[75] The major producers, meanwhile, were apparently not so willing to have their scripts vetted by British officials, or to tailor their films to the designs of the OWI. Instead they abandoned contemporary stories completely and returned to the past.

The change was remarkable. In 1942 and even in 1943, before the effect of these efforts was felt, the vast majority of 'British' films were set in the present and most had war-related plots.[76] In 1944 and 1945, however, contemporary British settings were seldom seen, and Hollywood embarked on a new cycle of historical and literary dramas that included *The Corn is Green* (1945), *Devotion* (1945), *Frenchman's Creek* (1944), *Gaslight* (1944), *Hangover Square* (1945), *Jane Eyre* (1944), *The Lodger* (1944) and *The Picture of Dorian Gray* (1945).[77] The logic behind this shift was simple. If Hollywood could not portray snobbery, class distinctions and extremes of wealth and poverty in wartime Britain, it would return to the past. The OWI did not object to this. When *Jane Eyre* was seen, for example, the reviewer noted that the film portrays an era that was 'particularly grim and joyless for anyone but the very wealthy', but the agency asked only that the date (1820) be displayed prominently at the outset of the film.[78] This became the policy toward 'British' costume dramas: so long as the historical setting was made clear in the beginning, the OWI would not submit the films to the scrutiny that contemporary films received.

Some of the costume dramas seem designed to appeal to the OWI's sense of social progress and destiny. *The Corn is Green*, for example, portrays the valiant efforts of an English school teacher in a poor Welsh mining village. When her prize pupil wins a scholarship to Oxford, it is understood that this is an early strike against social barriers and the harbinger of things to come.[79] Others did not offer a progressive message, but the OWI merely reiterated its request for a clear date at the outset of the film. Only *The Picture of Dorian Gray* drew criticism, and this supposedly was because of a sudden concern that audiences would confuse the past with the present. While it is true that the film emphasizes the contrast between the elegant West End and the squalid East End of London, as a parallel to Dorian's elegant facade and his impoverished soul, the extremes are certainly no more marked than in other films. One can only surmise that the OWI was uncomfortable with the air of decadent cynicism and the allusions to sexual depravity that run throughout this stylish adaptation of Oscar Wilde's novel. Despite declaring its historical setting, *The Picture of Dorian Gray* was considered 'unsuitable' for liberated territories.[80]

The distance of history was also emphasized in films set in the more recent past. Indeed, RKO clearly used this technique to soften the most unusual 'British' film made during the war years, *None but the Lonely Heart* (1944). This is the story of cockney drifter, Ernie Mott, whose life in the East End of London is characterized by abject poverty, crime and hopelessness. It was the bleakest of all 'British' films in 1944. Yet it begins with a spoken preamble, stating that the story is set in the 1930s, before Mott realized his 'higher destiny' as one of the 'warriors' of the Second World War. This slant was appreciated by BMP reviewers, who of course had a taste for dramas concerning the destiny of the common man. Thus, *None but the Lonely Heart* caused few difficulties. It received a 'suitable but not recommended' rating on the grounds that it was 'too sophisticated for mass audiences'.[81] The stategy was also adopted by MGM for *Lassie Come Home* (1943), a film that bears distinct similarities to *The White Cliffs of Dover*. Not only does it portray a similarly benevolent aristocracy and humble working class, but it also shares much of the same cast (Roddy McDowall, Elizabeth Taylor, Dame May Whitty). *Lassie Come Home* makes no mention of the war, though, and the

20   The OWI's preferred vision of Britain: Mickey Rooney, Elizabeth
Taylor and Jackie 'Butch' Jenkins star in *National Velvet* (1945)

opening titles clearly place the story 'in the pre-war days of
unemployment, empty pockets and the dole'. The combination of
historical distance, an utterly sentimental story and a canine star
seem to have allowed *Lassie Come Home* to escape the disapproval
which greeted so many of MGM's other 'British' films.[82]

Finally, at the end of the war, the OWI saw a 'British' film that
it could wholeheartedly endorse. MGM's *National Velvet* (1945)
also begins with titles that place its story in the past (in this case
the 1920s), but this was not a necessary measure as far as the
OWI was concerned. The reviewers revelled in this film, and
declared it to be an 'overwhelmingly favorable' portrait of Britain.
At first glance the setting may not seem too far removed from
those seen in MGM's other 'British' films. It is a rural village in the
south of England, and the date could just as easily be 1895 as
1925. The key difference is that there are neither manor houses
nor humble cottages, and the Brown family is authentically middle
class. Mr Brown is a butcher and the family home is a frugal and

simple one, particularly when compared with the luxurious Miniver home. Furthermore, the story does not involve aristocrats or class relations of any sort, but centres on family life and the aspirations of one daughter to enter her horse in the Grand National. The fact that this England bears some resemblance to the America of *Andy Hardy* films is not entirely due to the presence of star Mickey Rooney (playing the horse's trainer), or the fact that the California coast was used for location shooting instead of the Sussex coast. Rather, the resemblance stems from the wholesome small-town atmosphere, and the importance the story attaches to the ambition and enthusiasm of its young characters. For the OWI, it seems, the best way of portraying Britain was to make it more like the United States' own preferred vision of itself: family-centred, classless and energetic. *National Velvet* could not be called an authentic portrait of Britain, but it was one that made Britain look more like the United States. As such it was a Britain the OWI could heartily welcome and recommend.[83]

Conclusion

It is not surprising that the OWI and Hollywood could not agree upon how contemporary Britain should be portrayed. The OWI took a progressive view of the war. Film was seen as a means of educating the audience and the war was seen as an event important enough to warrant new approaches to film-making. The Hollywood studios, on the other hand, were in the business of making entertaining films. Their sense of patriotism and duty led them to include wartime themes and messages, but these had to be made palatable, and this most often was done by placing them within existing film genres and formulae. In regard to Britain, the two approaches simply could not be reconciled. The OWI's request for films that were set in a provincial, urban and working-class Britain had no precedent in Hollywood, and the scenario undoubtedly was thought to hold little interest for American audiences. The contemporary Britain that Hollywood preferred, meanwhile, seemed to reinforce the very aspects of Britain that the OWI knew to be politically troublesome for many Americans. This was the paradox of 'British' films, and the only solution to this paradox in wartime was to place the films in the past. The resulting change brought around in a full circle the cycle of 'British' films that had begun ten years earlier. Just as the leading 'British' films of the mid-1930s had been *David Copperfield*, *Mutiny on the Bounty* and *Captain Blood*, a similar mix of historical and literary films prevailed in the mid-1940s. In 1944 and

1945, and for the first time in several years, costume dramas proliferated and contemporary films were few and far between. By placing 'British' films in the past their political relevance was minimized, and yet Americans could still see on screen the Britain that they loved and loved to hate.

Notes

Introduction

1 *The Spectator* (7 May 1937); also reprinted in G. Greene, *The Pleasure Dome: The Collected Film Criticism, 1935–1940*, p. 149.

Chapter 1

1 See for example *The Motion Picture Herald* (9 September 1939), pp. 15–19; and *The Motion Picture Herald* (7 October 1939), p. 28; *Variety* (10 July 1940), p. 1; *The Motion Picture Herald* (17 August 1940), p. 31.

2 T. Ramsaye (ed.), *The 1935–1936 International Motion Picture Almanac*, pp. 997–1034.

3 T. Ramsaye (ed.), *The 1939–1940 International Motion Picture Almanac*, p. 944.

4 The earnings figures for Europe and Britain are cited in a *Motion Picture Herald* article concerning Hollywood's troubled foreign operations. This is one of the few instances in which figures are offered for foreign markets. However, at the time they were published, there was no longer a reason to be secretive about them. The European market had been closed, and the British figure had already been made public during the negotiations over the wartime currency regulations. *The Motion Picture Herald* (13 July 1940), p. 12.

5 K. Thompson, *Exporting Entertainment: America in the World Film Market*, pp. 159–161.

6 R. Moley, *The Hays Office*, p. 173.

7 Thompson, *Exporting Entertainment*, p. 126.

8 T. Ramsaye (ed.), *The 1933–1934 International Motion Picture Almanac*, pp. 672–673.

9 Ramsaye (ed.), *The 1939–1940 International Motion Picture Almanac*, pp. 827–829.

10 *Ibid.*

11 *Ibid.*

12 Ramsaye (ed.), *The 1933–1934 International Motion Picture Almanac*, p. 677.

13 *The Motion Picture Herald* (10 February 1945), p. 32.

14 T. Balio, *United Artists: The Company Built by the Stars*, pp. 167–168.

15 *Variety* (30 December 1936), p. 1.

16 *The Motion Picture Herald* (8 March 1941), p. 9.

17 *The Motion Picture Herald* (17 March 1945), p. 21.

18 Thompson, *Exporting Entertainment*, pp. 124–128.

19 T. Ramsaye (ed.), *The 1934–1935 International Motion Picture Almanac*, p. 987; *Variety* (3 April 1934), p. 13; *The Motion Picture Daily* (13 November 1934), p. 27.

20 Ramsaye (ed.), *The 1934–1935 International Motion Picture Almanac*, p. 1015.

21 *Variety* (31 July 1940), p. 93.

22 *The Motion Picture Herald* (19 October 1940), p. 46.

23 Both *The Motion Picture Herald* and *Variety* reported predictions that the Germans would not be able to supply the cinemas of Occupied Europe with enough films, and thus the Germans would have to begin importing American films again. See *The Motion Picture Herald* (13 July 1940), p. 7; and *Variety* (11 September 1940), p. 7.

24 *The Motion Picture Herald* (20 July 1940), p. 9.

25 The number of American films released in Finland dropped from 201 films in 1938 to 56 in 1942, and this was attributed to Nazi influence within the local film industry. *The Motion Picture Herald* (25 March 1944), p. 38.

26 *The Motion Picture Herald* (24 April 1943), p. 9.

27 It was stated that 'until recent events changed the film map of Europe, Lisbon was unimportant as a motion picture center'. *The Motion Picture Herald* (6 July 1940), p. 21.

28 *Variety* (4 September 1940), p. 19.

29 Thompson, *Exporting Entertainment*, pp. 141–144.

30 *The Motion Picture Herald* (9 December 1939), p. 50; and J. Alicoate (ed.), *The 1940 Film Daily Yearbook*, p. 57.

31 Ramsaye (ed.), *The 1933–1934 International Motion Picture Almanac*, pp. 673–674.

32 *The Motion Picture Herald* (19 May 1945), p. 60.

33 *The Motion Picture Herald* (31 January 1942), p. 43.

34 Tino Balio indicates that in 1940 United Artists derived 10 per cent of its foreign income from Latin America, and *The Motion Picture Herald* offered the same figure for the industry as a whole in 1940. See Balio, *United Artists*, p. 169; and *The Motion Picture Herald* (13 July 1940), p. 12.

35 *The Motion Picture Herald* (27 March 1943), p. 21; *The Motion Picture Herald* (27 May 1944), p. 34; and *The Motion Picture Herald* (11 November 1944), p. 9.

36 The statistics in table 3 were taken from *The Motion Picture Herald* (27 July 1940), p. 33.

37 J. Alicoate (ed.), *The 1932 Film Daily Yearbook*, pp. 977–1017.

38 *The Motion Picture Herald* (11 November 1944), pp. 9 and 42. See also J. Alicoate (ed.), *The 1943 Film Daily Yearbook*, pp. 955–957 and pp. 966–977.

39 *The Motion Picture Herald* (2 December 1944), p. 18.

40 The dubbed *Gaslight* was said to have broken box-office records in Buenos Aires, Lima, Mexico City and Santiago. See *The Motion Picture Herald* (2 December 1944), p. 18; *The Motion Picture Herald* (24 February 1945), p. 36; *The Motion Picture Herald* (17 March 1945), p. 24; and *The Motion Picture Herald* (31 March 1945), p. 56.

41 The region's dislike of war films is reported in *The Motion Picture Herald* (19 June 1943), p. 52. The belated release of war films in Argentina is reported in *The Motion Picture Herald* (21 April 1945), p. 42.

42 *Variety* (3 July 1940), p. 15.

43 *The Motion Picture Herald* (11 April 1942), p. 15; and *The Motion Picture Herald* (14 October 1944), p. 19.

44 The 1925 figure is taken from Thompson, *Exporting Entertainment*, p. 127. In 1940, it was reported that Hollywood earned between $35 million and $50 million annually in Britain, and that this was 50 per cent of gross foreign income and 70 per cent of the money that actually made it back to the USA. *The Motion Picture Herald* (13 July 1940), p. 12.

45 According to one report, Hollywood's foreign income 'dipped' in the early 1930s because of the advent of sound as well as the proliferation of quotas and restrictions throughout the world. But then 'rapidly increasing consumer markets in the English-speaking territories' in the 1930s compensated for losses elsewhere. *The Motion Picture Herald* (28 September 1940), p. 64.

46 I. Jarvie, *Hollywood's Overseas Campaign: The North Atlantic Movie Trade, 1920–1950*, p. 103.

47 Thompson, *Exporting Entertainment*, p. 125.

48 For a new and surprising analysis of the popularity of 1930s' British cinema in Britain, see J. Sedgwick, 'Cinema-going Preferences in Britain in the 1930s', in J. Richards (ed.), *The Unknown 1930s: An Alternative History of the British Cinema*, pp. 1–35.

49 M. Dickinson and S. Street, *Cinema and State: The Film Industry and the British Government, 1927–1984*, pp. 98–99.

50 R. Low, *Filmmaking in 1930s Britain*, p. 50.

51 Dickinson and Street, *Cinema and State*, pp. 120–129.

52 *Ibid.*

53 *The Motion Picture Herald* (7 December 1940), p. 50; and *The Motion Picture Herald* (10 January 1942), p. 47.

54 The quotation is taken from *Variety* (8 January 1947), p. 184. Numerous articles in the trade press signal the increasing concerns over the popularity of British films, and what this could mean in the post-war period. Concerns over the strength of J. Arthur Rank's empire are particularly acute. See *The Motion Picture Herald* (29 July 1944), p. 31; *The Motion Picture Herald* (14 April 1945), p. 28; and *Variety* (25 December 1946), p. 9.

55 *The Motion Picture Herald* (17 January 1942), p. 47; and *The Motion Picture Herald* (22 April 1944), p. 41.

56 These estimates were made by the managing director of Paramount

Studios' British distribution company. *The Motion Picture Herald* (23 December 1944), p. 26.

57 The Twentieth Century-Fox grosses were found in the United Artists' 'Black Book' on England. The document is dated 15 December 1944 and at the bottom of the page it is stated that 'these figures were furnished by a reliable source'. File 2, box 7, series 1F, United Artists Collection, Wisconsin State Historical Society (hereafter UA/WSHS).

58 *The Motion Picture Herald* (22 April 1944), p. 41.

59 Beginning in 1936, the top-grossing films of each year were calculated by *Kinematograph Weekly* and published in the first issue of each year. All of the films cited here were among the top ten films of their year.

60 *The Motion Picture Herald* (28 September 1940), p. 64.

61 J. Alicoate (ed.), *The 1944 Film Daily Yearbook*, p. 817; and J. Alicoate (ed.), *The 1945 Film Daily Yearbook*, p. 816; and *The Motion Picture Herald* (23 June 1945), p. 44.

62 *Variety* (8 January 1941), p. 1.

63 M. Walsh, 'Americanisation and Empire Loyalty: British Films in Australia, 1918–1933', a paper given to the 'Cinema, Identity, History' conference at the University of East Anglia, 12 July 1998.

64 Figures on the seventeen United Artists films can be found in file 3, box 38, series 3A, UA/WSHS. Figures on *Eagle Squadron* and *Arabian Nights* can be found in file 6, box 42 of The Walter Wanger Collection, Wisconsin State Historical Society (hereafter Wanger/WSHS).

65 MGM's figures are available in The Eddie Mannix Ledger, which is held as a special collection by The Margaret Herrick Library of the Academy of Motion Picture Arts and Sciences (Hereafter Mannix/Academy Library). The Warner Bros. figures are available in The William Schaefer Ledger, which is held as a special collection at the Doheny Library of the University of Southern California (Hereafter Schaefer/USC). The RKO figures are contained within the C.J. Tevlin Ledger, and have been analysed by the film historian Richard B. Jewell. See R. B. Jewell, 'RKO Film Grosses, 1929–1951: The C.J. Tevlin Ledger', *Historical Journal of Film, Radio and Television*, pp. 37–50.

Chapter 2

1 L. J. Leff and J.L. Simmons, *The Dame in the Kimono: Hollywood Censorship and the Production Code from the 1920s to the 1960s*, pp. 3–16.

2 R. Sklar, *Movie-Made America: A Cultural History of the Movies*, p. 76.

3 Leff and Simmons, *The Dame in the Kimono*, p. 7.

4 *Ibid.*, pp. 33–54.

5 R. Maltby, '*Baby Face*: Or How Joe Breen Made Barbara Stanwyck Atone for Causing the Wall Street Crash', *Screen*, pp. 22–45. See also F. Walsh, *Sin and Censorship: The Catholic Church and the Motion Picture Industry*.

6 For a full analysis of the Hays Office's foreign operations during the 1920s and 1930s see R. Vasey, *The World According to Hollywood, 1918–1939*.

7 The MPPDA Production Code of 1930 is reprinted in G. Mast (ed.),

The Movies in Our Midst, pp. 321–333.

8 Vasey, *The World According to Hollywood*, p. 152.

9 *Ibid.*, pp. 146–148.

10 *Ibid.*

11 Frederick Herron to Joseph Breen, 31 December 1935; *Captain Blood*, Production Code Administration Files, Margaret Herrick Library, Academy of Motion Picture Arts and Sciences (hereafter PCA/ Academy Library).

12 Joseph Breen to Brooke Wilkinson, 5 August 1937; Brooke Wilkinson to Joseph Breen, 6 August 1937; *The Citadel*, PCA/Academy Library.

13 James C. Robertson, *The British Board of Film Censors: Film Censorship in Britain, 1896–1950*, pp. 72–74.

14 Vasey, *The World According to Hollywood*, pp. 19–20 and p. 143.

15 Memo by Joseph Breen, 13 May 1938; *Ninotchka*, PCA/Academy Library.

16 Georg Gyssling to Joseph Breen, 28 May 1937; *Lancer Spy*, PCA/Academy Library.

17 F. Herron to Will Hays, 9 February 1937; *The Road Back*, PCA/Academy Library.

18 When *The Road Back* went into production in 1936, Gyssling informed Breen of the German government's earlier position on the film. Georg Gyssling to Joseph Breen, 30 September 1936; *The Road Back*.

19 *Ibid.*

20 Memo from Joseph Breen, 12 February 1937; *The Road Back*.

21 Gyssling to Breen, 20 September 1936; *The Road Back*.

22 For Breen's views see Joseph Breen to Harry Zehner (Universal Studios), 14 October 1936; and Breen to Zehner, 26 May 1937; *The Road Back*.

23 Breen's note, indicating that he would prefer to avoid Gyssling, was attached to a letter he had received from Gyssling. Georg Gyssling to Joseph Breen, 6 November 1936; *The Road Back*.

24 Memo from Joseph Breen, 12 February 1937; *The Road Back*.

25 Georg Gyssling to the cast and director of *The Road Back*, 6 April 1937; *The Road Back*.

26 The PCA files usually contain a typed sheet which lists any states, territories or countries where a film was cut or banned. In some instances, reasons for the cut or ban are offered. For example, *The Road Back* was banned in China 'because of the request of the German Consul General'; *The Road Back*.

27 Georg Gyssling to Joseph Breen, 29 December 1937; *Three Comrades*, PCA/Academy Library.

28 Joseph Breen to L.B. Mayer, 22 January 1938; *Three Comrades*.

29 Joseph Breen to L.B. Mayer, 27 May 1938; *Three Comrades*.

30 The article from *The New Masses* can be found in the PCA file for *Three Comrades*.

31 Quigley used the editorial page of *The Motion Picture Herald* to make his views known. See, for example, *The Motion Picture Herald* (21 January 1939), p. 14.

32 For an enlightening analysis of the Hollywood moguls' background and the way this influenced their films, see N. Gabler, *An Empire of Their Own: How the Jews Invented Hollywood*.

33 Vasey, *The World According to Hollywood*, p. 205.

34 *The Lady Vanishes*, PCA/Academy Library.

35 Four studios were in the bidding for *Idiot's Delight*: MGM, Pioneer, RKO and Warners. Breen felt sure that, given the play's subject matter and the author's asking price ($100,000), the studios would 'feel that it is too dangerous an undertaking at this time'. MGM, however, bought the rights for $125,000. Joseph Breen to Frederick Herron, 11 April 1936; *Idiot's Delight*, PCA/Academy Library.

36 Joseph Breen to James Beck (BBFC), 20 August 1936; *Idiot's Delight*.

37 James Beck to Joseph Breen, 15 September 1936; *Idiot's Delight*.

38 Breen's lunch and the Consul's terms are noted in Memorandum from Joseph Breen, 12 May 1937; *Idiot's Delight*.

39 The negotiations are discussed in Joseph Breen to Frederick Herron, 13 May 1937; R. Caracciolo (Italian Consul) to Joseph Breen, 8 June 1937; and Hunt Stromberg to Joseph Breen, 9 July 1937; *Idiot's Delight*.

40 Joseph Breen to Walter Wanger, 7 February 1938; *Blockade*, PCA/Academy Library.

41 John Hammell (Paramount) to Joseph Breen, 9 March 1937; *The Last Train from Madrid*, PCA/Academy Library.

42 C. R. Koppes and G. D. Black, *Hollywood Goes to War: How Politics, Profits and Propaganda Shaped World War Two Movies*, pp. 24–26.

43 *Blockade* was banned in Bulgaria, Czechoslovakia, El Salvador, Germany, Guatemala, Poland, Latvia, Peru, Portugal, Singapore, Spain and Yugoslavia.

44 Joseph Breen to Walter Wanger, 21 June 1938; *Foreign Correspondent*, PCA/Academy Library.

45 J. Warner with D. Jennings, *My First Hundred Years in Hollywood*, p. 249.

46 T. Doherty, *Projections of War: Hollywood, American Culture, and World War Two*, p. 311.

47 Georg Gyssling to Joseph Breen, 6 December 1938; *Confessions of a Nazi Spy*, PCA/Academy Library.

48 Robert Lord to Joseph Breen, 24 December 1938, *Confessions of a Nazi Spy*.

49 Luigi Luraschi to Joseph Breen, 10 December 1938; *Confessions of a Nazi Spy*.

50 Memo initialled 'K.L.', undated; *Confessions of a Nazi Spy*.

51 Joseph Breen to Jack Warner, 30 June 1938; *Confessions of a Nazi Spy*.

52 *Confessions of a Nazi Spy* was banned in Argentina, Chile, the Dominican Republic, Ireland, The Netherlands, Norway, Peru, South Africa, Spain, the Straits Settlements, Sweden, Switzerland and Venezuela. Chile and Venezuela lifted their bans on 9 May 1940, and Peru lifted its ban on 8 December 1941.

53 The BBFC's reasons for passing the film are quoted in a memorandum that was forwarded to Joseph Breen from Paramount's London office. The memorandum comments that the film 'is doing big business in cosmopolitan London' but questions how popular it would be

in the provinces. Memorandum from Paramount Studios Foreign Department, 30 June 1939; *Confessions of a Nazi Spy*. See also Robertson, *The BBFC*, pp. 100–101.

54 The MGM figures are taken from The Eddie Mannix Ledger; Mannix/Academy Library. The United Artists figures are taken from file 3, box 38, series 3A of the United Artists Collection; UA/WSHS.The Warner Bros.' figures are taken from The William Schaefer Ledger; Schaefer/USC.

55 A Gallup poll conducted in the United States in 1940 found that 96.5 per cent of respondents did not want the USA to enter the war, but 84 per cent were hoping for an Allied victory. See C. Shindler, *Hollywood Goes to War: Films and American Society, 1939–1952*, p. 12.

56 *The Motion Picture Herald* (4 November 1939), p. 18.

57 A PCA memo on *Escape* indicates that it 'did not seem to fall into the category of "hate pictures" in as much as many of the Germans are shown to be decent people'. However, Breen later complained to MGM of the 'illicit sex affair' between the General (Conrad Veidt) and the Countess (Norma Shearer). PCA memo, 9 October 1939; Joseph Breen to L.B. Mayer, 1 April 1940; *Escape*, PCA/Academy Library. No objections were raised to *The Mortal Storm*. Joseph Breen to L.B. Mayer, 15 September 1939; *The Mortal Storm*, PCA/Academy Library.

58 *Four Sons* and *The Man I Married*; PCA/Academy Library.

59 C. Chaplin, *My Autobiography*, p. 386.

60 Breen replied to Gyssling that he had 'no knowledge' of Chaplin's plans, but that Gyssling's letter would be forwarded to Chaplin's manager. Georg Gyssling to Joseph Breen, 31 October 1938; Joseph Breen to Georg Gyssling, 2 November 1938; *The Great Dictator*, PCA/Academy Library.

61 Brooke Wilkinson to Joseph Breen, 2 March 1939; *The Great Dictator*. Breen responded by saying that 'upon enquiring I find that the whole thing is pretty nebulous. Chaplin has no script and he has no fixed story in mind. However, he has before him your cablegram and I think he understands what the situation is.' Joseph Breen to Brooke Wilkinson, 13 March 1939; *The Great Dictator*.

62 British Foreign Office to Brooke Wilkinson, 16 June 1939; FO 395/663, Public Record Office, London.

63 Joseph Breen to Charlie Chaplin Film Corporation, 6 September 1940; *The Great Dictator*, PCA/Academy Library.

64 Joseph Breen to William Hays, 4 March 1941; and Breen to Hays, 11 March 1941; *Man Hunt*, PCA/Academy Library.

65 Memo on Meeting with United Artists, 10 June 1940; *Pastor Hall*, PCA/Academy Library.

66 It was noted that Korda had given his approval for the commentary. PCA Memo, 1 December 1939, *The Lion has Wings*, PCA/Academy Library.

67 The British film *Contraband* was retitled *Blackout* for its American release, undoubtedly to emphasize its topicality. When the film was submitted to the Hays Office the reviewer stated that:

> Note was taken of the fact that the foreword of this film stated that it was made with the cooperation of the British Admiralty, the British Ministry of Economic Warfare and the British Ministry of Information. In our opinion, it is important that this statement should appear in all prints publicly exhibited in this country, in

order that before seeing the picture individuals in America may have this fact in mind.

Francis Harmon to Daniel O'Shea, 17 May 1940; *Blackout*, PCA/Academy Library.

68 Wanger's opinion was offered at a meeting between United Artists producers and Francis Harmon of the PCA. The purpose of the meeting seems to have been to persuade Samuel Goldwyn against purchasing the US distribution rights for *Pastor Hall*. Francis Harmon to Joseph Breen, 8 June 1940; *Pastor Hall*, PCA/Academy Library.

69 Memo on Meeting with United Artists, 10 June 1940; *Pastor Hall*

70 Joseph Breen to James Roosevelt, 19 July 1940; *Pastor Hall*.

71 *Goodbye Mr Chips*; *Lloyds of London, A Yank at Oxford*; PCA/Academy Library.

72 *The Sea Hawk*; *That Hamilton Woman*; PCA/Academy Library.

73 Joseph Breen to William Hays, 18 March 1940; *Foreign Correspondent*, PCA/Academy Library.

74 Joseph Breen to Walter Wanger, 21 February 1941; *Sundown*, PCA/Academy Library.

75 Joseph Breen to Colonel Jason Joy, 24 March 1941; PCA review by Shurlock and Metzger, 8 August 1941; *A Yank in the RAF*, PCA/Academy Library.

76 United States Senate, Seventy-Seventh Congress, First Session, *Propaganda in Motion Pictures, Hearing Before a Subcommittee of the Committee on Interstate Commerce, on Senate Resolution 152, September 9–26, 1941.*

77 *Ibid.*, pp. 6 and 48.

78 The seventeen films included thirteen American films and four British films that had been released in the United States. The thirteen American films were *The Devil Commands* (Columbia, 1941), *Escape* (MGM, 1940), *Four Sons* (TCF, 1940), *Foreign Correspondent* (UA, 1940), *The Great Dictator* (UA, 1940), *The Man I Married* (TCF, 1940), *Man Hunt* (TCF, 1941), *The Mortal Storm* (MGM, 1940), *Mystery Sea Raider* (Paramount, 1941), *One Night In Lisbon* (Paramount, 1941), *So Ends Our Night* (UA, 1941), *That Hamilton Woman* (UA, 1941) and *They Dare Not Love* (Columbia, 1941). The four British films were *Blackout/Contraband* (UA, 1940), *Night Train/Night Train to Munich* (TCF, 1940), *Pastor Hall* (UA, 1940) and *Voice in the Night/Freedom Radio* (Columbia, 1941). Many more films were mentioned and discussed throughout the hearings. See *The Motion Picture Herald* (13 September 1941), p. 24.

79 US Senate, *Propaganda in Motion Pictures*, pp. 117–121.

80 Nye and many of the other isolationist Senators had been opposed to the Lend-Lease provisions accorded to Britain and Russia. Hence, the reference to 'Empire and Communism'. *Ibid.*, p. 43.

81 *Ibid.*, p. 56.

82 *Ibid.*, pp. 38–40.

83 *Ibid.*, p. 73.

84 *Ibid.*, p. 54.

85 Charles Higham describes Alexander Korda as the 'famous producer and agent of the British Intelligence Service MI6', and then claims that Korda was instrumental in recruiting Saville to work for MI6 while he was in Hollywood. Little evidence is offered to support these

claims. C. Higham, *Merchant of Dreams: Louis B. Mayer, MGM and the Secret Hollywood*, p. 268.

86 Koppes and Black, *Hollywood Goes to War*, pp. 44–45.

87 A copy of Wendell Willkie's statement is held in a special collection, '1941 War Film Hearings', at The Margaret Herrick Library, Academy of Motion Pictures Arts and Sciences (hereafter Film Hearings/Academy Library).

88 A wide selection of press clippings on the hearings is included in Film Hearings/Academy Library.

89 *Variety* (3 September 1941), p. 1.

Chapter 3

1 Sidney Franklin's comments on the origins of *Mrs Miniver* are made in his unpublished autobiography, *We Laughed and We Cried*, pp. 296–297. In an (untitled) speech, Franklin also recalls that MGM intended to release *Mrs Miniver* at advanced prices, but that Roosevelt urged MGM to release the film as quickly as possible 'at the usual prices'. This, Franklin claims, reduced the gross by between $3 million and $5 million. Both the autobiography and the speech are held in the Kevin Brownlow Collection.

2 Franklin, *We Laughed and We Cried*, p. 298.

3 The Eddie Mannix Ledger; Mannix/Academy Library.

4 *Main Street after Dark* (1944), a very inexpensive 'B' film, is the only film in the ledger without any foreign earnings.

5 S. Morley, *Tales from the Hollywood Raj: The British Film Colony On Screen and Off*, p. 108.

6 Aubrey Solomon claims that *Cavalcade* earned as much as $3 million in the domestic market, but this would have made it one of the most popular films of the decade. Sheridan Morley's assertion that the film 'did badly at the box office' undermines that claim. A. Solomon, *Twentieth Century-Fox: A Corporate and Financial History*, p. 16. Morley, *Tales from the Hollywood Raj*, p. 109.

7 K. Kulik, *Alexander Korda: The Man Who Could Work Miracles* (1990), p. 96.

8 *Ibid.*, p. 97.

9 S. Marx, *Mayer and Thalberg: The Make-Believe Saints* (1988), pp. 208–209.

10 David Selznick's production memos from *David Copperfield* are published in R. Behlmer (ed.), *Memo from David O. Selznick* (1989), pp. 72–75.

11 *Ibid.*, p. 72.

12 George Cukor is quoted in G. Lambert, *On Cukor*, pp. 83–84.

13 Behlmer, *Memo from David O. Selznick*, p. 58.

14 T. Schatz, *The Genius of the System: Hollywood Film-making in the Studio Era*, p. 169.

15 G. Lambert, *Norma Shearer: A Life*, p. 159.

16 See S. Callow, *Charles Laughton: A Difficult Actor*, pp. 97–100; and P. Hay, *MGM: When the Lion Roars*, pp. 125–127.

17 Apart from *Romeo and Juliet* the only 'British' failure was *Parnell* (1937), which starred Clark Gable and Myrna Loy. Gable had few

flops in the 1930s, but this was one of them. The film lost $637,000. Excursions into French history fared far worse, though, as Greta Garbo's *Conquest* (1937) and Norma Shearer's *Marie Antoinette* (1938) cost nearly $3 million each and had combined losses of over $2 million. These films put an end to MGM's quest for prestige via costume dramas for many years.

18 It has been said that films such as *Romeo and Juliet* were made for prestige alone, and that MGM realized that they would not be profitable. It seems highly unlikely, though, that studio executives would agree to losses of this magnitude. See Gary Carey, *All the Stars There Are in Heaven: Louis B. Mayer and MGM*, pp. 197–198.

19 Lambert, *On Cukor*, p. 96.

20 Carey, *All the Stars There Are in Heaven*, p. 197.

21 Schatz, *The Genius of the System*, p. 172.

22 When Selznick was planning to produce *David Copperfield* in Britain, he proposed filming *Beau Brummel* at the same time, but the latter was not made until 1954. See Behlmer (ed.), *Memo from David O. Selznick*, p. 72. Selznick also proposed a production of Dickens' *A Christmas Carol*, to be made 'at very low cost' in 1935 (Behlmer, p. 82). This was made by MGM in 1938 on a low budget ($289,000). Selznick proposed an adaptation of Galsworthy's *The Forsyte Saga* in 1933 (Behlmer, p. 62), but MGM did not make *That Forsyte Woman* until 1949. *Jane Eyre* set box-office records on the Odeon Circuit in Britain in 1944 (see *The Motion Picture Herald*, 22 April 1944, p. 14).

23 See, for example, *Kinematograph Weekly* (29 August 1934), p. 3.

24 L. J. Leff, *Hitchcock and Selznick: The Rich and Strange Collaboration of Alfred Hitchcock and David O. Selznick*, p. 23. K. Barrow, *Mister Chips: The Life of Robert Donat*, p. 102. M. Balcon, *Michael Balcon Presents ... A Lifetime in Films*, p. 100.

25 Seven writers received screen credit for *A Yank at Oxford*: Malcolm Stuart Boylan, Walter Ferris, Sidney Gilliat, Leon Gordon, Michael Hogan, George Oppenheimer and John Monk Saunders (for the original scenario). The script files show that twenty-eight other writers worked on the script. They were: Chandos Balcon, R.V.C. Bodley, David Boelim, J.P. Carstairs, Lenore Coffee, John Considine, Frank Davis, Virginia Faulkner, F. Scott Fitzgerald, K. Fitzpatrick, Harold Goldman, John Higgins, Monkton Hoffe, Samuel Hoffenstein, Arthur Hyman, Bradley King, Sidney Kingsley, Charles Lederer, Joseph Mankiewicz, Elliot Morgan, Roland Pertwee, Gottfried Reinhardt, H.E. Rogers, Ben Travers, Catherine Turney, Hugh Walpole, Maurice Watkins and Frank Wead. *A Yank at Oxford* script files, MGM Script Collection, Doheny Library, University of Southern California (hereafter MGM/USC).

26 'Notes from Hyman, Rogers, Lederer', 11 February 1935; *A Yank at Oxford*, MGM/USC.

27 'Notes from R.V.C. Bodley', 16 March 1935; *A Yank at Oxford*.

28 'Notes by Mr Thalberg', 16 July 1936; *Goodbye Mr Chips*, MGM/USC.

29 K.R.M. Short reports that Franklin's 'pronounced anglophilia was occasionally embarrassing even for his English colleagues'. K.R.M. Short, 'Cinematic Support for the Anglo-American Detente', in Philip M. Taylor (ed.), *Britain and the Cinema in the Second World War*, p. 128.

30 R.C. Sherriff, Claudine West and Eric Maschwitz received screen credit for the script of *Goodbye Mr Chips*, but the film's legal file indi-

cates that five other writers were paid for their contributions: James Ricard, Monkton Hoffe, Chum Nelson, Lorraine Noble, Ian Dalrymple. *Goodbye Mr Chips*, legal file, Turner Entertainment Corporation (hereafter MGM/Turner).

31 Franklin was known as a slow and costly director, and so MGM was eager to give him a different role at the studio. Franklin, *We Laughed and We Cried*, p. 262.

32 The publicity for *Goodbye Mr Chips* was found in the British Film Institute's microfiche file on the film.

33 The Ministry of Information document, 'Programme for Film Propaganda', is quoted in Ian Christie (ed.), *Powell, Pressburger and Others*, p. 54.

34 *The Listener* (25 January 1940), p. 160.

35 K. Vidor, *A Tree is a Tree*, p. 99.

36 *The Citadel* was placed second to *Pygmalion* (1939) in the review of box-office performance for 1939. See *Kinematograph Weekly* (11 January 1940), p. 7. MGM's British manager, Sam Eckman, reported to studio head Louis B. Mayer that the film was likely to achieve a gross of £250,000 in Britain. Sam Eckman to L.B. Mayer, 5 January 1939; *The Citadel*, legal file, MGM/Turner.

37 Kulik, *Alexander Korda*, pp. 276–277. *The Motion Picture Herald* (11 March 1944), p. 46. Franklin, *We Laughed and We Cried*, p. 290.

38 Lambert, *Norma Shearer*, p. 282.

39 This opening is described in 'Sidney Franklin's Notes', 31 January 1941; *Mrs Miniver*, MGM/USC.

40 K. Brownlow, 'Sidney Franklin: The Modest Pioneer', *Focus on Film*, p. 31.

41 Franklin, *We Laughed and We Cried*, p. 290.

42 *Ibid.*, p. 291.

43 *Waterloo Bridge*, legal file, MGM/Turner.

44 *Kinematograph Weekly* (9 January 1941), p. 26.

45 Ben Goetz to Sam Eckman, 8 April 1942; Sam Eckman to Ben Goetz, 16 April 1942. *Random Harvest*, legal file, MGM/Turner.

46 J. Richards, *Visions of Yesterday*, p. 110.

47 *Variety* (6 January 1943), p. 58. *Kinematograph Weekly* (14 January 1943), p. 46.

48 *Kinematograph Weekly* (13 January 1944), p. 51.

49 *Kinematograph Weekly* (12 January 1945), p. 41.

50 American interest in 'British' films did return sporadically. In the 1950s, for example, MGM enjoyed substantial box-office success with the medieval adventure films *Ivanhoe* (1952) and *Knights of the Round Table* (1953), both of which were filmed in Britain.

Chapter 4

1 N. Roddick, *A New Deal in Entertainment: Warner Brothers in the 1930s*, pp. 235–248.

2 The financial figures for these films were found in the William Schaefer Ledger; Schaefer/USC.

3 Roddick, *A New Deal in Entertainment*, p. 246.

4 Hal Wallis to Harry Joe Brown, 13 December 1935; *The Sea Hawk*, Warner Brothers Script Collection, Wisconsin State Historical Society (hereafter WB/WSHS).

5 Miller's comment is reported in Rudy Behlmer and Tino Balio (eds), *The Sea Hawk*, p. 16.

6 Miller's first treatment, dated 25 August 1938, was entitled 'Beggars of the Sea'. The issue of Queen Elizabeth's reluctance to build a new fleet, and her final speech, emerged in the scripts dated 28 August 1939 through those dated 30 January 1940. *The Sea Hawk*, WB/WSHS.

7 The script dated 28 August 1939 was the first to contain the Queen's speech and also the final shots: 'the wooden masts dissolve to the steel super-structure of modern war-ships'. Both the speech and the final shots are also present in the shooting script dated 30 January 1940. *The Sea Hawk*, WB/WSHS.

8 Joseph Breen to Jack Warner, 24 January 1940; *The Sea Hawk*, PCA/ Academy Library.

9 Howard Koch was interviewed by Barry Norman in 'Talking Pictures', BBC Television, 22 February 1988, Transmission.

10 *The Daily Mail* (2 August 1940); *The London Evening News* (2 August 1940); *The Daily Express* (2 August 1940).

11 *Kinematograph Weekly* (9 January 1941).

12 Luigi Luraschi admitted as much to Joseph Breen when he pointed out that the pink pages attached to the scripts he was sending to Breen were 'protection takes ... covering the British propaganda in the script'. Luraschi to Breen, 30 December 1940; *One Night in Lisbon*, PCA Files.

13 N. J. Cull, *Selling War: The British Propaganda Campaign Against American Neutrality in World War Two*, pp. 51–52.

14 *Ibid.*

15 R.C. Sherriff, *No Leading Lady: An Autobiography*, pp. 335–336. Korda's nephew, Michael Korda, states bluntly that 'Winston Churchill suggested the subject of Nelson and Lady Hamilton [to Alexander Korda]'. See M. Korda, 'A Knight in Hollywood', *New York Magazine*, p. 32. The film's origins are discussed more cautiously in K. Kulik, *Alexander Korda: The Man Who Could Work Miracles* (1990), p. 245; and in K.R.M. Short, 'That Hamilton Woman: Propaganda, Feminism and the Production Code', *Historical Journal of Film, Radio and Television*, pp. 7–8.

16 Jeffrey Richards, *Visions of Yesterday*, pp. 2–7.

17 Laurence Olivier, *Confessions of an Actor*, p. 91.

18 Sherriff, *No Leading Lady*, p. 335.

19 Rozsa was interviewed for 'The Golden Years of Alexander Korda', a BBC documentary on Korda. The transcripts of the interviews for this programme are held as a special collection at the British Film Institute in London.

20 Joseph Breen to Alexander Korda, 16 September 1940; Breen to Korda, 15 October 1940; Korda to Breen, 25 October 1940; Breen to Korda, 30 October 1940; *That Hamilton Woman*, PCA/Academy Library.

21 *The New Republic* (21 April 1941); *The New York Times* (4 April 1941); *The New Yorker* (5 April 1941).

22 Kulik, *Alexander Korda*, p. 249.

23 The domestic gross for *That Hamilton Woman* was found in file 3, box 38, series 3A, UA/WSHS. *Wuthering Heights* earned a domestic gross of $1,083,884; file 3, box 38, series 3A, UA/WSHS. *Pride and Prejudice* earned a domestic gross of $1,001,000; Mannix/Academy Library.

24 *Kinematograph Weekly* (10 January 1941).

25 Wanger abandoned *Personal History* in June 1938. The *Foreign Correspondent* production file begins with Alfred Hitchcock going on the payroll on 26 September 1939. The British writers working with Hitchcock were Alma Reville (though she did not receive screen credit), Joan Harrison, Charles Bennett and James Hilton. The American humourist Robert Benchley also contributed dialogue. File 24, box 78, Wanger/WSHS.

26 F. Truffaut, *Hitchcock: The Definitive Study* (1986), pp. 191–193.

27 *Variety* (28 August 1940).

28 The Paris setting is indicated in the 'shooting script' dated 3 June 1940; *Foreign Correspondent*, file 24, box 78, Wanger/WSHS.

29 D. Reynolds, *Rich Relations: The American Occupation of Britain, 1942–1945*, p. 33.

30 The American and British earnings figures for *Foreign Correspondent* can be found in file 3, box 38, Series 3A, UA/WSHS. Its ranking among British releases is listed in *Kinematograph Weekly* (10 January 1940), p. 34.

31 *Documentary News Letter* (December 1940), p. 19.

32 Apparently Goebbels was able to obtain a print of the film from Switzerland. Truffaut, *Hitchcock*, pp. 190–191; and L. Halliwell, *Halliwell's Film Guide* (1977), p. 367.

33 The production files for *Eagle Squadron* contain a 'clippings file' of articles on the actual Eagle Squadron. A typical article from *The Los Angeles Daily News*, dated 4 August 1941, centres on one member of the squadron, Gregory Daymond. The article states that:

> His sister Loretta and his close friend George Hampton say that they have noticed a big change in his attitude since reaching Britain. He was just a big, shy long-legged nineteen-year-old youngster when he went across, full of the spirit of adventure. Now he writes long philosophical letters: 'when you get over here and see what's happening and you can really take a punch at those fellows, democracy really has some meaning. It isn't just a two bit word that's shouted over the radio.'

Eagle Squadron Clippings File, box 77, Wanger/WSHS.

34 Cull, *Selling War*, pp. 89–90.

35 The story credit for *A Yank in the RAF* went to Melville Crossman, a pseudonym often used by Darryl Zanuck. Story outline ('The Eagle Squadron') by Darryl Zanuck dated 25 October 1940; *A Yank in the RAF*, Twentieth Century-Fox Script Collection, Theater Arts Library, University of California at Los Angeles (hereafter Fox/UCLA).

36 Memo from Mr Zanuck dated 14 January 1941; *A Yank in the RAF*, Fox/UCLA.

37 The instructions to model the film on *A Yank at Oxford* are stated in 'The Eagle Flies Again: Story Conference with Mr Zanuck', 2 December 1940; and in 'Story Conference with Mr Zanuck, on the revised outline dated 23 November 1940'; *A Yank in the RAF*.

38 'The Eagle Flies Again', story conference notes dated 5 November 1940; *A Yank in the RAF*.

39 This sequence is based on fact. The Lockheed Aircraft Company built planes for the RAF, but under the US Neutrality Act of 1939 the planes could not be delivered directly to a 'belligerent' nation. Hence, Lockheed bought a plot of flat land in North Dakota, on the Canadian border. The planes were flown to North Dakota by American pilots, towed across the border, and flown on to Britain by RAF pilots. See R. Dimbleby and R. Reynolds, *An Ocean Apart*, p. 124.

40 The Air Ministry's earliest discussions with Zanuck and Walter Wanger, about the Eagle Squadron films and the film title, are described in a letter from Air Commodore Peake to Sidney Bernstein (at the Ministry of Information), dated 9 January 1941; and in a letter from Squadron Leader Williams to Jack Beddington (at the Ministry of Information) dated 25 May 1941. *Eagle Squadron* file, Public Record Office, London, Ministry of Information 1/625 (hereafter INF 1/625).

41 In the notes from a story conference dated 31 January 1941, it is stated that Zanuck 'discussed' the ending of the film 'unofficially with some British officials'; and that 'they do not want us to show any more deaths than are absolutely essential to our story, and especially, they do not think that the American should die ... We are going to revise our continuity [script] accordingly.' Two weeks earlier, Zanuck had sent the script for *A Yank in the RAF* to the Air Ministry for approval. Darryl Zanuck to British Air Ministry, 16 January 1941; 'Conference with Mr Zanuck', 31 January 1941; *A Yank in the RAF*, Fox/UCLA

42 Darryl Zanuck to Hal Wallis, 3 March 1941, *International Squadron*, Warner Brothers Script Collection, Doheny Library, University of Southern California (hereafter WB/USC).

43 The cost and earnings figures for *International Squadron* are taken from the William Schaefer Ledger; Schaefer/USC. Reports on the box-office performance of *A Yank in the RAF* can be found in *Variety* (31 December 1941) and *Kinematograph Weekly* (14 January 1943).

44 Walter Wanger to Quentin Reynolds, 6 November 1940; and Sidney Bernstein to Walter Wanger, 13 February 1941; file 23, box 77, Wanger/WSHS.

45 'Minutes from a meeting of the board of directors of Walter Wanger Productions, Incorporated', dated 2 May 1941, file 2, box 37, Wanger/WSHS.

46 Walter Wanger to George Archibald, 24 April 1941; INF 1/625. George Archibald to Walter Wanger, 28 April 1941; Sidney Bernstein to Walter Wanger, 29 April 1941; file 18, box 77, Wanger/WSHS.

47 Walter Wanger to George Archibald, 24 April 1941; Air Commodore Peake to Sidney Bernstein, 9 January 1941; INF 1/625.

48 Merian Cooper to Walter Wanger, 1 April 1941; file 18, box 77, Wanger/WSHS.

49 The brief scenario was written by the project's associate producer, Louis Huot. The fact that it was written by hand and on hotel stationery gives some indication of the haste with which it was put together. Louis Huot to Sidney Bernstein and Air Commodore Peake, 19 May 1941; INF 1/625.

50 Squadron Leader Williams to Jack Beddington, 25 May 1941; INF 1/625.

51 Notes from a meeting attended by Lord Willoughby de Broke, Squadron Leader Twist and Mr Beddington, 28 August 1941; INF 1/625.

52 Harry Watt to Walter Wanger, 22 September, 1941; file 19, box 77, Wanger/WSHS.

53 T. Balio, *United Artists: The Company Built By The Stars*, pp. 174–176.

54 *Eagle Squadron* production costs; file 24, box 77, Wanger/WSHS.

55 Walter Wanger to Sidney Bernstein, 17 April 1942; INF 1/625.

56 Wanger also used shots from the British documentaries *Moscow*, *Ack-Ack*, *Dover Front Line*, *London Can Take It*, *Squadron 992* and *Ferry Pilot*; Ministry of Information Memo, 30 March 1942; INF 1/625.

57 The earnings and profit figures on *Eagle Squadron* are listed in a report dated March 1945; file 24, box 77, Wanger/WSHS. The British ranking is from *Kinematograph Weekly* (14 January 1943), p. 46.

Chapter 5

1 R. Sklar, *Movie-Made America: A Cultural History of the Movies*, pp. 95–99.

2 D. Reynolds, *The Creation of the Anglo-American Alliance, 1937–1941: A Study in Competitive Cooperation*, p. 23.

3 *Ibid.*

4 'The Eagle Flies Again', story conference notes dated 5 November 1940; *A Yank in the RAF*, Fox/UCLA.

5 E. Knight, *This Above All*.

6 *The Times Literary Supplement* (15 November 1941), p. 565. A review of *This Above All* in *The New Yorker* (12 April 1941) gave Eric Knight 'credit' for being 'the first [author] to attack a big Second World War theme in the pages of a long and very serious novel'. Similarly, in *The Saturday Review of Literature* (5 April 1941), the critic stated that '*This Above All* is a much better book as a novel than we have any reason to expect, coming as it does so early in the war'.

7 P. Rotha (ed.), *Portrait of a Flying Yorkshireman: Letters from Eric Knight in the United States to Paul Rotha in England*, p. 177.

8 'Report to Mr Zanuck on *The Rains Came* from Philip Dunne and Julien Josephson [undated]' and 'Story Conference with Mr Zanuck, 13 May 1939; *The Rains Came*, Fox/UCLA.

9 'Conference with Mr Zanuck', 14 April 1941; and 'Conference with Mr Zanuck', 22 May 1940; *How Green Was My Valley*, Fox/UCLA.

10 'Treatment by R.C. Sherriff', 17 July 1941; *This Above All*, Fox/UCLA.

11 'Conference With Mr Zanuck (on script dated 17 September 1941)', 19 September 1941; *This Above All*.

12 'Conference with Mr Zanuck', 30 July 1941; *This Above All*.

13 'Conference with Mr Zanuck', 21 July 1941; 'Conference with Mr Zanuck, 30 July 1941; 'Conference with Mr Zanuck', 27 August 1941; *This Above All*. The Hays Office had no political objections to *This Above All*, but had many moral reservations. Zanuck was forced to make several concessions as the writing proceeded. Clive and Prudence have separate bedrooms when they go on holiday together, she does not become pregnant, and they marry in the ending. Zanuck, however, insisted that the film must include the haystack scene. The Hays Office protested, but Zanuck compromised by inserting a subse-

quent scene in which Prudence tells her father that she and Clive 'did nothing to be ashamed of'. Joseph Breen to Jason Joy, 23 September 1941; Joseph Breen to Jason Joy, 3 November 1941; Darryl Zanuck to Joseph Breen, 10 November 1941; *This Above All*, PCA/Academy Library.

14 'Conference with Mr Zanuck', 21 July 1941; *This Above All*, Fox/UCLA.

15 *Ibid.*

16 'Conference with Mr Zanuck', 27 August 1941; *This Above All*.

17 'Conference with Mr Zanuck', 30 July 1941; *This Above All*.

18 Rotha (ed.), *Portrait of a Flying Yorkshireman*, p. 193.

19 *Ibid.*, p. 214.

20 E.M. Forster, 'The Top Drawer But One', *The New Statesman and Nation* (4 November 1939), p. 648.

21 Jan Struther was the pen-name for Joyce Maxtone Grahame. She apparently based the stories on her own life. A recent reissue of the collected Mrs Miniver stories by the Virago Press contains a biographical essay on Grahame by Valerie Grove. The stories mentioned in the text are 'Mrs Miniver Comes Home' and 'The New Car'. Jan Struther, *Mrs Miniver* (1989).

22 *Ibid.*, pp. 122–123.

23 S. Franklin, *We Laughed and We Cried*, p. 296.

24 Franklin's activities are recorded in his diary, which is held in the Kevin Brownlow Collection.

25 'Treatment by R.C. Sherriff', 17 October 1940; *Mrs Miniver*, MGM/USC.

26 Hilton, George Froeschel and Arthur Wimperis wrote the 'complete dialogue script' dated February 1941. This was sent to the screenwriter Paul Osborn for revisions in July 1941, and Claudine West wrote the 'revised continuity script' dated 11 September 1941. *Mrs Miniver*, legal file, MGM/Turner.

27 Struther, *Mrs Miniver* (1989), p. 122.

28 *Mrs Miniver*, revised continuity script dated 11 September 1941, pp. 5–6. The William Wyler Collection, Theater Arts Library, University of California at Los Angeles (hereafter Wyler/UCLA).

29 'Notes from Sidney Franklin: After the Munich Crisis', 31 October 1940; *Mrs Miniver*, MGM/USC.

30 'Notes From Sidney Franklin', 10 December 1940; *Mrs Miniver*.

31 'Sidney Franklin's Notes to Mr Hilton and Mr Froeschel: The Romance of Vin and Carol and the Communism Episode', 28 November 1940; also 'Script Conference with Franklin, Hilton and Froeschel', 2 December 1940; *Mrs Miniver*.

32 'Changes', 18 October 1941; *Mrs Miniver*.

33 'Notes From Sidney Franklin', 2 November 1940; *Mrs Miniver*.

34 'Notes From Sidney Franklin', 10 December 1940; *Mrs Miniver*.

35 'Script Conference with Franklin, Hilton and Froeschel', 2 December 1940; *MrsMiniver*.

36 'Last Sequence of *Mrs Miniver*', by Sidney Franklin and George Froeschel, 15 January 1941; *Mrs Miniver*.

37 Wyler was released to MGM for fourteen weeks beginning on 29

September 1941, at a salary of $6,250 per week. Contract between Wyler and MGM dated 5 September 1941; file 10, box 53, Wyler/UCLA.

38 Axel Madsen, *William Wyler*, p. 214.

39 *Mrs Miniver*, scripts dated 18 October 1941 and 9 February 1942.

40 Sidney Franklin to Paul Osborn, 18 July 1941; *Mrs Miniver*, legal file, MGM/Turner.

41 'Story Notes from George Froeschel', 30 December 1940; *Mrs Miniver*, MGM/USC.

42 Madsen, *William Wyler*, p. 215. The Hays Office had no objections, of any sort, to an 18 August 1941 script of *Mrs Miniver*. The revised script for the German flyer scene was also approved, but it was submitted on 27 December 1941, after the United States had entered the war. Breen to Mayer, 18 September 1941; Breen to Mayer, 11 January 1942; *Mrs Miniver*, PCA/Academy Library.

43 *Mrs Miniver*, revised continuity script dated 11 September 1941, pp. 115–116; Wyler/UCLA.

44 Madsen, *William Wyler*, p. 216.

45 'Script Changes' (handwritten by Wyler), 10 October 1941; Wyler/UCLA.

46 *Mrs Miniver*, revised continuity script dated 9 February 1942; 'Retakes', 12 March 1942; *Mrs Miniver*, MGM/USC. Sidney Franklin's diary notes that *Mrs Miniver* finished filming on 7 February 1942.

47 Sidney Franklin informed William Wyler, in a letter dated 6 May 1942, of 'the last days of *Mrs Miniver*'. Franklin indicates that he and Margaret Booth had been editing the film for several weeks, and that they had seen the completed version three times the previous day. He also says he 'had an awful time getting that woman [Mrs Miniver] out of my hair'. Franklin to Wyler, 6 May 1942; Sidney Franklin Documents, The Kevin Brownlow Collection.

48 The final version of the vicar's speech was not written until 31 March 1942. 'Final Scene'; *Mrs Miniver*, MGM/USC.

49 *Mrs Miniver*, script dated 11 September 1941, p. 159; Wyler/UCLA.

50 Prior to *Mrs Miniver*, only three films had lasted for six weeks at Radio City Music Hall: *Rebecca* (1940), *The Philadelphia Story* (1940) and *Woman of the Year* (1941). *Mrs Miniver's* record was broken, though, when *Random Harvest* – another 'British' film produced by Franklin and starring Greer Garson – had an eleven-week run at Radio City Music Hall beginning in December 1942. These statistics are reported in *The Motion Picture Herald* (6 March 1943), p. 25.

51 Speech by Sidney Franklin, undated; Sidney Franklin Papers, The Kevin Brownlow Collection.

52 *Kinematograph Weekly* (14 January 1943), p. 43.

53 The critic in *Look* (11 August 1942) said: 'by concentrating on one family, *Mrs Miniver* becomes universal. It shows, with remarkable power, how every man, woman and child becomes a fighter in modern war.' And in *Life* (8 June 1942), the critic had similar praise: 'Wyler directs these family affairs with such warmth and good taste that *Mrs Miniver* packs more emotional wallop than any other fictional war film to date.'

54 Franklin, *We Laughed and We Cried*, p. 320.

55 *The New York Times* (5 June 1942).

56 *The Monthly Film Bulletin* (31 July 1942).

57 *The Spectator* (17 July 1942).

58 *The Documentary News Letter* (August 1942), p. 112.

59 Harry Ashbrook, 'She's A Disgrace to the Women of Britain', *The Sunday Pictorial* (26 July 1942).

60 *Variety* (6 January 1943), p. 58.

61 *Kinematograph Weekly* (14 January 1943), p. 46.

62 *The Motion Picture Daily* (12 June 1942); *The Hollywood Reporter* (13 May 1942); *Variety* (13 May 1942).

63 *The Sunday Times* (20 September 1942).

64 *The New Statesman* (20 September 1942).

Chapter 6

1 S. Morley, *Tales from the Hollywood Raj: The British Film Colony On Screen and Off*.

2 *Ibid.*, pp. 85–88.

3 Selznick was speaking particularly about Darryl Zanuck's tendency to cast American stars in British roles. In TCF's *Man Hunt* (1941) and *Confirm or Deny* (1941), Joan Bennett plays British roles, and in *The Rains Came* (1939) Myrna Loy plays Lady Esketh. Zanuck also cast Tyrone Power in British parts in *Lloyds of London* (1937), *This Above All* (1942) and *Son of Fury* (1942). R. Behlmer (ed.), *Memo from David O. Selznick* (1989), pp. 407–408.

4 D. Thomson, *Showman: The Life of David O. Selznick*, p. 308.

5 Niven is the first to admit this and, in fact, he pays tribute to Colman in his memoirs. See D. Niven, *Bring on the Empty Horses* (1976), pp. 177–186.

6 Morley, *Tales from the Hollywood Raj*, p. 129.

7 E. Flynn, *My Wicked, Wicked Ways*, p. 165.

8 G. McCann, *Cary Grant: A Class Apart*, p. 54.

9 J. Fontaine, *No Bed of Roses: An Autobiography*, p. 134.

10 Garson's actual background only emerged when she died. It was also revealed that she was not born in 1908, as her studio biography stated, but in 1904. This meant that, contrary to an often stated view, she was not too young to play Mrs Miniver. See *The Guardian* obituary (8 April 1996) and also the subsequent letters to the editor from those who knew her in London: *The Guardian* (13 April 1996). For MGM's preferred view of Garson's background, see *The New York Times* (15 March 1942).

11 R. Milland, *Wide-Eyed in Babylon*, p. 125.

12 As Sheridan Morley states, the Hollywood British 'were, by and large, a second-rate lot'. See Morley, *Tales from the Hollywood Raj*, pp. 90–91.

13 Niven, *Bring on the Empty Horses*, pp. 191–192.

14 Fontaine, *No Bed of Roses*, p. 116.

15 R.C. Sherriff, *No Leading Lady: An Autobiography*, p. 334.

16 *Picturegoer and Film Weekly* (27 January 1940), pp. 6–7.

17 *Picturegoer and Film Weekly* (11 May 1940), p. 11.

18 *The Times* (24 May 1940).

19 B. Aherne, *A Proper Job: The Autobiography of an Actor's Actor*, p. 289.

20 *Variety* (10 July 1940).

21 *Ibid.*

22 Lord Lothian's letter to Lord Halifax is reproduced in Aherne, *A Proper Job*, p. 290.

23 *The Sunday Dispatch* (25 August 1940).

24 Priestley's broadcast is mentioned in the letter from Lord Lothian to Lord Halifax. See Aherne, *A Proper Job*, p. 290.

25 *The New York Daily News* (26 August 1940).

26 *Variety* (10 July 1940). Despite the fact that he was supposedly an Irishman, Flynn is listed in this article as one who is beyond the age of conscription.

27 Aherne, *A Proper Job*, pp. 291–293; Fontaine, *No Bed of Roses*, p. 130; A. Neagle, *There's Always Tomorrow*, p. 126; *Variety* (10 July 1940).

28 RKO's legal file on *Forever and a Day* contains numerous letters and memos between studio executives and the producers, as well as production reports and financial documents. The file also contains the minutes of several of the board of directors' meetings. Cedric Hardwicke, Alfred Hitchcock, Victor Saville and Herbert Wilcox attended nearly all of the meetings. They were attended less frequently by Edmund Goulding, W.P. Lipscomb, Frank Lloyd and Robert Stevenson. The invitations to take part in the film, and the subsequent replies are noted in 'Minutes from a Board of Directors Meeting of Charitable Productions', 20 March 1940, 'Memorandum of Meeting Held at United Artists Studios', 10 May 1940; *Forever and a Day* legal file, RKO legal files, Turner Entertainment Corporation (hereafter RKO/Turner).

29 The news that Chaplin would appear made the front page of *Variety* (17 July 1940).

30 It appears that Lipscomb and Stevenson wrote the story outline only, and that it was then left to the producers to find writers to complete a continuity script for each episode. Unfortunately, there is no record of the authorship of the individual episodes. 'Accumulation on Deferred Production Number 1789', 23 November 1940; and Charles Koerner (RKO/Los Angeles) to Peter Rathvon (RKO/New York City), 10 November 1942; *Forever and a Day*, RKO/Turner.

31 *The Motion Picture Herald* (3 August 1940).

32 Samuel Goldwyn's interest is noted in Samuel Goldwyn to Herbert Wilcox, 29 April 1940; *Forever and a Day*, RKO/Turner. MGM's offer to house the production (in 1940) is noted in a letter from the producers' lawyer, Henry Herzbrun, to Charles Koerner, the head of production at RKO in 1942. However, no details of MGM's offer are mentioned. Henry Herzbrun to Charles Koerner, 10 November 1942; *Forever and a Day*.

33 RKO's enthusiasm for the film is expressed in numerous letters: George Schaefer to Ned Depinet, 15 May 1941; Reg Armour to B.D. Lion, 9 May 1941; Phil Reisman to Charles Julian, 3 February 1942; *Forever and a Day*.

34 'Contract Between RKO Studios and Charitable Productions', 5 December 1940; *Forever and a Day*.

35 *Ibid.*

36 Bosley Crowther is quoted in Morley, *Tales from the Hollywood Raj*, pp. 140–141.

37 The dates of filming are included in a memorandum which explains the many delays and problems the production encountered. One problem was that the producers could not agree upon a title for the film. At the time of this memo, it was being called 'This Changing World'. 'Report on This Changing World', 31 December 1941; *Forever and a Day*, RKO/Turner.

38 By this time, Herbert Wilcox had gone back to Britain and RKO's Reg Armour kept him abreast of the film's progress and problems. Reg Armour to Herbert Wilcox, 27 November 1941; *Forever and a Day*.

39 Problems with the third episode are reported in 'Minutes of a Board of Directors Meeting', 15 August 1941; 'Memo [from RKO] to Herbert Wilcox', 3 September 1941; George Schaefer to Victor Saville, 5 August 1941; *Forever and a Day*.

40 Ida Lupino is quoted in E. Katz, *The Macmillan International Film Encyclopedia* (1994), p. 855.

41 'Report on This Changing World', 31 December 1941; *Forever and a Day*.

42 R.C. Dale, 'René Clair in Hollywood', *Film Quarterly*, p. 38.

43 'Minutes from the Board of Directors Meeting', 17 April 1942; *Forever and a Day*, RKO/Turner.

44 *Ibid.*

45 Frank Lloyd to Charles Koerner, 15 July 1942; *Forever and a Day*.

46 T. Lloyd Richards (RKO) to Eric Cleugh (British Consulate, Los Angeles), 22 July 1942; and T. Lloyd Richards to Victor Saville, 24 July 1942; *Forever and a Day*.

47 Frank Lloyd to Charles Koerner, 15 July 1942; *Forever and a Day*.

48 By this time, Charitable Productions had been renamed Anglo-American Productions. Charles Koerner to Anglo-American Productions, 27 August 1942; *Forever and a Day*.

49 'Report on This Changing World', 31 December 1941; *Forever and a Day*.

50 'Preview Comment Cards', 29 December 1942; *Forever and a Day*.

51 *The New York Times* (13 March 1943); *The Evening Standard* (19 June 1943); *The Observer* (20 June 1943); *The Sunday Times* (20 June 1943).

52 *Variety* (3 March 1943); *Kinematograph Weekly* (26 April 1943).

53 The figures for the domestic earnings of *Forever and a Day*, and all subsequent references to the film's international earnings, are taken from 'Anglo-American Productions Report on *Forever and a Day* as at 28 March 1946'; *Forever and a Day*, RKO/Turner.

54 *Variety* (5 January 1944).

55 As a means of generating publicity for the film, the producers arranged for the head of the government of each country in which the film played to designate which charity the film's proceeds would benefit. In the United States, President Roosevelt named the National Foundation for Infant Paralysis, which received $253,692. US proceeds also went to the Community Chest of Los Angeles ($57,195) and the British Actors' Orphanage Fund ($66,362). In Britain, $284,066 went to the Red Cross, $113,626 went to the King's Fund and $28,407 went to the Cinematograph Trade Benevolent Fund. In

virtually every other country, the Red Cross was designated as the charity. The charitable contributions are specified in 'Anglo-American Productions Report on *Forever and a Day* as at 28 March 1946'; *Forever and a Day*, RKO/Turner.

56 Aherne, *A Proper Job*, p. 301.

57 Warners' overwhelmingly patriotic *This is the Army*, which includes the debut of the song 'God Bless America', was by far the most successful of these films. In the domestic market alone, the film earned $8,301,000. Yet the cast (Ronald Reagan, George Murphy, Joan Leslie) was hardly the best the studio could offer. WB's top stars (Humphrey Bogart, Bette Davis, Errol Flynn, Olivia De Havilland) did appear in *Thank Your Lucky Stars*, which earned $2,501,000. (The William Schaefer Ledger, Schaefer/USC). MGM's *Thousands Cheer* features appearances by Judy Garland, Gene Kelly, Mickey Rooney and many others, and it earned a domestic gross of $3,751,000 (The Eddie Mannix Ledger, Mannix/Academy Library). *Stage Door Canteen* and *Hollywood Canteen* feature an impressive array of Broadway stars and Hollywood stars, respectively, and each was reported to earn over $4,000,000. See J. Finler, *The Hollywood Story*, p. 276.

Chapter 7

1 C.R. Koppes and G.D. Black, *Hollywood Goes to War: How Politics, Profits and Propaganda Shaped World War Two Movies*, pp. 51–58.

2 Script Review, 14 December 1942; *Jane Eyre*, box 567/3519, Records of the Office of War Information, Record Group 208, Washington National Records Center (hereafter OWI Files).

3 For a survey of the films made in the immediate aftermath of Pearl Harbor, see Koppes and Black, *Hollywood Goes to War*, pp. 60–81.

4 Hollywood's reaction to Mellett's request is made clear in *The Hollywood Reporter* (11 January 1943), pp. 7–8. His apparent retraction is discussed in *The Hollywood Reporter* (22 February 1943), p. 8. Quigley and Wanger previously had disagreed in print over the Hays Office's policy of 'pure entertainment' in the late 1930s, when Wanger struggled to produce *Blockade* and was stopped from producing *Personal History*. Now, both the conservative businessman and the liberal producer agreed that the OWI was too concerned with ideology and too little concerned with entertainment. They both cited OWI opinions of 'British' films as part of their argument. Quigley found the OWI's criticism of *Random Harvest* to be ridiculous, while Wanger was furious that his *Eagle Squadron* had received a negative review. See Martin Quigley, 'The OWI: Policy and Performance', *The Motion Picture Herald* (6 March 1943), pp. 7–8; and Walter Wanger, 'The OWI and Motion Pictures', *Public Opinion Quarterly* (Spring 1943), pp. 43–47.

5 Koppes and Black, *Hollywood Goes To War*, pp. 105–106.

6 *Ibid.*, pp. 125–126.

7 *The Motion Picture Herald* (16 January 1943), p. 17.

8 Arnold Picker to Morton Spring, 6 March 1945; *Mrs Miniver*, box 567/3522, OWI Files.

9 Koppes and Black, *Hollywood Goes to War*, pp. 138–141.

10 *The Government Information Manual for the Motion Picture Industry*, p. 3; box 264/1433, OWI Files.

11 'American Attitudes Toward the British: Memorandum Number 65,

August 21, 1943'. This nineteen-page report is contained within Volume 2 ('The Allies') of a fifteen-volume series, *American Attitudes Toward World War Two: Intelligence Reports*. The series is held as a special collection by the Widener Library of Harvard University, Cambridge, Massachusetts.

12 'American Attitudes Toward the British', p. 6.

13 *Ibid.*, p. 12.

14 *Ibid.*

15 *Ibid.*, p. 1.

16 *Ibid.*, p. 13.

17 *Ibid.*, p. 1.

18 Among Walter Wanger's collected papers is an OWI 'confidential report' that was sent to him by Nelson Poynter. The report gives details of the age and income groups of Americans who were most likely to be hostile to the British, and offers the following comments on isolationist and anti-British feeling:

> Isolationist newspapers have begun an attack on Churchill and it seems that their anti-British efforts will be intensified. The *Chicago Tribune*, for example, is refurbishing the old complaints about 'British Imperialism'. The superficial unity which succeeded Pearl Harbor seems to have ended.

'Selected Comments on American Opinion', 13 April 1943; file 17, box 14, Wanger/Madison.

19 S. Morley, *Tales from the Hollywood Raj: The British Film Colony On Screen and Off*, pp. 134–135.

20 *Gunga Din* had a production cost of $1,915,000, making it RKO's most expensive film of the decade. When it earned $1,507,000 in the domestic market and $1,300,000 in foreign markets, it became the studio's second largest earner, after *Top Hat*. Yet because of print, distribution and publicity costs, it still showed a loss of $193,000. The re-release in 1942 was thus necessary to make the film profitable, and it is not surprising that the studio was reluctant to withdraw it. The earnings accumulated before it was withdrawn provided another $705,000 and enabled a profit of $445,000. See Appendix One of R.B. Jewell, 'RKO Film Grosses, 1929–1951: The C.J. Tevlin Ledger', *Historical Journal of Film, Radio and Television*.

21 Lowell Mellett to Nelson Poynter, 25 June 1942, box 264/1439, OWI Files.

22 Depinet's comments are reported in a OWI memorandum. Samuel Spewack to Lowell Mellett, 29 June 1942; box 264/1439, OWI Files.

23 Feature Review, 29 September 1942; *Gunga Din*, box 567/3517, OWI Files.

24 Victor Saville to Lowell Mellett, 15 September 1942; box 264/1441, OWI Files.

25 MGM had been considering an adaptation of *Kim* since January 1934, when it was considered as a vehicle for stars Jackie Cooper and Johnny Weissmuller. The story went through many treatments, and the plot indicated here is based on Leon Gordon and Richard Schayer's synopsis of their own script. '*Kim*: Story Synopsis', 9 September 1942, *Kim*; MGM/USC.

26 Nelson Poynter to Lowell Mellett, 4 August 1942; *Kim*, box 567/3520, OWI Files.

27 Victor Saville to Lowell Mellett, 18 September 1942; box 264/1441,

OWI Files.

28 Lowell Mellett to Victor Saville, 23 September 1942; and Victor Saville to Lowell Mellett, 30 September 1942; *Kim*, box 567/3520; OWI Files.

29 Ulric Bell to Robert Riskin, 6 January 1943; *Adventure in Iraq*, box 567/3511, OWI Files.

30 'Comments on *Adventure in Iraq*', Nelson Poynter to Steve Trilling (Warner Bros.), 28 December 1942; *Adventure in Iraq*.

31 Ulric Bell informed Robert Riskin (OWI/Washington DC) that Watterson Rothacker only agreed to revoke the export license when 'the State Department stepped in'. No further details are offered. Ulric Bell to Robert Riskin, 6 January 1943; *Adventure in Iraq*. The William Schaefer Ledger indicates that every other Warner Bros. film released in the 1940s had at least some foreign earnings, but there are none indicated for *Adventure in Iraq*. The film cost a mere $130,000 and earned only $147,000 in the domestic market. The William Schaefer Ledger, Schaefer/USC.

32 It was also regretted that the film portrays wartime London as 'anarchic and dangerous', that the murderer is anti-Nazi and thus a sympathetic character, and that the police seem to be inept. Feature Review, 2 December 1942; *The London Blackout Murders*, box 567/3519, OWI Files. The studio's avoidance tactics are reported in Ulric Bell to Robert Sherwood, 14 January 1943; *The London Blackout Murders*.

33 Feature Review, 18 December 1942; *The Great Impersonation*, box 567/3517, OWI Files.

34 The reviewer disliked the film enough to state, 'If the OWI launches a campaign for fewer and better war pictures, this is the kind of thing that should be eliminated.' Feature Review, 14 August 1942; *Sherlock Holmes and the Voice of Terror*, box 567/3525, OWI Files.

35 Feature Review, 12 April 1944; *The Secrets of Scotland Yard*, box 567/3525, OWI Files.

36 Feature Review, 17 October 1944; *Ministry of Fear*, box 567/3522, OWI Files.

37 Lord Halifax to William Wyler, 3 July 1942; box 10, Wyler/UCLA. Lord Halifax to Sidney Franklin, 3 July 1942, reproduced in the manuscript of S. Franklin, *We Laughed and We Cried*, p. 299; the Kevin Brownlow Collection.

38 See C. Moorehead, *Sidney Bernstein: A Biography*, pp. 141–142.

39 *The Daily Herald* (21 July 1942) and *The Spectator* (17 July 1942).

40 The *Times* reviewer expressed 'gratitude' for *Mrs Miniver* but also said that 'the picture of England at war suffers from the distortion which seems inevitable whenever Hollywood cameras are trained on it'; *The Times* (8 July 1942), p. 6. In Argentina, the country's foreign minister 'evidently wished to be seen applauding the film'; *The Times* (23 November 1942), p. 3. It was 'received enthusiastically' in Sweden, too; *The Times* (3 December 1942), p. 3. And in Switzerland *Mrs Miniver* was regarded as 'the outstanding event of the year in the cinema world' because it was playing to 'full houses' in Lausanne, Zurich and Geneva; *The Times* (1 January 1943), p. 3. Reaction to the film in the USA was reported in *The Times* (17 August 1942), p. 3.

41 Feature Review, 4 August 1942; *Mrs Miniver*, box 567/3522, OWI Files.

42 *Eagle Squadron* was said to be 'trivial' and 'disappointing'. Feature Review, 25 June 1942; *Eagle Squadron*, box 567/3515, OWI Files. Oddly, the reviewers never mentioned the English setting of *This Above All*, but praised the film for posing the question, 'What is the common man fighting for?' Feature Review, 25 June 1942; *This Above All*, box 567/3527, OWI Files.

43 Feature Review, 24 August 1942; *Mrs Miniver*, box 567/3522, OWI Files.

44 Memorandum by Ferdinand Kuhn, 7 January 1943; box 566/3509, OWI Files.

45 Ferdinand Kuhn to Lowell Mellett, 10 December 1942; *Random Harvest*, box 567/3524, OWI Files. The studio's response is indicated in Nelson Poynter to Lowell Mellett, 26 December 1942; *Random Harvest*.

46 The Provost of Eton recalled his earlier contact with MGM and his current view of the matter in a letter to Brendan Bracken. Lord Quickswood to Brendan Bracken, 16 March 1942; *A Yank at Eton*, legal file, MGM/Turner.

47 MGM's correspondence with Eton is recounted in an internal MGM memo; D. Decker to I. Prinzmetal, 24 February 1942; *A Yank at Eton*.

48 Mayer's comments are reported in Sam Eckman to Brendan Bracken, 8 April 1942; *A Yank at Eton*.

49 *A Yank at Eton*: Report by Florence Browning and James Fadiman, 17 April 1942; *A Yank at Eton*.

50 This arrangement is reported in Robert Rubin to David Decker, 11 June 1942; *A Yank at Eton*.

51 One of the scenes to be cut showed a 'free-for-all fight' in a night club, while the other showed the entire school being whipped as a punishment. Lord Halifax to L.B. Mayer, 31 July 1942; *A Yank at Eton*.

52 Feature Review, 30 September 1942; *A Yank at Eton*, box 567/3530, OWI Files.

53 'False Representations of Great Britain: Memorandum from Ferdinand Kuhn', 7 January 1943; box 566/3509, OWI Files. The memorandum itself was to be read by OWI staff only, but they were meant to use it as the basis for the advice they gave to film-makers. Ulric Bell, for example, used Kuhn's ideas as the basis for a speech he gave to the Independent Producers Association in Hollywood. This was then reported in *The Motion Picture Herald* without reference to specific films. See *The Motion Picture Herald* (27 February 1943), p. 21.

54 Ferdinand Kuhn to Ulric Bell, 17 February 1943; box 566/3509, OWI Files.

55 Kuhn reported his idea to Ulric Bell in a letter concerning *Forever and a Day*:

     After all that we and the British have been trying to do in this country to give the picture of a progressive, true-to-life England, it is discouraging to have an Englishman like [Cedric] Hardwicke suggest a picture that does just the reverse ... In this case I think I shall ask the British here in Washington to work on people like Hardwicke and other expatriates in Hollywood.

     Kuhn to Bell, 17 February 1943; box 566/3509, OWI Files. However, when Bell saw *Forever and a Day* he thought that its good points outweighed its tendency toward 'the England of the old order'. Ulric Bell to Ferdinand Kuhn, 10 March 1943; *Forever and a Day*, 567/3516, OWI Files.

56 The meeting is recounted in letters between Ulric Bell and Ferdinand Kuhn. Ulric Bell to Ferdinand Kuhn, 16 March 1943; box 566/3509, OWI Files. Ferdinand Kuhn to Ulric Bell, 24 March 1943; box 567/3529, OWI Files. The meeting was also reported in the trade papers. See *The Hollywood Reporter* (15 March 1943), p. 2.

57 Ulric Bell proposed that the director of the OWI, Elmer Davis, should request that British Information Services write guidelines for Hollywood film-makers on how to portray Britain in films. This would serve to 'reinforce the opinions now being given by the OWI and reduce the possibility of these opinions becoming capricious'. But Ferdinand Kuhn thought that this was a bad idea, because it would give the impression that 'the British government is setting up rules about what can and cannot be said about Great Britain'. The idea was then dropped. Ulric Bell to Ferdinand Kuhn, 15 March 1943; Ferdinand Kuhn to Ulric Bell, 26 March 1943; box 566/3509, OWI Files.

58 *The Hollywood Reporter* (22 February 1943), p. 6.

59 The script files for both films begin in June 1942, which was the month that *Mrs Miniver* opened at Radio City Music Hall in New York City.

60 Dialogue Continuity Script by Arthur Wimperis, 27 July 1942; *If Winter Comes*, MGM/USC.

61 Russell's comments are offered in Marjorie Russell to Ulric Bell, 26 May 1943; *If Winter Comes*, box 567/3518, OWI Files. The MGM and OWI files for *If Winter Comes* end without explanation in June 1943. The film was not made until 1947 (see the Filmography for details).

62 Russell and Butler's views were reported in Ulric Bell to Ferdinand Kuhn, 29 March 1943; box 566/3509, OWI Files.

63 Ulric Bell told Ferdinand Kuhn that 'MGM is being tough about *White Cliffs*, mainly, I am told, because of Sidney Franklin's prima donna status'. Ulric Bell to Ferdinand Kuhn, 29 March 1943; box 566/3509, OWI Files. Earlier, Nelson Poynter had sent comments on the screenplay to MGM executive Eddie Mannix with a cover letter stating that he realized the criticisms would not be welcomed, because the film was a 'tremendously important and expensive picture' and because 'you have unusual problems of temperament involved'. Nelson Poynter to Eddie Mannix, 12 March 1943; *The White Cliffs of Dover*, box 567/3529, OWI Files.

64 Franklin wrote of his enthusiasm for *The White Cliffs of Dover*, and his belief that it would improve Anglo-American understanding in a letter to his friend, the British screenwriter Chum Nelson:
It's really the story of America and England and I think it will be very timely and will help to unify our two countries, which is most important for the peace of the world. A subject like this is interesting to work on. There is not a propaganda thought, unless truth is propaganda.
Franklin's letter is reproduced in Franklin, *We Laughed and We Cried*, p. 320.

65 Sidney Franklin later told Poynter that he 'was indeed shocked' when he first read the comments. S. Franklin to N. Poynter, 10 May 1943; *The White Cliffs of Dover*, box 567/3529, OWI Files.

66 Script Review, 2 March 1943; *The White Cliffs of Dover*.

67 Notes from C. West, 31 March 1943; *The White Cliffs of Dover*, MGM/USC.

68 The technical adviser was C.S. Ramsay-Hill a retired major in the

British Army. He admitted feeling 'misgivings' after reading the script, particularly in regard to its emphasis upon arguments between the British and American characters. Whereas Miller's poem had 'essentially well bred characters' these arguments made them seem 'harsh if not offensive'. He also complained that 'it seems a pity that there is not more of the modern England, the England of 1943'. MGM Inter-Office Communication from Major C.S. Ramsay-Hill, 3 April 1943; *The White Cliffs of Dover*, MGM/USC.

69 Lowell Mellett to Nelson Poynter, 22 March 1943; *The White Cliffs of Dover*, box 567/3529, OWI Files.

70 It was in the spring of 1943 that both Walter Wanger and Martin Quigley wrote articles complaining of the OWI's incompetence. And, in fact, in January 1943 the OWI had already been reprimanded publicly by MGM over remarks that one of the officials from the British division had made about *Mrs Miniver*. The official told a reporter from *Film Daily* that the British public 'disliked *Mrs Miniver* intensely'. The manager of MGM's international department, Dave Blum, promptly wrote letters to both Elmer Davis and the editor of *Film Daily*, which listed every accolade the film had received in Britain and suggested that the OWI was elitist and out of touch with the public. Dave Blum to Elmer Davis, 8 January 1943, *Mrs Miniver* legal file, MGM/Turner. See also *Film Daily* (8 January 1943).

71 Feature Review, 10 March 1944; *The White Cliffs of Dover*, box 567/3529, OWI Files.

72 Ulric Bell to Ferdinand Kuhn, 27 May 1943; box 566/3509, OWI Files.

73 It appears that Kuhn was worried about *Flare Path* because its story focuses on officers and not 'ordinary English people'. Rattigan's story was later filmed in Britain as *The Way to the Stars* (1945). In the same letter, there is also a comment about an unnamed studio that was planning a film entitled *Mr Bullfinch Takes a Walk*. This too bothered Kuhn, who thought that 'the use of Churchill in this film would be highly objectionable to the British'. This seems to be another project that was cancelled. Ferdinand Kuhn to Ulric Bell, 17 February 1943; box 566/3509, OWI Files.

74 The reviewer was pleased with both the final comment and the fact that the film had little relevance to the war. Feature Review, 17 June 1943; *Sherlock Holmes Faces Death*, box 567/3525, OWI Files.

75 The OWI originally had many objections to Republic's *Thumbs Up*, which centres on an American singer working in a British factory. But they were all overcome after Russell 'worked closely with Republic' revising the script. Ulric Bell to Nelson Poynter, 29 March 1943, *Thumbs Up*, box 567/3524, OWI Files.

76 There were eleven 'British' films made in 1942 and twelve made in 1943, but only three of these were set in the past: *The Moon and Sixpence*, *Son of Fury* and *Forever and a Day*.

77 There were thirteen 'British' films made in 1944 and nine made in 1945, yet apart from the *Sherlock Holmes* films, which avoided war issues, only four were set during wartime: *The White Cliffs of Dover*, *Ministry of Fear*, *Scotland Yard Investigator* and *Vacation from Marriage*.

78 Script Review, 30 November 1942; *Jane Eyre*, box 567/3519, OWI Files.

79 Feature Review, 9 February 1945; *The Corn is Green*, box 567/3514, OWI Files.

80 Feature Review, 19 October 1944; *The Picture of Dorian Gray*, box 567/3523, OWI Files.

81 Feature Review, 22 September 1944; *None but the Lonely Heart*, box 567/3523, OWI Files.

82 Feature Review, 6 August 1943; *Lassie Come Home*, box 567/3520, OWI Files.

83 *National Velvet* was praised for being 'a subtle and profound illustration of the values inherent to living in a democracy'. William Cunningham (OWI) to Louis Chappelear (MGM), 9 October 1944; *National Velvet*, box 567/3523, OWI Files.

Filmography: Hollywood's 'British' films, 1930–50

Key:

US film title/British film title (film distributor, year of release)

pro   producer(s)

dir   director(s)

sc   author(s) of screenplay (orginal source of screenplay)

c   cast

Adventure in Iraq (WB, 1943)

pro: William Jacobs

dir: D. Ross Lederman

sc: George Bilsen, Robert E. Kent (based on the play by William Archer)

c: John Loder, Ruth Ford, Warren Douglas, Paul Cavanagh, Barry Bernard, Peggy Carson

The Adventures of Robin Hood (WB, 1938)

pro: Henry Blanke

dir: Michael Curtiz

sc: Norman Reilly Raine, Seton I. Miller

c: Errol Flynn, Olivia De Havilland, Basil Rathbone, Claude Rains, Ian Hunter, Eugene Pallette, Alan Hale, Melville Cooper, Patric Knowles, Herbert Mundin, Una O'Connor, Montagu Love, Robert Noble, Robert Warwick, Reginald Sheffield, Holmes Herbert

The Adventures of Sherlock Holmes/Sherlock Holmes (TCF, 1939)

pro: Gene Markey

dir: Alfred Werker

sc: Edwin Blum, William Drake (based on characters created by Arthur Conan Doyle)

c: Basil Rathbone, Nigel Bruce, George Zucc, Ida Lupino, Alan Marshal, E.E. Clive, Mary Gordon, Terry Kilburn, Henry Stephenson, Arthur Hohl,

May Beatty, Holmes Herbert

The Barretts of Wimpole Street (MGM, 1934)

pro: Irving Thalberg

dir: Sidney Franklin

sc: Ernest Vajda, Claudine West, Donald Ogden Stuart (based on the play by Rudolf Besier)

c: Norma Shearer, Fredric March, Charles Laughton, Maureen O'Sullivan, Katharine Alexander, Una O'Connor, Ralph Forbes, Ian Wolfe, Leo Carroll, Marion Clayton

Beau Geste (Paramount, 1939)

pro: William Wellman

dir: William Wellman

sc: Robert Carson (based on the novel by P.C. Wren)

c: Gary Cooper, Ray Milland, Robert Preston, Brian Donlevy, J. Carroll Naish, Susan Hayward, Heather Thatcher, James Stephenson, Donald O'Connor, G.P. Huntley Jr

Berkeley Square (Fox, 1933)

pro: Jesse L. Lasky

dir: Frank Lloyd

sc: Sonya Levien, John L. Balderston (based on the play by John L. Balderston)

c: Leslie Howard, Heather Angel, Valerie Taylor, Irene Browne, Beryl Mercer, Colin Keith Johnson, Alan Mowbray

The Bishop Misbehaves/The Bishop's Misadventures (MGM, 1935)

pro: Lawrence Weingarten

dir: E.A. Dupont

sc: Leon Gordon, George Auerbach (based on the play by Frederick Jackson)

c: Lucile Watson, Maureen O'Sullivan, Edmund Gwenn, Reginald Owen, Dudley Digges

Blond Cheat (RKO, 1938)

pro: William Sistrom

dir: Joseph Santley

sc: Charles Kaufman, Paul Yawitz, Viola Brothers Shore, Harry Segall (based on the story by Aladar Lazlo)

c: Cecil Kellaway, Joan Fontaine, Lilian Bond, Derrick De Marney, Cecil Cunningham

The Body Snatcher (RKO, 1945)

pro: Val Lewton

dir: Robert Wise

sc: Philip MacDonald, Carlos Keith (based on the story by Robert Louis Stevenson)

c: Boris Karloff, Bela Lugosi, Henry Daniell, Edith Atwater, Russell Wade, Sharyn Moffett

The Brighton Strangler (RKO, 1943)

pro: Sid Rogell, Herman Schlom

dir: Max Nosseck

sc: Max Nosseck, Arnold Phillips, Hugh Gray

c: John Loder, June Duprez, Michael St Angel, Miles Mander, Rose Hobart, Gilbert Emery, Rex Evans, Matthew Boulton, Olaf Hytten, Lydia Bilbrook, Ian Wolfe

British Intelligence/Enemy Agent (WB, 1940)

pro: Brian Foy

dir: Terry Morse

sc: Lee Katz (based on the play by Anthony Paul Kelly)

c: Boris Karloff, Margaret Lindsay, Maris Wrixon, Bruce Lester, Leonard Mudie, Holmes Herbert

Bulldog Drummond (UA, 1929)

pro: Samuel Goldwyn

dir: F. Richard Jones

sc: Sidney Howard (based on the play by H.C. McNeile and Gerald Du Maurier)

c: Ronald Colman, Joan Bennett, Claud Allister, Lilyan Tashman, Montagu Love

Bulldog Drummond at Bay (Col, 1947)

pro: Louis Appleton Jr, Bernard Small

dir: Sidney Salkow

sc: Frank Gruber (based on the novel by H.C. McNeile)

c: Ron Randell, Anita Louise, Pat O'Moore, Terence Kilburn, Holmes Herbert

Bulldog Drummond Escapes (Congress Films, 1937)

pro: not listed

dir: James Hogan

sc: Edward T. Lowe (based on the story by H.C. McNeile)

c: Ray Milland, Sir Guy Standing, Heather Angel, Reginald Denny, Fay Holden, E.E. Clive.
This was the first in a series of eight 'Bulldog Drummond' films made by Congress Films. All were based on stories by H.C. McNeile, and all of the seven films that followed feature actors John Howard, Reginald Denny and E.E. Clive. The list below gives the title, year of production and the other principal cast members:

Bulldog Drummond Comes Back (1937): John Barrymore, Louise Campbell

Bulldog Drummond's Revenge (1937): John Barrymore, Louise Campbell

Bulldog Drummond's Peril (1938): John Barrymore, Louise Campbell

Arrest Bulldog Drummond! (1938): Heather Angel, H.B. Warner

Bulldog Drummond in Africa (1938): Heather Angel, H.B. Warner

Bulldog Drummond's Bride (1939): Heather Angel, H.B. Warner

Bulldog Drummond's Secret Police (1939): Heather Angel, H.B. Warner

Bulldog Drummond Strikes Back (UA, 1934)

pro: Joseph M. Schenk

dir: Roy Del Ruth

sc: Nunnally Johnson (based on the novel by H.C. McNeile)

c: Ronald Colman, Loretta Young, C. Aubrey Smith, Charles Butterworth, Warner Oland, Una Merkel, Arthur Hohl, Ethel Griffies, E.E. Clive, Halliwell Hobbes, Billy Bevan

Bulldog Drummond Strikes Back (Col, 1947)

pro: Louis Appleton Jr, Bernard Small

dir: Frank McDonald

sc: Edna Anhalt, Edward Anhalt, L.E. Taylor (based on the novel by H.C. McNeile)

c: Ron Randell, Gloria Henry, Pat O'Moore, Terence Kilburn, Holmes Herbert

But the Flesh is Weak (MGM, 1932)

pro: Irving Thalberg

dir: Jack Conway

sc: Ivor Novello (based on his play *The Truth Game*)

c: Robert Montgomery, Heather Thatcher, C. Aubrey Smith, Edward Everett Horton, Nora Gregor, Nils Asther, Fred Kerr, Forrester Harvey

The Canterville Ghost (MGM, 1944)

pro: Arthur L. Field

dir: Jules Dassin

sc: Edwin Harvey Blum (based on the story by Oscar Wilde)

c: Robert Young, Margaret O'Brien, Charles Laughton, Reginald Owen, Peter Lawford, Elizabeth Risdon, Una O'Connor, Lumsden Hare, William Gargan, Rags Raglan

Captain Blood (WB, 1935)

pro: Hal B. Wallis, Harry Joe Brown, Gordon Hollingshead

dir: Michael Curtiz

sc: Casey Robinson (based on the novel by Rafael Sabatini)

c: Errol Flynn, Olivia De Havilland, Lionel Atwill, Basil Rathbone, Ross Alexander, Guy Kibbee, Henry Stephenson, Robert Barrat, Hobart Cavanaugh, Donald Meek, Jessie Ralph, Forrester Harvey, Holmes Herbert, E.E. Clive, David Torrence, J. Carrol Naish, Leonard Mudie

Cavalcade (Fox, 1932)

pro: Winfield Sheehan

dir: Frank Lloyd

sc: Reginald Berkeley (based on the play by Noel Coward)

c: Clive Brook, Diana Wynyard, Ursula Jeans, Herbert Mundin, Una O'Connor, Irene Browne, Merle Tottenham, Beryl Mercer, Frank Lawton, Billy Bevan, John Warburton

The Challenge (TCF, 1948)

pro: Ben Pivar, Bernard Small

dir: Jean Yarbrough

sc: Frank Gruber, Irving Elman (based on the story by H.C. McNeile)

c: Tom Conway, June Vincent, Richard Stapley, Eily Manyon, Terence Kilburn

The Charge of the Light Brigade (WB, 1936)

pro: Hal B. Wallis, Sam Bischoff

dir: Michael Curtiz

sc: Michael Jacoby, Rowland Lee (based on an original historical story by Michael Jacoby and the poem by Alfred, Lord Tennyson)

c: Errol Flynn, Olivia De Havilland, Patric Knowles, Henry Stephenson, Nigel Bruce, Donald Crisp, David Niven, C. Henry Gordon, G.P. Huntley Jr, Spring Byington, E.E. Clive, Lumsden Hare, Holmes Herbert, Reginald Sheffield, Robert Barret

A Christmas Carol (MGM, 1938)

pro: Joseph Mankiewicz

dir: Edwin L. Marin

sc: Hugo Butler (based on the story by Charles Dickens)

c: Reginald Owen, Gene Lockhart, Kathleen Lockhart, Terry Kilburn, Leo G. Carroll, Lynne Carver, Lionel Braham, Ann Rutherford, Halliwell Hobbes, Billy Bevan

A Chump at Oxford (MGM, 1939)

pro: Hal Roach

dir: Alfred Goulding

sc: Charles Rogers, Harry Langdon, Felix Adler

c: Stan Laurel, Oliver Hardy, James Finlayson, Forrester Harvey, Wilfred Lucas

The Citadel (MGM, 1938)

pro: Victor Saville

dir: King Vidor

sc: Ian Dalrymple, Frank Wead, Elizabeth Hill, Emlyn Williams (based on the novel by A.J. Cronin)

c: Robert Donat, Rosalind Russell, Ralph Richardson, Rex Harrison, Emlyn Williams, Mary Clare, Cecil Parker, Francis L. Sullivan, Penelope Dudley Ward, Nora Swinburne

Clive of India (UA, 1934)

pro: Darryl F. Zanuck, Willian Goetz

dir: Richard Boleslawski

sc: W.P. Lipscomb, R.J. Minney (based on their play Clive)

c: Ronald Colman, Loretta Young, Colin Clive, Francis Lister, C. Aubrey Smith, Cesar Romero, Montagu Love, Lumsden Hare, Ferdinand Munier, Gilbert Emery, Leo G. Carroll, Eily Manyon, Leonard Mudie, Francis Lister

Confirm or Deny (TCF, 1941)

pro: Len Hammond

dir: Archie Mayo

sc: Jo Swerling (based on the story by Henry Wales and Samuel Fuller)

c: Don Ameche, Joan Bennett, Roddy McDowall, Arthur Shields, Raymond Walburn, John Loder, Eric Blore, Queenie Leonard, Billy Bevan, Alan Napier, Lumsden Hare

The Corn is Green (WB, 1945)

pro: Jack Chertok

dir: Irving Rapper

sc: Casey Robinson, Frank Cavett (based on the play by Emlyn Williams)

c: Bette Davis, Nigel Bruce, Rhys Williams, Rosalind Ivan, Mildred Dunnock, Arthur Shields, Gwyneth Hughes, Billy Roy, Thomas Louden, John Dall, Joan Lorring

Cynara (UA, 1933)

pro: Samuel Goldwyn

dir: King Vidor

sc: Frances Marion, Lynn Starling (based on the play by H.M. Harwood and Robert Gore-Brown and its source novel, *An Imperfect Lover*, by Robert Gore-Brown)

c: Ronald Colman, Kay Francis, Phyllis Barry, Henry Stephenson, Paul Porcasi

The Dark Angel (UA, 1935)

pro: Samuel Goldwyn

dir: Sidney Franklin

sc: Lillian Hellman, Mordaunt Shairp (based on the play by H.B. Trevelyan)

c: Merle Oberon, Fredric March, Herbert Marshall, Janet Beecher, John Halliday, Henrietta Crosman, Frieda Inescort, George Breakston, Claud Allister, Fay Chaldecott

David Copperfield (MGM, 1934)

pro: David O. Selznick

dir: George Cukor

sc: Hugh Walpole, Howard Estabrook (based on the novel by Charles Dickens)

c: Edna May Oliver, Elizabeth Allan, Jessie Ralph, Freddie Bartholomew, Basil Rathbone, Herbert Mundin, Una O'Connor, Lionel Barrymore, Violet Kemble-Cooper, W.C. Fields, Elsa Lanchester, Lennox Pawle, Roland Young, Lewis Stone, Frank Lawton, Madge Evans, Maureen O'Sullivan, Arthur Treacher, Hugh Walpole

The Devil to Pay (Goldwyn, 1930)

pro: Samuel Goldwyn

dir: George Fitzmaurice

sc: Frederick Lonsdale, Benjamin Glazer (based on the play by Frederick Lonsdale)

c: Ronald Colman, Loretta Young, Myrna Loy, Frederick Kerr, David Torrence, Mary Forbes, Paul Cavanagh, Florence Britton

Devotion (WB, 1945)

pro: Robert Buckner

dir: Curtis Bernhardt

sc: Keith Winter (original story by Theodore Reeves)

c: Ida Lupino, Paul Henreid, Olivia De Havilland, Sydney Greenstreet, Nancy Coleman, Arthur Kennedy, Dame May Whitty, Montagu Love, Ethel Griffies, Eily Malyon, Forrester Harvey, Edmund Breon, Billy Bevan

Disraeli (WB, 1929)

pro: not indicated

dir: Alfred Green

sc: Julien Josephson (based on the play by Louis N. Parker)

c: George Arliss, Joan Bennett, Florence Arliss, Anthony Bushell, David Torrence

Dracula (Uni, 1931)

pro: Carl Laemmle Jr

dir: Tod Browning

sc: Garrett Fort (based on the novel by Bram Stoker)

c: Bela Lugosi, Helen Chandler, David Manners, Dwight Frye, Edward Van Sloan

Dr Jekyll and Mr Hyde (Par, 1932)

pro: Rouben Mamoulian

dir: Rouben Mamoulian

sc: Samuel Hoffenstein, Percy Heath (based on the novel *The Strange Case of Dr Jekyll and Mr Hyde* by Robert Louis Stevenson)

c: Fredric March, Miriam Hopkins, Rose Hobart, Holmes Herbert, Halliwell Hobbes

Dr Jekyll and Mr Hyde (MGM, 1941)

pro: Victor Fleming

dir: Victor Fleming

sc: John Lee Mahin (based on the novel *The Strange Case of Dr Jekyll and Mr Hyde* by Robert Louis Stevenson)

c: Spencer Tracy, Ingrid Bergman, Lana Turner, Donald Crisp, Ian Hunter, C. Aubrey Smith, Barton MacLane, Sara Allgood, Frederick Worlock, Billy Bevan, Forrester Harvey, Lumsden Hare

Eagle Squadron (Uni, 1942)

pro: Walter Wanger

dir: Arthur Lubin

sc: Norman Reilly Raine (based on the story by C.S. Forester)

c: Robert Stack, Diana Barrymore, John Loder, Eddie Albert, Nigel Bruce, Leif Erikson, Edgar Barrier, John Hall, Evelyn Ankers, Isobel Elsom, Gladys Cooper, Alan Hale Jr., Robert Warwick, Rhys Williams, Paul Cavanagh, Alan Napier, Jill Esmond, Queenie Leonard, Ian Wolfe, with commentary by Quentin Reynolds

The Earl of Chicago (MGM, 1940)

pro: Victor Saville

dir: Richard Thorpe

sc: Lesser Samuels, Gene Fowler, Charles de Grandcourt (based on the book by Brock Williams)

c: Robert Montgomery, Edward Arnold, Edmund Gwenn, Reginald Owen, E.E. Clive, Ronald Sinclair, Norma Varden, Halliwell Hobbes, Ian Wolfe, Billy Bevan

Foreign Correspondent (UA, 1940)

pro: Walter Wanger

dir: Alfred Hitchcock

sc: Charles Bennett, Joan Harrison, James Hilton, Robert Benchley, Ben Hecht

c: Joel McCrea, Laraine Day, Herbert Marshall, George Sanders, Albert Basserman, Robert Benchley, Edmund Gwenn, Harry Davenport, Eduardo Ciannelli, Martin Kosleck, Frances Carson, Ian Wolfe, Emory Parnell, Holmes Herbert, Leonard Mudie

Forever and a Day (RKO, 1943)

pro/dir: René Clair, Edmund Goulding, Cedric Hardwicke, Frank Lloyd, Victor Saville, Robert Stevenson, Herbert Wilcox

sc: Charles Bennett, Alan Cambell, Norman Corwin, C.S. Forester, Peter Godfrey, Jack Hartfield, Lawrence Hazard, S.M. Herzig, James Hilton, Michael Hogan, Christopher Isherwood, Emmet Lavery, W.P. Lipscomb, Gene Lockhart, Frederick Lonsdale, Alice Duer Miller, R.C. Sherriff, Donald Ogden Stewart, John Van Druten, Claudine West, Keith Winter

c: Brian Aherne, Harry Allen, Claud Allister, Wendy Barrie, May Beatty, Billy Bevan, Eric Blore, Anita Bolster, Nigel Bruce, Clyde Cook, Gladys Cooper, Robert Coote, Alec Craig, Donald Crisp, Robert Cummings, June Duprez, Alan Edmiston, Isobel Elsom, Barbara Everest, Emily Fitzroy, Marta Gale, Reginald Gardiner, Ethel Griffies, Ernest Grooney, Edmund Gwenn, Sir Cedric Hardwicke, Lumsden Hare, Joy Harrington, Richard Haydn, Halliwell Hobbes, Dennis Hoey, Edward Everett Horton, Wendell Hulett, Ian Hunter, Charles Irwin, June, Buster Keaton, Cecil Kellaway, Walter Kingsford, George Kirby, Patric Knowles, Elsa Lanchester, Charles Laughton, Anna Lee, Connie Leon, Queenie Leonard, Doris Lloyd, Gene Lockhart, June Lockhart, Montague Love, Ida Lupino, Victor McLaglen, Herbert Marshall, Aubrey Mather, Jessie Matthews, Ray Milland, Doreen Monroe, Daphne Moore, Arthur Mulliner, Odette Myrtil, Anna Neagle, Merle Oberon, Una O'Connor, Reginald Owen, Helena Pickard, Jean Prescott, Claude Rains, Stuart Robertson, Clifford Severn, Ivan Simpson, C. Aubrey Smith, Gerald Oliver Smith, Kent Smith, Arthur Treacher, Pax Walker, Ruth Warrick, Ben Webster, Dame May Whitty, Roland Young

The Fountain (RKO, 1934)

pro: Pandro S. Berman

dir: John Cromwell

sc: Jane Murfin, Samuel Hoffenstein (based on the novel by Charles Morgan)

c: Ann Harding, Brian Aherne, Paul Lukas, Jean Hersholt, Ralph Forbes, Violet Kemble-Cooper, Sara Haden, Ian Wolfe

Four Men and a Prayer (TCF, 1938)

pro: Kenneth MacGowan

dir: John Ford

sc: Richard Sherman, Sonya Levien, Walter Ferris (based on the novel by David Garth)

c: David Niven, George Sanders, Richard Greene, William Henry, Loretta Young, C. Aubrey Smith, J. Edward Bromberg, John Carradine, Alan Hale, Reginald Denny

Frenchman's Creek (TCF, 1944)

pro: B.G. De Sylva

dir: Mitchell Leisen

sc: Talbot Jennings (based on the novel by Daphne du Maurier)

c: Joan Fontaine, Arturo De Cordova, Basil Rathbone, Nigel Bruce, Cecil Kellaway

Gaslight/Murder in Thornton Square (MGM, 1944)

pro: Arthur Hornblow Jr

dir: George Cukor

sc: John Van Druten, Walter Reisch, John Balderston (based on the play by Patrick Hamilton)

c: Ingrid Bergman, Charles Boyer, Joseph Cotton, Angela Lansbury, Dame May Whitty, Barbara Everest, Emil Rameau, Edward Breon, Halliwell Hobbes, Tom Stevenson

Goodbye Mr Chips (MGM, 1939)

pro: Victor Saville

dir: Sam Wood

sc: R.C. Sherriff, Eric Maschwitz, Claudine West (based on the novel by James Hilton)

c: Robert Donat, Greer Garson, Paul Henreid, Terry Kilburn, John Mills, Lyn Harding, Austin Trevor, Edmund Breon, David Tree, Judith Furse

Great Expectations (Uni, 1934)

pro: Stuart Walker

dir: Stuart Walker

sc: Gladys Ungar (based on the novel by Charles Dickens)

c: Phillips Holmes, Jane Wyatt, Henry Hull, Florence Reed, Alan Hale, Rafaela Ottiano, Francis L. Sullivan, Eily Manyon, Forrester Harvey

The Great Impersonation (Uni, 1935)

pro: Edmund Grainger

dir: Alan Crosland

sc: Frank Wead, Eva Greene (based on the novel by E. Phillips Oppenheim)

c: Edmund Lowe, Valerie Hobson, Vera Engels, Henry Mollison, Lumsden Hare, Spring Byington, Charles Waldron, Dwight Frye, Leonard Mudie

The Great Impersonation (Uni, 1942)

pro: Paul Malvern

dir: John Rawlins

sc: W. Scott Darling (based on the novel by E. Phillips Oppenheim)

c: Ralph Bellamy, Evelyn Ankers, Aubrey Mather, Edward Norris, Henry Daniell

The Green Goddess (WB, 1930)

pro: not indicated

dir: Alfred E. Green

sc: Julien Josephson (based on the play by William Archer)

c: George Arliss, Alice Joyce, Ralph Forbes, H.B. Warner, Ivan Simpson, Reginald Sheffield

Gunga Din (RKO, 1939)

pro: George Stevens

dir: George Stevens

sc: Joel Sayre, Fred Guiol, Ben Hecht, Charles MacArthur (based on the poem by Rudyard Kipling)

c: Cary Grant, Douglas Fairbanks, Victor McLaglen, Sam Jaffe, Joan Fontaine, Eduardo Ciannelli, Montagu Love, Abner Biberman, Lumsden Hare, Cecil Kellaway

Hangover Square (TCF, 1945)

pro: Robert Bassler

dir: John Brahm

sc: Barré Lyndon (based on the novel by Patrick Hamilton)

c: Laird Cregar, Linda Darnell, George Sanders, Glenn Langan, Faye Marlowe, Alan Napier, Frederick Worlock

Haunted Honeymoon/Busman's Honeymoon (MGM, 1940)

pro: Howard Huth

dir: Arthur B. Woods

sc: Monkton Hoffe, Angus McPhail, Harold Goldman (based on the novel by Dorothy Sayers)

c: Robert Montgomery, Constance Cummings, Leslie Banks, Googie Withers

The Hound of the Baskervilles (TCF, 1939)

pro: Gene Markey

dir: Sidney Lanfield

sc: Ernest Pascal (based on the novel by Arthur Conan Doyle)

c: Basil Rathbone, Nigel Bruce, Richard Greene, Wendy Barrie, Lionel Atwill, Morton Lowry, John Carradine, Barlowe Borland, Beryl Mercer, Ralph Forbes, E.E. Clive, Eily Malyon, Mary Gordon

How Green Was My Valley (TCF, 1941)

pro: Darryl F. Zanuck

dir: John Ford

sc: Philip Dunne (based on the novel by Richard Llewellyn)

c: Walter Pidgeon, Maureen O'Hara, Roddy McDowall, Donald Crisp, Sara Allgood, Anna Lee, John Loder, Barry Fitzgerald, Patric Knowles,

Morton Lowry, Arthur Shields, Frederick Worlock, Rhys Williams, Ethel Griffies, Clifford Severn, Mary Gordon

If Winter Comes (MGM, 1947)

pro: Pandro S. Berman

dir: Victor Saville

sc: Arthur Wimperis, Marguerite Roberts (based on the novel by A.S.M. Hutchinson)

c: Walter Pidgeon, Deborah Kerr, Angela Lansbury, Janet Leigh, Binnie Barnes, Dame May Whitty, Reginald Owen, Rhys Williams, Halliwell Hobbes, John Abbott, Dennis Hoey

International Lady (UA, 1941)

pro: Edward Small

dir: Tim Whelan

sc: Howard Estabrook, E. Lloyd Sheldon, Jack De Witt

c: George Brent, Basil Rathbone, Ilona Massey, Gene Lockhart, George Zucco, Francis Pierlot, Martin Kosleck, Marjorie Gateson, Frederick Worlock

International Squadron (WB, 1941)

pro: Edmund Grainger

dir: Lewis Seiler

sc: Barry Trivers, Kenneth Gamet (suggested by a play by Frank Wead)

c: Ronald Reagan, James Stephenson, Julie Bishop, Cliff Edwards, Reginald Denny, Olympe Bradna, William Lundigan, John Ridgely, Holmes Herbert

The Invisible Man (Uni, 1933)

pro: Carl Laemmle Jr

dir: James Whale

sc: R.C. Sherriff, Philip Wylie (based on the novel by H.G. Wells)

c: Claude Rains, Gloria Stuart, William Harrigan, Henry Travers, E.E. Clive, Una O'Connor, Forrester Harvey, Dudley Digges, Holmes Herbert

Ivy (Uni, 1947)

pro: William Cameron Menzies

dir: Sam Wood

sc: Charles Bennett (based on the novel *The Story of Ivy* by Mrs Marie Belloc Lowndes)

c: Joan Fontaine, Herbert Marshall, Patric Knowles, Richard Ney, Cedric Hardwicke, Lucile Watson, Sara Allgood, Henry Stephenson, Una O'Connor, Isobel Elsom, Alan Napier, Paul Cavanagh, Gavin Muir, Norma Varden

Jane Eyre (Mon, 1934)

pro: Ben Verschleiser

dir: Christy Cabanne

sc: Adele Comandini (based on the novel by Charlotte Brontë)

c: Virginia Bruce, Colin Clive, Beryl Mercer, Jameson Thomas, Eileen Pringle

Jane Eyre (TCF, 1944)

pro: William Goetz, Orson Welles

dir: Robert Stevenson

sc: Aldous Huxley, Robert Stevenson, John Houseman (based on the novel by Charlotte Brontë)

c: Joan Fontaine, Orson Welles, Margaret O'Brien, Henry Daniell, John Sutton, Agnes Moorehead, Elizabeth Taylor, Peggy Ann Garner, Sara Allgood, Aubrey Mather, Hillary Brooke, Edith Barrett, Ethel Griffies, Barbara Everest, John Abbott, Eily Manyon

Journey for Margaret (MGM, 1942)

pro: B.P. Fineman

dir: W.S. Van Dyke

sc: David Hertz, William Ludwig (based on the book by William Allen White)

c: Robert Young, Laraine Day, Margaret O'Brien, William Severn, Fay Bainter, Nigel Bruce, Elisabeth Risdon, Doris Lloyd, Jill Esmond, Halliwell Hobbes, Heather Thatcher

Kidnapped (TCF, 1938)

pro: Darryl F. Zanuck

dir: Alfred L. Werker

sc: Sonya Levien, Richard Sherman, Walter Ferris (based on the novel by Robert Louis Stevenson)

c: Warner Baxter, Freddie Bartholomew, Arleen Whelan, John Carradine, C. Aubrey Smith, Nigel Bruce, Reginald Owen, Miles Mander, E.E. Clive, Halliwell Hobbes, H.B. Warner

Kim (MGM, 1950)

pro: Leon Gordon

dir: Victor Saville

sc: Leon Gordon, Helen Deutsch, Richard Schayer (based on the novel by Rudyard Kipling)

c: Errol Flynn, Paul Lukas, Dean Stockwell, Thomas Gomez, Cecil Kellaway, Arnold Moss, Reginald Owen, Walter Kingsford, Ivan Triesault

Lancer Spy (TCF, 1937)

pro: Darryl Zanuck, Samuel G. Engel

dir: Gregory Ratoff

sc: Philip Dunne (based on a novel by Marthe McKenna)

c: Dolores Del Rio, George Sanders, Peter Lorre, Joseph Schildkraut, Virginia Field, Sig Rumann, Maurice Moscovich, Lionel Atwill, Holmes Herbert, Leonard Mudie

Lassie Come Home (MGM, 1943)

pro: Samuel Marx

dir: Fred M. Wilcox

sc: Hugo Butler (based on the story by Eric Knight)

c: Roddy McDowall, Nigel Bruce, Elsa Lanchester, Donald Crisp, Dame May Whitty, Ben Webster, Edmund Gwenn, Elizabeth Taylor, Arthur

Shields, Alan Napier, Ben Webster

The Last of Mrs Cheyney (MGM, 1929)

pro: Irving Thalberg

dir: Sidney Franklin

sc: Hans Kraly, Claudine West (based on the play by Frederick Lonsdale)

c: Norma Shearer, Basil Rathbone, George Barraud, Hedda Hopper, Maude Turner Gordon

The Last of Mrs Cheyney (MGM, 1937)

pro: Lawrence Weingarten

dir: Richard Boleslawski

sc: Leon Gordon, Samson Raphaelson, Monkton Hoffe (based on the play by Frederick Lonsdale)

c: Joan Crawford, Robert Montgomery, William Powell, Frank Morgan, Jessie Ralph, Nigel Bruce, Benita Hume, Melville Cooper, Sara Haden, Lumsden Hare

Let's Try Again/The Marriage Symphony (RKO, 1934)

pro: Pandro Berman, Myles Connolly

dir: Worthington Miner

sc: Worthington Miner (based on the play *Sour Grapes* by Vincent Lawrence)

c: Diana Wynyard, Clive Brook, Helen Vinson, Irene Hervey, Theodore Newton

The Light That Failed (Par, 1939)

pro: William Wellman

dir: William Wellman

sc: Robert Carson (based on the novel by Rudyard Kipling)

c: Ronald Colman, Walter Huston, Ida Lupino, Dudley Digges, Muriel Angelus, Fay Helm

Little Lord Fauntleroy (UA, 1936)

pro: David O. Selznick

dir: John Cromwell

sc: Richard Schayer, Hugh Walpole, David O. Selznick (based on the novel by Frances Hodgson Burnett)

c: Freddie Bartholomew, Dolores Costello, C. Aubrey Smith, Guy Kibbee, Mickey Rooney, Jessie Ralph, Henry Stephenson, E.E. Clive, Constance Collier, Una O'Connor

The Little Princess (TCF, 1939)

pro: Gene Markey

dir: Walter Lang

sc: Ethel Hill, Walter Ferris (based on the novel by Frances Hodgson Burnett)

c: Shirley Temple, Richard Greene, Anita Louise, Ian Hunter, Cesar Romero, Arthur Treacher, Mary Nash, Sybil Jason, Miles Mander, Marcia Mae Jones, Beryl Mercer

Lives of a Bengal Lancer (Par, 1935)

pro: Louis D. Lighton

dir: Henry Hathaway

sc: Waldemar Young, John L. Balderston, Achmed Abdullah (based on the novel by Francis Yeats-Brown)

c: Gary Cooper, Franchot Tone, Richard Cromwell, Sir Guy Standing, C. Aubrey Smith, Kathleen Burke, Douglass Dumbrille, Monte Blue, Colin Tapley, Lumsden Hare

Lloyds of London (TCF, 1937)

pro: Kenneth MacGowan

dir: Henry King

sc: Ernest Pascal, Walter Ferris (based on the story by Curtis Kenyon)

c: Freddie Bartholomew, Madeleine Carroll, Sir Guy Standing, Tyrone Power, C. Aubrey Smith, Virginia Field, Douglas Scott, George Sanders, J.M. Kerrigan, Una O'Connor, Forrester Harvey, Gavin Muir, E.E. Clive, Miles Mander, Montagu Love, Lumsden Hare, Billy Bevan, May Beatty, Holmes Herbert, Leonard Mudie

The Lodger (TCF, 1944)

pro: Robert Bassler

dir: John Brahm

sc: Barré Lyndon (based on the novel by Mrs Marie Belloc Lowndes)

c: Merle Oberon, George Sanders, Laird Cregar, Cedric Hardwicke, Sara Allgood, Aubrey Mather, Queenie Leonard, Doris Lloyd, Lumsden Hare, Frederick Worlock

The London Blackout Murders/Secret Motive (Rep, 1942)

pro: George Sherman

dir: George Sherman

sc: Curt Siodmak

c: John Abbott, Mary McLeod, Lloyd Corrigan, Lester Matthews, Anita Bolster, Billy Bevan, Frederick Worlock, Lumsden Hare

London by Night (MGM, 1937)

pro: Sam Zimbalist

dir: William Thiele

sc: George Oppenheimer (based on the play by Will Scott)

c: George Murphy, Rita Johnson, Leo G. Carroll, George Zucco,Virginia Field, Montagu Love, Eddie Quillan, Leonard Mudie, Forrester Harvey

Man Hunt (TCF, 1941)

pro: Kenneth MacGowan

dir: Fritz Lang

sc: Dudley Nichols (based on the novel Rogue Male by Geoffrey Household)

c: Walter Pidgeon, Joan Bennett, George Sanders, John Carradine, Roddy McDowall, Ludwig Stossel, Heather Thatcher, Frederick Worlock, Holmes Herbert, Eily Manyon

Mary of Scotland (RKO, 1936)

pro: Pandro Berman

dir: John Ford

sc: Dudley Nichols (based on the play by Maxwell Anderson)

c: Katherine Hepburn, Fredric March, Donald Crisp, Florence Eldridge, Douglas Walton, John Carradine, Robert Barrat, Monte Blue, Frieda Inescort, Alan Mowbray

Ministry of Fear (Par, 1944)

pro: Seton I. Miller

dir: Fritz Lang

sc: Seton Miller (based on the novel by Graham Greene)

c: Ray Milland, Marjorie Reynolds, Carl Esmond, Hillary Brooke, Dan Duryea, Percy Waram, Alan Napier, Erskine Sanford

The Miniver Story (MGM, 1950)

pro: Sidney Franklin

dir: H.C. Potter

sc: Ronald Millar, George Froeschel (based on characters created by Jan Struther)

c: Greer Garson, Walter Pidgeon, Cathy O'Donnell, John Hodiak, Leo Genn, Reginald Owen, Henry Wilcoxon, William Fox, Anthony Bushell, Reginald Owen

The Moon and Sixpence (UA, 1942)

pro: Stanley Kramer, David L. Loew

dir: Albert Lewin

sc: Albert Lewin (based on the novel by Somerset Maugham)

c: George Sanders, Herbert Marshall, Steve Garay, Doris Dudley, Elena Verdugo, Florence Bates, Heather Thatcher, Eric Blore, Albert Basserman

Moss Rose (TCF, 1947)

pro: Gene Markey

dir: Gregory Ratoff

sc: Jules Furthman, Tom Reed, Niven Busch (based on the novel by Joseph Shearing)

c: Peggy Cummins, Victor Mature, Ethel Barrymore, Vincent Price, George Zucco, Billy Bevan, Rhys Williams

Mrs Miniver (MGM, 1942)

pro: Sidney Franklin

dir: William Wyler

sc: Arthur Wimperis, George Froeschel, James Hilton, Claudine West (based on characters created by Jan Struther)

c: Greer Garson, Walter Pidgeon, Teresa Wright, Richard Ney, Dame May Whitty, Henry Travers, Reginald Owen, Henry Wilcoxon, Helmut Dantine, Rhys Williams, Aubrey Mather, Clare Sandars, Christopher Severn, Brenda Forbes, Marie De Becker, Billy Bevan, Ben Webster, Aubrey Mather, Forrester Harvey, Ian Wolfe, Peter Lawford

Mutiny on the Bounty (MGM, 1935)

pro: Irving Thalberg, Albert Lewin

dir: Frank Lloyd

sc: Talbot Jennings, Jules Furthman, Carey Wilson (based on the novel by Charles Nordhoff and James Norman Hall)

c: Charles Laughton, Clark Gable, Franchot Tone, Herbert Mundin, Eddie Quillan, Dudley Digges, Donald Crisp, Henry Stephenson, Francis Lister, Spring Byington, Movita, Ian Wolfe

My Name is Julia Ross (Col, 1945)

pro: Wallace Macdonald

dir: Joseph H. Lewis

sc: Muriel Roy Bolton (based on the novel *The Woman in Red* by Anthony Gilbert)

c: Nina Foch, Dame May Whitty, George Macready, Roland Varno, Doris Lloyd, Leonard Mudie, Joy Harrington, Queenie Leonard, Reginald Sheffield

The Mystery of Edwin Drood (Uni, 1935)

pro: Edmund Grainger

dir: Stuart Walker

sc: John L. Balderston, Gladys Unger, Bradley King, Leopold Atlas (based on the unfinished novel by Charles Dickens)

c: Claude Rains, Douglass Montgomery, Heather Angel, David Manners, E.E. Clive, Valerie Hobson, Francis L. Sullivan, Walter Kingsford, Vera Buckland, Forrester Harvey

The Mystery of Mister X (MGM, 1934)

pro: Lawrence Weingarten

dir: Edgar Selwyn

sc: Howard Emmett Rogers, Philip MacDonald, Monckton Hoffe (based on the novel by Philip MacDonald)

c: Robert Montgomery, Elizabeth Allan, Lewis Stone, Ralph Forbes, Henry Stephenson, Forrester Harvey, Alec B. Francis, Leonard Mudie

National Velvet (MGM, 1945)

pro: Pandro S. Berman

dir: Clarence Brown

sc: Theodore Reeves, Helen Deutsch (based on the novel by Enid Bagnold)

c: Mickey Rooney, Donald Crisp, Elizabeth Taylor, Anne Revere, Angela Lansbury, Juanita Quigley, Reginald Owen, Arthur Treacher, Norma Varden, Terry Kilburn, Arthur Shields, Jackie 'Butch' Jenkins, Alec Craig, Aubrey Mather, Frederick Worlock, Billy Bevan

Night Must Fall (MGM, 1937)

pro: Hunt Stromberg

dir: Richard Thorpe

sc: John Van Druten (based on the play by Emlyn Williams)

c: Robert Montgomery, Rosalind Russell, Dame May Whitty, Alan Marshall, Merle Tottenham, Kathleen Harrison, Matthew Boulton, E.E. Clive, Eily Manyon

None but the Lonely Heart (RKO, 1944)

pro: David Hempstead

dir: Clifford Odets

sc: Clifford Odets (based on the novel by Richard Lewellyn)

c: Cary Grant, Ethel Barrymore, June Duprez, Barry Fitzgerald, Jane Wyatt, George Coulouris, Dan Duryea, Konstantin Shayne, Morton Lowry, Helene Thimig

Nurse Edith Cavell (RKO, 1939)

pro: Herbert Wilcox

dir: Herbert Wilcox

sc: Michael Hogan (based on the play *Dawn* by Reginald Berkeley)

c: Anna Neagle, Edna May Oliver, George Sanders, May Robson, Zasu Pitts, H.B. Warner

Of Human Bondage (RKO, 1934)

pro: Pandro S. Berman

dir: John Cromwell

sc: Lester Cohen (based on the novel by Somerset Maugham)

c: Leslie Howard, Bette Davis, Frances Dee, Reginald Owen, Reginald Denny, Kay Johnson, Alan Hale, Reginald Sheffield

Of Human Bondage (WB, 1946)

pro: Henry Blanke

dir: Edmund Goulding

sc: Catherine Turney (based on the novel by Somerset Maugham)

c: Paul Henreid, Eleanor Parker, Alexis Smith, Edmund Gwenn, Patric Knowles, Janis Paige, Henry Stephenson, Isobel Elsom, Una O'Connor

The Old Dark House (Uni, 1932)

pro: Carl Laemmle Jr

dir: James Whale

sc: Benn W. Levy, R.C. Sherriff (based on the novel *Benighted* by J.B. Priestley)

c: Melvyn Douglas, Charles Laughton, Raymond Massey, Boris Karloff, Ernest Thesiger

Old English (WB, 1930)

pro: not indicated

dir: Alfred E. Green

sc: Walter Anthony, Maude T. Howell (based on the play by John Galsworthy)

c: George Arliss, Doris Lloyd, Harrington Reynolds, Reginald Sheffield, Betty Lawford

Oliver Twist (Mon, 1933)

pro: I.E. Chadwick

dir: William Cowen

sc: Elizabeth Meehan (based on the novel by Charles Dickens) c: Dickie Moore, Irving Pichel, William Boyd, Doris Lloyd, Barbara Kent, Alec B. Francis

One More River/Over the River (Uni, 1934)

pro: James Whale

dir: James Whale

sc: R.C. Sherriff (based on the novel *Over The River* by John Galsworthy)

c: Colin Clive, Diana Wynyard, C. Aubrey Smith, Jane Wyatt, Lionel Atwill, Mrs Patrick Campbell, Frank Lawton, Reginald Denny, Henry Stephenson, Alan Mowbray, E.E. Clive

One Night in Lisbon (Par, 1941)

pro: Edward H. Griffith

dir: Edward H. Griffith

sc: Virginia Van Upp (based on the play *There's Always Juliet* by John Van Druten)

c: Madeleine Carroll, Fred MacMurray, Edmund Gwenn, Patricia Morrison, Billie Burke, John Loder, Dame May Whitty, Reginald Denny, Billy Gilbert

The Paradine Case (Selznick Releasing Orgānization, 1947)

pro: David O. Selznick

dir: Alfred Hitchcock

sc: David O. Selznick, Alma Reville (based on the novel by Robert Hichins)

c: Gregory Peck, Alida Valli, Ann Todd, Louis Jourdan, Charles Laughton, Charles Coburn, Ethel Barrymore, Leo G. Carroll, John Goldsworthy, Isobel Elsom

Parnell (MGM, 1937)

pro: John M. Stahl

dir: John M. Stahl

sc: John Van Druten, S.N. Behrman (based on the play by Elsie T. Schauffler)

c: Clark Gable, Myrna Loy, Edmund Gwenn, Edna May Oliver, Alan Marshal, Donald Crisp, Billy Bevan, Billie Burke, Berton Churchill, Donald Meek, Montagu Love

Payment Deferred (MGM, 1932)

pro: Irving Thalberg

dir: Lothar Mendes

sc: Ernest Vajda, Claudine West (based on the play by Jeffrey F. Dell)

c: Charles Laughton, Maureen O'Sullivan, Ray Milland, Dorothy Peterson, Veree Teasdale, Billy Bevan, Halliwell Hobbes

Piccadilly Jim (MGM, 1936)

pro: Harry Rapf

dir: Robert Z. Leonard

sc: Charles Brackett, Edwin Knopf (based on the novel by P.G. Wodehouse)

c: Robert Montgomery, Madge Evans, Frank Morgan, Billie Burke, Eric

Blore, Robert Benchley, Ralph Forbes, Cora Witherspoon, E.E. Clive, Billy Bevan

The Picture of Dorian Gray (MGM, 1945)

pro: Pandro S. Berman

dir: Albert Lewin

sc: Albert Lewin (based on the novel by Oscar Wilde)

c: George Sanders, Hurd Hatfield, Donna Reed, Angela Lansbury, Peter Lawford, Lowell Gilmore, Richard Fraser, Douglas Walton, Morton Lowry, Miles Mander, Billy Bevan

Pride and Prejudice (MGM, 1940)

pro: Hunt Stromberg

dir: Robert Z. Leonard

sc: Aldous Huxley, Jane Murfin (based on the novel by Jane Austen)

c: Greer Garson, Laurence Olivier, Frieda Inescort, Edward Ashley, Mary Boland, Edmund Gwenn, Maureen O'Sullivan, Edna May Oliver, Ann Rutherford, Heather Angel

The Prince and the Pauper (WB, 1936)

pro: Hal B. Wallis, Robert Lord

dir: William Keighley

sc: Laird Doyle (based on the story by Mark Twain)

c: Errol Flynn, Claude Rains, Henry Stephenson, Barton MacLaine, Billy Mauch, Bobby Mauch, Alan Hale, Eric Portman, Halliwell Hobbes, Montagu Love, Forrester Harvey

The Prisoner of Zenda (Selznick, 1937)

pro: David O. Selznick

dir: John Cromwell

sc: John L. Balderston, Wells Root, Donald Ogden Stewart (based on the novel by Anthony Hope and the play by Edward Rose)

c: Ronald Colman, Madeleine Carroll, Mary Astor, Raymond Massey, C. Aubrey Smith, David Niven, Douglas Fairbanks Jr, Montagu Love, Ben Webster

Private Lives (MGM, 1931)

pro: Irving Thalberg

dir: Sidney Franklin

sc: Hans Kraly, Claudine West, Richard Schayer (based on the play by Noel Coward)

c: Norma Shearer, Robert Montgomery, Reginald Denny, Una Merkel, Jean Hersholt

The Private Lives of Elizabeth and Essex (WB, 1939)

pro: Hal B. Wallis, Robert Lord

dir: Michael Curtiz

sc: Norman Reilly Raine, Aeneas MacKenzie (based on the play *Elizabeth the Queen* by Maxwell Anderson)

c: Bette Davis, Errol Flynn, Olivia De Havilland, Donald Crisp, Henry

Daniell, Alan Hale, Vincent Price, Henry Stephenson, James Stephenson, Nanette Fabares, Ralph Forbes, Robert Warwick, Leo G. Carroll, Forrester Harvey, John Sutton

Raffles (UA, 1930)

pro: Samuel Goldwyn

dir: Harry D'Abbadie D'Arrast, George Fitzmaurice

sc: Sidney Howard, George Fitzmaurice (based on short stories by E.W. Hornung)

c: Ronald Colman, Kay Francis, Bramwell Fletcher, Francis Dade, David Torrence

Raffles (UA, 1940)

pro: Samuel Goldwyn

dir: Sam Wood

sc: John Van Druten, Sidney Howard (based on short stories by E.W. Hornung)

c: David Niven, Olivia De Havilland, Dame May Whitty, Dudley Digges, E.E. Clive

Rage in Heaven (MGM, 1940)

pro: Gottfried Reinhardt

dir: W.S. Van Dyke

sc: Christopher Isherwood, Robert Thoeren (based on the novel by James Hilton)

c: Robert Montgomery, George Sanders, Ingrid Bergman, Lucile Watson, Oscar Homolka, Philip Merivale, Mathew Boulton, Gilbert Emery, Aubrey Mather, Frederick Worlock

The Rains Came (TCF, 1939)

pro: Darryl F. Zanuck, Harry Joe Brown

dir: Clarence Brown

sc: Philip Dunne, Julien Josephson (based on the novel by Louis Bromfield)

c: Tyrone Power, Myrna Loy, George Brent, Nigel Bruce, Brenda Joyce, Joseph Schildkraut, H.B. Warner, Maria Ouspenskaya, Henry Travers

Random Harvest (MGM, 1942)

pro: Sidney Franklin

dir: Mervyn LeRoy

sc: Arthur Wimperis, George Froeschel, James Hilton, Claudine West (based on the novel by James Hilton)

c: Ronald Colman, Greer Garson, Philip Dorn, Susan Peters, Reginald Owen, Henry Travers, Aubrey Mather, Rhys Williams, Ian Wolfe, Jill Esmond, Norma Varden, Arthur Shields, Edmund Gwenn, Margaret Wycherley, Bramwell Fletcher, Una O'Connor, Peter Lawford

Rebecca (UA, 1940)

pro: David O. Selznick

dir: Alfred Hitchcock

sc: Robert E. Sherwood, Joan Harrison (based on the novel by Daphne du Maurier)

c: Laurence Olivier, Joan Fontaine, George Sanders, Judith Anderson, Nigel Bruce, Gladys Cooper, Florence Bates, Reginald Denny, C. Aubrey Smith, Melville Cooper, Leo G. Cooper, Leonard Carey, Forrester Harvey, Lumsden Hare

The Return of the Vampire (Col, 1943)

pro: Sam White

dir: Lew Landers

sc: Griffin Jay, Randolf Faye

c: Bela Lugosi, Nina Foch, Frieda Inescort, Miles Mander, Matt Willis, Billy Bevan

Romeo and Juliet (MGM, 1936)

pro: Irving Thalberg

dir: George Cukor

sc: Talbot Jennings (based on the play by William Shakespeare)

c: Norma Shearer, Leslie Howard, John Barrymore, Basil Rathbone, Edna May Oliver, Henry Kolker, C. Aubrey Smith, Violet Kemble-Cooper, Reginald Denny

Safari (Par, 1940)

pro: Anthony Veiller

dir: Edward H. Griffith

sc: Delmer Davies (based on the story by Paul Hervey-Fox)

c: Douglas Fairbanks Jr, Madeleine Carroll, Tullio Carminati, Billy Gilbert

The Saint in London (RKO, 1939)

pro: William Sistrom

dir: John Paddy Carstairs

sc: Lynn Root, Frank Fenton (based on the story *The Million Pound Day* by Leslie Charteris)

c: George Sanders, Sally Gray, David Burns, Gordon McLeod, Athene Seyler, Henry Oscar

Scotland Yard (TCF, 1941)

pro: Sol M. Wurtzel

dir: Norman Foster

sc: Samuel G. Engel, John Balderston (based on the play by Denison Clift)

c: Edmund Gwenn, Henry Stephenson, Nancy Kelly, Henry Wilcoxon, John Loder, Melville Cooper, Gilbert Emery, Norma Varden, Leo G. Carroll, Billy Bevan

Scotland Yard Investigator (Rep, 1945)

pro: George Blair

dir: George Blair

sc: Randall Faye

c: C. Aubrey Smith, Erich Von Stroheim, Stephanie Bachelor, Forrester Harvey, Richard Fraser, Frederick Worlock

The Sea Hawk (WB, 1940)

pro: Hal B. Wallis, Henry Blanke

dir: Michael Curtiz

sc: Seton I. Miller, Howard Koch

c: Errol Flynn, Brenda Marshall, Claude Rains, Donald Crisp, Flora Robson, Alan Hale, Henry Daniell, Montagu Love, Gilbert Roland, Una O'Connor, William Lundigan, Robert Warwick, Alec Craig, Halliwell Hobbes

Secrets of Scotland Yard (Rep, 1943)

pro: Armand Schaefer, George Blair

dir: George Blair

sc: Denison Clift (based on his novel *Room 40, O.B* by Denison Clift)

c: C. Aubrey Smith, Edgar Barrier, Stephanie Bachelor, Lionel Atwill, Henry Stephenson, John Abbott, Walter Kingsford, Martin Kosleck, Frederick Worlock, Forrester Harvey

Sherlock Holmes (Fox, 1932)

pro: William K. Howard

dir: William K. Howard

sc: Bertram Milhouser (based on characters created by Arthur Conan Doyle)

c: Clive Brook, Reginald Owen, Ernest Torrence, Miriam Jordan, Alan Mowbray

Sherlock Holmes and the Voice of Terror (Uni, 1942)

pro: Howard Benedict

dir: John Rawlins

sc: Lynn Riggs, John Bright, Robert D. Andrews (based on the story *His Last Bow* by Arthur Conan Doyle)

c: Basil Rathbone, Nigel Bruce, Reginald Denny, Thomas Gomez, Evelyn Ankers, Henry Daniell, Montagu Love, Hillary Brooke, Mary Gordon, Arthur Blake.

This was the first in a series of twelve *Sherlock Holmes* films produced by Universal Studios. Each of the twelve films that followed star Basil Rathbone and Nigel Bruce, and each was directed by Roy William Neill:

Sherlock Holmes and the Secret Weapon (1942)

Sherlock Holmes in Washington (1943)

Sherlock Holmes Faces Death (1943)

Sherlock Holmes and the Spider Woman (1944)

The Scarlet Claw (1944)

The Pearl of Death (1944)

The House of Fear (1945)

The Woman in Green (1945)

Pursuit to Algiers (1945)

Terror by Night (1946)

Dressed to Kill/Sherlock Holmes and the Secret Code (1946)

Smilin' Through (MGM, 1932)

pro: Irving Thalberg

dir: Sidney Franklin

sc: Ernest Vajda, Donald Ogden Stewart, Claudine West, James Fagan (based on the play by Jane Murfin and Jane Cowl)

c: Norma Shearer, Fredric March, Leslie Howard, O.P. Heggie, Ralph Forbes, Beryl Mercer, Margaret Seddon, Forrester Harvey, Cora Sue Collins

Smilin' Through (MGM, 1941)

pro: Victor Saville

dir: Frank Borzage

sc: Donald Ogden Stewart, John Balderston (based on the play by Jane Murfin and Jane Cowl)

c: Jeanette MacDonald, Brian Aherne, Gene Raymond, Ian Hunter, Frances Robinson

Son of Fury (TCF, 1942)

pro: William Perlburg

dir: John Cromwell

sc: Philip Dunne (based on the novel Benjamin Blake by Edison Marshall)

c: Tyrone Power, Gene Tierney, George Sanders, Frances Farmer, Roddy McDowall, John Carradine, Elsa Lanchester, Dudley Digges, Harry Davenport, Halliwell Hobbes

Stanley and Livingstone (TCF, 1939)

pro: Darryl F. Zanuck, Kenneth MacGowan

dir: Henry King

sc: Philip Dunne, Julien Josephson, Hal Long, Sam Hellman

c: Spencer Tracy, Cedric Hardwicke, Richard Greene, Nancy Kelly, Walter Brennan, Charles Coburn, Henry Hull, Henry Travers, Miles Mander, Holmes Herbert

Step Lively, Jeeves (TCF, 1938)

pro: John Stone

dir: Eugene Forde

sc: Frances Hyland, Frank Fenton, Lynn Root (based on the character 'Jeeves' created by P.G. Wodehouse)

c: Arthur Treacher, Patricia Ellis, Robert Kent, Alan Dineheart, George Givot, Helen Flint, John Harrington, George Cooper, Arthur Houseman, Max Wagner, Franklin Pangborn

Sundown (UA, 1941)

pro: Walter Wanger

dir: Henry Hathaway

sc: Barré Lyndon

c: Gene Tierney, George Sanders, Bruce Cabot, Cedric Hardwicke, Reginald Gardiner

The Sun Never Sets (Uni, 1939)

pro: Rowland V. Lee

dir: Rowland V. Lee

sc: W.P. Lipscomb, Jerry Horwin, Arthur Fitzrichard

c: Basil Rathbone, Douglas Fairbanks Jr, Barbara O'Neill, Lionel Atwill, Virginia Field

The Suspect (Uni, 1944)

pro: Islin Auster

dir: Robert Siodmak

sc: Bertram Milhauser, A.T. Harman (based on the novel *This Way Out* by James Ronald)

c: Charles Laughton, Henry Daniell, Rosalind Ivan, Ella Raines, Molly Lamont

Suspicion (RKO, 1941)

pro: Harry Edington

dir: Alfred Hitchcock

sc: Samson Raphaelson, Joan Harrison, Alma Reville (based on the novel *Before the Fact* by Francis Iles)

c: Cary Grant, Joan Fontaine, Nigel Bruce, Cedric Hardwicke, Dame May Whitty, Isobel Jeans, Heather Angel, Leo G. Carroll, Aubrey Mather, Reginald Sheffield, Ben Webster, Lumsden Hare, Billy Bevan

Sylvia Scarlett (RKO, 1935)

pro: Pandro Berman

dir: George Cukor

sc: Gladys Unger, John Collier, Mortimer Offner (based on the play by Compton Mackenzie)

c: Katherine Hepburn, Cary Grant, Edmund Gwenn, Brian Aherne, Lennox Pawle

A Tale of Two Cities (MGM, 1935)

pro: David O. Selznick

dir: Jack Conway

sc: W.P. Lipscomb, S.N. Behrman (based on the novel by Charles Dickens)

c: Ronald Colman, Elizabeth Allan, Basil Rathbone, Edna May Oliver, Blanche Yurka, Reginald Owen, Henry B. Walthall, Donald Woods, Walter Catlett, H.B. Warner, Claude Gillingwater, Fritz Leiber, Billy Bevan, Eily Manyon, E.E. Clive

Tartu/The Adventures of Tartu (MGM, 1943)

pro: Irving Asher, Howard Huth

dir: Harold S. Bucquet

sc: John Lee Mahin, Howard Emmet Rogers, John Higgins

c: Robert Donat, Valerie Hobson, Glynis Johns, Walter Rilla, Martin Miller, David Ward

Tarzan the Ape Man (MGM, 1932)

pro: Irving Thalberg

dir: W.S. Van Dyke

sc: Cyril Hume, Ivor Novello (based on characters created by Edgar Rice Burroughs)

c: Johnny Weissmuller, C. Aubrey Smith, Neil Hamilton, Maureen O'Sullivan, Forrester Harvey

Temple Tower (Fox, 1930)

pro: not indicated

dir: Donald Gallagher

sc: Llewellyn Hughes (based on the story by H.C. McNeile)

c: Kenneth MacKenna, Marceline Day, Henry B. Walthall

Thank You, Jeeves (TCF, 1936)

pro: Sol M. Wurtzel

dir: Arthur Greville Collins

sc: Joseph Hoffman, Stephen Gross (based on the story by P.G. Wodehouse)

c: David Niven, Arthur Treacher, Virginia Field, Lester Matthews, Colin Tapley

That Forsyte Woman/The Forsyte Saga (MGM, 1949)

pro: Leon Gordon

dir: Compton Bennett

sc: Jan Lustig, Ivan Tors, James B. Williams, Arthur Wimperis (based on the novel *Man of Property* by John Galsworthy)

c: Greer Garson, Errol Flynn, Walter Pidgeon, Robert Young, Janet Leigh, Harry Davenport, Aubrey Mather, Lumsden Hare, Halliwell Hobbes, Billy Bevan

That Hamilton Woman/Lady Hamilton (UA, 1941)

pro: Alexander Korda

dir: Alexander Korda

sc: Walter Reisch, R.C. Sherriff

c: Laurence Olivier, Vivien Leigh, Gladys Cooper, Alan Mowbray, Sara Allgood, Henry Wilcoxon, Halliwell Hobbes, Heather Angel, Gilbert Emery, Miles Mander

Thirteen Lead Soldiers (TCF, 1948)

pro: Ben Pivar, Bernard Small

dir: Frank McDonald

sc: Irving Elman (based on the story by H.C. McNeile)

c: Tom Conway, Maria Palmer, Helen Westcott, John Newland, Terry Kilburn

This Above All (TCF, 1942)

pro: Darryl F. Zanuck

dir: Anatole Litvak

sc: R.C. Sherriff (based on the novel by Eric Knight)

c: Tyrone Power, Joan Fontaine, Thomas Mitchell, Henry Stephenson, Gladys Cooper, Nigel Bruce, Philip Merivale, Alexander Knox, Melville Cooper, Sara Allgood, Queenie Leonard, Jill Esmond, Holmes Herbert,

Arthur Shields, Dennis Hoey, Thomas Louden, Miles Mander, Rhys Williams, Holmes Herbert, Forrester Harvey, Billy Bevan

Thumbs Up (Rep, 1943)

pro: Albert J. Cohen

dir: Joseph Santley

sc: Frank Gill Jr, Roy Golden, Henry Moritz

c: Brenda Joyce, Richard Fraser, Elsa Lanchester, Arthur Margetson, J. Pat O'Malley, Gertrude Neisen, André Charlot, Queenie Leonard, Molly Lamont, George Byron

To Each His Own (Par, 1946)

pro: Charles Brackett

dir: Mitchell Leisen

sc: Charles Brackett, Jacques Thery

c: Olivia De Havilland, John Lund, Roland Culver, Mary Anderson, Philip Terry

Tom Brown's Schooldays (RKO, 1940)

pro: Gene Towne, Graham Baker

dir: Robert Stevenson

sc: Walter Ferris, Frank Cavell, Gene Towne, Grahame Baker, Robert Stevenson (based on the novel by Thomas Hughes)

c: Jimmy Lydon, Cedric Hardwicke, Billy Halop, Freddie Bartholomew, Gale Storm

Tower of London (Uni, 1939)

pro: Rowland V. Lee

dir: Rowland V. Lee

sc: Robert N. Lee

c: Basil Rathbone, Boris Karloff, Barbara O'Neil, Ian Hunter, Vincent Price, Nan Grey, John Sutton, Leo G. Carroll, Miles Mander

Treasure Island (MGM, 1934)

pro: Hunt Stromberg

dir: Victor Fleming

sc: John Lee Mahin (based on the novel by Robert Louis Stevenson)

c: Wallace Beery, Jackie Cooper, Lewis Stone, Lionel Barrymore, Otto Kruger, Douglass Dumbrille, Nigel Bruce, Chic Sale, William V. Mong, Charles McNaughton

Vacation from Marriage/Perfect Strangers (MGM, 1945)

pro: Alexander Korda

dir: Alexander Korda

sc: Clemence Dane, Anthony Pelissier

c: Robert Donat, Deborah Kerr, Glynis Johns, Ann Todd, Roland Culver, Elliot Mason

Vanessa, Her Love Story (MGM, 1935)

pro: David O. Selznick

dir: William K. Howard

sc: Lenore Coffee, Hugh Walpole (based on the novel *Vanessa* by Hugh Walpole)

c: Helen Hayes, Robert Montgomery, May Robson, Otto Kruger, Lewis Stone, Henry Stephenson, Violet Kemble-Cooper, Jessie Ralph, Donald Crisp

The Verdict (WB, 1946)

pro: William Jacobs

dir: Don Siegel

sc: Peter Milne (based on the novel *The Big Bow Mystery* by Israel Zangwill)

c: Sidney Greenstreet, Peter Lorre, Joan Lorring, George Coulouris, Rosalind Ivan, Paul Cavanagh, Arthur Shields, Morton Lowry, Holmes Herbert

Waterloo Bridge (Uni, 1931)

pro: Carl Laemmle Jr

dir: James Whale

sc: Tom Reed, Ben W. Levy (based on the play by Robert E. Sherwood)

c: Mae Clarke, Kent Douglass, Doris Lloyd, Ethel Griffies, Enid Bennett, Frederick Kerr

Waterloo Bridge (MGM, 1940)

pro: Sidney Franklin

dir: Mervyn LeRoy

sc: S.N. Behrman, George Froeschel, Hans Rameau (based on the play by Robert E. Sherwood)

c: Vivien Leigh, Robert Taylor, Virginia Field, Maria Ouspenskaya, Lucile Watson, C. Aubrey Smith, Steffi Duna, Leo G. Carroll

We Are Not Alone (WB, 1939)

pro: Henry Blanke

dir: Edmund Goulding

sc: James Hilton, Milton Krims (based on the novel by James Hilton)

c: Paul Muni, Jane Bryan, Flora Robson, Raymond Severn, Una O'Connor, Henry Daniell, Montagu Love, James Stephenson, Cecil Kellaway, Eily Manyon, Billy Bevan

Wee Willie Winkie (TCF, 1937)

pro: Darryl F. Zanuck, Gene Markey

dir: John Ford

sc: Ernest Pascal, Julien Josephson (based on the story by Rudyard Kipling)

c: Shirley Temple, Victor McLaglen, C. Aubrey Smith, June Lang, Cesar Romero

Werewolf of London (Uni, 1935)

pro: Stanley Bergerman, Robert Harris

dir: Stuart Walker

sc: John Colton, Harvey Gates, Robert Harris

c: Henry Hull, Warner Oland, Lester Matthews, Spring Byington, Valerie Hobson

The White Cliffs of Dover (MGM, 1944)

pro: Sidney Franklin

dir: Clarence Brown

sc: Claudine West, George Froeschel, Jan Lustig (based on the narrative poem 'The White Cliffs' by Alice Duer Miller)

c: Irene Dunne, Alan Marshal, Frank Morgan, C. Aubrey Smith, Gladys Cooper, Elizabeth Taylor, Roddy McDowall, Peter Lawford, Dame May Whitty, Ian Wolfe, Arthur Shields, Jill Esmond, Brenda Forbes, Norma Varden, Van Johnson, June Lockhart, Isobel Elsom

The Wolf Man (Uni, 1941)

pro: George Waggner

dir: George Waggner

sc: Curt Siodmak

c: Lon Chaney Jr, Claude Rains, Warren William, Ralph Bellamy, Bela Lugosi, Maria Ouspenskaya, Patric Knowles, Evelyn Ankers, Fay Helm, Forrester Harvey

Wuthering Heights (UA, 1939)

pro: Samuel Goldwyn

dir: William Wyler

sc: Ben Hecht, Charles MacArthur (based on the novel by Emily Brontë)

c: Laurence Olivier, Merle Oberon, David Niven, Hugh Williams, Flora Robson, Geraldine Fitzgerald, Donald Crisp, Leo G. Carroll, Cecil Kellaway, Miles Mander

A Yank at Eton (MGM, 1942)

pro: John Considine Jr

dir: Norman Taurog

sc: George Oppenheimer, Lionel Houser, Thomas Phipps

c: Mickey Rooney, Freddie Bartholomew, Tina Thayer, Ian Hunter, Edmund Gwenn, Alan Mowbray, Marta Linden, Peter Lawford, Terry Kilburn, Raymond Severn

A Yank at Oxford (MGM, 1938)

pro: Michael Balcon

dir: Jack Conway

sc: Sidney Gilliat, Michael Hogan, Leon Gordon, Malcolm Stuart Boylan, Walter Ferris, George Oppenheimer (based on a scenario by John Monk Saunders)

c: Robert Taylor, Maureen O'Sullivan, Lionel Barrymore, Vivien Leigh, Edmund Gwenn, Griffith Jones, C.V. France, Edward Rigby, Edmund Breon, Robert Coote

A Yank in the RAF (TCF, 1941)

pro: Lou Edelman

dir: Henry King

sc: Karl Tunberg, Darrell Ware (based on a scenario by Melville Crossman (pseudonym for Darryl F. Zanuck))

c: Tyrone Power, Betty Grable, John Sutton, Reginald Gardiner, Donald Stuart, Morton Lowry, Richard Fraser, Frederick Worlock, Gladys Cooper, Forrester Harvey

Bibliography

Archival and Unpublished Document Sources:
The British Film Institute Library (London, United Kingdom)
Alexander Korda Papers

The Kevin Brownlow Collection (London, United Kingdom)
Sidney Franklin Diaries
Sidney Franklin Papers
Sidney Franklin, *We Laughed and We Cried* (unpublished autobiography)

The Doheny Library of the University of Southern California (Los Angeles, California, USA):
The Metro-Goldwyn-Mayer Script Collection
The Warner Brothers Script Collection
The William Schaefer Ledger

The Margaret Herrick Library of the Academy of Motion Picture Arts and Sciences (Beverly Hills, California, USA)
1941 War Film Hearings Collection
The Eddie Mannix Ledger
The MPPDA Production Code Administration Files

The Public Record Office (Kew, London, United Kingdom)
INF 1/625: Ministry of Information, *Eagle Squadron* File

The Theater Arts Library of The University of California at Los Angeles
Radio-Keith-Orpheum Script Collection
Twentieth Century-Fox Script Collection
The William Wyler Collection

The Turner Entertainment Corporation (Los Angeles, California, USA)
Metro-Goldwyn-Mayer Legal Files
Radio-Keith-Orpheum Legal Files

The Washington National Records Center (Suitland, Maryland, USA)

Record Group 208: Records of the Office of War Information

The Widener Library of Harvard University (Cambridge, Massachusetts, USA)

American Attitudes Toward World War Two: Intelligence Reports

The Wisconsin State Historical Society (Madison, Wisconsin, USA)

The United Artists Collection
The Walter Wanger Papers
Warner Brothers Legal Files
The Warner Brothers Script Collection

Memoirs and published documents, letters and interviews

Aherne, B., *A Proper Job: The Autobiography of an Actor's Actor*, Boston, Hugh Mifflin, 1969.

Balcon, M., *Michael Balcon Presents ... A Lifetime in Films*, London, Hutchinson, 1969.

Behlmer, R. (ed.), *Memo from Darryl F. Zanuck: The Golden Years at Twentieth Century-Fox*, New York, Grove Press, 1993.

Behlmer, R. (ed.), *Memo from David O. Selznick*, Hollywood, Samuel French, [1972] 1989.

Chaplin, C., *My Autobiography*, New York, Simon and Schuster, 1964.

Flynn, E., *My Wicked, Wicked Ways*, London, Heinemann, 1960.

Fontaine, J., *No Bed of Roses: An Autobiography*, New York, William Morrow, 1978.

Hardwicke, C., *A Victorian in Orbit*, London, Methuen, 1961.

Lambert, G., *On Cukor*, New York, G.P. Putnam's Sons, 1972.

Loder, J., *Hollywood Hussar: The Life and Times of John Loder*, London, Howard Baker Press, 1977.

Mast, G. (ed.), *The Movies in Our Midst*, Chicago, University of Chicago Press, 1982.

Milland, R., *Wide-Eyed in Babylon*, New York, William Morrow, 1974.

Neagle, A., *There's Always Tomorrow*, London, W.H. Allen, 1974.

Niven, D., *Bring on the Empty Horses*, London, Coronet, [1975] 1976.

Olivier, L., *Confessions of an Actor*, London, Weidenfeld and Nicolson, 1982.

Rotha, P. (ed.), *Portrait of a Flying Yorkshireman: Letters from Eric Knight in the United States to Paul Rotha in England*, London, Chapman and Hall, 1952.

Sherriff, R.C., *No Leading Lady: An Autobiography*, London, Victor Gollancz, 1968.

Truffaut, F., *Hitchcock: The Definitive Study*, London, Paladin, [1967] 1986.

United States Senate, Seventy-Seventh Congress, First Session, *Propaganda in Motion Pictures: A Hearing Before a Sub-committee of the Committee on Interstate Commerce on Senate Resolution 152, September 9–26, 1941*, Washington DC, United States Senate Record, 1941.

Vidor, K., *A Tree is a Tree*, New York, Harcourt Brace, 1953.

Warner, J. with D. Jennings, *My First Hundred Years in Hollywood*, New York, Random House, 1975.

Watt, H., *Don't Look at the Camera*, London, Elek Books, 1974.

Wilcox, H., *Twenty-Five Thousand Sunsets*, London, Bodley Head, 1967.

Biographies

Allen, D.R., *Sir Aubrey: A Biography of C. Aubrey Smith*, London, Elm Tree, 1982.

Barrow, K., *Mister Chips: The Life of Robert Donat*, London, Methuen, 1985.

Berg, A.S., *Goldwyn: A Biography*, London, Hamish Hamilton, 1989.

Bernstein, M., *Walter Wanger: Hollywood Independent*, London, University of California Press, 1994.

Callow, S., *Charles Laughton: A Difficult Actor*, London, Methuen, 1987.

Gatiss, M., *James Whale: A Biography*, London, Cassell, 1995.

Gussow, M., *Zanuck: Don't Say Yes Until I've Finished Talking*, London, W.H. Allen, 1971.

Higham, C., *Merchant of Dreams: Louis B. Mayer, MGM and the Secret Hollywood*, London, Sidgwick and Jackson, 1993.

Kessler, R., *The Sins of the Father: Joseph P. Kennedy and the Dynasty He Founded*, London, Hodder and Stoughton, 1996.

Korda, M., *Charmed Lives: The Fabulous World of the Korda Brothers*, London, Allen Lane, 1980.

Kulik, K., *Alexander Korda: The Man Who Could Work Miracles*, London, Virgin Books, [1975] 1990.

Lambert, G., *Norma Shearer: A Life*, London, Hodder and Stoughton, 1990.

McCann, G., *Cary Grant: A Class Apart*, London, Fourth Estate, 1996.

McGilligan, P., *George Cukor: A Double Life*, New York, St Martin's Press, 1991.

Madsen, A., *William Wyler*, New York, Thomas Y. Crowell, 1973.

Moorehead, C., *Sidney Bernstein: A Biography*, London, Jonathan Cape, 1984.

Mosley, L., *Zanuck: The Rise and Fall of Hollywood's Last Tycoon*, London, Panther, 1985.

Spoto, D., *Laurence Olivier: A Biography*, London, HarperCollins, 1991.

Spoto, D., *The Life of Alfred Hitchcock: The Dark Side of Genius*, London, Collins, 1983.

Taylor, J. R., *Hitch: The Authorized Biography of Alfred Hitchcock*, London, Faber and Faber, 1978.

Thomson, D., *Showman: The Life of David O. Selznick*, New York, Alfred Knopf, 1992.

Thornton, M., *Jessie Matthews: A Biography*, London, Hart, Davis and MacGibbon, 1974.

Walker, A., *Elizabeth*, London, Weidenfeld and Nicolson, 1991.

Books and monographs

Allen, R.C. and D. Gomery, *Film History: Theory and Practice*, New York,

Alfred Knopf, 1985.

Balio, T. (ed.), *The American Film Industry*, Madison, The University of Wisconsin Press, 1976.

Balio, T. (ed.), *Grand Design: Hollywood as a Modern Business Enterprise, 1930–1939*, New York, Charles Scribner's Sons, 1993.

Balio, T., *United Artists: The Company Built by the Stars*, London, University of Wisconsin Press, 1976.

Barr, C. (ed.), *All Our Yesterdays: Ninety Years of British Cinema*, London, British Film Institute, 1986.

Basinger, J., *The World War Two Combat Film: Anatomy of a Genre*, New York, Columbia University Press, 1986.

Baxter, J., *The Hollywood Exiles*, London, MacDonald and Jane's, 1976.

Behlmer, R., *Behind the Scenes*, Hollywood, Samuel French, [1982] 1990.

Behlmer, R. and T. Balio (eds), *The Sea Hawk*, Madison, The University of Wisconsin Press, 1982.

Black, G., *Hollywood Censored: Morality Codes, Catholics and the Movies*, Cambridge, Cambridge University Press, 1994.

Brown, G., *Launder and Gilliat*, London, British Film Institute, 1977.

Calder, A., *The Myth of the Blitz*, London, Jonathan Cape, 1991.

Calder, A., *The People's War: Britain, 1939–1945*, London, Jonathan Cape, 1969.

Carey, G., *All the Stars There Are in Heaven: Louis B. Mayer and MGM*, London, Robson Books, 1982.

Christie, I. (ed.), *Powell, Pressburger and Others*, London, British Film Institute, 1978.

Crowther, B., *The Lion's Share*, New York, Henry Holt, 1957.

Cull, N.J., *Selling War: The British Propaganda Campaign Against American Neutrality in World War Two*, Oxford, Oxford University Press, 1995.

Curran, J. and V. Porter (eds), *British Cinema History*, London, Weidenfeld and Nicolson, 1983.

Dick, B.F., *The Star-Spangled Screen: The American World War Two Film*, Lexington, University of Kentucky Press, 1985.

Dickinson, M. and S. Street, *Cinema and State: The Film Industry and the British Government, 1927–1984*, London, British Film Institute, 1985.

Dimbleby, R. and D. Reynolds, *An Ocean Apart*, London, Hodder and Stoughton, 1988.

Divine, R., *The Reluctant Belligerent: American Entry into the Second World War*, New York, Alfred Knopf, 1965.

Doherty, T., *Projections of War: Hollywood, American Culture, and World War Two*, New York, Columbia University Press, 1993.

Eames, J.D., *The MGM Story*, New York, Crown Publishers, 1976.

Finler, J., *The Hollywood Story*, London, Octopus Books, 1988.

Fraser, G.M., *The Hollywood History of the World*, New York, William Morrow, 1988.

Furhammer, L. and F. Isaksson, *Politics and Film*, London, Studio Vista, 1971.

Gabler, N., *An Empire of Their Own: How the Jews Invented Hollywood*, New York, Crown Publishers, 1989.

Gomery, D., *The Hollywood Studio System*, London, Macmillan Press, 1986.

Greene, G., *The Pleasure Dome: The Collected Film Criticism, 1935–1940*, London, Secker and Warburg, 1972.

Harper, S., *Picturing the Past: The Rise and Fall of the British Costume Film*, London, British Film Insitute, 1994.

Hay, P., *MGM: When The Lion Roars*, Atlanta, Turner Publishing, 1991.

Hitchens, C., *Blood, Class and Nostalgia: Anglo-American Ironies*, London, Chatto and Windus, 1990.

Izod, J., *Hollywood and the Box-Office*, London, Macmillan, 1988.

Jarvie, I., *Hollywood's Overseas Campaign: The North Atlantic Movie Trade, 1920–1950*, Cambridge, Cambridge University Press, 1992.

Jowett, G., *Film: The Democratic Art*, Boston, Little Brown, 1976.

Knight, E., *This Above All*, London, Cassell and Company, 1941.

Koppes, C.R. and G.D. Black, *Hollywood Goes to War: How Politics, Profits and Propaganda Shaped World War Two Movies*, London, I.B. Tauris, 1987.

Lant, A., *Blackout: Reinventing Women for Wartime British Cinema*, Oxford, Princeton University Press, 1991.

Leff, L.J., *Hitchcock and Selznick: The Rich and Strange Collaboration of Alfred Hitchcock and David O. Selznick*, New York, Weidenfield and Nicolson, 1987.

Leff, L.J. and J.L. Simmons, *The Dame in the Kimono: Hollywood Censorship and the Production Code from the 1920s to the 1960s*, London, Weidenfeld and Nicolson, 1990.

Low, R., *Filmmaking in 1930s Britain*, London, George Allen and Unwin, 1985.

Manvell, R., *Films and the Second World War*, London, J.M. Dent, 1974.

Marx, S., *Mayer and Thalberg: The Make-Believe Saints*, Hollywood, Samuel French, [1975] 1988.

Moley, R., *The Hays Office*, Indianapolis, Bobbs-Merrill, 1945.

Mordden, E., *The Hollywood Studios: House Style in the Golden Age of Hollywood*, New York, Alfred Knopf, 1988.

Morley, S., *Tales from the Hollywood Raj: The British Film Colony On Screen and Off*, London, Weidenfeld and Nicolson, 1983.

O'Neill, W.L., *A Democracy At War: America's Fight at Home and Abroad in World War Two*, Cambridge, Harvard University Press, 1993.

Reynolds, D., *The Creation of the Anglo-American Alliance, 1937–1941: A Study in Competitive Cooperation*, London, Europa, 1981.

Reynolds, D., *Rich Relations: The American Occupation of Britain, 1942–1945*, London, HarperCollins, 1996.

Richards, J., *The Age of the Dream Palace: Cinema and Society in Britain, 1930–1939*, London, Routledge and Kegan Paul, 1984.

Richards, J., *Films and British National Identity: From Dickens to Dad's Army*, Manchester, Manchester University Press, 1997.

Richards, J., *The Swordsmen of the Screen*, London, Routledge and Kegan Paul, 1977.

Richards, J., *Visions of Yesterday*, London, Routledge and Kegan Paul, 1973.

Richards, J. (ed.), *The Unknown 1930s: An Alternative History of the British Cinema*, London, I.B. Tauris, 1998.

Richards, J. and A. Aldgate, *Britain Can Take It: The British Cinema in the Second World War*, Oxford, Basil Blackwell, 1986.

Richards, J. and D. Sheridan, *Mass Observation at the Movies*, London, Routledge and Kegan Paul, 1987.

Robertson, J., *The British Board of Film Censors: Film Censorship in Britain, 1896–1950*, London, Croom Helm, 1985.

Robertson, J., *The Hidden Cinema: British Film Censorship In Action, 1913–1975*, London, Routledge and Kegan Paul, 1989.

Roddick, N., *A New Deal in Entertainment: Warner Brothers in the 1930s*, London, British Film Institute, 1983.

Schatz, T., *The Genius of the System: Hollywood Film-making in the Studio Era*, New York, Pantheon Books, 1988.

Schatz, T., *Hollywood Genres: Formulas, Film-making and the Studio System*, London, McGraw Hill, 1981.

Shindler, C., *Hollywood Goes to War: Films and American Society, 1939–1952*, London, Routledge and Kegan Paul, 1979.

Shindler, C., *Hollywood in Crisis: Cinema and American Society, 1929–1939*, London, Routledge, 1996.

Short, K.R.M. (ed.), *Feature Films as History*, London, Croom Helm, 1981.

Sklar, R., *Movie-Made America: A Cultural History of the Movies*, New York, Random House, 1975.

Solomon, A., *Twentieth Century-Fox: A Corporate and Financial History*, London, The Scarecrow Press, 1988.

Sorlin, P., *The Film in History: Re-staging the Past*, Oxford, Basil Blackwell, 1980.

Struther, J., *Mrs Miniver*, London, Virago, [1939] 1989.

Sussex, E., *The Rise and Fall of British Documentary*, Berkeley, University of California Press, 1975.

Taves, B., *The Romance of Adventure: The Genre of Historical Adventure Movies*, Jackson, University Press of Mississippi, 1993.

Taylor, J.R., *Strangers in Paradise: The Hollywood Emigrés, 1933–1950*, London, Faber and Faber, 1983.

Taylor, P. M. (ed.), *Britain and the Cinema in the Second World War*, London, Macmillan, 1988.

Thompson, K., *Exporting Entertainment: America in the World Film Market*, London, British Film Institute, 1985.

Vasey, R., *The World According to Hollywood, 1918–1939*, Madison, The University of Wisconsin Press, 1997.

Vidal, G., *Screening History*, London, André Deutsch, 1992.

Walker, A., *The Shattered Silents: How the Talkies Came to Stay*, London, Hamish Hamilton, 1978.

Walsh, F., *Sin and Censorship: The Catholic Church and the Motion Picture Industry*, London, Yale University Press, 1996.

Reference books

Alicoate, J. (ed.), *The 1932 Film Daily Yearbook*, New York, Film Daily Publications, 1933.

Alicoate, J. (ed.), *The 1939 Film Daily Yearbook*, New York, Film Daily Publications, 1940.

Alicoate, J. (ed.), *The 1940 Film Daily Yearbook*, New York, Film Daily Publications, 1941.

Alicoate, J. (ed.), *The 1941 Film Daily Yearbook*, New York, Film Daily Publications, 1942.

Alicoate, J. (ed.), *The 1942 Film Daily Yearbook*, New York, Film Daily Publications, 1943.

Alicoate, J. (ed.), *The 1943 Film Daily Yearbook*, New York, Film Daily Publications, 1944.

Alicoate, J. (ed.), *The 1944 Film Daily Yearbook*, New York, Film Daily Publications, 1945.

Alicoate, J. (ed.), *The 1945 Film Daily Yearbook*, New York, Film Daily Publications, 1946.

Halliwell, L., *Halliwell's Film Guide: A Survey of 8,000 English Language Movies*, London, Paladin Books, 1977.

Katz, E., *The Macmillan International Film Encyclopedia*, London, Harper-Collins, 1994.

Michael, P., *The Academy Awards: A Pictorial History*, New York, Crown Publishers, 1982.

Ramsaye, T. (ed.), *The 1932–1933 International Motion Picture Almanac*, New York, Quigley Publications, 1933.

Ramsaye, T. (ed.), *The 1933–1934 International Motion Picture Almanac*, New York, Quigley Publications, 1934.

Ramsaye, T. (ed.), *The 1934–1935 International Motion Picture Almanac*, New York, Quigley Publications, 1935.

Ramsaye, T. (ed.), *The 1935–1936 International Motion Picture Almanac*, New York, Quigley Publications, 1936.

Ramsaye, T. (ed.), *The 1936–1937 International Motion Picture Almanac*, New York, Quigley Publications, 1937.

Ramsaye, T. (ed.), *The 1937–1938 International Motion Picture Almanac*, New York, Quigley Publications, 1938.

Ramsaye, T. (ed.), *The 1938–1939 International Motion Picture Almanac*, New York, Quigley Publications, 1939.

Ramsaye, T. (ed.), *The 1939–1940 International Motion Picture Almanac*, New York, Quigley Publications, 1940.

Thomas, N. (ed.), *The International Dictionary of Films and Filmmakers: Second Edition*, Chicago and London, St James Press, 1990.

Articles and chapters

Altman, C.F., Towards a Historiography of American Film, *Cinema Journal*, 16:2 (1977).

Barr, C., War Record, *Sight and Sound*, 58:4 (1989).

Brownlow, K., Sidney Franklin: The Modest Pioneer, *Focus on Film*, 10 (1972).

Dale, R.C., René Clair in Hollywood, *Film Quarterly*, 24 (1970–1971).

Davis, J., Notes on Warner Brothers' Foreign Policy, *Velvet Light Trap Review of Cinema*, 4 (1972).

Dening, G., *Mutiny on The Bounty*, in M. Carnes (ed.), *Past Imperfect: History According to the Movies*, New York, Henry Holt, 1995.

Forester, E.M., The Top Drawer But One, *New Statesman and Nation* (4 November 1939).

Jacobs, L., World War Two and the American Film, *Cinema Journal*, 7 (1967–1968).

Jarvie, I., Dollars and Ideology: Will Hays' Economic Foreign Policy, 1922–1945, *Film History*, 2 (1988).

Jewell, R.B., RKO Film Grosses, 1929–1951: The C.J. Tevlin Ledger, *Historical Journal of Film, Radio and Television*, 14:1 (1994).

Jones, D.B. The Hollywood War Film, 1942–45, *Hollywood Quarterly*, 1:1 (1945).

Koppes, C.R. and G.D. Black. What to Show the World: The Office of War Information and Hollywood, *Journal of American History*, 64 (1977).

Korda, M., A Knight in Hollywood, *New York Magazine* (22 October 1979).

Maltby, R., *Baby Face*: Or How Joe Breen Made Barbara Stanwyck Atone for Causing the Wall Street Crash, *Screen*, 27:2 (1986).

Poole, J., British Cinema Attendance in Wartime: Audience Preference at the Majestic, Macclesfield, 1939–1946, *Historical Journal of Film, Radio and Television*, 7:1 (1987).

Quigley, M., The OWI: Policy and Performance, *Motion Picture Herald* (6 March 1943), pp. 7–8.

Richards, J., Wartime British Cinema Audiences and the Class System: The Case of *Ships With Wings*, *Historical Journal of Film, Radio and Television*, 7:2 (1987).

Short, K.R.M., Cinematic Support for the Anglo-American Detente, in P. Taylor (ed.), *Britain and the Cinema in the Second World War*, London, Macmillan, 1988.

Short, K.R.M., *That Hamilton Woman* (1941): Propaganda, Feminism and the Production Code, *Historical Journal of Film, Radio and Television*, 11:1 (1991).

Short, K.R.M., *The White Cliffs of Dover* (1944): Promoting the Anglo-American Alliance in Wartime, *Historical Journal of Film, Radio and Television*, 2:1 (1982).

Street, S., The Hays Office and the Defence of the British Market, *Historical Journal of Film, Radio and Television*, 5:1 (1985).

Wanger, W., 120,000 Ambassadors, *Foreign Affairs*, 18 (1939).

Wanger, W., The OWI and Motion Pictures, *Public Opinion Quarterly* (Spring 1943), pp. 43–47.

Index